觀察‧類推‧條理化 下冊
分析性的英語語法

湯廷池——編著　許淑慎——監修

SYNTAX

ENGLISH GRAMMAR

元華文創

〈永世夫妻〉

青梅竹馬，笑開懷於寒冬中。

新竹高中與新竹女中教書時，嬉戲於竹中操場。

兒子一家人返臺探親，歡樂於新竹照相館。

與學生共度 80 歲生日，悲喜交織於臺北餐聚。

〈教學相長〉

以「誤人子弟，天誅地滅」互勉，切磋於竹中宿舍。

與學生參加國際研討會，留影於中研院蓮花池。

〈有你真好〉

湯廷池老師生前熱愛慢跑，經常帶著學生在新竹十八尖山跑步，
亦師亦友，輔導課業與生活於綠意盎然小徑中。

清華大學語言學研究所追思網址

https://ling.site.nthu.edu.tw/p/406-1400-187636,r5972.php?Lang=zh-tw

http://ling.hss.nthu.edu.tw/tingchitang/

http://140.114.116.1/tingchitang/

編著者自序

湯廷池：新竹中學 1951 年第四屆畢業

摘　　自：新竹中學 1961 年第十四屆畢業生《2011 年五十週年同學會紀念冊》

　　我並不是一個十分用功的學生，只是喜歡靠自己讀書，尤其是喜歡靠自己觀察、分析、思考、推論。我對於教育這個工作懷有深厚的使命感，臺大法律系畢業以後，就與臺大外文系畢業的妻子，分別回到母校新竹高中與新竹女中擔任英文教員。我們時常以「誤人子弟，天誅地滅」互勉，幾乎課本裡的每一個生字都查詢家裡的每一部英文辭典，不但準備了非常詳盡的教案，還在家裡預演如何上課。1963 年與 1971 年我前後兩次出國，都在極短時間內順利獲得學位歸國。這樣的表現並非由於我特別的聰明或用功，而是來自平時的「教學相長」，是學生對我的期望與我對學生的責任感造就了今天的我。

　　我的專業領域是語言學，特別是華語、英語、日語的語法理論與分析，而我今生的志願則是把現代語言學的理論與方法傳授給學生，好讓現代語言學在國內生根茁壯。教學生涯已五十五年，五十五年如一日，一直樂在其中，不改其樂。教學為的是回報，著書為的是薪傳。活到老學到老，人盡其才而物盡其用。無論自己的年紀多大，都願意把自己當做資源回收與廢物利用的對象來繼續努力，一直到最後回歸大地為止。

編著者介紹

　　湯廷池，臺灣苗栗縣通霄人，一九三一年生，一九五七年與畢業於臺灣大學外文系的青梅竹馬許淑慎小姐共結連理。臺灣大學法學學士、美國德州大學奧斯汀分校語言學碩士、美國德州大學奧斯汀分校語言學博士。曾任臺灣師範大學英語學系與研究所教授、清華大學外國語文學系教授兼創系主任與語言學研究所教授、輔仁大學語言學研究所兼任教授、東吳大學日本語文學系兼任教授、元智大學應用外語系教授兼創系主任、輔仁大學翻譯學研究所兼任教授、交通大學語言與文化研究所兼任教授、新竹教育大學臺灣語言與語言教育研究所兼任教授、東吳大學日本語文學系所客座教授、輔仁大學外語學院野聲講座教授、輔仁大學跨文化研究所兼任教授。二〇二〇年九月二十一日與愛妻一起長眠於家鄉通霄。

　　曾獲得「行政院圖書出版金鼎獎」、「教育部六藝獎章」、「中華民國語文獎章」、「行政院國家科學委員會傑出研究獎」、「行政院國家科學委員會優等研究獎」、「行政院國家科學委員會特約研究人員」、「中華民國英語教師學會終身貢獻獎」、「傑出人才發展基金會傑出人才講座」、「中華民國私立教育事業協會大仁獎章」、「教育部教育文化獎章」、「元智大學績敘獎勵研究特優獎」、「元智大學第七屆研究獎傑出教授獎助一等獎」、「臺灣語言學學會終身成就獎」等獎勵。著有六十多本專書，以及數百篇期刊論文與會議論文。

主要專書

1968.（與楊景邁共編）《如何教英語》臺北：東華書局。

1969a. *A Transformational Analysis of Japanese Verbs and Verb Phrases.* 臺北：海國書局。

1969b. *A Transformational Approach to Teaching English Sentence Patterns.* 臺北：海國書局。

1972a.《國語格變語法試論》臺北：海國書局。

1972b. (with co-editors C. H. Tung and Y. T. Wu) Papers in linguistics in honor of A. A. Hill. 臺北：臺灣虹橋書店。

1973.（與許淑慎共編）《現代高中英文：社會組》臺北：海國書局。

1974.（與許淑慎共編）《現代高中英文：自然組》臺北：海國書局。

1973-1976.《實用高級英語語法》（共六冊）臺北：海國書局。

1975.《國語格變語法動詞的分類研究》臺北：海國書局。

1977a.《國語變形語法研究第一集：移位變形》臺北：臺灣學生書局。

1977b.《英語教學論集》臺北：臺灣學生書局。

1978. (with co-editors R. L. Cheng and Y.-C. Li) Proceedings of Symposium on Chinese Linguistics. (1977 Linguistic Institute of the Linguistic Society of America). 臺北：臺灣學生書局。

1978-1979.《最新實用高級英語語法》（共兩冊）臺北：海國書局。

1979a.《國語語法研究論集》臺北：臺灣學生書局。

1979b. (with co-editors F. F. Tsao and I. Li) Proceeding of 1979 Asian and Pacific Conference on Linguistics and Language Teaching, August 24-26. 臺北：臺灣學生書局。

1980. 主編《一九七九年亞太地區語言教學研討會論集》臺北：臺灣學生書局。

1981.《語言學與語文教學》臺北：臺灣學生書局。

1984a.《英語語法修辭十二講：從傳統到現代》臺北：臺灣學生書局。

1984b.《英語語言分析入門：英語語法教學問答》臺北：臺灣學生書局。

1985.《最新實用高級英語語法（修訂本）》（共兩冊）臺北：海國書局。

1988a.《英語認知語法：結構、意義與功用（上集）》臺北：臺灣學生書局。

1988b.《漢語詞法句法論集》臺北：臺灣學生書局。

1989a.《漢語詞法句法續集》臺北：臺灣學生書局。

1989b.《國中英語教學指引》臺北：臺灣學生書局。

1992a.《英語認知語法：結構、意義與功用（中集）》臺北：臺灣學生書局。

1992b.《漢語詞法句法三集》臺北：臺灣學生書局。

1992c.《漢語詞法句法四集》臺北：臺灣學生書局。

1994a.《英語認知語法：結構、意義與功用（下集）》臺北：臺灣學生書局。

1994b.《漢語詞法句法五集》臺北：臺灣學生書局。

1999a.《日語語法與日語教學》臺北：臺灣學生書局。

1999b.《閩南語語法研究試論》臺北：臺灣學生書局。

2000a.《極小主義分析導論：基本概念與原則》臺北：金字塔出版社。

2000b.《漢語詞法論集》臺北：金字塔出版社。

2000c.《漢語語法論集》臺北：金字塔出版社。

2000d.《英語語法論集》臺北：金字塔出版社。

2002a.（與姚榮松等共編）《古典散文選》（共三冊）臺北：國立編譯館出版。

2002b.（與姚榮松等共編）《古典散文選‧教師手冊》（共三冊）臺北：國立編譯
館出版。

2010a.（許淑慎監修）《語言學、語言分析與語言教學（上冊）》臺北：致良出版社。

2010b.（許淑慎監修）《語言學、語言分析與語言教學（下冊）》臺北：致良出版社。

2012a.（許淑慎監修）《日語形容詞研究入門（上冊）》臺北：致良出版社。

2012b.（許淑慎監修）《日語形容詞研究入門（下冊）》臺北：致良出版社。

2014a.（許淑慎監修）《英語應用語言學研究入門（上冊）》臺北：致良出版社。

2014b.（許淑慎監修）《英語應用語言學研究入門（下冊）》臺北：致良出版社。

2014c.（許淑慎監修）《英語語法研究入門》臺北：致良出版社。

2014d.（許淑慎監修）《華語詞法研究入門（上冊）》臺北：致良出版社。

2015a.（許淑慎監修）《對比分析研究入門（上冊）》臺北：致良出版社。

2015b.（許淑慎監修）《對比分析研究入門（下冊）》臺北：致良出版社。

2015c.（許淑慎監修）《華語詞法研究入門（中冊）》臺北：致良出版社。

2015d.（許淑慎監修）《華語詞法研究入門（下冊）》臺北：致良出版社。

2016.（許淑慎監修）《華語語言分析入門》臺北：致良出版社。

2018a.（許淑慎監修）《河洛語語法研究入門（上冊）》臺北：致良出版社。

2018b.（許淑慎監修）《河洛語語法研究入門（下冊）》臺北：致良出版社。

2019a.（許淑慎監修）《英語形式句法分析導論（上冊）》臺北：致良出版社。

2019b.（許淑慎監修）《英語形式句法分析導論（中冊）》臺北：致良出版社。

2019c.（許淑慎監修）《英語形式句法分析導論（下冊）》臺北：致良出版社。

2019d.（許淑慎監修）《語言學 英、日、華 術語對照與簡介（上冊）》臺北：致良出版社。

2019e.（許淑慎監修）《語言學 英、日、華 術語對照與簡介（下冊）》臺北：致良出版社。

2021a.（許淑慎監修）《日本語言語学研究入門（上）》臺北：致良出版社。

2021b.（許淑慎監修）《日本語言語学研究入門（中）》臺北：致良出版社。

2021c.（許淑慎監修）《日本語言語学研究入門（下）》臺北：致良出版社。

2022a.（許淑慎監修）《日本語文法研究入門（上）》臺北：致良出版社。

2022b.（許淑慎監修）《日本語文法研究入門（下）》臺北：致良出版社。

2022c.（許淑慎監修）《觀察、類推、條理化：分析性的英語語法（上）》臺北：元華文創。

《觀察 · 類推 · 條理化：分析性的英語語法》
——傳授顯性語言知識的一個典範

英語教學一直存在兩種不同的觀點：一種觀點認為，傳授語法知識是重要的，不僅需要讓學生在使用英語的時候符合語法規則，而且還要讓學生了解語言形式背後所蘊含的規則，就是說學生需要具備顯性語言知識；另一種觀點則認為，教授英語應該以有效的練習和強化方法，讓學生培養聽說讀寫能力，在日常交際中運用自如。能做到這點，就表示已經掌握了語法規則，至於是否了解英語語法規則，並不重要。湯廷池教授 30 多年前出版的《最新實用高級英語語法》(修訂本)，是傳授顯性語言知識的一個典範，至今仍然有極大的參考價值。舊版的檔案雖然早已遺失，幸好隨著科技的進步，掃描舊版原書後，更名為《觀察·類推·條理化：分析性的英語語法》，由元華文創重新編排，分成上下兩冊出版。

《最新實用高級英語語法（修訂本）》成書於 1985 年，正是英語教學熱衷於宣揚傳意語言教學（communicative language teaching）的年代（Wilkins 1976; Widdowson 1978; Johnson 1982）。在這之前的 1950-1960 年代，英語教學法受美國行為主義影響，盛行機械式口語練習（oral drills），認為通過強化某些句式，口語能力就能得到顯著提高，這種客觀的語言能力提升是對學員最大的鼓勵，其激勵作用不亞於有趣生動的課堂教學（Lado 1964）。這種強調句式操練的教學法，過分突出語法形式而忽略語意和語境，很快就顯示其弱點。學員們往往死記硬背了許多語法規則和句子結構，也難以真正把結構掌握好；由於脫離語境，不一定能用得上，或者用在不恰當的場景。因此，自 1970 年中期開始，就有許多應用語言學專家提倡，語言教學法應以語意和傳意為基礎，認為學員只要能在特定語境準確使用恰當的語句，就意味著他 / 她們掌握了傳意語法（communicative grammar）。

在 1970 年代當英語老師的時候，有一位資深英國老師就跟我推薦一種實用的傳意語言教學觀點，認為針對一種情景（例如問候，問路、或者承諾）只需要學一

兩種恰當而管用的固定句式，能夠在相關情景下運用自如，這樣就足夠了，不需要學那麼多不同的句法形式。我們的確常遇到一種情況：學員上課時學了各種不同句式，但碰到特定的情景，如問候、問路、承諾等，就要思索該用哪種形式，反而變得結結巴巴，說不出口，達不到語言溝通的基本功能。傳意語言教學法以交際互動、語言功能為基礎，對英語學習者來說似乎很管用，用這種方法很快就能用英語來實現某種傳意功能，滿足交際需要。

　　然而，對二語學習者來說，傳意教學法的局限也是顯而易見的。任何一個語言都有豐富的詞彙，裡面的名詞、動詞、形容詞都有著複雜的內容，儘管普遍語法規定了人類語言的普遍通則，讓我們對句法形式和語意的搭配有一些基本的認識，但畢竟語言之間具有許多差異，每個語言都存在著一定的獨特個性和偏離常規的例外，這些都需要我們對語法形式反覆推敲，對語言細微之處有所體會，否則是無法提高到高級水平層次的。例如，高級英語學習者在用關於「建議、推薦、要求」等動詞的時候，常會犯如（1a-1c）裡面的錯誤。英語中 *suggest, recommend, demand* 等動詞後面的子句，需要用假設法現在式（subjunctive mood，上冊第 7 章），而不是用不定詞動詞（infinitive –to）。就是說，必須使用光杆動詞原形 "V" 或者用 "should +V" 這種格式，如（2a-2c）所示。

（1）　a. *John suggested us to invite our teacher to the party.

　　　　b. *The artist recommended us to design a poster for the event.

　　　　c. *The residents demanded the mayor to build a bridge.

（2）　a. John suggested that we invite our teacher to the party.

　　　　John suggested that we should invite our teacher to the party.

　　　　b. The artist recommended that we design a poster for the event.

　　　　The artist recommended that we should design a poster for the event.

　　　　c. The residents demanded that the mayor build a bridge.

　　　　The residents demanded that the mayor should build a bridge.

　　為何英語需要用假設語氣來表達子句所表述的未然情況，而不用普通的不定詞 "to VP" 子句結構，這涉及英語本身一些特殊情況，學習英語時需要特加注意，否則會不斷犯錯而不察覺，強化了這種錯誤。

　　為何連英語程度不錯的學員也會犯這種錯誤？因為在一定程度上，用 "to VP" 格式來表達「建議、推薦、要求」等言語行為的物件，是符合語法規律的。原因有二：首先，"to VP" 這個形式一般表達未然情況或事件，而相對於表達「建議、推薦、要求」等言語行為來說，子句所表達的都屬於尚未發生的行動或情況。第二，許多語義上跟 "suggest, recommend, demand" 近似的動詞，如 "request, advise, require" 等動詞，卻容許帶 "to VP" 作為子句補語，從（3a-3c）例句可見。如果學員們用類比（analogy）推算就很容易認為，既然（3）裡面的例子成立，例子（1）裡面的句子應該也符合語法。這些與英語具體動詞相關的細節，需要學習者仔細掌握。對於高階英語學員來說，關於英語語法的顯性知識（explicit knowledge）是必須具備的，否則難以糾正自己常犯的語法錯誤，無法自我提升英語水平。

（3）a. John requested us to invite our teacher to the party.

　　　b. The artist advised us to design a poster for the event.

　　　c. The law requires us to put on our seat belt while driving.

　　湯廷池教授的《觀察・類推・條理化：分析性的英語語法》正是一本弘揚顯性語法知識的典範英語語法參考書，具有以下幾個特點，值得讀者注意。

（一）定義清晰；清楚區分形式與語義

　　本書以簡單清晰的語言來定義語法術語，並把一些容易混淆的概念清楚界定。例如，Time（時間）和 tense（時式）的區分，以及可數名詞與不可數名詞的區分，對初次接觸英語語法的讀者來說，都是容易混淆的概念。本參考語法把這些基本語法概念都梳理得非常清楚，把語言形式及其所表達的語意加以嚴格區分。

・時間（time）和時式（tense）的區分

　　第三章「十二種動詞時變式」對時式和時間的區分就有以下說明：「英語的動詞只有兩種『時式』（tense）：現在式（present）與過去式（past）」。「我們必須區別時式與時間（time）這兩個不同的概念。時間指過去、現在、未來所有的時間；時式卻指動詞的形式。我們用各種不同的時式來表示各種不同的時間，但是現在式不一定表示現在時間，過去式也不一定代表過去時間。」既然英語只有現在式和過去式，而沒有未來時式，如何表達未來時間，書中就有詳細的討論，和更進一

步的複習，鞏固讀者對這個區別的認識。

· 可數名詞與不可數名詞的區分

有些傳統英語語法著作，把可數名詞和不可數名詞用語義標準加以區分，認為可數名詞指向可以數數的物體（如 *person*「人」、*table*「桌子」、*car*「汽車」、*computer*「電腦」等名詞），而不可數名詞則描述不可數的物質（如 *water*「水」、*milk*「牛奶」、*meat*「肉」、*air*「空氣」等名詞）。語言學家很早就指出，以語意區分可數與不可數名詞是站不住腳的（Gleason 1965），這個語法區別只能用形式分佈來加以定義。本書上冊第 11 章就是以形式和分佈對這個區分進行說明的。

「名詞如果可以有『單數形』（singular）與『複數形』（plural），就叫做可數名詞（count nouns）」。「可數名詞的單數形，必須加上冠詞 *a*（*an*），*the* 或其他『限定詞』（如 *this, that* 等）」。「僅有單數形、不能有複數形的名詞叫做不可數名詞（noncount nouns）」；「不可數名詞不能加上 *a*（*an*），但是可以加上 some, the, this, that 等。」按照這個清晰的標準，*person, table, car, computer* 都是可數名詞，因為既有單數形，也有複數形 *persons, tables, cars, computers*。而 *water, milk, meat, air* 則只有單數形，而且不能在名詞前面加不定冠詞 *a*（*n*），因此屬不可數名詞。[1]

· 助動詞的詞類定義

本書對助動詞這個詞類的定義，也是嚴格用語言形式來界定的。上冊第 1 章就開宗明義說，英語的句型按照動詞可以劃分為三種；含有 *be* 的句型；含有助動詞的句型；以及含有 *be* 和助動詞以外的動詞。英語助動詞不多，就以列舉定義，包括 *will, would; shall, should; can, could; may, might; must; have, has, had; ought to*。當然，在談到助動詞特點的時候，會介紹各個助動詞所表達的語意，但關鍵是在定義這個詞類時，只列出形式準則，沒有用語意標準。

---

[1] 這幾個詞如果加了 -s，變成 *waters, milks, meats, airs*，當然也符合語法，但就不是原來名詞的涵義了。

（二）本參考語法介紹了大量的語法規則細節，主要不是用抽象的符號
規則或語言學課上常用的樹形圖，而是通過示範和大量的例句。
在介紹規則的時候，也注重詞彙的個性和例外。

以下用五個實例來說明湯教授參考語法的豐富內容。

．假設法（subjunctive mood）的使用

本書第 7 章在介紹假設法（subjunctive mood）的使用時，清楚列舉哪些動詞
和形容詞需要用上這種句型。

「在表示『提議』、『請求』或『命令』的動詞（如 suggest, request, order 等）
後面的子句，常用動詞的基本式（「假設法現在」）：

The doctor suggested that the patient stop smoking.

We requested that he give us another chance.

The judge ordered that the prisoner be set free.

She demanded that she be given a fair trial.」

所選的子句都用第三人稱單數作為主語，因為這樣才能顯示假設法現在式的語
法特點。還進一步說明，如果子句為否定句，否定詞 not 應該放在什麼位置；並指
出，除了用動詞基本式（即動詞原形）外，還可以用 "should" 與動詞的基本式來
代替假設法現在式。

此外，本書還指出，假設法現在式的使用並不限於動詞，有些形容詞也需要
用這種句式：「在表示『重要』、『需要』或『適當』的形容詞（如 important,
necessary, proper 等）後面的子句，也常用動詞的基本式。這是一般英語語法書極
少會談到的細節。

It is important that he follow the doctor's directions.

It is necessary the he be there by noon.

It is essential that I not be disturbed before I finish my letter.」

．*Tough-* 前移句型

英語有些句式，涉及主賓語位置的互換，有一種句型將不定式子句（infinitival
clause）的賓語前移到主句的主語位置，英語語法書常稱作「*tough-* 前移句型」。

本書下冊第 15 章對此句型做了以下介紹：

「拿『不定詞子句』做主語，因此也可以改成『It is + 形容詞 + 不定詞子句』的句型：

For them to solve the question is difficult.

It is difficult for them to solve the question.

這種句型，不定詞的賓語可以取代句首的 it 而變成主句的主語：

The question is difficult for them to solve.」

書上接著指出，能否有「*tough-* 前移句型」要看動詞和述語而定。例如，impossible 可以容納這種句型，但 possible 就不行，如下列句子所示。事實上，如 "He is possible to reason with" 這樣的句子，正是高階英語學習者常犯的錯誤。本書一方面詳細介紹語法規則細節，也同時關注一些具體特例，兩方面都兼顧。

It is impossible to reason with him.

He is impossible to reason with.

It is possible to reason with him.

*He is possible to reason with.

·助動詞的使用

上冊第五章介紹表示情態的助動詞，指出這些助動詞在屈折形式形態上的特點。「助動詞與主動詞不同，不因為主語的身與數而變化。因此助動詞只有現在式（can, may, will, shall, must）與過去式（could, might, would, should, must），沒有第三身單數現在式（V-s），也沒有現在分詞式（V-ing）或過去分詞式（V-en）」。除了描述典型的助動詞外，還談到 ought to, need, dare, used to 等比較特別的助動詞的用法。在介紹 need 的時候，指出這個詞可以當主動詞用，也可以當助動詞用，但當助動詞用的時候，「只限於否定句與帶有否定意味的問句裡。」

（主動詞用法）

He needs to work so late.

Does he need to work so late?

He doesn't need to work so late, does he?

（助動詞用法）

Need he work so late?

He needn't work so late, need he?

在介紹 used to 作為助動詞的時候，則指出 used 的否定式與問句式，美式英語多用 did not use to 於 did...use to 這些句型。

He didn't use to talk much.

Did he use to play tennis?

You used to play tennis, didn't you?

·關係代詞 whose 的使用問題

對高階英語語法學習者來說，如何處理所有格關係代詞 whose 是令人困惑的問題，何時能用，何時不能用，如何界定？關於這個細節，本書下冊第 17 章解釋如下：

「關係代名詞 whose 用來代替名詞（或代名詞）的所有格。這個名詞主要的是表示人的名詞，但是偶爾也可能是表示物或動物的名詞。注意：這個時候 whose 後面的名詞也要一起提前放在關係子句的句首。」

You bought the man's car./

（I met）the man whose car you bought.

The editor of the newspaper was fired./

（Have you read）the newspaper whose editor was fired?

The windows of the house are broken./

（Can you see）the house whose windows are broken?

（Can you see）the house of which the windows are broken?

作者一方面指出所有格關係代詞可以代替無生名詞，但從修辭效果考慮則主張避免使用，建議改用其他句式來表達同樣意思：「無生名詞的所有格，一般都避免用關係代名詞 whose 或 of which 來代替，而改用由 with 引導的介詞片語。

Can you see the house whose windows/of which the windows are broken?（欠通順）

Can you see the house with broken windows?（較通順）」

‧關係代詞和「介詞流落」（preposition stranding）

英語關係子句中當關係代詞為介詞的賓語的時候，介詞與關係代詞一起前移，還是讓介詞留在動詞後面，這是一個「介詞流落」（preposition stranding）的語法現象。本書下冊第 17 章對何時介詞留在動詞後頭，何時不能，都有詳細描述。對不同的關係代詞和介詞出現的語法環境都有明確規定，讓讀者一目了然。

「當關係代名詞 whom 是介詞賓語的時候，介詞可以放在關係代名詞的前面，也可以放在關係子句的句尾：

the man with whom you dined（較文的說法）

the man who（m）you dined with（口語的說法）」

「在下列情況中，介詞只能放在關係子句的後面。」

（a）當關係代名詞被省略的時候：

This is the house we have been invited to.

（b）當關係代名詞是 that, as 或 but 的時候：

This is the very book that I am looking for.

There is no one but he can find fault with.

（c）當關係代名詞同時做兩個以上介詞的賓語的時候：

What is the subject（that）you have seen an increasing interest in and controversy over?

「在下列的情形，介詞常放在關係代名詞（whom, which）的前面。」

（a）連接關係子句：

George, with whom I used to go to school, is now a well-known novelist.

（b）關係代名詞前面有「數量詞」all, both, some, many, none, neither, one 等。

I have two friends, both of whom are on holiday at the moment.

（c）介詞與關係代名詞 which 所代替的名詞形成一種固定的狀態副詞片語：

the courage with which he faced the enemy

（d）beyond, around, opposite, besides, than, as to, outside, except, during, considering 等介詞，一般都放在關係代名詞的前面。

the man opposite whom I'm sitting

the fountain around which they are standing

　　高階英語學習者在掌握上述假設式子句、*tough* 子句賓語前提、典型與非典型助動詞、以及關係代詞等虛詞和句式特點的時候，既需要掌握規律，也需要瞭解常規之外的情況，需要學習許多句式和虛詞的獨特性，否則學不好英文。由於這些虛詞和句式的特點和限制，對一般二語學員來說，不一定出現在平日接觸到的語料裡面，因此只能靠顯性知識去掌握。湯教授的參考語法提供了豐富的參考指引。

（三）本書雖然強調語法形式的重要性，沒有依循傳意語法的路子，但卻對詞彙之間的細微差異以及句式和語意的搭配非常重視，因為語言形式之間的語意和語用差別，是學員所必須掌握的。以下也用五個實例來說明本書這個特點。

・內動詞和外動詞的區別

　　英語的表達聽覺和視覺具備兩套動詞，一套表達積極的知覺模態，即個體行動者主動地、有意識地去注意一些現象，如 look at, listen to；還有一套描述非積極的知覺模態，即由於外部環境的感知或外部因素而得到了某種知覺或產生了某種變化，如 see, hear。這種積極與非積極模態的區別也體現在其他動詞的差別上，如 look for 和 find 的差別，前者表達積極的尋找，而後者表示「找到了」，達到了目的。本書把前者稱為「外動詞」（public verbs），把後者稱為「內動詞」（privative verbs），在上冊第 4 章有詳細的列舉。

　　"I *see* him now.（「看見、看到」：內動詞）

　　I *am looking at* him now.（「看」：外動詞）

　　I *hear* the music now.（「聽見、聽到」：內動詞）

　　I *am listening to* the music now.（「聽」：外動詞）

・追問句的語調

　　語法和語調的相互作用，對英語學習者來說是不好掌握的，這方面具備語法和語用知識，懂得其中規律，會有很大的幫助。本書上冊第 1 章對追問句（tag question）的語調特點有很好的說明，指出如 "He's an American, isn't he?" 這樣的句子，如果尾部追問部分 "isn't he?" 是降調，表示說話者對所說的話相當有把握；

如果尾部追問部分是升調，則表示說話者對所說的話沒有多大把握。同樣一串詞語和句式，如果語調不一樣，問句的預設將會截然不同。這種句法與語調的複雜界面現象，對於英語學習者來說，是非常重要的資訊。

以下的例子更能說明，本書對語法與語意之間的關係非常重視，而且所提出的描述分析，是其他英語參考語法不一定提到的。書中下冊第 16 章，對英語動詞的過去分詞兩種用法，有如下介紹：

‧動詞過去分詞作為形容詞

「動詞的『過去分詞』或『en 式動詞』也可以放在名詞的前面做修飾語。這個時候，及物動詞的過去分詞含有『被動（被……的）』的意思；不及物動詞的過去分詞含有「完成（已經……的）」意思。」

文中還提醒讀者注意，過去分詞作為形容詞，放在名詞前作為修飾語和放在系動詞後面作為補語，意思是不一樣的。例如，"the broken cup" 的涵義是「被打破的杯子」而 "the cup is broken" 描述一種靜態的狀況「那個杯子是破的」。同樣的，"a wounded soldier" 涵義是「一個受傷的士兵」；而 "a soldier was wounded"，除了可以表示「有一個士兵被打傷了」這個意思外，還可以描述有一個過去的狀態，即「有一個士兵曾經是受過傷的」，目前這個狀態已不再存在。另外，如 "fall" 這樣的非及物動詞，"a fallen leaf" 描述一片已經墜落在地上的樹葉，但 "a leaf has fallen" 可以描述一片正在墜落的樹葉。

the broken cup（比較：The cup is broken.）

a wounded soldier（比較：A soldier was wounded.）

a fallen leaf（比較：A leaf has fallen.）

書中還進一步指出，不是所有動詞的過去分詞都可以作為形容詞的，有些過去分詞具有形容詞特點，可以出現在名詞前作為修飾語，被加強詞修飾，也可以作補語，如 *tired, surprised, pleased* 等過去分詞。但也有一些過去分詞並不是形容詞，不能被加強詞（如 very）修飾而出現在名詞前或者系詞後面，如 *wounded, punished, beaten*。[2] 這些細緻的差別，是高級英語學習者不一定能察覺到的，通過

---

2 對於什麼動詞的過去分詞能充當形容詞，後來的語法著作有更詳細的二語習得分析，請參看 Wang and Lee（1999）.

語法書來掌握相關知識，是有效的途徑。

The boy was very tired/surprised/pleased.

*The boy was very wounded/punished/beaten.

‧動名詞

本書對動名詞（gerundive nominal）一些形式及語意上的差別，也有詳細解說。例如，"I don't like your coming late" 和 "I don't like you coming late"，或者 "I hate Bob's borrowing money from me" 和 "I hate Bob borrowing money from me"，前者用了所有格 's，後者則只是賓格，到底有什麼差別？這種問題是高階英語學習者常有的疑惑。下冊第 43 頁詳細列出哪些動詞可以帶動名詞 V-ing 形式（gerund）作為賓語，並區分兩種動名詞，一種如 like, prefer, fancy, hate, dislike, detest, mind, dread, fear, regret, understand, remember 等動詞，可以出現在「主語＋動詞＋所有格（代）名詞＋ V-ing…」句型，而另一種如 finish, avoid, advise, suggest, deny, begin, continue, postpone, need, want 等動詞，則只出現在「主語＋動詞＋ V-ing…」句型。書中並指出「主語＋動詞＋所有格（代）名詞＋ V-ing…」可以變成「主語＋動詞＋賓格（代）名詞＋ V-ing…」，但兩者有細微的語義差別：「在日常口語中常把所有格（代）名詞改為賓格，以表示所強調的是引起事件的人而非事件本身。」

‧時間介詞的特點

作者對語意的重視，從對動詞的分類可見。上冊第 4 章就提出，表示瞬間的動詞和表示持續時段的動詞，其搭配情況是不一樣的，需要區分。「根據能否有表示時間長短的副詞，英語的動詞可以分為兩種。『持續性動詞』（如 live, stay, wait, sit, stand, sleep, lie, work, study, read, write, listen 等）可以有由 for, till, until 引導的期間副詞。」因此可以說以下句子：

They waited for a long time.

He slept till/until nine o'clock.

「『瞬間性動詞』（如 come, go, leave, start, arrive, die, appear, disappear 等）不可以有由 for, till, until 引導的期間副詞。」因此不能說以下句子：

*They came for a long while.

*He left till/until nine o'clock.

　　書中同時指出，持續性的動詞可以出現在由 while 引導的副詞子句中，而瞬間性的動詞卻不能。因此可以說 The band was playing while I waited；但不能說 *The band was playing while I left。相反地，持續性動詞不能出現在由 when 引導的副詞子句中，而瞬間性的動詞卻能。因此不能說 *The band was playing when I waited; 但可以說 The band was playing when I left。

　　書中對時間介詞一些細微的差別，有精確的描述。例如，下冊第 19 章對 for 和 during 的時間特點有以下補充：「for 一般表示『不特定的期間』；during 表示『特定的期間』。」例如，在下列句子，for 都是跟表不定時間段的短語搭配，如 for two weeks, for several months；而 during 則跟特定時間段搭配，如 during the summer, during the vacation 等短語。這些精細而重要的語義差別，在書中處處可見，讓讀者常有驚喜。

　　We waited for a week/two weeks/several months.

　　I hope to see you some time during the week/the summer/ the vacation.

　　He was in Japan for the month of May.「整個五月都在日本」

　　He was in Japan during May.「不一定整個五月都在日本」

（四）本書的第四個特點，在於書中所描述的許多語法細節，吸收了當代語言學（尤其是生成語法學）1960-1980 年代的最新研究成果，從書中的參考書目可見作者的研究素養和功力。

‧動詞的補語子句

　　在 1970 年代生成語法對動詞補語子句有深入的分析，將動詞按照子句類型的不同，加以分類，並以此作為基礎揭示各種語法現象，讓人能對複雜句結構有一個通盤的認識（Bresnan 1972; Grimshaw 1979）。本書下冊第十五章將動詞的補語子句稱為「名詞子句」，指出有四種名詞子句：[that- 子句]、[wh- 子句]、[不定詞 -子句]、[動名詞子句]，並舉例說明：

　　I know that he has arrived.（ [that- 子句]）

　　I know when we should start.（[wh- 子句]）

　　It is easy for us to study English.（ [不定詞子句]）

Nobody knows my going to Japan.（[動名詞子句]）

該章節詳細列出，哪些動詞和形容詞可以接受 [that- 子句] 做為賓語，哪些接受 [wh- 子句] 做為賓語。及後更指出，有些動詞可以容許子句中的 wh- 詞提前移到句首，有些動詞卻不可以。同時提醒讀者，疑問句中子句中的 wh- 詞，移到兩個位置，表達兩種不同的語義；wh- 詞在句首表達一個特指問句；wh- 詞在子句之首，則表達是非問句。名詞子句（即補語子句 complement clause）中的 wh- 詞，與主句動詞和句子語義之間的關係，生成語法對 wh- 結構的深入研究，在一定程度上反映在書中對名詞子句的詳細論述。

Do you know <u>when</u> he will come?（yes/no 問句）

<u>When</u> do you think he will come?（wh- 問句）

‧關係子句的限制和非限制用法

語法學家在 1970 年代對關係子句的限制和非限制用法，在句法形式和語意特點的分析上，都有不少研究（Peranteau, Levi and Phares 1972; Stockwell, Schachter and Partee 1973），也反映在本書對關係子句的描寫。下冊第 17 章對這兩種關係子句的語義區別有非常簡要準確的說明：

「關係子句在性質上是一個形容詞子句，其功用在修飾前面的名詞。例如在下面的句子裡，關係子句 that was nearest to his house 修飾前面的名詞 the garage，即從眾多的修車廠裡面特地指出離他家最近的那一家修理廠來。

He walked to the garage that was nearest to his house.

『他走到離家最近的修車廠。』

這種用法就叫做關係子句限制的用法（the restrictive use），因為這個時候關係子句的功用在修飾或限制前面的名詞。

另外有些關係子句，其功用並不在修飾前面的名詞，而在連接這個關係子句，以便接著繼續把話說下去。例如在下面的句子裡，我們已經知道他去的是最近的一家修車廠，用不著再用關係子句來告訴我們究竟指的是哪一家。所以這裡關係子句 which was a mile away 的主要目的是，補充說明或者順便提一提這家修車廠座落在一里遠的地方。

He walked to the nearest garage, which was a mile away.

『他走到最近的一家修車廠，而這家修車廠離他家有一里之遠。』

這種用法就叫做連接的用法（the continuative use）。」

本書對關係子句的非限制性用法稱為「連接的用法」，更能帶出這種用法的實質特點，因為這種用法就是針對所修飾的名詞作出補充說明。

・子句的時式

本書對一些語意現象的描述，也反映了當時語言學界對相關現象的研究成果。如何表達子句裡面的時式（tense），是令高階英語學習者困惑的問題。上冊第 4 章對間接陳述句的時式問題，通過下列例句作出概括。

I said, "I am tired" → I said that I was tired.

He said that honesty is the best policy.

She said that she takes a walk in the park every morning.

「如果傳達動詞是過去式的話，那麼按照時式一致的原則，間接引句裡面的動詞也要改為過去式」。「但是如果間接引句的內容時表示普遍的真理、常習的動作或歷史的事實的話，那麼就不一定要改成過去式或過去完成式。」上面的概括，基本上與語言學家對時式序列（sequence of tenses）所總結的規律一致（Comrie 1985）。

・論元結構的承襲（argument structure inheritance）

一個動詞具有論元結構，例如在句子 John refused to help 中，及物動詞 refuse「拒絕」有兩個論元，一個是作為施事的主語 John，另一個是作為客體的不定名詞子句 to help。問題是假如這個動詞名詞化了之後，它的論元結構是否仍然存在，是否為衍生的名詞所承襲？就是說，在 refuse 變成名詞 refusal 後，能否說 "John's refusal to help"？這種語法問題在生成語法著作裡面有所討論（Lees 1963; Grimshaw 1990），但在一般參考語法書中極少涉及。本書下冊第 15 章有以下描述，指出一些動詞在名詞化後仍然保留了原來的論元結構和補語特點，有些動詞卻不能：

「含有動詞（如 need, desire, tend, fail, hesitate, guarantee, plan, arrange, agree, request, refuse, promise, decide, threaten, intend, advise, invite, remind 等）與不定詞的

子句可以直接把動詞改為名詞（need, desire, tendency, failure, hesitation, guarantee, plan, arrangement, agreement, request, refusal, promise, decision, threat, intention, advice, invitation, reminder）以後當名片語用。這個時候動詞的主語要用所有格。」

He failed to get the job.

His failure to get the job（made her very unhappy）.

They agreed to help him.

（They forgot all about）their agreement to help him.

有些動詞（如 need, like, prefer）改為名詞（need, liking, preference）以後還要把後面的不定詞改為 for+ V-ing.

→ His preference for eating alone（is quite well known）.

・有定冠詞 *the* 語義的描述

由於漢語是一種沒有冠詞的語言，對母語為漢語的英語學習者來說，英語的冠詞是很難掌握的一個系統，何時該用不定冠詞 a（n），何時用有定冠詞 the，高級學習者也會常犯這方面的錯誤。為何冠詞系統如此難以掌握，其中困難之處在於長久以來對冠詞的句法語意分析，尚未總結出較全面的規律，對冠詞所涉及的各種指稱涵義，也缺乏清晰的界定。這個局面在 1960 年後有了許多突破。例如，Baker（1966）關於定指和不定指的研究引進了 specific/ non-specific（實指 / 虛指）這組指稱概念。Hawkins（1978）的專著比較全面地描述了英語中定指和不定指（definite/ indefinite）的表達方式，從聆聽者的角度，分析了含有定冠詞的名詞短語「the + 名詞」的各種使用情況；有時候 the N 在前文有明顯的先行語，即其所指向的物體，前文已經提過；有時候 the + 名詞可以直接指向語境中的特定物體；但有時候它和前文的連接是比較間接的，需要說話者利用對客觀世界的認識來建立。本書上冊第 12 章對有定冠詞 the 的用法，提出四條規律：

「（1）『後指』：指在前文裡已經出現過的名詞。注意，這些名詞前後用不同的冠詞。」書中並不是孤立看有定冠詞，而是對比不定冠詞 *a*（*n*）和有定冠詞 *the* 的用法。在以下例子，前者 *a cat* 引進一個話語對象，後者 *the cat* 回指先行語 *a cat* 已經引進的對象。

I saw *a cat* in the tree this morning, but when I looked again this afternoon, *the cat* was gone.

「（2）『明指』：名詞的前後有修飾語，足以認定某一個特定的人或物。」在以下例子，「the＋名詞」直接指向語境中的一些物體，是一種直指或明指（deictic）的情況。

Hand me *the longer piece of chalk* on the desk, please.

This is *the book* I have been looking for.

「（3）『暗指』：名詞的前後雖然沒有修飾語，但是從生活經驗或語言情況中仍可以判定所指的是一個特定的人或物。」在下列書中例子，聽話者聽到 the post office，可以憑生活經驗和話語語境判斷，就是指常去的那個郵政局；至於聽到 the letter 也可以憑生活經驗判斷為一般去郵政局時投寄的信件。

He went to *the post office* to mail *the letter.*

「（4）『泛指』：用在單數可數名詞之前，以表示一類的所有分子。」書中指出，定冠詞表類指，有一定的限制，例如只限於單數可數名詞。

The horse is a noble animal.

總的來說，本書關於英語有定冠詞用法的說明，反映了 1960-1970 年代語言學研究這方面取得的成果，從聆聽者的角度來總結有定／無定名詞的使用規律，描述的相當精確。表達指稱概念所採用的中文術語有些也屬作者原創，跟後來語言學研究者常用的一些術語互相輝映。例如，書中用「後指」來代表 anaphora，而不用「回指」；用「明指」來涵蓋一些 deixis（直指）的情況；以「暗指」來代表一種常被稱為 associative use 的有定冠詞用法。這些術語「望文生義」，有助讀者把握術語背後的含義。

如上所述，湯廷池教授的《觀察　‧　類推　‧　條理化：分析性的英語語法》是一本弘揚顯性語法知識的典範英語語法參考書，對語法規則以及各種虛詞和句型的語意特點都有詳細精要的描述，充分反映現代語言學界的研究成果，許多討論都是一般語法參考書所不會涉及的。湯教授基於多年英語教學的經驗，在介紹相關語法結構的時候，避開抽象的符號，而用具體示範和豐富事例來說明，書中在不同章節都提供了大量的練習，以便讀者鞏固對相關句型結構的理解。英語的語法規則，有

些基本適用與某個語法範疇的所有成員（例如，動詞第三身單數屈折形式 -s）；另外有些規則適用與某個語法範疇的大部分成員，但仍然有不少例外的情況（例如複數標記 -s 加在可數名詞後面）；還有許多其他語法規則（如假設法 subjunctive mood，或者 tough- 前移規則），都只適用與某些動詞。這些都是需要英語學習者特加注意，用詞彙學習的方法去掌握的。作者除了介紹語法規律，還花了大量篇幅討論詞彙獨特的情況，這是本書一大特色。

此書是一本適合英語老師和高階英語學習者參考的中文著作，如果將之跟同時代一些流行的英文著作相比，例如 Michael Swan 的 *A Practical English Usage*（Swan 1980），絲毫不會遜色，而且處處顯示作者的心得和心血。用中文來講解英文語法，對母語為漢語的學習者更有針對性，所強調的主題和選擇的題材更能照顧學習者的需要。用中文向華語讀者介紹最前沿的語言學概念和研究成果，是湯廷池教授畢生信奉的寫作原則，這本英語參考語法體現了湯教授這種學術理念，也是他留給英語教學界的重要貢獻。

李行德

香港中文大學語言學及現代語言系榮休教授

大學通識教育部主任

2022.04.08

References

Baker, C. L. (1966). *Definiteness and Indefiniteness in English*. Master Thesis. University of Illinois. Reproduced by the Indiana University Linguistics Club.

Bresnan, Joan. 1979 [1972]. *Theory of complementation in English syntax*. New York: Garland.

Comrie, Bernard. 1985. *Tense*. Cambridge: Cambridge University Press.

Gleason, H. A. 1965. *Linguistics and English grammar*. New York: Holt, Rinehart and Winston.

Grimshaw, Jane. 1985 [1977]. *English Wh-constructions and the theory of grammar*. New York: Garland.

Grimshaw, Jane. 1990. *Argument structure*. Cambridge, MA: MIT Press.

Hawkins, John. 1978. *Definiteness and indefiniteness: a study in reference and grammatical prediction*. London: Croom Helm.

Johnson, Keith. 1982. *Communicative syllabus design and methodology*. New York: Pergamon.

Lado, Robert. 1964. *Language teaching: a scientific approach*. New York: McGraw Hill.

Lees, Robert. 1968. [1963]. *The grammar of English nominalizations*. The Hague: Mouton.

Peranteau, Paul, J. Levi and G. Phares. eds. 1972. *The Chicago which hunt: papers from the Relative Clause Festival*. Chicago: Chicago Linguistic Society.

Stockwell, Robert, P. Schachter and B. Partee. 1973. *The major syntactic structures of English.* New York: Holt, Rinehart, and Winston.

Swan, Michael. 1980. *A practical English usage*. Oxford: Oxford University Press.

Wang, Chuming and Thomas H.-T. Lee. 1999. L2 acquisition of conflation classes of prenominal adjectival participles. *Language Learning* 49(1), 1-36.

Widdowson, H. 1978. *Teaching language as communication*. Oxford: Oxford University Press.

Wilkins, David. 1976. *Notional syllabuses: a taxonomy and its relevance to foreign language curriculum development*. Oxford: Oxford University Press.

推薦序二

最體貼的經師與人師

　　個人追隨湯師二十多年，是老師從清華大學退休之後的追隨者之一。我們這群號稱「湯家班」也獲得老師首肯認證的小團體，從老師退休後在東吳大學博士班任教以來，長年追隨老師的成員多數是日文專業背景。由於老師英日語左右逢源，日文造詣更勝母語者，故在授課之際總是鼓勵我們為學宜廣宜深，並能英日語並用。我也就不知不覺深受感召，聽從老師的教導，十餘年來逐步涉獵英語並開啟探索英美社會文化的興趣。

　　而本書正是老師推薦我研讀的英語文法書。可惜，我當時上網買來的，和這本書的格式、編排都大不相同。如果不是如今有機會翻閱這個版本，恐怕始終不知自己當年讀來著實吃力的內容，原來跟原始版本竟有如此巨大的差異！

　　從本書的版面、圖式、簡表，乃至例句對比、編排順序等，都可以看出老師為學習者投注的貼心設想。這些設計環節都是他認為需要熟記的內容，因而透過視覺化的認知途徑，儘可能地減輕學習者負擔的巧思。同時，他以語言學者的知識高度，卻要求自己不輕易使用學術語言；舉重若輕的行文表達，做的正是他自己知行合一、奉行多年的寫作心法——「把輕鬆理解留給讀者，苦心煎熬留給自己」。

　　本書為了高三生英語總複習而設計了直截淺白、有效易懂等有助認知記憶的表達形式之外，老師身為語言學者的嚴謹自是如影隨形。例如，他引述了所有的語料來源，並強調本書例句採集自英語母語者的原則。此外，從三個重要句型、十個基本句型、十二種動詞時變式，再到各種變式的用途等，一路由淺入深的「華麗」展開，處處透露出一位巨人般的語言學者，俯身對待小朋友的溫柔用心。

　　甚至，他還照顧到英語課堂上的老師，指出後續的練習方式，可以透過口頭問答，取代習題的書寫。這也反映了老師一向不喜書呆子式的苦讀之道，而「靈活權變、與書對話」，則是他認為不會被書讀死的康莊大道。而之所以匯集了豐富的習題，則是為了讓學習者透過實踐熟能生巧。個人有幸聽聞老師曾經提起本書匯集眾

多語料與習題的緣由，披露於此或可供讀者或外語教師印證所學與經驗。

　　感謝志真與志永老師重新出版此書，不僅對老師思念甚深的學生受惠，如今為學英語不得其門而入的莘莘學子必定獲益良多。重展此書，環顧現今的學術環境，願為高中生寫語法書的語言學者恐怕將成絕響了。更何況，以湯師在語言學上無人能及的洞見與博學，能夠惠澤青年學生的基礎教育，當是所有讀者難能可貴的緣分與福分！

楊承淑

輔仁大學學術特聘教授

於 2021 年 9 月 28 日教師節

悼念恩師

推薦序三

勤練習是內化文法規則的不二法門

　　六月時收到湯志真轉寄來信告知，在新竹中學圖書館黃大展主任和退休蔡肇慶老師的協尋下，臺南女中圖書館劉文明主任和新竹中學退休曾義興老師，分別收藏了一套湯廷池老師 1985 年由海國書局出版的絕版文法書《最新實用高級英語語法（修訂本）》和習題解答本，書況還算不錯，決定由元華文創重新出版這上下兩冊為一套的文法書，並定名為《觀察・類推・條理化：分析性的英語語法》以追思湯老師，我很高興這套文法書能重新出版並為在天上最敬愛的湯老師寫一序文。

　　元華文創李欣芳主編寄來當時由海國書局出版的原始文法書電子掃描檔後，我翻著一頁頁泛黃並有著斑點的 PDF 文件，不知不覺地時光回到過去，一幕幕老師站在講臺上教我如何觀察、分析、思考、推論的容顏又浮上腦海，同時也讓我想起 35 年前在清華大學讀語言學研究所時和這套文法書的因緣。研究所二年級時，我為了家教一高中生英文，就是跟湯老師借這套文法書來當教材使用。當時就覺得這是一部與眾不同的文法書，好學又好記。此番重讀，依然覺得這文法書有其獨特之處，是一部值得時常查閱並終生收藏的好文法書。

　　這套文法書共二十二章，第一章到第十四章分為上冊，第十五到第二十二章為下冊，兩冊近 1100 頁，專供高中三年英語教學之用，現重新出版，依然保留原始章節安排，但開本加大，以方便空白處作筆記。看到近 1100 頁的頁數，很多人也許會嚇壞了，免不了懷疑這怎麼讀得完？背得起來嗎？要回答這個問題之前，我說說一個我個人的小故事。在大四那年還是讀研究所時的暑假，我想提升自己的英文實力，但單字是個門檻，能主動使用的詞彙有限。後來在報上看到有人建議單字其實不用背，最好的方法是大量閱讀，閱讀中不懂的字因為會重複出現而自動記憶。所以那年暑假我跟圖書館借了多本英文著名小說，從早讀到晚。除了被小說故事吸引外，發現許多不懂的單字真的會重複出現，而且只需第一、二次查一下字典或猜意思，那個字就記起來了，因而那個暑假我學會也記得了許多新單字。

　　上面那個學單字的方法，和湯老師文法書上所體現的教學方法其實有異曲同工之妙。老師的文法書雖然看似有 1100 頁之多，但真正的文字敘述只佔據了很小一部份。湯老師把大部分的文法，特別是需要熟記的部分，都整理歸納成簡單的句型或圖表，並有例外規則的參考說明，以方便記憶。但更重要的是文法書上的所有規則及句型都有豐富的例句演示，並且提供大量由簡到難的不同練習題來反覆操作。這些練習的目的就是要透過次數來強化牢固規則的記憶，其道理就和單字不用死記死背是一樣的，只要同一個單字重複地出現，腦中就容易記得那個單字的意思和用法。同理，重複地利用不同的句子來練習同一種句型，想不記得那個句型也難。人家常說，同樣一件事，能做一百次，就會成為那件事的專家，我相信勤練習也是在學習英文時內化其文法規則的不二法門。湯老師的文法書正是希望所有讀者都能成為文法專家，所以練習題佔據了很大的空間，而不是文字說明。

　　大學上湯老師課時，他常說他是個不喜歡死記死背的人，他喜歡用自己的推理推論來獲得規則。但就如同他文法書上所說，學習語言不能完全離開熟記，而熟記的最有效方法就是用多次練習來強化記憶。湯老師的文法書在這方面真的是下足了一番功夫，所以不怕你學不會，記不來，只怕你不練習，肯練習就一定記得住。我在此序文向所有想學好英文文法的人大力推薦，一定要在案頭擺上湯老師的這套文法書，相信你將因此終生受用。

林若望

中央研究院語言學研究所所長

2021.09.28

推薦序四

書香飄兩岸，桃李念師恩

2011 年，兩岸實現高等教育學歷互認，首批大陸學生赴臺灣就讀大學和研究所，這是兩岸教育合作史上的一個里程碑。受益於這項政策，我得以於 2017 年從北京跨越海峽到輔仁大學攻讀口譯研究博士，並在輔仁大學有幸成為湯廷池先生的學生。

最早聽說先生名號是在我的博士生導師楊承淑教授（2010）的一本專著序言裡。她提及曾拜師於湯廷池先生門下，以學徒的方式學習語言學長達 20 年之久。楊教授是在兩岸四地都很有影響力的口譯研究學者，我斷定，能吸引她追隨學習如此之久的湯先生，必定是一位品格高潔的飽學之士。

自新竹清華大學退休後，湯先生長期在輔仁大學擔任講座教授，為研究生講授語言學課程。為了方便先生授課，學校專門就近先生住所在臺北大安森林公園附近租賃了教室。從新莊輔大校園去上課不免舟車勞頓，卻擋不住同學們的學習熱情，先生課上總是有很多人。

先生當時已經年逾八旬，講話緩慢但有力，思路特別清晰。艱深抽象的語言學理論，在先生的口中變得深入淺出。在先生的課堂上，我頓悟了不少曾經百思不得其解的生成語法的概念。除了學習知識外，從先生的言傳身教中，更是學到寶貴的為學之道，燃起了對學術研究的熱愛。

先生在生活中隨身攜帶小筆記本，隨時記錄自己看到和聽到的新詞或特別的語言現象，拿到課堂上與同學們一起進行語言分析。我在先生課上交的第一篇作業題目是《語法「三品說」評述》。先生對我的作業給予了鼓勵，作業紙上卻留下密密麻麻的紅筆批註。

先生改作業時，不僅要看行文結構和學術觀點，任何遣詞造句甚至標點使用的不當之處都難逃他的「金睛火眼」。先生一直諄諄教誨我們，要建立起「觀察」、「類推」和「條理化」的思維，才能透過現象看本質，做好學問。

　　我是那一期語言學班上唯一的陸生。知道我來自遙遠的北京後，先生給予了我特別的關照。在課堂上給我更多回答問題的機會，在課堂外對我在臺灣的生活也關心有加。他告訴我，看到大陸地區近些年在各個領域的快速發展，他的內心充滿了喜悅。他鼓勵我多做一些促進兩岸學術交流的事。

　　湯先生 1992 年曾主編過一套由臺灣學生書局出版的《現代語言學論叢》。在先生的推動下，該叢書中包含了一本大陸學者石毓智的專著，他親筆為該書作序。該書應該是那個時期大陸語言研究者在臺出版的第一本新書。在該書序文中，湯先生表示，出版一本大陸學者的書所花的心血與時間，遠超出版臺灣學者的十本書，但是他覺得有責任來努力縮短海峽兩岸在學術空間上的人為距離。1997 年，先生曾訪問北京大學。據那次訪問的北大對接人趙楊教授回憶，先生就美國語言學發展、認知語法等主題與北大教師開展了對話。訪問期間，先生還非常興奮地登上了長城。

　　除了做好語言研究，先生的另一個宏願是幫助更多學子學好英語。我的臺灣同學告訴我，先生曾經擔任臺灣高中英文教科書的編輯委員長，他編寫的《最新實用高級英語語法（修訂本）》曾經是幾代臺灣人英語學習的啟蒙。大陸《語言文字週報》有篇文章對先生在生成語法的推廣與普及方面所做的貢獻給予了高度的評價，稱先生「善於將高深的理論用淺顯的語言表述出來」（丁健，2017）。《最新實用高級英語語法（修訂本）》就是這樣一本在高深理論指導下編寫而成的淺顯易懂的語法書。

　　聽聞此書在臺灣的影響力後，大陸地區的不少英語學子紛紛在網路上的豆瓣、知乎等平臺表達對此書的濃厚興趣，同時也因找不到此書而抱憾。先生的女兒湯志真也是一位語言學教授，退休前在臺灣中研院語言所就職。我從她那裡得知，她不時也會收到一些大陸地區學子表達類似訴求的郵件，讀者的熱情期盼是促成此書得以再版的最重要的力量之一。

　　新技術賦予了圖書更強大的生命力。此書將以「電子書＋紙質書」的組合形式再版，讀者可以獲得更加豐富的閱讀經驗。乘著新技術的翅膀，這部經典之作還將跨越地域限制，惠及兩岸乃至全球更多的讀者。

　　我在臺灣於 2021 年取得博士學位後，來到北京第二外國語學院任教。作為一名教師，我相信此書會給大陸地區的英語學子帶來不同的學習視角；作為湯先生的

學生，我希望他的更多著作能得到再版，讓更多學子受益；而作為兩岸教育合作與交流的受益者，我盼望未來兩岸在學術領域能有更多類似的建設性互動。

齊濤雲

北京第二外國語學院 副教授

2021 年 9 月北京

編　輯　大　意

一、本書根據教育部頒高級中學英語課程標準編輯，分上、下兩冊，專供高級中學
　　三年英語語法教學之用。

二、語法說明力求淺顯，以冀學生能自行閱讀。同時附有許多圖式、例句與比較，
　　以幫助學生了解。

三、語法術語力求簡化，並盡量採用語言學上最近通用的術語。凡是不必要的定義，
　　無意義的分類，都一概刪去。

四、學習語言不能完全離開熟記，因此需要學生熟記的部分都列成簡單的表式，以
　　幫助記憶。

五、有關參考資料如用字、發音以及比較瑣碎的語法問題都列在參考裡，排列的次
　　序大致是由重要到次要。老師們可以視實際需要做適當的取捨，不必全部教
　　授。

六、練習的分量不少，每一種練習的安排大致是由易到難。其目的在供給老師充足
　　的補充教材，以免除蒐集的麻煩。同時，每一位老師的教授對象不同，程度有
　　差異，老師們可以自行斟酌選擇適量的習題。如果學生的程度較高，則簡易習
　　題可以省略不做。或者可以採用口頭練習，回答正確，習題即可算做完。老師
　　們不必擔心習題過多，負擔過重。

七、本書的英語，無論是例句與習題，都盡量採用參考資料中英美人士所實際使用
　　的句子，盡量避免自己造句。

目　次

第15章
名詞子句

15-1. 名詞子句

　　除了名詞或名詞組以外，整個句子也可以當主語、賓語或補語用。當整個句子做名詞用的時候，這個句子就叫做**名詞子句**（noun clause）。英語的名詞子句主要的有四種：「that- 子句」、「wh- 子句」、「不定詞子句」、「動名詞子句」。比較：

> The news was a surprise.
> *That he passed the examination* was a surprise.（that- 子句）

> I know his arrival.
> I know *that he has arrived*.（that- 子句）

> The question hasn't been decided yet.
> *Who will be in charge of the project* hasn't been decided yet.（wh- 子句）

> I know the time.
> I know *when we should start*.（wh- 子句）

> English is easy.
> It is easy *for us to study English*.（不定詞子句）

> Nobody knows the truth.
> Nobody knows *my going to Japan*.（動名詞子句）

15-2. that- 子句

　　that- 子句（*that*-clause），在句子的前面加連詞 that 而成：

Sentence	（句子）	⇒	Noun	Clause	（名詞子句）
NP	VP		Subj	NP	VP

John has arrived.
I know that. ⎫ → I know *that John has arrived*.

She was wrong.
She admitted that to me. $\Big\}$ → She admitted to me *that she was wrong.*

that- 子句前面的介詞一定要刪去：

You come along with me.
My brother insists on that. $\Big\}$ → My brother insists *that you come along with me.*

She was sick.
Bob told me about that. $\Big\}$ → Bob told me *that she was sick.*

I will succeed.
I am sure of that. $\Big\}$ → I am sure *that I will succeed.*

如果 that- 子句出現在主語或賓語的位置，那麼這個 that- 子句可以移到句尾，並且用 it 去填補原來主語的位置：

$$\boxed{\text{that + Sentence} \cdots} \Rightarrow \boxed{\text{It} \cdots \text{that + Sentence}}$$

⟨ That he finished his job all by himself ⟩ is impossible. →

It is impossible *that he finished his job all by himself.*

習 題 272

依照例句用 that 連接下列句子。

Examples:

He has left the city.
They believe it. $\Big\}$ →

　They believe that he has left the city.

You work hard.
It is important. $\Big\}$ →

　That you work hard is important.

　It is important that you work hard.

They got married last week.
I found it true. $\Big\}$ →

　I found it true that they got married last week.

　　He has a bad cold. ⎫
　　　　　　　　　　　⎬ →
　　It seems so. ⎭

　　　It seems that he has a bad cold.

1. We don't have to go to school today. ⎫
　　　　　　　　　　　　　　　　　　　⎬
　　I forgot it. ⎭

2. He is not coming. ⎫
　　　　　　　　　　⎬
　　I don't know about it. ⎭

3. I cannot go. ⎫
　　　　　　　　⎬
　　I am sorry about it. ⎭

4. He is right. ⎫
　　　　　　　　⎬
　　He is sure of it. ⎭

5. You go there at once. ⎫
　　　　　　　　　　　　⎬
　　It is necessary. ⎭

6. He hes left school. ⎫
　　　　　　　　　　　⎬
　　Is it true? ⎭

7. He didn't have enough money. ⎫
　　　　　　　　　　　　　　　　⎬
　　It appeared so. ⎭

8. We would see each other every week. ⎫
　　　　　　　　　　　　　　　　　　　⎬
　　We agreed on it. ⎭

9. You get there in time. ⎫
　　　　　　　　　　　　⎬
　　They consider it important. ⎭

10. He won the election. ⎫
　　　　　　　　　　　　⎬
　　It was fortunate. ⎭

參考：(1) 可以接「that- 子句」做賓語的動詞有 say (to someone), write (to someone), explain (to someone), report (to someone), reveal (to someone), deny, hope, mean, think, suppose, consider, dream, assume, conclude, expect, imagine, guess, suspect, believe, know, find (out), figure (out), learn, understand, see (= understand), hear (= learn), notice, feel, gather, (not) mind, trust pretend, bet, remember, recall, forget, realize, discover, prove (to someone), doubt, fear, regret, prefer, agree, complain, decide, argue, claim, insist, tell someone, inform someone, warn someone, remind someone, assure someone, notify someone, promise (someone), take care, make clear, see to it 等；形容詞有 glad, pleased, (un)satisfied, (un)happy, sorry, afraid, anxious, lucky, grateful, thankful, sure, certain, positive, confident, convinced, aware, consious, careful, excited, upset, annoyed, disappointed, disturbed, worried, ashamed, surprised, amazed 等。

(2) 可以接「that- 子句」做主語的形容詞有 good, nice, fine, great, wonderful, marvelous, too bad, pitiful, shameful, right, wrong, sure, certain, clear, evident, apparent, obvious, true, natural, (un)likely, (im)possible, probable, lucky, (un)fortunate, strange, miraculous, sad, necessary, important, tragic, incredible, interesting, curious 等。注意，這個句型通常都改成「It is + 形容詞 + that- 子句」的句型：

That he will never win is possible.

　→ *It is possible that he will never win.*

尤其是問句，非改成這個句型不可：

$\begin{cases} \text{Is it possible that he will never win?（○）} \\ \text{Is that he will never win possible?（×）} \end{cases}$

與上面的形容詞意思相近的名詞（如 a good thing, a shame, a pity, a miracle, no wonder 等）也可以出現在這個句型：

It's *a good thing* that you have brought an umbrella with you.

Isn't it *a pity* that he failed again?

It's *no wonder* (*small wonder*) that she is popular with her friends.

(3) seem (to someone), appear (to someone), look (to someone), (so) happen, (so) chance, follow, occur to someone, (not) matter, stand to reason, turn out, may be, must be, can(not) be, help a lot, hurt a lot 等動詞只能出現在「It ⋯ that- 子句」的句型：

It *seems to me* that he is very rich.

It *turned out* that I was wrong.

It *may be* that he missed the bus.

It *helped a lot* that they lent us that extra money.

Because he is good it does not *follow* that he is wise.

It (*so*) *happened* that he was out of London at that time.

習　題　273

依照例句用 that 連接下列句子，並且把連接以後的句子改為被動式。

Examples:

She is very rich.⎫
⎬ →
They say it.　　⎭

They say that she is very rich.

It is said that she is very rich.

He has succeeded.⎫
⎬ →
It suprises me.　　⎭

It surprises me that he has succeeded.

I am surprised that he has succeeded.

1. He will go.　　⎫
　They expect it.⎭

2. She speaks English so fluently.⎫
　It amazes me.　　　　　　　⎭

3. The project would never succeed.⎫
　Someone explained it to me.　　⎭

4. She never answered his letters.⎫
　It bothered him.　　　　　　⎭

5. He was selfish.　　　⎫
　You must never say so.⎭

6. We eat with chopsticks.
   It amuses her. }

7. The examination would take place the next week.
   We thought so. }

8. He kept asking for more money.
   It annoyed his brother. }

9. A new branch will be opened next year.
   They have decided on it. }

10. Twenty students failed the course.
    It shocked their teacher. }

參考一：表「令人 …」的動詞，如 surprise, amaze, shock, frighten, stun, alarm, scare, please, delight, satisfy, amuse, interest, excite, fascinate, intrigue, annoy, upset, bother, irritate, disgust, worry, impress, disturb, disappoint 等，可以出現在「It + 動詞 + 人 + that- 子句」的句型：

It *pleases* me that you look so well.

It doesn't *bother* me that they don't like each other any longer.

這些動詞可以改成被動式：

I *am pleased* that you look so well.

I *am not bothered* that they don't like each other any longer.

有許多動詞在字尾加 -ing 後還可以變成形容詞。比較：

It *amazes* me that he speaks English so well.

It *is amazing* (to me) that speaks English so well.

It *amuses* her that he acts like a child.

It *is very amusing* (to her) that he acts like a child.

參考二：「that- 子句」如果出現在賓語或補語的位置，連詞 that 通常都可以省略。比較：

> *That* he passed the course was a surprise.（主語，不能省略）
>
> I know (*that*) he passed the course.（賓語，可以省略）
>
> It's strange (*that*) he failed the course.（補語，可以省略）
>
> It seems a shame (*that*) he failed the course.（補語，可以省略）
>
> The fact is (,) we know very little about gorillas.（補語，that 省略後可以留下逗號）

習 題 274

依照例句連接下列句子。

Examples:

Modern airplanes are fast. Everybody recognizes the fact. →

Everybody recognizes the fact that modern airplanes are fast.

He would leave soon. The idea disturbed his wife. →

The idea that he would leave soon disturbed his wife.

The idea disturbed his wife that he would leave soon.

1. I would be on time. The thought pleased me.

2. The enemy were near. The news alarmed the citizens.

3. Fire burns. No one can deny the fact.

4. There will be a general election. The rumor goes around.

5. They should consider seriously. They did not pay attention to the advice.

6. He forgot all about his appointment. The realization embarrassed Bob.

7. We reconsider the plan. The suggestion never came up.

8. They adopt the resolution. We passed the proposal.

9. The enemy were launching an attack. The information was passed on to the commander in chief.

10. Should we or shouldn't we contribute? The question came up during the discussion.

參考：「that- 子句」除了可以做動詞或形容詞的主語或賓語以外，還可以放在表示「事實、主意、消息」的名詞（如 fact, idea, news, information, thought, rumor, realization, suggestion, proposal 等）後面做「同位語」（appositive）：

He cannot face the fact *that he is a total failure.*

The idea *that he might get killed* scared him.

如果「that- 子句」是主語的同位語，還可以移到句尾：

The idea scared him 〔*that he might get killed.*〕

如果「that- 子句」是主語的補語，常用逗號「，」來代替連詞 that：

The fact is $\left\{ \begin{array}{c} \text{that} \\ , \end{array} \right\}$ he is a total failure.

表示「疑問」的名詞（如 question, puzzle, problem 等）常用「wh- 子句」做同位語：

The question *when we will start* hasn't been decided yet.

習 題 275

依照例句把斜體部分的動詞改為否定式。

Examples:

I know he *will* come. → *I know he won't come.*

I *knew* he will come. → *I didn't know he will come.*

I *think* he *will* come. → *I don't think he won't come.*

1. I hope he *will* fail.

2. I *imagine* he will pass.

3. I imagine he *will* pass,

4. I learned that there *was* enough time.

5. He *realized* that time was getting short.

6. I *realized* he *could* hear very well.

7. He's sure he *will* succeed.

8. He *is* sure he will succeed.

9. She found that you *missed something.*

10. I guess *somebody* told you that.

參考：主句的否定與從句的否定表示不同的意思：

$\begin{cases} \text{I know he } won't \text{ come.「我知道他不會來」。} \\ \text{I } didn't \text{ know he will come.「我不知道他會來」。} \end{cases}$

含有 think, believe, expect, suppose, imagine, be sure 等動詞或形容詞的句子，主句的否定與從句的否定所表示的意思很相近，但不盡相同。比較：

$\begin{cases} \text{I think he } won't \text{ come.「我認為他不會來。（比較有把握的說法）」} \\ \text{I } don't \text{ think he will come.「我不認為他會來。（比較無把握的說法）」} \end{cases}$

習 題 276

依照例句，用 Yes, I think so; No, I don't think so 或 No, I think not 回答下列問句。

Examples:

  Will it be fine tomorrow? (think) →

   Yes, I think so.

   No, I don't think so. / No, I think not.

1. You haven't caught cold, have you? (think) →

2. It's time to go, isn't it? (believe) →

3. Do you think it will keep fine today? (afraid) →

4. Will you be at the party tonight? (hope) →

5. Can't you ask for help? (guess) →

6. He left a week ago, didn't he? (believe)

7. Is there time for another cup of coffee?

8. Were you very late? (afraid)

9. The Volga is the longest river in Europe, isn't it? (guess) →

10. You are having a holiday this year, aren't you? (hope) →

參考：think, guess, suppose, expect, believe, imagine, gather, assume, hope, be afraid 後面的「that- 子句」，在答句中可以用 so 或 not 來代替：

  Will it be fine tommorrow?

   Yes, I think *so* (= that it will be fine tomorrow).

   No, I don't think *so* (= that it will be fine tomorrow).

   No, I think *not* (= that it won't be fine tomorrow).

習 題 277

把括號裡面的動詞改為適當的形式。

1. I suggested to him that he (give) up smoking.

2. John insisted that we (be) here by noon.

3. He proposed that they (not go) there any more.

4. She wishes that she (have) her new coat on.

5. I'm not a millionaire, but I wish I (be).

6. Is it necessary he (get) there on time?

7. She demanded that you (be not) told.

8. It's about time you (get) married and (settle) down.

9. I would rather you (pay) in cash.

10. He has made some mistakes, but he wishes he (have not).

11. It is essential that you (not tell) it to anyone.

12. The teacher ordered that they (be) quiet and (not make) any noise.

參考：(1) 「that- 子句」如果在表示、「提議」、「請求」或「命令」的動詞（如 suggest, recommend, advise, propose, move, ask, require, request, pray, plead, demand, insist, urge, maintain, order, command, instruct, direct, intend, arrange, prefer 等）後面當賓語用，裡面的動詞通常用動詞原形（或 should ＋動詞原形）、否定式用 not ＋動詞原形（或 should not＋動詞原形）：

I suggested that he (*should*) *do* it right away.

I suggested that we (*should*) *not do* it now.

(2) 「that- 子句」如果在表示「重要」、「需要」或「適當」的形容詞（如 important, proper, necessary, urgent, essential, fitting, imperative, right, advisable, better, preferable, traditional 等）後面當補語用，裡面的動詞也常用動詞原形或 should ＋動詞原形

It is important she (should) *follow* the doctor's directions.

(3) wish, it is time, would rather 後面的「that- 子句」，動詞常用過去式：

I wish you *were* not so excited.

It's time we *started*.

I would rather you *came* with me.

15-3. wh- 子句

由「wh- 詞」或「疑問詞」（who, whom, whose, which, what, when, where, why, whether, how）帶頭的名詞子句叫做 **wh- 子句**（wh-clause）。Wh- 子句與間接 wh- 問句一樣，由 (1) 先以適當的 wh- 詞代替句子中的某些語詞、(2) 然後把這個 wh- 詞移前放在句首而得來。

Somebody broke th record.
I know *who*. } →

　I know *who broke the record*.

John bought *something yesterday*.
He asked me *what*. } →

　He asked me *what John bought yesterday*.

Some student won the prize.
She didn't tell me *which*. } →

　She didn't tell me *which student won the prize*.

You are reading *someone's book*.
Could you tell me *whose*? } →

　Could you tell me *whose book you are reading*?

They came home *sometime*.
I wonder *when*. } →

　I wonder *when they came home*.

You met her *someplace*.
Do you remember *where*? } →

　Do you remember *where you met her*?

She came to know the truth *somehow*.
May I ask you *how*? } →

May I ask you *how she came to know the truth*?

He didn't attend the meeting *for some reason.*

Nobody knows *why.* $\Big\}\rightarrow$

Nobody knows *why he didn't attend the meeting.*

wh- 子句，除了出現在賓語的位置以外，還可以出現在主語的位置：

He comes from *somewhere.*

It is not important. $\Big\}\rightarrow$

Where he comes from is not important.

這個時候 wh- 子句還可以移到句尾，並且用 it 去填補原來主語的位置。

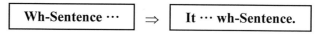

| **Wh-Sentence ⋯** | ⇒ | **It ⋯ wh-Sentence.** |

It is not important *where he comes from.*

習　題　278

依照例句用「wh- 詞」連接下列句子。

Examples:

I have seen her before.

I can't remember where. $\Big\}\rightarrow$

I can't remember where I have seen her before.

1. He saw her last.

    He forgot when. $\Big\}$

2. She decided not to do it.

    They don't care why. $\Big\}$

3. He got that idea.

    I don't know where. $\Big\}$

4. Somebody paid the bill.

    I wonder who. $\Big\}$

5. Something is bothering him.

    I don't know what. $\Big\}$

6. He is going to accomplish it. ⎫
   They can't figure out how. ⎭

7. Quite a few people attended the meeting. ⎫
   You can't imagine how many. ⎭

8. She spent a lot on her dresses. ⎫
   We wonder how much. ⎭

參考：可以接「wh- 子句」做賓語的動詞有 say, know, learn, realize, understand, see, wonder, decide, guess, ask (someone), discover discuss, find (out), figure (out), remember, forget, tell someone, inform someone, advise someone, show someone, teach someone, explain (to someone), (not) care, (not) imagine, have (no) idea, be (not) sure 等。

習 題 279

依照例句改寫下列句子。

Examples:

　　We know she did (…). → *We know what she did.*

1. We know (…) did it.
2. We know she went (…).
3. We know she left home (at …).
4. We know she left for America (by …).
5. We know she couldn't come (because …).
6. We know she went downtown with (…).
7. We know she wants to buy (…).
8. We know she wants to buy a present for (…).
9. We know she wants (…) to go with her.
10. We know she wants to go (…) to buy a present.
11. I wonder they're going to stay (…) when they get here.
12. I wonder they're going to get where they're going (…).

習 題 280

依照例句連接下列句子。

Examples:

Where do they live? (I don't know …)

I don't know where they live.

1. Which one did she want? (She showed us …)

2. Who rang the bell? (Could you tell me …)

3. When did they leave? (I wonder …)

4. Where does the problem lie? (We'll discuss …)

5. What happened? (Nobody knew …)

6. Why isn't the idea popular? (I ask him …)

7. Which one does she want? (I'm not sure …)

8. What is the trouble? (Let's find out …)

9. How did they bring down the government? (He explained to us …)

10. What's the matter with you? (May I ask you …)

習 題 281

依照例句改寫下列各句。

Examples:

I followed his advice. → *I followed what he advised.*

He knows my intention. → *He knows what I intend.*

1. She follows her liking.

2. Is that his preference?

3. This does not come up to my expectation.

4. They paid no attention to my warning.

5. Is that their guarantee?

6. Their threat was never carried out.

7. She always makes good her promise.

8. You failed to follow his order.

9. He carries out our decisions.

10. We'll discuss your plan after.

習 題 282

依照例句把下列各句改為問句。

Examples:

You can ask him what time it is. →

Can you ask him what time it is?

What time he comes is important. →

Is what time he comes important?

1. He knows where she comes from.

2. Where she comes from is a secret.

3. He said how he managed.

4. Why he came is a mystery.

5. She told you who paid the bill.

6. When he arrives will be an open question.

7. You know what's bothering him.

8. Where he went that night is a matter for investigation.

9. You always agree with what he says.

10. What he says is usually interesting.

習 題 283

依照例句把下列各句改為問句。

Examples:

I know (…) got the nomination. →

Do you know who got the nomination?

I think (…) won the election. →

Who do you think won the election?

1. She remembered she put the book (…).

2. He guessed you were going to buy (…).

3. You forget (…) will come tomorrow.

4. You suppose (…) has been elected captain.

5. Bob found out the meeting would take place (…).

6. Jane believes her father will give (…) a new watch.

7. He discovered he could send the message (by …).

8. She realizes she has to finish her job (by …).

9. They think their teacher lives (with …).

10. You suppose these scholars come from (…).

參考：在含有動詞 think, guess, suppose, believe, expect, gather, imagine, dream 等的問句中，wh- 子句中的 wh- 詞，要提前移到句首來；在含有 know, remember, realize, notice, discover, find (out) 等的問句中，wh- 子句中的 wh- 詞不能移到句首來。比較：

$$\begin{cases} \textit{When} \text{ do you think he will come?（wh- 問句）} \\ \quad (\text{I think he will come tomorrow.}) \\ \text{Do you know } \textit{when} \text{ he will come?（yes / no 問句）} \\ \quad (\text{Yes, I do. He'll come tomorrow.}) \end{cases}$$

但是如果 wh- 詞原來就在主句中，那麼當然要提前移到句首：

When did you find out he will come?（wh- 問句）

(I found it out yesterday.)

習　題　284

依照例句改寫下列問句。

Examples:

Who won the election?

Who was it that won the election?

Why do you want to go to Japan to study?

Why is it (that) you want to go to Japan to study?

Why doesn't John want to go to the party?

Why is it (that) John doesn't want to go to the party?

1. When did she leave?

2. Who made the plan?

3. Where did they see each other?

4. What finally occurred?

5. What are you worried about?

6. Why didn't you tell the truth?

7. Who didn't know the answer?

8. Who are you angry with?

9. What does he want to be sent to the post office?

10. How does the government think it can reduce taxes?

參考：「疑問詞＋is it (that)＋直述句」所表達的意思與「wh- 問句」差不多一樣，
但是語氣上顯得比較委婉些。比較：

　　　{ Why did you fail?
　　　{ Why is it (that) you failed?

如果疑問詞是句子的主語，那麼 that 不能省略：

　　　{ Whatis on the desk?
　　　{ What is it that is on the desk?

習　題　285

依照例句改寫下列各句。

Examples:

　　We don't know how he did it. → *How he did it we don't know.*

　　I wonder where she went. → *Where did she go, I wonder?*

1. He didn't say where it was.

2. I wonder where it is.

3. She didn't ask who the others were.

4. He can't remember when he saw them last.

5. She won't tell which one she is going to buy.

6. We wonder how much he really knows about it.

7. He can't imagine how she is going to accomplish it.

8. I can't figure out why he would ever do anything like that.

9. I wonder where they're going to stay when they get here.

10. I didn't realize who it was knocking at the door.

參考：如果主動詞是否定式，那麼出現在賓語位置的 wh- 子句便可以直接移到句首：

> I don't know how he did it.
>
> ⇒ *How he did it I don't know.*

如果主動詞是，wonder「wh- 子句」要改成「wh- 問句」以後才可以移到句首：

> I wonder how he did it.
>
> ⇒ *How did he do it, I wonder?*

15-4. 不定詞與不定詞子句

不定詞（infinitive）或「**to 動詞**」（to-verb）是由動詞的基本式或原形前面加 to 而得來。例如：

come	to come
walk in the rain	to walk in the rain.
teach him English after class	to teach him English after class
be shot at in the dark	to be shot at in the dark
have troubled you again	to have troubled you again
have been working for an hour	to have been working for an hour
have been punished before	to have been punished before

不定詞子句（infinitive clause）是在句子的主語前面加介詞 for，在動詞原形前面加 to 而得來：

Sentence　（句子）	⇒	Noun　　Clause（名詞子句）
NP　　　　VP		for NP　　　　to V …

You help your friends.
It is right. } →

　　For you to help your friends is right.

We protect our country.
It is our duty. } →

　　For us to protect our country is our duty.

Henry won the prize.
It was lucky. } →

　　For Henry to win the prize was lucky.

John has passed the exam.
It is surprising. } →

　　For John to have passed the exam is surprising.

He was punished.
It was necessary. } →

　　For him to be punished was necessary.

　　如果不定詞子句出現在動詞賓語的位置，那麼不定詞子句前面的介詞 for 通常都要省去：

John is clever.
I believe it. } →

　　I believe *John to be clever*.

Paul has studied French.
They know it. } →

　　They know *Paul to have studied French*.

John will be elected captain.
I expect it. } →

　　I expect *John to be elected captain*.

Her daughter would marry a millionaire.

She wished for it. $\Big\}\rightarrow$

She wished (*for*) *her daughter to marry a millionaire.*

不定詞子句的主語，如果與主句的主語或賓語一樣，就要刪掉：

I go to the United States this summer.

I plan it. $\Big\}\rightarrow$

I plan *to go to the United States this summer.*

You stop singing.

I must ask *you*. $\Big\}{\rightarrow}\atop\vdash\rightarrow$

I must ask you *to stop singing.*

如果不定詞子句的主語指不言而喻的人物，也可以刪掉：

We protect our country.

It is our duty. $\Big\}\rightarrow$

To protect our country is our duty.

　　如果不定詞子句出現在主語或賓語的位置，那麼就可以把這個不定詞子句移到句尾，然後用 it 去填補原來主語的位置：

| for NP to V … *** | ⇒ | It *** for NP to V … |

For you to help your friends is right. →

　　It is right *for you to help your friends.*

To protect our country is our duty. →

　　It is our duty *to protect our country.*

For him to be punished was necessary. →

　　It was necessary *for him to be punished.*

You help your friends.

I think it right. $\Big\}\rightarrow$

　　I think *it* right *for you to help your friends.*

We protect our country. ⎫
We consider it our duty. ⎭ →

We consider *it* our duty (*for us*) *to protect our country*.

習　題　286

依照例句完成下列句子。

Examples:

You watch the man. (His orders are ⋯) →

His orders are for you to watch the man.

I watch the man. (My orders are ⋯)

My orders are (*for me*) *to watch the man.*

1. You practice every day. (The improtant thing is ⋯)
2. His family spends the vacation at the seaside. (His plan is ⋯)
3. She looks after the children. (Her duty is ⋯)
4. She must not be late any more. (The important thing is ⋯)
5. He gives advice to foreign students. (His job is ⋯)
6. I remind her to be there. (His orders are ⋯)
7. He collects stamps. (His hobby is ⋯)
8. You take a couple of weeks off. (His advice is ⋯)
9. I get there on time. (The important thing is ⋯)
10. He makes airplane models. (His favorite pastime is ⋯)

習　題　287

依照例句連接下列句子。

Examples:

John beat his sister. ⎫
It was wrong. ⎭ →

For John to beat his sister was wrong.

It was wrong for John to beat his sister.

You cheat your friends.
It is wrong. } →

For you to cheat your friends is wrong.

It is wrong for you to cheat your friends.

To cheat your friends is wrong.

It is wrong to cheat your friends.

1. A young boy smokes.
   It isn't good. } →

2. We learn difficult, words.
   It is useless. } →

3. You learn how to use a word.
   It is more useful. } →

4. Bob told the truth.
   It was right. } →

5. You practice English every day.
   It is important. } →

6. My sister invents a new machine.
   It is impossible. } →

7. John paid in cash.
   It wasn't necessary. } →

8. You finish the job in a week.
   Is it possible? } →

9. I will take the book back.
   Is it all right? } →

10. I am to wear white gloves.
    Do you think it proper? } →

參考：可以拿「不定詞子句」做主語的形容詞有 nice, good, wonderful, right, wrong, shameful, useful, useless, important, necessary, essential, imperative, advisable, preferable, (im)proper, urgent, fitting, better, traditional, (im)possible, strange, odd, unusual, sad, impolite, unreasonable, illegal, discouraging, annoying, interesting, helpful, awful, funny, wise, stupid, hard, difficult, easy, dangerous, risky, harmful; a shame, a pity, fun, a good idea, a pleasure, rerief 等：

For me to cheat my friends is wrong.

但是為了避免句子的「頭重腳輕（主語長、述語短）」，通常都改成「It is ＋形容詞＋不定詞子句」的句型：

It is wrong for me to cheat my friends.

尤其是問句，非改成這個句型不可。比較：

{Is it wrong for me to cheat my friends?（○）
{Is wrong for me to cheat my friends?（×）

如果「不定詞子句」的主語指一般不特定的人或物，那麼可以連同 for 一起省掉：

It's wrong (for you) to cheat (your) friends.

習　題　288

依照例句改寫下列各句。

Examples:

To work hard is your duty. →

Your duty is to work hard.

It is your duty to work hard.

To waste all that food is shameful. →

It is shameful to waste all that food.

1. To type letters is her job.

2. To leave early was his idea.

3. To supply everybody with enough paper is their business.

4. To see you again is nice.

5. To warn them all to stay away is my duty.

6. To be home again is wonderful.

7. To hear from you again was a delight.

8. To receive the award was a great honor for him.

9. To climb up high always makes me dizzy.

10. To have failed the course was just bad luck.

習 題 289

依照例句連接下列句子。

Examples:

We study English. ⎫
It is easy. ⎭ →

For us to study English is easy.

It is easy (for us) to study English.

English is easy (for us) to study.

You study English. ⎫
I think it easy. ⎭ →

I think it easy (for you) to study English.

Henry won the prize. ⎫
It was lucky. ⎭ →

For Henry to win the prize was lucky.

It was lucky for Henry to win the prize.

Henry was lucky to win the prize.

1. They learn Chinese characters. ⎫
   It is difficult. ⎭

2. Henry has won the first place. ⎫
   It is lucky. ⎭

3. We asked him for help. ⎫
   It was foolish ⎭

4. You answer this question. ⎫
   It is much easier. ⎭

5. She learned the whole lesson by heart.
   I thought it impossible.

6. You agreed to such a proposal.
   It was crazy.

7. They deal with this case.
   Is it hard?

8. Jane has a lot of good friends.
   Isn't it fortunate?

9. You always talk like that.
   They consider it wrong.

10. We watched the dying child.
    It was really painful.

參考：(1) 表示「難易、好歹」的形容詞（如 easy, hard, difficult, (in)convenient, good, nice, wonderful, fun, dangerous, painful, interesting, (im)possible, useful, useless, strange, sad, all right 等）也可以拿「不定詞子句」做主語，因此也可以改成「It is + 形容詞 + 不定詞子句」的句型：

    For them to solve the question is difficult.

    It is difficult for them to solve the question.

這種句型，不定詞的賓語可以取代句首的 it 而變成主句的主語：

    The question is difficult for them to solve.

注意：impossible 可以出現於這個句型，但是 possible 卻不可以。

$$\text{He is} \left\{ \begin{array}{l} \text{impossible} \\ \text{possible}（×） \end{array} \right\} \text{to reason with.}$$

(2) 表示「幸運、智愚」的形容詞（如 (un)lucky, (un)fortunate, clever, smart, wise, (un)wise, foolish, stupid, silly, crazy, wrong 等）可以拿「不定詞子句」做主語，但是通常都改成「It is + 形容詞 + 不定詞子句」的句型：

    It was unlucky for John to fail again.

It was stupid for me to make the same mistake.

It is wrong for you to cheat your friends.

這種句型，不定詞的主語可以取代句首的 it 而變成主句的主語：

John was unlucky to fail again.

I was stupid to make the same mistake.

You are wrong to cheat your friends.

習 題 290

依照例句改寫下列各句。

Examples:

You are very kind. to say so.

It is very kind of you to say so.

How kind (it is) of you to say so!

1. You were unwise to accept his offer.

2. She was stupid to make such a mistake.

3. I was careless to leave my book in the train.

4. Mary was naughty to pull the kitten's tail.

5. Bob was foolish to lend money to Dick.

6. The boys were clever to answer the questions so quickly.

7. You were wrong to put the blame on him.

8. Harry was polite to offer his seat to his teacher.

9. He was very brave to go into the burning building to save the child.

10. They are very wicked to say such things behind my back.

參考：表示「善惡、智愚、勇怯」的形容詞（如 nice, good, (un)kind, sweet, wonderful, decent, civil, (in)considerate, (un)grateful, (im)polite, honest, wrong, absurd, naughty, ill-natured, rude, cruel, wicked, thoughtful（～ less), careful（～ less), (un)wise, clever, smart, silly, stupid, brave, bold 等）可以

出現在「主語＋形容詞＋不定詞」的句型，也可以出現在「It is＋形容詞＋不定詞子句」的句型。這個時候常用介詞 of 來代替 for。比較：

$\left\{\begin{array}{l}\text{You were very unwise to refuse his invitaton.} \\ \text{It was very unwise } \textit{of you} \text{ to refuse his invitation.}\end{array}\right.$

（= Your refusal of his invitation was very unwise.）

這個句型在口語中常改成「How 形容詞 it is 不定詞子句」的感嘆句：

How unwise (it was) of you to refuse his invitation!

或 How unwise of you (it was) to refuse his invitation!

習　題　291

依照例句連接下列句子。

Examples:

We see you again. We are happy. →

We are happy to see you again.

1. She attends the party. She is eager.

2. I see you. I am very pleased.

3. He must pass the examinaton. He is anxious.

4. She heard his success. She was delighted.

5. He learned that the game was over. He was disappointed.

6. I must see the principal. I am afraid.

7. Jane heard the good news. Jane was excited.

8. Tom realized his advantage. Tom was very quick.

9. Bob understood his mistake. Bob was slow.

10. Dick beat his sister. Dick was cruel.

11. Peter told me a lie. Peter was wicked.

12. You were born into a rich family. You were lucky.

13. Jim embarrassed me before my friends. Jim was naughty.

14. I gave him all my money. I was crazy.

15. She wanted to know who the man was. She was curious.

16. You can choose to go or stay. You are free.

17. I must trouble you. I am sorry.

18. I have troubled you. I am sorry.

參考：表示「情感」（如 glad, happy, pleased, delighted, sorry, afraid, surprised, shocked, amazed, astonished, ashamed, excited, disappointed, determined, eager, anxious, impatient, grieved, crazy 等）「機警」（如 quick, promp, ready, prepared, slow 等）與其他形容（如 free, willing, wild, mistaken, sure, certain, likely, apt, inclined, liable 等）可以出現在「主語＋形容詞＋不定詞」的句型。

> I am *glad to meet you.*
>
> He is *ready to help you.*
>
> It is *likely to rain.*

習　題　292

依照例句連接下列句子。

Examples:

> John is clever. ⎫
> I believe that. ⎭ →
>
> *I believe John to be clever.*
>
> *I believe John clever.*

1. He is a coward. ⎫
   We find that out. ⎭

2. She is wrong. ⎫
   We prove that. ⎭

3. They were my friends. ⎫
   I thought so. ⎭

4. He is President. ⎫
   He declares that. ⎭

5. This dictionary is very useful.
　 Everyone believes that.

6. They are in love with each other.
　 We understand that.

7. The task is difficult.
　 You must admit that.

8. This has been the case.
　 He denied that.

參考：表示「意見」的動詞（如 think, consider, deem, believe, expect, suppose, prove, imagine, remember, find, take, mistake, judge, guess, hold, understand 等）與「宣稱」的動詞（如 declare, admit, deny, profess, pronounce, announce 等）可以出現在「主語＋動詞＋賓語＋to be …」的句型。如果 to be 後面是表主觀評價或動作結果的名詞或形容詞的話，那麼這個 to be 常可以省略：

　　　　They consider him *a genius*.

　　　　The jury found him *guilty*.

　　　　The priest pronounced them *man and wife*.

　　但是：We took her *to be your sister*.

　　　　　I thought her *to be downstairs*.

習　題　293

依照例句完成下列句子。

Examples:

　　　　My coffee is strong. (I want …) →

　　　　　I want my coffee (to be) strong.

　　　　He is your brother. (I took …) →

　　　　　I took him to be your brother.

　　　　The book is on the desk. (I put) →

　　　　　I put the book on the desk.

1. The house is clean. (They want ⋯)

2. The door is open. (He has pushed ⋯)

3. The prisoner is free. (They set ⋯)

4. Her hat is downstairs. (She left ⋯)

5. His hair is long. (He likes to wear ⋯)

6. The wall is green. (He plans to paint ⋯)

7. The meat is in the refrigerator. (They keep ⋯)

8. She was your secretary. (We mistook ⋯)

9. He was my best friend. (I always thought ⋯)

10. His favorite vase was broken to pieces. (He found ⋯)

習　題　294

依照例句連接下列句子。

Examples:

I told you. Bring the book with you. →

I told you to bring the book with you.

He told me. Don't forget your assignment.

He told me not to forget my assignment.

1. He ordered them. Keep away from the dog.

2. She encouraged you. Try again and again.

3. They asked him. Leave at once.

4. We reminded you. Don't forget your appointment.

5. They will force you. Tell us the truth.

6. She begged them. Don't be so hard on me.

7. He urged us. Don't make any more mistakes.

8. We invited them. Have dinner with us.

9. We warned each of them. Don't expect any favors.

10. They instructed us. You all report to the embassy.

參考：下面的動詞可以出現在「主語 ＋ 動詞 ＋ 賓語 ＋ 不定詞」的句型：tell, ask,

beg, expect, teach, instruct, remind, want, like, prefer, get, prepare, invite, advise, request, permit, allow, require, persuade, convince, urge, challenge, encourage, order, force, help, train, authorize, cause。

習　題　295

依照例句完成下列句子。

Examples:

He goes to Europe next year. (He plans …) →

He plans to go to Europe next year.

I try again and again. (She encouraged …) →

She encouraged me to try again and again.

I try once more. (I encouraged …) →

I encouraged myself to try once more.

1. I stay home. (I expected …)

2. I stay home. (He told …)

3. I stay home. (I persuaded …)

4. He pays out money. (He hates …)

5. You take a job next semester. (Do you really intend …)

6. I keep the appointment. (I'll have to remind …)

7. He won the game. (We tried hard to help …)

8. Each one supports himself. (I train …)

9. Each one protects the other. (Each one trains …)

10. She pronounces the word correctly. (She doesn't even know how …)

參考：下面的動詞可以出現在「主語＋動詞＋不定詞」的句型：plan, intend, mean, expect, wish, hope, need, want, desire, choose, agree, refuse, arrange, ask, request, like, prefer, (not) care, tend, try, manage, learn, know how, start, begin, continue, get, decide, remember, forget, fail, hesitate, guarantee, threaten, seem, appear, happen, can afford。

習 題 296

依照例句連接下列句子。

Examples:

I took the examination.
The teacher encouraged me. $\Big\}$ →

　　The teacher encouraged me to take the examination.

She entered the room.
I saw it. $\Big\}$ →

　　I saw her enter the room.

He washed the car.
I made him. $\Big\}$ →

　　I made him wash the car.

1. We should practice English every day.
   The teacher told us. $\Big\}$

2. He walked across the street.
   She watched it. $\Big\}$

3. You finish your work.
   Let me help you. $\Big\}$

4. She should not tell his father.
   The child begged her. $\Big\}$

5. Someone broke a glass.
   She heard it. $\Big\}$

6. The earth moved.
   I felt it. $\Big\}$

7. The secretary left earlier than usual.
   The manager let her. $\Big\}$

8. The nurse worked until midnight.
   The doctor forced her. $\Big\}$

9. The burglar sneaked into the apartment. ⎤
　　The janitor noticed it. ⎦

10. The clerk opened the safe. ⎤
　　The robber made him. ⎦

參考：表示「感官、知覺」的動詞（如 see, watch, notice, perceive, witness, observe, hear, feel, smell, know, look at, listen to）與「使役」的動詞（如 make, have, let, bid, help）後面的不定詞補語要省去 to 而只用動詞原形：

Did you *see* him *come*?

I have *known* educated persons *make* this mistake.

Shall I *have* my brother *drive* you to the station?

I will *let* you share the secret.

He *helped* her (to) *cook* the meal.

習　題　297

依照例句把下列句子改為被動式。

Examples:

We believed him to be innocent. →

　　He was believed to be innocet.

I saw her enter the room. →

　　She was seen to enter the room.

They said that he was very rich. →

　　He was said to be very rich.

1. They asked her to come in.

2. I saw the boy hit the dog.

3. They advised me to start early.

4. His parents made him take up medicine.

5. I have never known her lose her temper.

6. It is rumored that he has escaped to South America.

7. Did you hear John leave the room?

8. They say that he has a lot of money.

9. They say that he had a lot of money.

10. They believe that he made acquaintance with many artists.

參考一：「知覺動詞」與「使役動詞」的不定詞補語，雖然在主動句中省略不定詞記號 to，但是在被動句中卻必須加以保留：

    I saw her smile at him. → She was seen to smile at him.

    有些動詞只能用被動式，不能用主動式：

    He is said to be a genius. （○）

    They say him to be a genius. （×）

（比較： They say that he is a genius. （○）

    He is rumored to have made a fortune. （○）

    They rumor him to have made a fortune. （×）

（比較： It is rumored that he has made a fortune. （○）

參考二：完成式不定詞表示這個不定詞所代表的事態比主句動詞所代表的事態先發生。比較：

$\begin{cases} \text{He seems to be rich. (= It seems that he is rich.)} \\ \text{He seems to have been rich. (= It seems that he was / has been rich.)} \end{cases}$

習 題 298

依照例句把下列句子改成被動式。

Examples:

    He wants everybody to like him. →

        He wants to be liked by everybody.

    Everybody tends to like him. →

        He tends to be liked by everybody.

1. Something seems to displease him.

2. He expects someone to contact him.

3. Something continues to annoy him.

4. He likes everyone to respect him.

5. Everyone tends to misunderstand him.

6. Everyone began to like him.

7. He wants someone to teach him.

8. He asked everyone to believe him.

9. Somebody happened to have seen him.

10. He requested everybody to listen to him.

參考：有些被動句，改成被動式的不是主動詞而是後面的不定詞：

> Everybody seems to like him. →
>
> > He seems to *be liked* by everybody.
>
> He needs someone to scold him. →
>
> > He needs to *be scolded* by someone.

這種被動式，與含有助動詞 be going to 或 used to 的句子的被動式很相似：

> Someone is going to interview him. →
>
> > He is going to *be interviewed* by someone.
>
> Everyone used to criticize him. →
>
> > He used to *be criticized* by everyone.

習　題　299

依照例句改寫下列各句。

Examples:

> She was taught to be a singer. →
>
> > *They taught her to be a singer*.
>
> She was thought to be a singer. →
>
> > *They thought that she* was a singer.

1. He was trained to be a dancer.

2. He was said to be a dancer.

3. She was known to be a novelist.

4. He was invited to be a speaker.

5. She was supposed to be a typist.

6. He was encouraged to be a doctor.

7. She was understood to be a secretary.

8. He was expected to be an engineer.

9. He was believed to be a Christian.

10. He was found to be a Muslin.

習　題　**300**

依照例句改寫下列句子。

Examples:

I expect that she will succeed. → *I expect her to succeed.*

She hopes that she can succeed. → *She hopes to succeed.*

I think he is a fool. → *I think him (to be) a fool.*

It seems that he is heavily in debt.

→ *He seems to be heavily in debt.*

1. She advised that we wait another semester.

2. I wish that I could get there in time.

3. We understand that you come from Germany.

4. I prefer that you take a taxi.

5. He asked that you not speak English.

6. He didn't ask that you speak English.

7. We found that he was a coward.

8. I thought that he was outside.

9. They know that Paul has been abroad.

10. We believe that he is innocent.

11. She declared that she was Queen.

12. It seemed that no one knew what happened.

13. It happened that he was out of work at that time.

14. It chanced that we were out when she called.

15. It appears that this is the only exception to the rule.

習 題 301

依照例句用 "*No, but he plans to*" 等句子回答下列問句。

Examples:

        Does he have to go? (plan) → *No, but he plans to.*

1. Did you go to Tainan? (hope)

2. Do you like to get up at five o'clock? (have)

3. Did you get a letter? (expect)

4. Do you want to study tonight? (ought)

5. Must you take a four-year course? (want)

6. Did you see the new play? (would like)

7. Did Bob talk to his teacher? (intend)

8. Are you going to go to a movie tonight? (would like)

9. Does she understand French? (hope)

10. Did he pay for the ticket? (plan)

參考：在日常口語中，常用「不定詞記號 to」來代替整個不定詞：

        He didn't go last month, but he plans *to* (= to go) next month.

        Did you get a letter from your brother?

        No, but I expect *to* (= to get a letter from my brother).

習 題 302

依照例句把「wh- 子句」改成「wh- 不定詞」。

Examples:

        I don't know what I should do. → *I don't know what to do.*

        We showed him how he should do it.

        → *We showed him how to do it.*

1. I wonder how I should do it.

2. Please tell me which I should take.

3. Can you tell me who I should see?

 4. Can you advise me which I should buy?

 5. They told the girl where she could get tickets.

 6. She doesn't know what dress she is to wear.

 7. Tell me when I should be there, and I'll not be late.

 8. They were not sure which room they should give you.

 9. He can't decide whether he should attend the party.

10. I don't really know who I should recommend you to apply to.

參考：「wh- 子句」裡的主語，如果與主句裡的主語或賓語一樣，就可以省掉。這個時候，「wh- 子句」的動詞一定要改成不定詞：

$$\boxed{\textbf{wh-X NP VP}} \;\Rightarrow\; \boxed{\textbf{wh-X to V} \cdots}$$

I am wondering which *I* should buy. →

　　I am wondering *which to buy*.

　　Tell *him* whether *he* should come or not. →

　　Tell him *whether to come or not*.

如果「wh- 子句」的主語指不特定的人或物，也可以改成「wh- 不定詞」：

Do you know where $\left\{ \begin{array}{c} \text{we can} \\ \text{to} \end{array} \right\}$ get a good meal in this town?

Ask your teacher how $\left\{ \begin{array}{c} \text{you should} \\ \text{to} \end{array} \right\}$ pronounce the word.

以 why 引導的「wh- 子句」不能改為不定詞。

習 題 303

依照例句把下列句子改為問句。

Examples:

　　I asked (⋯) to help me. → *Who did you ask to help you?*

　　She wants me to do (⋯). → *What does she want you to do?*

 1. We reminded (⋯) to call you up.

 2. (⋯) encouraged us to be patient.

3. She is allowing them to sit (…).

4. You advised her to do (…).

5. She expected us to get up (…).

6. I instructed her to contact (…).

7. They warned everybody not to forget (…).

8. He likes you all to be there (…).

9. She told her children not to do (…).

10. We are telling them to bring (…) many chairs.

15-5. 動名詞與動名詞子句

動名詞（gerund）或「**ing 動詞**」（ing-verb），係在動詞原形的字尾加 -ing 而來。例如：

come	coming
go to the museum	going to the museum
shoot the bird with a gun	shooting the bird with a gun
be shot by a robber	being shot by a robber
have seen him once	having seen him once
have been told before	having been told before

動名詞子句（gerund clause），把句子的主語改為所有格，把動詞改為動名詞而得來：

Sentence　　（句子）	⇒	Noun　　Clauses（名詞子句）
NP　　　　VP		NP's　　　　　　V-ing …

Bob borrows money from me. }　→
I hate it.

　I hate *Bob's borrowing money from me.*

John had won the first prize. }　→
It surprised everybody.

　John's having won the first prize surprised every body.

You wear a red necktie.
She doesn't like it. } →

She doesn't like *your wearing a red necktie*.

I open the window.
Do you mind it? } →

Do you mind *my opening the window?*

動名詞子句的主語，如果與主句的主語一樣，就要省掉：

I borrow money from you.
I hate it. } →

I hate *borrowing money from you*.

She wears a red necktie.
She doesn't like it. } →

She doesn't like *wearing a red necktie*.

You open the window for me.
Do *you* mind it? } →

Do *you* mind *opening the window for me?*

習　題　304

依照例句改寫下列各句。

Examples:

His job is teaching English. → *Teaching English is his job.*

His business is picking up. → *His business is picking up.*

1. His hobby is collecting stamps.

2. His only interest is making lots of money.

3. His business is selling.

4. His business is falling off.

5. His job is changing.

6. His job is changing money.

7. His business is turning out automobiles.

8. His factory is turning out automobiles.

9. His favorite pastime is becoming his occupation.

10. His favorite pastime is getting together for an evening of bridge.

參考：「動名詞」與「現在分詞」在形式上一樣，但是用法不同：

> His business is selling cars.「他的生意是推銷汽車。」（動名詞）
> His business is picking up.「他的生意漸有起色。」（現在分詞）

注意，只有動名詞能從補語變成主語。比較：

> Selling cars is his business.（○）
> Picking up is his business.（×）

習　題　305

依照例句連接下列句子。

Examples:

> You come late. I don't like that. →
>
> *I don't like your coming late.*
>
> *I don't like you coming late.*
>
> I am late. I don't like that. →
>
> *I don't like being late.*
>
> She walked in the rain. She enjoyed that. →
>
> *She enjoyed walking in the rain.*
>
> You told him what to do. He objected to that. →
>
> *He objected to your telling him what to do.*

1. I have written my paper. I have just finished that.

2. I smoke a pipe. Do you mind that?

3. He went there himself. He insisted on that.

4. I help others. I belive in that.

5. He had seen him before. He denied that.

6. Some people say "It's me." Some people admit to that.

7. They'll be able to lend him some money. He's counting on that.

8. He help others. I believe in that.

9. Your composition is improved. Your composition needs that.

10. I correct your papers. I'll get around to that tomorrow.

11. You leave me without knowing where you are going. I can't risk that.

12. He married a girl with a temper like hers. Can you imagine that?

參考：(1) 下面的動詞可以出現在「主語＋動詞＋所有格（代）名詞＋V-ing …」或「主語＋動詞＋V-ing」的句型：like, prefer, fancy, hate, dislike, detest, mind, dread, fear, risk, regret, resent, (cannot) stand, (cannot) bear, understand, remember, recall, mention, forget, picture, imagine, forgive, excuse, enjoy, appreciate.

在日常口語中常把所有格（代）名詞改為賓格，以表示所強調的是引起事件的人而非事件本身。比較：

> I don't like *your* coming late.「我不喜歡你遲到」。
> I don't like *you* coming late.「我不喜歡你遲到」。

I hate $\begin{Bmatrix} Bob's \\ Bob \end{Bmatrix}$ borrowing money from me.

(2) 下面的動詞出現在「主語＋動詞＋V-ing…」的句型：finish, avoid, practice, hesitate, advise, suggest, admit, deny, resist, oppose, escape, delay, postpone, put off, hold off, begin, start, continue, go on, keep on, keep up, stop, cease, let up, cannot help, feel like, need, want. 比較：

> I will remember *to mail* the letter.「我會記得要宿信。（還沒有寄信）」
>
> (= I am going to mail the letter, and I will remember that.)
>
> I remember *mailing* the letter.「我記得已經寄了信。」
>
> (= I mailed the letter, and I remember that.)

> He tried (= made an attempt) *to sleep*, but he couldn't.「他想法子人睡，但是睡不著。」
>
> He tried (= made an experiment with) *sleeping*, but when he got up his head was still aching.「他睡過了，但是起來的時候頭還是很痛。」

$$\begin{cases} \text{I stopped (in order) } \textit{to talk} \text{ to him.} 「我停下來跟他講話。」 \\ \quad (= \text{I stopped doing something else and talked to him.}) \\ \text{I stopped } \textit{talking} \text{ to him.} 「我沒有再跟他講話。」 \\ \quad (= \text{I was talking to him, but I stopped doing so.}) \end{cases}$$

$$\begin{cases} \text{What do you like as a pastime?} \\ \quad \text{I like } \textit{walking} \text{ (in the rain).} 「我喜歡在雨中散步。（一般的情形）」 \\ \text{How would you like to go downtown?} \\ \quad \text{I'd like } \textit{to walk} \text{ (rather than take a taxi).} 「我上街寧願走路也不坐計} \end{cases}$$

　　程車。（特定的情形）」。

下面的兩個句子意思一樣，但是動名詞用主動式，不定詞用被動式：

$$\begin{cases} \text{Your clothes needs / wants } \textit{mending}. \\ \text{Your clothes needs } \textit{to be mended}. \end{cases}$$

(3) 與下面的動詞合用的 to 是介詞，不是不定詞記號。因此 to 後面要用名詞或「ing 動詞」：take to (= Iike), object to, refer to, admit to, confess to, allude to, be/get used to, be/get accustomed to, dedicate…to, devote…to, contribute…to, sacrifice…to, apply…to, look forward to, get around to, get down to, settle down to, knuckle down to, feel up to, measure up to, come/go near (to), with a view to.

　　He confessed to *taking* the money.

　　She devoted all her life to *helping* the poor.

　　We're looking forward to *seeing* you.

　　I am used to *getting* up early.「我已經習慣早起（並不覺得苦）。」

　　（比較：I used to *get* up early.「我過去常早起（現在卻不一定）。」

習　題　306

依照例句改寫下列各句。

Examples:

I'm happy that I take courses. →

I'm happy to take courses.

I'm happy about taking courses.

We're sorry that we have to leave. →

We're sorry to have to leave.

We're sorry about having to leave.

1. We are careful that we say the right thing.

2. We were surprised that we saw you in town.

3. He was lucky that he won the election.

4. I was ashamed that I made a mistake.

5. She is afraid that she may fail the examination.

6. They were annoyed that they had to do it all over again.

7. I am glad that I'm taking this course.

8. Is she satisfied that she'll have a chance to compete?

9. They are anxious that they arrive home safely.

10. I'm disappointed that I can't see you.

參考：下面的形容詞，後面可以接「that 子句」，「不定詞」或「介詞＋動名詞」：lucky (at), surprised (at), amazed (at), ashamed (of), sure (of), afraid (of), certain (of), happy (about), careful (about), excited (about), glad (about), worried (about), sorry (about), anxious (about), upset (over), disturbed (over), annoyed (with), delighted (with), pleased (with), disappointed (with).

習 題 307

依照例句完成下列句子，然後改成被動式。有些句子可能沒有被動式。

Examples:

He was walking down the street. (I saw …) →

I saw him walking down the street.

He was seen walking down the steet.

The boy was standing outside. (They left …) →

They left the boy standing outside.

The boy uas left standing outside.

1. The train was leaving the station. (We watched …)

2. She was working at her desk. (I found …)

3. I was waiting in the lobby. (He kept …)

4. A plane was coming nearer and nearer. (They heard …)

5. Something is burning in the kitchen. (I smell …)

6. The band is playing the national anthem. (They listened to …)

7. He was stealing apples from his garden. (They caught …)

8. I was wondering what would happen next. (The news left …)

9. All of us are thinking seriously. (His question set …)

10. My heart was beating rapidly. (I could feel …)

參考：下面的動詞可以出現在「主語＋動詞＋賓語＋V-ing …」的句型：表示「知覺」的動詞（如 see, watch, notice, perceive, witness, observe, look at, listen to, find, catch, feel, recognize, smell）與 keep, leave, get, start, set, have, want 等。這些句子通常部可以改成被動式，但是有例外。這種 V-ing 一般部分析為現在分詞，做為賓語的補語用。

The boy saw the thief running away. →

The thief was seen running away by the boy.

（比較：The thief was looked at running away.（ ✕ ））

比較：

I saw him *walking* across the street.「我看見他正在橫過馬路。」

　(= He *was walking* across the street, and I saw that.)

I saw him *walk* across the street.「我看見他橫過了馬路。」

　(= He *walked* across the street, and I saw that).

I feel the earth *moving*.「我覺得地在動。」

　(= The earth is moving, and I feel that.)

I felt the earth *move*.「我發覺地（剛才）動了一下。」

　(The earth moved, and I felt that.)

— 89 —

習 題 308

依照例句連接下列句子。

Examples:

I finished my letter.
It took two hours.
$\Big\}$ →

It took me two hours to finish my letter.

I prepared my lesson.
I spent two hours.
$\Big\}$ →

I spent two hours preparing my lessons.

1. He completed the experiment.
   It took three weeks.

2. She looked up all the new words.
   She spent the whole day.

3. The teacher explained the problem to us.
   It took half an hour.

4. John watched TV.
   John had a good time.

5. The committee will investigate the matter.
   It will take almost a year.

6. You study English.
   Do you have trouble?

7. We worked together on the project.
   We had an excellent time.

8. I fixed my radio.
   I spent a lot of time.

9. They will look for a job.
   They will have a hard time.

10. You explained the word to a foreign student. ⎫

    Did you have any diffculty? ⎭

參考：在 spend + 時間，have a good (/ fine / wonderful / excellent / hard) time, have
trouble (/ difficulty) 等後面常用「ing 動詞」做補語。

習　題　309

依照例句連接下列句子。

Examples:

He arrived so early. It was surprising.

→ *That he arrived so early was surprising.*

It was surprising that he arrived so early.

For him to arrive so early was surprising.

It was surprising for him to arrive so early.

His arriving so early was surprising.

1. He passed the course. It was a surprise.

2. She is leaving so suddenly. It is unfortunate.

3. You are alone without companions. It seems sad.

4. They came home safely. It was a miracle.

5. He was not able to remember her name. It was very odd.

習　題　310

依照例句把 *He practices every day.* 改為適當的名詞子句做動詞的賓語。

Examples:

I told →

I told him to practice every day.

I told him that he practice every day.

I said →

I said him to practice every day.

I said that he practiced every day.

I didn't want →

   I didn't want him to practice every day.

   I didn't want him practicing every day.

I can't picture →

   I can't picture him practicing every day.

I need →

   I need him to practice every day.

It is easy →

   It's easy for him to practice every day.

I let →

   I let him practice every day.

I criticized →

   I criticized his practicing every day.

I noticed →

   I noticed him practicing every day.

   I noticed that he practices every day.

I suggested →

   I suggested that he practice every day.

1. I asked

2. I wish

3. I objected to

4. I wouldn't pay

5. I'm surprised

6. I encouraged

7. It wasn't good

8. I helped

9. I can't imagine

10. I'm telling you

11. I'd rather

12. I assume

13. I made

14. I didn't mind

15. I'm aware

16. He looked as if

17. It is high time

18. Are you sure

19. I'll have

20. Don't you appreciate

習　題　311

依照例句連接下列句子。

Examples:

He's eager to try. I'm impressed with that. →

I'm impressed with his being eager to try.

I'm impressed with his eagerness to try.

They're willing to work hard. We're surprised about that. →

We're surprised about their being willing to work hard.

We're surprised about their willingness to work hard.

1. He's able to play well. We're confident of that.

2. They're inclined to drink a little. He's used to that.

3. She's eligible to vote. Vm glad about that.

4. I'm qualified to register. They're sure of that.

5. We're free to move around. She's opposed to that.

6. He's ready to take the exam. We're satisfied with that.

7. They're unable to finish on time. He's tired of that.

8. She's ineligible to vote. I'm sorry about that.

9. We're unwilling to do more. They're disappointed with that.

10. He's reluctant to see a doctor. I'm concerned about that.

參考：含有形容詞（如 eager, ready, willing, inclined, reluctant, (un) able, (in) eligible, qualified, careful 等）與不定詞的句子，除了可以變成「動名詞子句」以外，也可以直接把形容詞改為名詞（eagerness, readiness, willingness, inclination, reluctance, (in)ability, (in)eligibility, qualification, care）變成名詞組。這個時候，Be 動詞必須刪略：

He is eager to try. → *his eagerness to try*

They are willing to work hard. →

their willingness to work hard

習 題 312

依照例句連接下列句子。

Examples:

They agreed to do it. They forgot about it. →

They forgot about their agreement to do it.

You reminded him to come early. It was useless. →

Your reminder to him to come early was useless.

1. He decided to leave home. No one knew about it.

2. She failed to keep her promise. He was angry at it.

3. She intends to go abroad. I have heard about it.

4. They invited her to attend the party. She was very pleased with it.

5. You promised to lend him money. You broke it.

6. She refused to marry her boss. It surprised nobody.

7. He hates to attend parties. It is a well-known fact.

8. They threatened to call the police. He ignored it.

9. She likes to wear jewels. Everybody knows it.

10. I advised him to study harder. It was all in vain.

參考：含有動詞（如 need, desire, tend, fail, hesitate, guarantee, plan, arrange, agree, request, refuse, promise, decide, threaten, intend, advise, invite, remind 等）與不定詞的子句可以直接把動詞改為名詞（need, desire, tendency, failure, hesitation, guarantee, plan, arrangement, agreement, request, refusal, promise, decision, threat, intention, advice, invitation, reminder）以後當名詞組用。

這個時候動詞的主語要用所有格：

He failed to get the job.

→ *His failure to get the job* (made her very unhappy).

They agreed to help him.

→ (They forgot all about) *their agreement to help him.*

有些動詞（如 need, like, prefer）改為名詞（need, liking, preference）以後還要把後面的不定詞改為 for＋V-ing：

　　He prefers to eat alone.

　　→ *His preference for eating alone* (is quite well known).

另外有些動詞（如 hope, hate, expect, intend, threat）則改為名詞（hope, hatred, expectation, intention, threat）以後，要把後面的不定詞改為 of＋V-ing：

　　She intended to be here.

$$→ \text{(Nobody realized) } \textit{her intention} \begin{cases} \textit{of being here.} \\ \textit{to be here.} \end{cases}$$

習　題　313

依照例句把下列句子改為名詞組。

Examples:

　　　　He suggested that you go there right away. →

　　　　　　his suggestion that you go there right away

　　　　　　his suggestion for you to go there right away

　　　　It is necessary that he be there. →

　　　　　　the necessity that he be there

　　　　　　the necessity for him to be there

　　　　　　the necessity of his being there

1. We demand that you investigate the matter.

2. It requires that he take the course without delay.

3. It is possible that she may arrive on time.

4. He ordered that she not sell the car.

5. It is likely that he arrived here in 1960.

6. We proposed that he not be punished.

7. George claims that you were there with him.

8. It is certain that tomorrow will be warm and sunny.

9. We expect that they would have a lot of things to think about.

10. The expert announced that the government's estimate was accurate.

習　題　314

依照例句連接下列句子。

Examples:

I arrived late in the evening. Nobody knows that. →

Nobody knows my arriving late in the evening.

Bob takes no interest in mathematics. I know that fact.

I know the fact of Bob's taking no interest in mathematics.

They drowned the cats. That is against the law. →

Their drowning of the cats is against the law.

John drew the pictures skillfully. That fascinated me. →

John's skillful drawing of the pictures fascinated me.

1. John agreed to the proposal. I regret that.

2. Jane won first prize in the speech contest. They're glad to hear that.

3. The girl sang the national anthem. That brought the audience to their feet.

4. He doesn't want to go to college. I cannot understand that.

5. She gave money to him. You must keep in mind that fact.

6. Jane sang "Annie Lawrie" sweetly. It delighted everybody.

7. He questioned her motives. She found that very annoying.

8. Her boss questioned her motives constantly. It annoyed her.

9. Jack left the town suddenly. Do you know that?

10. jack left the town suddenly. It caught us by surprise.

參考：「動名詞子句」有兩種用法。

（1）表示事實：

Nobody knows (the fact of) *my arriving late in the evening.*（事實可以知道）

(The fact of) *John's driving a new car is no news to us.*

（2）表示動作：

They saw *my arriving late in the evening.*（事實不能看見，只有動作才能看見）

John's driving of a new car startled them.

注意：表示動作的動名詞與賓語之間要放介詞 of。如果原來的動詞有副詞修飾語，那麼可以改成形容詞後放在動名詞的前面。比較：

> John drew the pictures *skillfully.*
> *John's skillful drawing of the pictures* (fascinated me).

> Mary told the story tearfully.
> *Mary's tearful telling of the story* (moved the audience to tears).

習 題　315

把括號裡的動詞與代名詞改成適當的形式。

Examples:

> I don't like (come) late. →
> *I don't like to come late.*
> *I don't like coming late.*

> I don't like (you, come) late. →
> *I don't like you to come late.*
> *I don't like your coming late.*
> *I don't like you coming late.*

> I must ask you (stop, interfere). →
> *I must ask youto stop interfering.*
> *I must ask youto stop to interfere.*

> I don't want (make) him (do) what I say. →
> *I don't want to make him do what I say.*

1. We watch the trees (sway) in the wind.
2. Didn't Mrs. Brown make her children (obey)?
3. Did you listen to the man (speak)?
4. We like (see) young people (enjoy) themselves.

5. He admitted (take) the money.

6. We have decided not (go).

7. The club endeavored (raise) five thousand dollars for charity.

8. I don't care (see) him again.

9. They encouraged me (study) abroad.

10. I promised him not (tell) you.

11. I dread (think) about it.

12. They intend (call) her tomorrow.

13. The traffic continued (move) slowly.

14. Imagine (he, win) the first prize!

15. We expect (they, leave) tonight.

16. The child begged (I) not (go).

17. They allow (we, smoke) here.

18. They don't allow (smoke) here.

19. Do they permit (we, camp) here?

20. Do they permit (camp) here?

21. I can't bear (see) her (cry).

22. I can't stand (hear) that again.

23. He neglected (file) his income tax return.

24. I remember (write) to him every week.

25. She prefers (type) her own letters.

26. I saw him (help) her (cook) the dinner.

27. We finally got (he, accept) the offer.

28. I advise (you, see) a lawyer.

29. I didn't mean (hurt) your feelings.

30. We dislike (play) bridge tonight.

31. I plan (take) French next year.

32. My mother objected to (go) there.

33. Are you used to (get) up early?

34. I used to (buy) my clothes at Dixon's.

35. Paper is used to (make) a lot of things.

36. The butler took to (hide) the dishes he broke.

37. I am accustomed to (work) late.

38. They are looking forward to (see) you.

39. Mr.Wilson has dedicated himself to (help) the poor.

40. The teacher couldn't get around to (correct) our papers.

41. Philip devotes all his money to (study) music.

42. They went on (talk) for hours.

43. Let's keep on (work) for a while.

44. You had better hold off (write) that letter until tomorrow.

45. I put off (do) my assignment until the last minute.

46. I don't feel like (go) out today.

47. I don't feel up to (talk) with anybody else now.

48. If you keep (you, talk) up, you will be sorry.

49. I have avoided (meet) him so far.

50. He escaped (be hurt) in the accident.

51. I'm sorry that I missed (see) you.

52. Mr. Jackson considered (buy) a car.

53. The guard commanded (we, halt).

54. Don't start (refuse) (listen) before I've begun.

55. Let me (help) you (get) it right.

56. He was encouraged (start) (look) for a job immediately.

57. We have decided (allow) her (do) as she wishes.

58. She heard him (say) he wanted (buy)the house.

59. I would love (hear) that orchestra (play).

60. The manager let us (watch) the actors (rehearse).

61. They promised (help) me (prepare) for the party.

62. We found the trip (be) very dull, and we couldn't help (say) so.

63. Can you (manage) (finish) (pack) these parcels by yourself?

64. She endeavored (arrange) (come) early (help) (cut) the bread and butter.

65. Have you ever watched people (try) (catch) fish?

66. Try (avoid) (offend) him.

67. Are you going (keep) me (wait) all day?

68. Do you remember (I, return) those books to the library?

69. My mother hates (I, smoke) in the bathroom.

70. I dislike (you, remind) me continually of the things I ought to have done.

71. I always enjoy (watch) (he, act) Shakespeare.

72. Do you mind (I, close) the window?

73. I can't risk (you, leave) me without (know) where you're going.

74. I don't think she will forgive (we, eat) all the rest of the pie.

75. I dread (he, come) back when I'm alone.

76. I advise you (stop) (think) of (carry) out such a dangerous plan.

77. Please excuse (I, say) so.

78. Would you mind (watch) the instructor (demonstrate) so as to (learn) (swim) more quickly?

79. I beg you (hesitate) before (decide) (accept) his proposal.

80. Could I trouble you (arrange)(travel) with my young brother?

81. She loves (powder) her nose.

82. I'd like (powder) my nose.

83. She told me how (make) clothes (last) longer.

84. She forgot (remind) you (give) the servants orders (prepare) for their arrival.

85. The witness was compelled (swear) (speak) the truth.

86. They took her (be) a foreigner on (hear) her (speak).

87. I beseech you (persuade) her (be) reasonable.

88. They noticed him (hesitate) (sign) the agreement.

89. Don't let me (find) you (day-dream) again.

90. They dislike (be interrogated) while (try) (finish) a piece of work.

91. This loss went near to (ruin) him.

92. The army came near (obtain) a complete victory.

第**16**章
名詞的修飾語（一）

16-1. 名詞的修飾語

　　英語的名詞，除了可以用「限定詞」、「數量詞」或「限制詞」來限制以外，還可以用「形容詞」、「名詞」、「現在分詞」、「過去分詞」、「不定詞」、「場所副詞」、「介詞片語」、「關係子句」等加以修飾。

　　　　this student（限定詞＋名詞）

　　　　this clever student（限定詞＋形容詞＋名詞）

　　　　a girl studeht（限定詞＋名詞＋名詞）

　　　　these three students（限定詞＋數量詞＋名詞）

　　　　only these three students（限制詞＋限定詞＋數量詞＋名詞）

　　　　the smiling student（限定詞＋現在分詞＋名詞）

　　　　the wounded student（限定詞＋過去分詞＋名詞）

　　　　the student *to help you*（限定詞＋名詞＋不定詞）

　　　　the student *there*（限定詞＋名詞＋場所副詞）

　　　　the student *in the next room*（限定詞＋名詞＋介詞片語）

　　　　the student *who came late*（限定詞＋名詞＋關係子句）

　　國語的名詞修飾語，不管字數多少，都要放在名詞的前面；英語的名詞修飾語卻有的放在名詞的前面，有的放在名詞的後面。
比較：

　　　　yellow flowers「黃色的花」

　　　　boy students「男學生」

　　　　the bicycle *outside*「外面的腳踏車」

　　　　the car *in the garage*「車庫裡面的汽車」

　　　　the boy *who won first prize*「得到第一獎的男孩」

習 題 316

在名詞的修飾語下面畫線, 被修飾的名詞上面加圈。

Examples:

Please give me (something) to drink.

The office (girl) who is typing is Miss Lee.

1. That pretty girl is John's sister.

2. The car outside belongs to my uncle.

3. The building with a red roof is the school library.

4. That is a very disappointing answer indeed.

5. I have never seen a girl more beautiful than Mary.

6. The hat on the counter is different from the one on the shelf.

7. He gave me some coffee to drink.

8. The mother tenderly kissed the sleeping baby.

9. A child whose parents are dead is an orphan.

10. I don't know the place he lives.

16-2. 放在名詞前面的修飾語

放在名詞前面的修飾語，主要的有 (1) 形容詞、(2) 現在分詞、(3) 過去分詞、(4) 名詞與動名詞。

(1) **形容詞**：形容詞是最常見的名詞修飾語。

Modifier（修飾語）	Headword（被修飾語）
Adj 形容詞	**N** 名詞

a *sad*   story   （比較：The story is sad.）

this *high*   building   （比較：This building is high.）

the *sweet*   girl   （比較：The girl is sweet.）

that *happy*   family   （比較：That family is happy.）

形容詞前面常加上表示程度的「加強詞」（intensifier），如 very, quite, rather, somewhat 等：

a	very	sad	story
the	rather	high	price
the	quite	sweet	girl
these	somewhat	unfamiliar	faces

形容詞修飾名詞的時候，形容詞要念輕，名詞要念重。但是如果形容詞與名詞合成一個複合名詞，那麼形容詞要念重，名詞要念輕。

比較：

> blâck bóard (= a board that is painted black)「一塊塗成黑色的板」
>
> bláckbòard (= a large piece of wood, painted black and used in schools)「上課用的黑板」

> grêen hóuse (= a house that is painted green)「漆成綠色的房屋」
>
> gréenhòuse (= a glass-covered house where green things are raised)「栽培植物的溫室」

(2) **現在分詞**：不及物動詞的現在分詞或「ing 式動詞」也可以做為名詞的修飾語用。現在分詞含有「進行（正在…）」的意思。

Modifier（修飾語）	Headword（被修飾語）
V-ing 現在分詞	**N** 名詞

a *sleeping*	baby	（比較：A baby is sleeping.）
the *burning*	house	（比較：The house is burning.）
the *dying*	soldier	（比較：The soldier was dying.）

注意：現在分詞前面不能加 very, quite, rather, somewhat 等「加強詞」。比較：

> a very *interesting* story（○）（形容詞）
>
> a very *sleeping* baby（×）（現在分詞）

> a quite *charming* girl（○）（形容詞）
> a quite *burning* house（×）（現在分詞）

interesting, charming, surprising, amusing 等是由及物動詞的現在分詞變出來的形容詞，因此，可以用加強詞修飾、可以用 more, most 變成比較級或最高級、也可以放在動詞 seem, look 等後面做補語。比較：

> This book is more *interesting* than that.（○）
> This baby is more *sleeping* than that.（×）

> The book seems *interesting*.（○）
> The baby seems *sleeping*.（×）

(3) **過去分詞**：動詞的「過去分詞」或「en 式動詞」也可以放在名詞的前面做修飾語。這個時候，及物動詞的過去分詞含有「被動 (被…的)」的意思；不及物動詞的過去分詞含有「完成（已經…的）」意思。

Modifier（修飾語）	Headword（被修飾語）
V-en	N
過去分詞	名詞

the *broken*　　　　cup　　　　（比較：The cup is broken.）

a *wounded*　　　　soldier　　　（比較：A soldier was wounded.）

a *fallen*　　　　　leaf　　　　（比較：A leaf has fallen.）

these *faded*　　　　flowers　　　（比較：These flowers have faded.）

注意：過去分詞前面不能加 very, quite, rather, somewhat 等「加強詞」。比較：

> a very *wounded* soldier（×）
> a very *tired* soldier（○）

tired, surprised, pleased 等是由及物動詞的過去分詞變出來的形容詞，因此可以用加強詞修飾、可以用 more, most 變成比較級或最高級、也可以放在動詞 seem, look 等後面做補語。

比較：

> The boy was very *tired* / *surprised* / *pleased*.（○）
> The boy was very *wounded* / *punished* / *beaten*.（×）

$$\begin{cases} \text{The boy was more } \textit{tired / surprised / pleased } \text{than you.（○）} \\ \text{The boy was more } \textit{wounded / punished / beaten } \text{than you.（×）} \end{cases}$$

$$\begin{cases} \text{The boy seems } \textit{tired / surprised / pleased}.（○） \\ \text{The boy seems } \textit{wounded / punished / beaten}.（×） \end{cases}$$

現在分詞或過去分詞修飾名詞的時候，分詞要念輕，名詞要念重。

　　a slêeping báby, a flŷing pláne, a brôken lég, a wounded sóldier

(4) **名詞與動名詞**：名詞也可以放在名詞的前面做修飾語。

Modifier（修飾語）	Headword（被修飾語）
N	N
名詞	名詞

the *spring*	vacation	「春假」
a *girl*	friend	「女朋友」
the *chemistry*	teacher	「化學老師」

「動名詞」具有名詞的功用，因此也可以做名詞修飾語用。

the *dining*	room	「餐廳」
a *racing*	horse	「比賽用的馬」
these *rocking*	chairs	「搖椅」

名詞修飾名詞的時候，第一個名詞要念重，第二個名詞要念輕。

　　bóy stùdent（男學生），círcus lìon（在馬戲團表演的獅子），

　　ócean lìner（郵輪），táxi drìver（計程車司機）

比較：

$$\begin{cases} \text{a Frênch teácher (= a teacher whose nationality is French)「法國籍的老師」} \\ \text{a Frénch teàcher (= a teacher who teaches French)「教法文的老師」} \end{cases}$$

動名詞修飾名詞的時候，動名詞要念重，名詞要念輕。

　　líving ròom（起居室、客廳），smóking ròom（吸煙室），flŷing òfficer（飛行官），móving vàn（搬運車），wáshing machìne（洗衣機），spínning whèel（紡車）

比較：

$\begin{cases} \text{a slêeping báby (= a baby who is sleeping)「睡眠中的嬰孩」} \\ \text{a sléeping càr (= a car for sleeping)「臥車」} \end{cases}$

$\begin{cases} \text{a dâncing gírl (= a girl who is dancing)「正在跳舞的女孩子」} \\ \text{a dáncing gìrl (= a girl whose profession is dancing)「舞女」} \end{cases}$

習　題　317

高聲念出下面的語詞，並說出中文的意思。

Examples:

a beautiful singer; a folk-song singer

a *bêautiful sínger*（美麗的歌手）

a *fólk-sòng sìnger*（民謠歌手）

1. a new master; a head master

2. a high wall; a brick wall

3. a big ball; a cannon ball

4. an evening paper; some white paper

5. a beautiful flower; a garden flower

6. a strange name; a family name

7. a long spoon; a silver spoon

8. an old lamp; a desk lamp

9. a spare ticket; a return ticket

10. useless furniture; dining-room furniture

11. a singing bird; a reading room

12. an English gentleman; an English teacher

參考：表原料、材料或質料的名詞修飾名詞的時候，通常念成前輕後重（ˏ ́），而非前重後輕（́ ˏ）。比較：

$\begin{cases} \text{âpple júice（蘋果汁）} \\ \text{ápple trèe（蘋果樹）} \end{cases}$ $\qquad$ $\begin{cases} \text{stône bridge（石橋）} \\ \text{stóne brèaker（碎石機）} \end{cases}$

同樣地，如果表時間與處所的名詞修飾名詞，在語義上沒有發生什麼特別變化，通常也念成前輕後重（＾＇）。比較：

$$
\begin{cases}
\text{êvening páper（晚報）} \\
\text{évening drèss（晚禮服）}
\end{cases}
\qquad
\begin{cases}
\text{môrning práyer（晨禱）} \\
\text{mórning síckness（害喜）}
\end{cases}
$$

$$
\begin{cases}
\text{schôol lánd（學校的土地）} \\
\text{schóol bùs（校車）}
\end{cases}
\qquad
\begin{cases}
\text{fìeld evénts（田賽）} \\
\text{fíeld spòrts（野外運動）}
\end{cases}
$$

習　題　318

依照例句，改寫下列各句。

Examples:

The story is sad. → *It's a sad story.*

The game is very tiring. → *It's a very tiring game.*

The glass is broken. → *It's a broken glass.*

The city has fallen. → *It's a fallen city.*

The car is for racing. → *It's a racing car.*

These people live in a city. → *They're city people.*

1. The wife is happy.
2. The story is very interesting.
3. The money was stolen.
4. The hero has returned.
5. The building is burning.
6. The stick is for walking.
7. The general has retired.
8. The students live in the dormitory.
9. The economy is growing.
10. The patients are moaning.
11. The girl was very much frightened.
12. The convict has escaped.
13. The students are failing.
14. The matter has been settled.
15. The water is running.
16. The paper is for writing.
17. The officer flies (an airplane).
18. The mob is angrily shouting.
19. The guests have newly arrived.
20. The price was surprisingly high.

習　題　319

依照例句改寫下列各句。

Examples:

He made progress rapidly. → *He made rapid progress.*

She makes decisions fast. → *She makes fast decisions.*

1. I gave an answer honestly.

2. She makes contributions regularly.

3. He does odd jobs occasionally.

4. They suffered defeats frequently.

5. We need repair continually.

6. I'll do an analysis carefully.

7. He offered advice enthusiastically.

8. He has his tea usually.

9. They held a demonstration peacefully.

10. I must have an explanation immediately.

習　題　320

依照例句改寫下列各句。

Examples:

The news surprised me.

→ *The news was surprising (to me).*

→ *I was surprised (at the news).*

The speech bored the audience.

→ *The speech was boring (to the audience).*

→ *The audience was bored (by the speech).*

1. The party pleased the guests.

2. The questions confused the students.

3. His long talk tired us.

4. The children amused the parents.

5. The concert disappointed the audience.

6. The performer fascinated the spectators.

7. The horror movie frightened the children.

8. The TV program never bored him.

9. Yesterday's events upset them.

10. His argument convinced everybody.

11. Her remarks do not interest me.

12. Did the results amaze you?

參考：許多表示情感的動詞（如 surprise, shock, astonish, amaze, frighten, alarm, please, amuse, entertain, charm, fascinate, interest, intrigue, disturb, confuse, annoy, excite, thrill, bore, upset, convince, irritate, discourage, disgust, move, strike, refresh, tire, exhaust 等）加了「-ing」或「-ed」的字尾以後可以當形容詞用。注意，這個時候「ing 式」含有主動的意思；「ed 式」含有被動的意思。比較：

> The news is very surprising.「消息非常令人驚訝。」
> I was very (much) surprised.「我非常感到驚訝。」

習 題 321

選出適當的字。

1. The grapes are drying in the sun. Raisins are (drying, dried) grapes.

2. Mother baked some apples. She often serves (baking, baked) apples for dessert.

3. The (losing, lost) child was crying for his mother.

4. After the incident she inspected her (damaging, damaged) automobile.

5. When I dine out, I prefer (broiling, broiled) meat.

6. I replaced the (fading, faded) carpet with a new rug.

7. The newly (constructing, constructed) highway is a pleasure to drive on.

8. We will get it (finishing, finished) as soon as we can.

9. The secret finally became (knowing, known) to the public.

10. The (exciting, excited) crowd gathered around the speaker.

11. One of our heroes lies (burying, buried) here.

12. They are looking at the (sparkling, sparkled) stars.

13. We can hear the (whistling, whistled) wind outside.

14. They have decided to adopt the (proposing, proposed) plan.

15. The dog ran after the (startling, startled) deer.

16. They are holding their meeting behind the (closing, closed) door.

17. I am sorry I have kept you (waiting, waited) so long.

18. He bought the camera at the (reducing, reduced) price.

19. A (typing, typed) paper is much easier to read than a (writing, written) paper.

20. I waited for my friend at the airport. He had telephoned me the (expecting, expected) arrival time of his flight.

習 題 322

依照例句改寫下列各句。

Examples:

It's a winning team.

　→ *It's a winning team. / The team is winning.*

It's a disappointing campaign.

　→ *It's a very disappointing campaign. / The campaign is very disappointing.*

She has a winning smile.

　→ *She has a very winning smile. / Her smile is very winning.*

1. It's a moving train.

2. It was a moving experience.

3. It's a striking resemblance.

4. They're striking workers.

5. He's the commanding officer.

6. He had a commanding presence.

7. It was not a convincing argument.

8. Was it a thrilling race?

習 題 323

依照例句完成下列各句。

Examples:

Just throw any *waste* paper in this *basket*. It's a <u>wastebasket</u>.

He wears a *watch* on the *wrist*. It's a <u>wristwatch</u>.

The *factory* produces *automobiles*. It's an <u>automobile factory</u>.

1. Mrs. Brown bought a *shade* for the *lamp*. She bought a _____.

2. Mr. Brown likes to go *sailing* in his *boat*. He has a _____.

3. That *student* studies in *college*. He is a _____.

4. A small *boat* saved her *life*. It was a_____.

5. The *tree* bears *apples*. It's an _____.

6. Jack deposited the *mail* in the *box*. He put the letters in the _____.

7. The *lamp* is on the *desk*. It's a _____.

8. We drink *tea* from *cups*. We drink from _____.

9. These *lights* regulate the *traffic*. They're _____.

10. She went into the *store* to buy some *shoes*. She went intothe _____.

11. The *bells* of the *church* rang out. I heard the _____.

12. He was carrying the *hat* in a *box*. He was carrying a _____.

13. Charles gave Susan a *ring* for their *engagement*. He gave her an _____.

14. The *man* is holding the *door*. He's a _____.

15. Bill bought a *ticket* for a *baseball game*. He bought a _____.

16. This *store* has a number of different *departments*. It's _____.

17. The *stamp* costs *ten cents*. It's a _____.

18. You need a *coat* to wear in the *rain*. You'll have to buy a _____.

19. That *man* has the highest *sales* record. He's the best _____ in the company.

20. The streetlights were off, but I could see by the *light* of the *moon*.

The street was lit up by the _____.

參考：名詞修飾名詞而成為複合名詞的時候，有的拼成一個字（如 wastebasket, wristwatch），有的分開寫成兩個字（如 automobile factory, department store），有的中間用連號（如 window-cleaner, air-conditioning, pay-day）。如有問題，最好查字典。

習　題　**324**

依照例句把下列語詞排成適當的名詞組。

Examples:

　　　　　a, street, village, narrow → *a narrow village street*

1. large, dormitory, college, this

2. players, tall, shose, sophomore

3. photogenic, swimmer, that, girl

4. this, counselor, enthusiastic, senior

5. wool, blue, necktie, George's

6. leather, her, shoes, old

7. desk, hardwood, large, his

8. cheap, ballpoint, these, pens

9. typewriter, student, my, portable

10. fence, sturdy, garden, our

習　題　**325**

依照例句回答下列各句。

Examples:

　　　　What's that shelf for? (books)

　　　　　→ *It's a shelf for books. It's a bookshelf.*

　　　　What's this key to? (house)

　　　　　→ *It's the key to the house. It's the house key.*

1. What's that book about? (history)

2. What's that smoke from? (cigarettes)

3. What was the conference on? (disarmement)

4. What's he a member of? (faculty)

5. What's that a ticket for? (movies)

6. What is the polish for? (shoes)

7. What's that furniture for? (living room)

8. What was the movie about? (was)

9. What was the speech on? (election)

10. What are the loans for? (students)

<h1 style="text-align:center">習　題　326</h1>

依照例句改寫下列句子。

Examples:

It's a song of beauty. → *It's a beautiful song.*

It's a song of love. → *It's a love song.*

1. It's a matter of importance.

2. It's a matter of business.

3. He's a man of patience.

4. He's a man of the city.

5. They're people of wealth.

6. They're people of society.

7. It's a problem of traffic.

8. It's a problem of urgency.

9. It's a program of length.

10. If's a position of strength.

<h1 style="text-align:center">習　題　327</h1>

依照例句改寫下列名詞組。

Examples:

a place of meeting → a méeting plàce

water for drinking → drínking wàter

pictures that move → môving píctures

1. the price of selling

2. room for standing.

3. a danger that exists

4. the standard of living

5. paper for wrapping

6. a mind that inquires

7. the cost of living

8. a pill for sleeping

9. costs that rise

10. a game of guessing

11. the point of boiling

12. the business of printing

13. a place for parking

14. money for spending

15. gum for chewing

16. a need that presses

17. a door that revolves

18. the vote that decides

19. a career of acting

20. a committee for investigating

習　題　328

依照例句改寫下列名詞組。

Examples:

> the turning point → the point of turning
>
> a hearing aid → an aid for hearing
>
> a crying shame → a shame (that) cries

1. the editing job

2. a frying pan

3. the opposing side

4. a hiding place

5. voting privileges

6. a measuring cup

7. a working agreement

8. the beraking point

9. cleaning fluid

10. recording facilities

11. a shifting current

12. stifling heat

13. a dictating machine

14. identifying marks

15. purchasing power

16. differing opinions

17. cutting remark

18. cutting edge

19. a grôwing páin

20. grówing pàins

習　題　329

依照例句回答下列問句。

Examples:

> What's water that runs? *Running water.*
>
> What's water that's for drinking? *Drinking water.*

1. What's a chair that folds?

2. What's a chair that's for rocking?

3. What are prices that are rising?

4. What are prices that are for selling?

5. What's a car that's speeding?

6. What's a car that's for racing?

7. What's a company that's in mining?

8. What's a company that are expanding?

9. What's an attorney who practices?

10. What's an attorney who's for prosecuting?

11. What's an experience that's in teaching?

12. What's an experience that was interesting?

習 題 330

依照例句改寫下列各句。

Examples:

The business is growing fast. → *It's a fâst-grôwing búsiness.*

The girl looks nice. → *She's a níce-lôoking gírl.*

The team breaks records. → *It's a rêcord-brêaking téam.*

The mail is coming in. → *It's an încoming máil.*

1. The cars are moving fast.

2. The students look happy.

3. The drugs form habits.

4. The decisions reach far.

5. The eggs smell bad.

6. The reforms range wide.

7. The citizens pay taxes.

8. The medicine works fast.

9. The sergeant drinks beer.

10. The men look forward.

11. The roast smells tempting.

12. The effects last long.

13. Your party sounds wonderful.

14. The tiger eats men.

15. The politicians know all.

16. The records play long.

17. The mail is going out.

18. The operation consumes time.

19. The diplomat ranks high.

20. The news breaks hearts.

參考：動詞常與後面的副詞、形容詞、賓語合成名詞修飾語，放在名詞的前面。這個時候，動詞、形容詞、賓語要調到動詞的前面，動詞要改成「ing 式」，中間常加連號‘－’。

$$\boxed{N \; V \left\{ \begin{array}{l} \textbf{Adv} \\ \textbf{Adj} \\ \textbf{N}' \end{array} \right\}} \quad \Rightarrow \quad \boxed{\left\{ \begin{array}{l} \textbf{Adv} \\ \textbf{Adj} \\ \textbf{N}' \end{array} \right\} \textbf{-V-ing N}}$$

The business is growing fast.

　　→ the fast-growing business「迅速發展的事業」

The girl looks nice.

　　→ the nice-looking girl「漂亮的女孩子」

The team breaks records.

　　→ the record-breaking team「破紀錄的隊伍」

The mail is coming in.

　　→ the incoming mail「寄來的信件」

習　題　331

依照例句改寫下列各句。

Examples:

　　The buses are for seeing the sights.

　　　　→ *They're buses for seeing sights.*

　　　　→ *They're sight (-) sèeing bùses.*

　　The organization is for gathering news.

　　　　→ *It's an organization for gathering news.*

　　　　→ *It's a néws-gàthering organization.*

1. The van is for moving furniture.

2. The society is for watching birds.

3. The committee is for finding the facts.

4. The department is for cleaning the streets.

5. The campaign is for getting the votes.

6. The apparatus is for fighting fires.

7. The time is for cleaning the house.

8. The equipment is for saving lives.

9. The party is for coming home.

10. The expedition is for climbing the mountain.

參考：表示目的（放在介詞 for 後面）的動名詞與賓語也可以合成名詞修飾語，放在名詞的前面：

$$\boxed{\textbf{N is for V-ing N}'} \Rightarrow \boxed{\textbf{N}'\textbf{-V-ing N}}$$

The bus is for seeing sights. → the sight (-) seeing bus

The organization is for gathering news.

→ the news-gathering organization

這個時候，賓語名詞一定要從複數形改為單數形（如 seeing sights → sightseeing, cleaning the streets → street-cleaning）。又注意，這裡「N-V-ing N」前重後輕的念法（ˇˇ）與上面的練習「N-V-ing N」前輕後重的念法（ˇˇˊ）不同。

習　題　332

依照例句改寫下列各句。

Examples:

The business was managed well.

→ *It was a well-managed business.*

The question was answered clearly.

→ *It was a clearly answered question.*

1. The gentleman is dressed well.

2. The bridge was erected hastily.

3. The ball was pitched well.

4. The target was bombed repeatedly.

5. The girl is educated well.

6. The party was planned perfectly.

7. The program was performed brilliantly.

8. The engagement was announced officially.

9. The tradition has been long established.

10. The glass was half filled.

11. The soldier was wounded seriously.

12. The bridge was damaged badly.

習　題　333

依照例句改寫下列各句。

Examples:

> The area is developing industry.
>
> > → *It's an industry-developing area.*
>
> The area is developed by industry.
>
> > → *It's an industry-developed area.*
>
> The story is made up.
>
> > → *It's a made-up story.*
>
> The man is taught by himself.
>
> > → *He's a self-taught man.*

1. The shoes are worn out.

2. The scholars are well known.

3. The woman is educated by herself.

4. The furniture is made by hand.

5. he gangs make troubles.

6. The rug is eaten by moths.

7. The workers have been laid off.

8. These citizens are well educated.

9. The property is owned by the government.

10. The official has elected himself.

11. The engine has been burned out.

12. The businessman employs himself.

13. The announcements are paid for.

14. The transportation is operated by the city.

15. The demonstration is organized by the students.

16. The spokesman has appointed himself.

17. The car has broken down.

18. The meal is cooked at home.

19. The territory is held by the enemy.

20. The peanuts are covered with chocolate.

習　題　334

依照例句改寫下列各句。

Examples:

The girl has blue eyes.

　→ *She's a girl with blue eyes.*

　→ *She's a blue-eyed girl.*

The program has five points. →

　→ *It's a program with five points.*

　→ *It's a five-point program.*

1. The boy has fair hair.

2. The train has ten cars.

3. The radical has a strong will.

4. The shirt has short sleeves.

5. The apartment has three rooms.

6. The traditions have deep roots.

7. The building has ten stories.

8. The boy has many talents.

9. The man has a narrow mind.

10. The shoes have high heels.

11. The jet has twin engines.

12. The animal has four feet.

13. The scientist has a mind like a computer.

14. The woman has her mind on a career.

15. The pudding has a flavor like an orange.

參考：形容詞與名詞可以合成複合形容詞來修飾名詞。這個時候，形容詞與名詞之間常加連號「-」，名詞的後面常加 -ed。

N has Adj N′.	⇒	N is Adj-N′ed.	⇒	Adj-N′ed N

The man has a bald head.

　　→ The man is *bâld-hêaded*.

　　→ He is a *bâld-hêaded mán*.

The girl has blue eyes.

　　→ The girl is *blûe-êyed*.

　　→ She is a *blûe-êyed gírl*.

但是 The comb has fine teeth.

　　→ It is a *fine-tooth* comb.

同樣地，數詞與名詞也可以合成複合形容詞。這個時候，名詞後常不加 -ed.

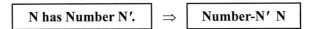

| **N has Number N'.** | ⇒ | **Number-N' N** |

The word has four letters.

　　→ It's a *fôur-lêtter wórd*.

The knife has a single edge.

　　→ It'a *síngle-êdge knífe*.

但是 The star has five points.

　　→ It's a *five-pôinted stár*.

注意，複合形容詞裡面的名詞部要改成單數形。

習　題　335

依照例句改寫下列詞句。

Examples:

　　　　a boy with (many) talents → a *(many-) talented boy*

　　　　an area with (thick) woods　→ a *(thickly) wooded area*

1. a driver with a license　　　　　2. shirts with stripes

3. police with helmets　　　　　　 4. a discussion with spirit

5. an opinion with a bias　　　　　 6. instruments with strings

7. an employee with a salary　　　　8. troops in uniform

9. a housewife with a simple mind　 10. a person with striking talents

11. an athlete with long legs

12. a performer with brilliant gifts

13. an official with a short temper

14. a photograph with clear details

15. a tradition with deep roots

16. a student with good manners

參考：有些形容詞是由名詞加 -ed 而得來：如 moneyed class「有錢階級」，aged man「老年人」，skilled labor「技能勞動」，barbed wire「鐵絲網」，experienced writer「有經驗的作家」，scented soap「加香料的肥皂」，tiled bathroom「舖瓷磚的浴室」，jeweled watch「嵌寶石的手錶」，detailed answer「詳細的回答」，helmeted police「戴鋼盔的警察」，talented boy「多才多藝的孩子」，wooded country「多樹木的鄉村」，spirited conversation「活潑的談話」，biased opinion「偏見」等。

習　題　336

依照例句回答下列問句。

Examples:

What's a voice with a high pitch?

It's a high-pitched voice.

What's a reply that's been expected for a long time?

It's a long-expected reply.

What's an area with thick woods?

It's a thickly wooded area.

What's a salaried employee who's good?

He's a good salaried employee.

1. What's a parent with a broad mind?

2. What's a vacation that's well-earned?

3. What's a performer with marvelous gifts?

4. What's a licensed driver who is young?

5. What's a lens with a wide angle?

6. What's a meal that's been cooked fast?

7. What's opinion with a strong bias?

8. What's a person with good intentions?

9. What's a hat with a broad brim?

10. What are glasses with a horn rim?

11. What's a hat that has three corners?

12. What's an apartment that has three rooms?

習　題　337

依照例句完成下列各句。

Examples:

> A broken chair is a chair which *is broken*.
>
> A quickly moving crowd is a crowd which *is moving quickly*.
>
> A fallen city is an city which *has fallen*.
>
> A one-eyed beggar is a beggar who *has one eye*.
>
> The record-breaking price is the price which *breaks the records*.

1. A burnt child is a child who …

2. A painted doll is a doll which …

3. A retired officer is an officer who …

4. A lying witness is a witness who …

5. A torn coat is a coat which …

6. A departed guest is a guest who …

7. The deeply moved audience is the audience who …

8. A well-educated gentleman is a gentleman who …

9. A fact-finding committee is a committee which …

10. A nerve-shattering experience is an experience which …

11. A two-storied house is a house which …

12. A broad-minded man is a man who …

13. A double-edged sword is a sword that …

14. The first-born child is the child who …

15. A housekeeping woman is a woman who …

16. A humble-looking clerk is a clerk who …

17. A paid-up bill is a bill which …

18. An upturned face is a face which …

19. Home-made cookies are cookies that …

20. Japanese-made cars are cars that …

21. The … clothing is the clothing that has been worn out.

22. A … man is a man who is dressed well.

23. The … news is the news that breaks our hearts.

24. A … woman is a woman who has a kind heart.

25. A … maid is a maid who has blue eyes.

26. A … boy is a boy who has weak sight.

27. A … room is a room that is furnished well.

28. A … article is an article that inspires thought.

29. A … face is a face that looks sulky.

30. A … maid is a maid who has slow wits.

31. A … man is a man who has short temper.

32. A … crowd is a crowd which is stricken with panic.

33. A … machine is a machine that saves labor.

34. A … officer is an officer who ranks high.

35. A … influence is an influence that reaches far.

36. A … man is a man who uses the left hand.

37. A … youth is a youth who looks shabby.

38. A … watch is a watch that is made in Switzerland.

39. A … boy is a boy who is good for nothing.

40. A … occasion is an occasion which has been looked for a long time.

16-3. 名詞前修飾語的次序

　　當有兩個以上的修飾語出現在名詞前面的時候，通常的次序是形容詞與分詞在前、名詞與動名詞在後：

Modifiers（修飾語）			Headword（被修飾語）
Determiner 限定詞	Adjective / Participle 形容詞 / 分詞	Noun / Gerund 名詞 / 動名詞	Noun 名詞
these	happy	girl	students
her	best	silver	spoons
that	smiling	dancing	girl
these	wounded	foot	soldiers

　　如果有兩個以上的形容詞修飾同一個名詞的時候, 通常的次序是 (1) 表示形狀大小的形容詞、(2) 表示性質的形容詞、(3) 表示年齡的形容詞、(4) 表示顏色的形容詞、(5) 表示質料的形容詞、(6) 專有形容詞：

Determiner 限定詞	Adjectives（形容詞）						Headword（被修飾語）
	Size 大小	Quality 性質	Shape 形狀	Age 年齡	Color 顏色	Material, Proper 質料、專有	Noun 名詞
a	tall	handsome			blond	French	student
these	big	juicy			red	Korean	apples
that	small		round		pink		face
this		beautiful		new		woolen	coat
those	big	dirty		old	black	wooden	boxes
these		attractive		oblong	green	Cape Colony	stamps

但是形容詞出現的次序, 並不是一定不變的。試比較：

　　　　{ his last brilliant book（他寫過幾本好書）
　　　　{ his brilliant last book（他可能只寫了一本好書）

　　　　{ his forceful and lucid remarks（forceful 與 lucid 修飾 remarks）
　　　　{ his forceful, lucid remarks（forceful 修飾 lucid remarks）
　　　　{ his lucid, forceful remarks（lucid 修飾 forceful remarks）

> { a tall fat man（比較自然）
> { a fat tall man

> { the two typical large country houses（比較自然）
> { the two large typical country houses

注意，有時候形容詞在名詞前面出現的次序，與在名詞後面出現的次序不一樣。例如：

> beautiful long hair = hair that is long and beautiful
>
> long straight hair = hair that is straight and long

參考：專有名詞與專有形容詞

專有形容詞除了當形容詞以外，還可以指 (1) 語言（不加冠詞）、(2) 民族（加有定冠詞 the)、(3) 國籍（加無定冠詞 a(n) 或用複數形）：

> He was born in *China*.（國家）
>
> He can speak *Chinese* (= the Chinese language).（語言）
>
> The *Chinese* are a peace-loving people.（民族）
>
> He is a *Chinese*. (What is his nationality?)（國籍）
>
> I saw one *Chinese*, two Japanese and three *Koreans*.

	Proper Noun	Adjective	Language	People	Individual	
					Singular	Plural
中　　國	China	Chinese	Chinese	the Chinese	a Chinese	Chinese
日　　本	Japan	Japanese	Japanese	the Japanese	a Japanese	Japanese
葡 萄 牙	Portugal	Portugese	Portugese	the Portugese	a Portugese	Portugese
瑞　　士	Switzerland	Swiss		the Swiss	a Swiss	Swiss
美　　國	America	American		the Americans	an American	Americans
德　　國	Germany	German	German	the Germans	a German	Germans
義 大 利	Italy	Italian	Italian	the Italians	an Italian	Italians
俄　　國	Russia	Russian	Russian	the Russians	a Russian	Russians
韓　　國	Korea	Korean	Korean	the Koreans	a Korean	Koreans
印　　度	India	Indian		the Indians	an Indian	Indians
澳 地 利	Austria	Austrian		the Austrians	an Austrian	Austrians

	Proper Noun	Adjective	Language	People	Individual	
					Singular	Plural
澳　　洲	Australia	Australian		the Australians	an Australian	Australians
加拿大	Canada	Canadian		the Canadians	a Canadian	Canadians
巴　　西	Brazil	Brazillian		the Brazillians	a Brazillian	Brazillians
挪　　威	Norway	Norwegian	Norwegian	the Norwegians	a Norwegian	Norwegians
埃　　及	Egypt	Egyptian	Egyptian	the Egyptians	an Egyptian	Egyptians
墨西哥	Mexico	Mexican	Mexican	the Mexicans	a Mexican	Mexicans
羅　　馬	Rome	Roman	(Latin)	the Romans	a Roman	Romans
波　　斯	Persia	Persian	Persian	the Persians	a Persian	Persians
亞　　洲	Asia	Asian			an Asian	Asians
非　　洲	Africa	African			an African	Africans
歐　　洲	Europ	European			an European	Europeans
英　　國	England	English	English	the English	an Englishman	Englishmen
法　　國	France	French	French	the French	a Frenchman	Frenchmen
愛爾蘭	Ireland	Irish	Irish	the Irish	an Irishman	Irishman
蘇格蘭	Scotland	{ Scots / Scottish }	{ Scots / Scottish }	{ the Scots / the Scottish }	a Scotsman / a Scotchman	Scotsmen / Scotchmen
荷　　蘭	Holland	Dutch	Dutch	the Dutch	a Dutchman	Dutchmen
希　　臘	Greece	Greek	Greek	the Greeks	a Greek	Greeks
瑞　　典	Sweden	Swedish	Swedish	the Swedes	a Swede	Swedes
丹　　麥	Denmark	Danish	Danish	the Danes	a Dane	Canes
西班牙	Spain	Spanish	Spanish	{ the Spanish / the Spaniards }	a Spaniard	Spaniards
土耳其	Turkey	Turkish	Turkish	the Turks	a Turk	Turks
波　　蘭	Poland	Polish	Polish	the Poles	a Pole	Poles

習 題 338

依照例句把括號裡面的修飾語放在句中適當的位置。

Examples:

The question was difficult. (examination, third)

The third examination question was difficult.

1. There were clouds in the sky. (many, rain)

2. Mr. Smith bought a suit yesterday. (gray, flannel)

3. That fence must be removed. (low, wire)

4. The women wore evening dresses to the opera. (new, their)

5. Let me see two knives. (steel, these)

6. Jack wants to be a teacher. (language, foreign)

7. There are some reports. (newspaper, other, bad)

8. Pranks are unworthy of you. (any, childish, such)

9. We need sand. (white, more, much)

10. Chapters are very important. (three, the, all, last)

11. Roommates want to go. (Chinese, studious, both, my)

12. I want sandwich. (no, cold, cheese)

13. Dogs never bite. (friendly, our, all, neighborhood)

14. Where can I get ornament? (glass, huge, another)

15. We need wires. (long, all, copper, the)

16. Rings are expensive. (lovely, engagement, her, both)

17. What are you going to do with flowers? (fresh, those, prairie, all)

18. Students come from China. (our, engineering, half, new)

19. This is a watch. (gold, old, valuable, very)

20. I want to buy a belt. (leather, long, brown)

21. There is a wall around the house. (brick, red, high)

22. Where did you get shoes? (brown, these, snakeskin, smart)

23. I've bought cabbages. (red, pickling, several, large)

24. This is stamp. (Cape-Colony, an, green, quite, triangular, attractive)

習　題　**339**

依照例句把括號裡面的語詞排成適當的名詞組。

Examples:

Do you have (a, book, new, telephone)?

　Do you have a new telephone book?

1. The library has (English, easy, books, very, several).

2. Mrs. Miller has (suit, pretty, a, green, very).

3. The church has (pictures, very, old, some, Spanish).

4. I like (two, silk, those, dresses, blue).

5. (black, dress, pretty, her, wool) is at the cleaner's.

6. The parents select (names, first, their, two, children's)

7. (these, bills, one-dollar, new, five) are for you.

8. (first, names, daughter's, her, two) are Mary Grant.

9. (lessons, six, first, our, reading) are not difficult.

10. (two, classes, interesting, teacher's, the, afternoon) are large.

11. (old, dress, evening, that, blue) is beautiful on her.

12. (programs, good, several, very, radio, American) are beginning this month.

習　題　**340**

依照例句改寫下列各句。

Examples:

Germany invaded France. →

　Germany's invasion of France

　the German invasion of France

　the invasion of France by Germany

Japan promised Germany to attack America. →

　Japan's promise to Germany to attack America

　the Japanese promise to Germany to attack America

1. Korea proposed to the United Nations.

2. China solved that problem.

3. France applied for membership.

4. Russia believes in subverting unfriendly governments.

5. Germany requested Japan to attack America.

6. France attempted to determine the Algerian government.

7. Britain realized that the Empire was doomed.

8. America wished Germany to attack Russia.

9. India exploded its first atomic bomb.

10. Spain justifies itself constantly.

16-4. 放在名詞後面的修飾語

放在名詞後面的修飾語主要的有 (1) 場所與時間副詞，(2) 介詞片語，(3) 不定詞片語，(4) 分詞片語，(5) 形容詞片語，(6) 同位語，(7) 關係子句。

(1) **場所與時間副詞**：表示場所與時間的副詞可以放在名詞的後面做修飾語用。

限定詞	名　詞	場所副詞	
the	people	here	（比較：The caris outside.）
the	car	outside	（比較：The people are here.）
those	guests	upstairs	（比較：Those guests are upstairs.）
the	paragraph	above	（比較：The paragarph is above.）
that	garage	three miles away	

（比較：That garage is three miles away.）

限定詞	名　詞	時間副詞
the	meeting	later

（比較：The meeting took place later.）

the	dinner	afterwards

（比較：They ate dinner afterwards.）

| this | game | tomorrow |

（比較：The game takes place tomorrow.）

| that | party | last night |

（比較：They gave the party last night.）

(2) **介詞片語**：介詞片語由介詞與名詞或動名詞合成，只能放在名詞後面做修飾語。

限定詞	名　詞	介詞片語
the	boy	with a dog
the	girl	without a friend
these	people	in the white car
that	picture	between the book and the map
the	machine	for washing clothes

(3) **不定詞片語**：不定詞片語（to V …）在動詞的基本式或原形前面加 to 而成。

限定詞	名　詞	不定詞片語（to V …）
the	boy	to send the message
the	message	for the boy to send
the	message	to send
the	message	to be sent by the boy

比較：The boy will send the message.

　　　The message will be sent by the boy.

(4) **分詞片語**：分詞片語分為現在分詞片語（V-ing …）與過去分詞片語（V-en …）。

限定詞	名　詞	現在分詞片語（V-ing …）
the	baby	sleeping in the cradle
the	man	standing at the gate
the	students	having finished their assignments

比較：The baby is sleeping in the cradle.

　　　The man was standing at the gate.

　　　The students have finished their assignments.

限定詞	名　詞	過去分詞片語（V-eii…）
the	cup	broken to pieces
the	soldier	wounded by a bullet
the	students	killed in an accident

比較：The cup was broken to pieces.

The soldier was wounded by a bullet.

The students were killed in an accident.

(5) **形容詞片語**：形容詞片語（Adj…）由形容詞與形容詞修飾語（如「加強詞」，不定詞，介詞片語等）合成。

限定詞	名　詞	形容詞片語（…Adj, Adj…）
a	girl	so lovely
a	soldier	afraid to die
a	man	angry with his wife
the	hills	right and left
the	boy	old enough to know better
the	salary	too small for us to live on

比較：The girl is so lovely.

The soldier is afraid to die.

The man is angry with his wife.

The hills are on the right and left.

The boy is old enough to know better.

The salary is too small for us to live on.

習　題　341

依照例句用第一個句子的副詞（片語）修飾第二個句子的名詞。

Examples:

The woman was inside.

The woman was my aunt.

→ *The woman inside was my aunt.*

The game will take place tomorrow. ⎫
Are you going to attend the game? ⎭

→ *Are you going to attend the game tomorrow?*

1. The branches were overhead. ⎫
   The branches were laden with fruit. ⎭

2. The discussion took palce yesterday. ⎫
   The discussion was informal and lively. ⎭

3. The laundry is outside. ⎫
   The laundry is almost dry. ⎭

4. The party is going on downstairs. ⎫
   The party is very noisy. ⎭

5. The clouds gathered above us. ⎫
   The clouds were dark and threatening. ⎭

6. The road stretched out ahead. ⎫
   The road was crowded with automobiles. ⎭

7. The noise occurred during the party. ⎫
   The noise annoyed the neighbors. ⎭

8. She longed for her home town. ⎫
   Her home town was thousands of miles away. ⎭

9. After the performance, the audience applauded. ⎫
   The applause was loud and enthusiastic. ⎭

10. Following the dance, the hostess served refreshments. ⎫
    The refreshments were delicious. ⎭

習　題　342

依照例句把下列每對句子連起來。

Examples:

⎰ The people are in the office.
⎱ The people are very helpful.

→ *The people in the office are very helpful.*

→ *The office people are very helpful.*

1. The clock says 4:30.

   The clock is on the wall.

2. They live in a room.

   The room is in a dormitory.

3. He is looking for a job.

   The job is for the summer.

4. She bought a book yesterday.

   The book is about psychology.

5. Don't forget to take the lunch with you.

   The lunch is in the box.

6. She's expecting to get a check today.

   The check is from the government.

7. Where did you get the frame?

   The frame is for the picture.

8. She sang a song.

   The song was of love.

9. They attended the conference.

   The conference was on disarmament.

10. Can I use your telephone to make a call?

    The call is out of town.

習　題　343

依照例句改寫下列各句。

Examples:

The door has a sign over it.

　　→ *the door with a sign over it*

The man isn't wearing a hat.

→ *the man without a hat*

1. The cup has a broken handle.

2. The boy doesn't have friends.

3. The coat has three pockets.

4. The clerk isn't wearing a necktie.

5. The baby has no clothes on.

6. The poor orphans don't have a home.

7. The woman wore an angry look in her eyes.

8. The man doesn't have a single penny with him.

9. The soldier carried a sword in his hand.

10. The lady didn't wear a hat or a coat.

習 題 344

依照例句把下列每一個句子改為含有 He's … man 的句子。

Examples:

He's big. → *He's a big man.*

He brings the mail. → *He's the mailman.*

He's in Taipei. → *He's the man in Taipei.*

1. He's honest.

2. He holds the door.

3. He's weaing sun glasses.

4. He's got only one eye.

5. He collects the garbage.

6. He's in business. He's from Brazil.

7. He's fat. He's wearing a moustache.

8. He's thin. He's not wearng a coat.

9. He's in in uniform. He serves in the navy.

10. He works on a newspaper. He's from New York.

習 題 345

依照例句把下列每對句子連起來。

Examples:

They watched the soldiers.
The soldiers were marching (to war).

→ *They watched the soldiers marching to war.*

→ *They watched the marching soldiers.*

The boy was sent to a hospital.
The boy was wounded (by a bullet).

→ *The boy wounded by a bullet was sent to a hospital.*

→ *The wounded boy mas sent to a hospital.*

1. They are looking for the person.
   The person is missing (from school).

2. Cet me the water.
   The water is boiling (on thr stove).

3. I can't hit the target.
   The target is moving (so fast).

4. Men can be engineers.
   The man are trained (in mathematics).

5. Did you hear the rumor?
   The rumor is spreading (around the town).

6. We are going to support the workers.
   The workers are striking (for higher salary).

7. The packages get special handling.
   The packages are insured (by the sender).

8. It was unsafeto enter the building.
   The building was damaged (by fire).

9. We went directly to the table.

The table was reserved (in our name).

10. A student must take no more than fifteen credits.

The student is beginning (his studies at this university).

習　題　346

依照例句連接下列每對句子。

Examples:

The English language is easy.

Learning it is easy.

　　→ *The English language is easy to learn.*

　　→ *English in an easy language to learn.*

Jane is a nice girl.

Sending her is nice.

　　→ *Jane is a nice girl to send.*

1. That statement was stupid.

Making it was stupid.

2. That comparison wasn't hard.

Making it wasn't hard.

3. George is wonderful person.

Working with him is wonderful.

4. Those places were dangerous.

Exploring them was dangerous.

5. She is an impossible person.

Arguing with her is impossible.

6. These offices are pleasant.

Working in them is pleasant.

7. Your analysis is funny.

Listening to it is funny.

8. A Volkswagen is an economical car.

   To drive it is economical.

9. Twenty-five dollars was a terrible price.

   Paying it was terrible.

10. "My Fair Lady" is a marvelous show.

    To go to it is marvelous.

習 題 347

依照例句把下面每一對句子連起來。

Examples:

He knows the man.

The man is at the door.

→ *He knows the man at the door.*

He is waiting for the bus.

The bus is leaving in an hour.

→ *He is waiting for the bus leaving in an hour.*

They gave me a question.

The question is too hard to answer.

→ *They gave me a question too hard to answer.*

1. He went to the bookstore.

   The bookstore is on the campus.

2. Pass me the newspaper.

   The newspaper is lying on the table.

3. We don't often see a movie.

   The movie is as good as that.

4. Fines are placed in the scholarship found.

   The fines are paid by students on overdue books.

5. Secretaries get additional pay.

   The secretaries work weekends.

6. They attended the conference.
   The conference was on public health. ⎱

7. A house is difficult to find.
   The house is as cheap as that. ⎱

8. You can buy your shirts at the shop.
   The shop is opposite the post office. ⎱

9. Do you know the girl?
   The girl is standing between Betty and Anne. ⎱

10. They sat down at the table.
    The table was reserved in their name. ⎱

16-5. 同位語

　　放在名詞組後面補充說明這個名詞組的名詞組，叫做**同位語** (ap-positive)。同位語通常都用逗號「,」劃開。

Headword（被修飾語）	Modifier（修飾語）
NP 名詞組	**NP (appositive)** 名詞組（同位語）

George,　　　　　　　　*my best friend*, (has moved away.)

Joe Adams,　　　　　　*a good student*, (got an A in math.)

Three of us　　　　　　—*George, Jack and I*— (went swimming.)

(The car stopped before) the house,

　　　　　　　　　a decorated Victorian mansion.

同位語有時候可以移到句首：

My best friend, George, has moved away.

A good student, Joe Adams, got an A in mathematics.

或移到句尾：

This, *a new Parker fountain pen*, is what I want.

　→ This is what I want, *a new Parker fountain pen*.

有些同位語（如 fact, report, realization, condition 等）還可以指前面整個句子：

> The woman has lived as a nurse in an English family, *a fact* which accounts for her acquaintance with English.

> The summer continued hot and dry, *a condition* which made the townspeople restless.

參考：注意同位語的音調：

> Dick, my cousin, is very good at chess.（名詞＋同位語）

（比較：My cousin Dick is very good at chess.（修飾語＋名詞）

> They stopped before the house, a decorated Victorian mansion.

習 題 348

在同位語下面畫線，被修飾的名詞上面加圈。

Examples:

> (Dick) my cousin, is very good at chess.

> There are only (two girls) there, namely, Mary and Ann.

> (We) all want to go.

1. Here comes George, your best friend.

2. Mr. Smith, the secretary, read the minutes of the last meeting.

3. The other, Miss Thompson, is very beautiful.

4. It was Sunday, always a dull day in London.

5. You Germans admire Hitle; we English do not.

6. Three boys were absent — namely, Tom, Dick and Harry.

7. There are many Latin words in present-day English, for example, *ratio* and *bonus*.

8. They were themselves busy that day.

9. They are neither of them very honest.

10. I have three ambitions: to live in peace, to have a few good friends, and to finish my life-work successfully.

11. The news that her son had been killed was a great shock to her.

12. It occurred to me that it was a good opportuity.

參考：(1) 同位語前面常用表示「說明」（如 namely, specifically, that is, or, in other words）或「舉例」（such as, forinstance, for example）的語調：

There are four elementary qualities of taste sensation, *that is*, sour, salt, sweet and bitter.

The features are common to languages coming from Latin *such as* French, Italian and Spanish.

(2) all, most, both, none, neither, each 等表示數量的代名詞與反身代名詞也常用做同位語：

The poets are not *all* alike.

We are *none of us* happy.

We gave them *each* an apple. / We gave them an apple *each*.

We were *ourselves* disappointed at the result of the election.

(3) 有時候不定詞子句，動名詞子句，that- 子句也可以當做同位語用：

It was difficult *for me to understand her French*.

It's a blessing *having you here*.

It never occurred to him *that he might have been wrong*.

The fact *that he is dead* is beyond dispute.（同位語子句）

比較：The fact (*that / which*) *he discovered* is beyond dispute.（關係子句）

習 題 349

依照例句把下面每對句子的第二個句子改為同位語。

Examples:

Dick plays chess. ⎱
Dick is my cousin. ⎰ →

Dick, my cousin, plays chess.

1. We saw Hamlet. ⎱
Hamlet is a play by Shakespeare. ⎰

2. Mr. Wilson moved away.

   Mr. Wilson was the oldest resident.

3. The president was called to Washington.

   The president was Harding.

4. The motorcycle was in good shape.

   The motorcycle was a secondhand contraption.

5. We inspected his new car.

   His new car was a long, sleek Humber.

6. "Trees" was included in the new collection.

   "Trees" was his favorite poem.

7. I felt what I always feel.

   What I always feel is a sense of frustration.

8. The dog can be an infernal nuisance.

   The dog is allegedly man's best friend.

9. The idea is ridiculous.

   The idea is that Alice is a thief.

10. The proposal was defeated.

    The proposal was that we send a telegram to the President.

習 題 350

把括弧裡的修飾語放在句中適當的位置。

Examples:

> That book is mine. (English, on the desk)
>
> That *English* book *on the desk* is mine.

1. The man is a professor. (old, music, with the gray hair)

2. The lecture was very interesting. (evening, on the life in the United States)

3. The question was difficult. (on the second page, examination, third)

4. Two knives are sharp. (steel, those, in the drawer)

5. Here are napkins. (paper, for you to wash, some)

6. The men are officers. (army, wearing the uniforms, young, Egyptian)

7. The boy is John's cousin. (talking to the professor, in the blue sweater, thin)

8. Do those magazines belong to you? (in the hall, on the table, new, English)

習　題　351

從括號裡面的語詞，選出適當的形容詞。

1. I always feel (sleepy, asleep) after I take a hot bath.

2. He fell (sleepy, asleep) during the class.

3. Who is the boy fast (sleepy, asleep) on the front seat?

4. Who is that (sleepy, asleep) looking boy?

5. He wasn't (content, contented) with what he had; he wanted more.

6. Some people are never (content, contented).

7. I am (content, contented) to live a quiet life in a small town.

8. He is a (content, contented) man.

9. She is three years (older, elder) than her sister.

10. She is much more intelligent than her (elder, older) sister.

11. I wonder who that (elder, older, elderly) man is.

12. Is the fish (live, alive) or dead?

13. She is purging (live, alive) fish in the kitchen.

14. Can you believe that he ate the whole fish (live, alive, lively)?

15. Who is the greatest man (live, alive, lively)?

16. He gave us a very (live, alive, lively) idea of what happened.

17. He is (shameful, ashamed) of his (shameful, ashamed) conduct.

18. More than one hundred people died at that (fearful, afraid) railroad accident.

19. The boy was very much (fearful, afraid) of his father.

20. The two sisters are very much (like, alike, likely).

21. (Like, Alike, Likely) causes produce (like, alike, likely) results.

22. Which are the most (like, alike, likely) candidates to win in this coming election?

23. She isn't (like, alike, likely) to come now; it's too late.

24. It isn't (like, alike, likely) that she should write such a letter.

參考：有些形容詞（如 afraid, asleep, alive, alike, awake, ashamed, accustomed, acquainted, content 等）只能放在名詞後面做補語，不能放在名詞前面做修飾語。這些形容詞通常都用「加強詞」very much 修飾：He is still very much alive.

又有些形容詞（如 elder, eldest, live「活的」等）只能放在名詞前面做修飾語，不能放在名詞後面做補語。比較：

$$\text{The fish is still} \begin{cases} \text{alive.}（○） \\ \text{live.}（×） \end{cases}$$

又注意有些形容詞（如 lively「活潑的，生動的」，elderly「年齡相當大的」，likely「可預期的」等）與副詞相像，帶有字尾 -ly：

We had a very *lively* discussion last night.

習 題 352

依照例句改寫下列各句。

Examples:

He lied poorly.

→ *He was a poor liar.*

The newspaper is published daily.

→ *It's a daily newspaper.*

The reason is chiefly that he didn't have enough money.

→ *The chief reason is that he didn't have enough money.*

1. She types poorly.

2. He was truly a poet.

3. The girl was totally a stranger in the town.

4. She was formerly his wife.

5. He is at present your friend.

6. He was regularly the champion.

7. The soprano sings beautifully.

8. The lawyer specializes in criminal cases.

9. The policeman works in a rural district.

10. He argues mainly that he needs more time to work on his project.

參考一：有些形容詞（如 chief「主要的」，main「主要的」，principal「主要的」，total「全然的」，sheer「全然的」，former「從前的」，late「已故的」，present「當前的」，poor「拙劣的」，particular「特別的」，regular「經常的」，only「僅有的」，daily「每天（出版）的」，rural「鄉村的」，criminal「刑法（方面）的」，只能放在名詞前面做修飾語，不能放在名詞後面做補語：

Rice is the *principal* food in China.

Her *late* husband was a musician.

Is there any *particular* reason for his objection to the proposal?

She is the *only* girl student in our class.

這些形容詞一般都不能有比較級或最高級，而且在語義上與副詞有密切的關係。

注意："She is a beautiful soprano" 可以有兩種解釋：

「她是長得很漂亮的女高音 (= The soprano is beautiful.)」

「她是唱得很漂亮的女高音 (= The soprano sings beautifully.)」

參考二：有些「名詞 + en」的形容詞（為 wooden, woolen, silken, golden, earthen）與「動詞 + en」的過去分詞（如 sunken, beaten, stricken, drunken, molten）也只能放在名詞前面做修飾語，不能放在名詞後面做補語。

第17章
名詞的修飾語（二）

17-1. 關係子句

名詞除了用單詞與詞組或片語修飾以外，還可以用整個子句來修飾。修飾名詞的子句，就叫做**關係子句**（relative clause）。

Headword（被修飾語）	Modifier（修飾語）
NP 名詞組	Relative Clause 關係子句

the girl	who won first prize
the book	that you took away
the money	which is for the tickets
the man	who is driving a truck
the place	where he lives
the hour	when we left
the reason	why we called you up

凡是含有關係子句的句子，都由兩個句子——**主句**（main sentence）與**從句**（subordinated sentence）連接而成。這個時候，這兩個句子必須含有一個名詞指同一個人或物。例如：

I know the girl *who won first prize.*

這個句子是由下面兩個句子連接而來的：

$\left\{ \begin{array}{l} \text{I know } \textit{the girl.}（主句）\\ \textit{She} \text{ won first prize.}（從句） \end{array} \right.$

而 the girl 與 she 是指同一個人。又如，

The book *that you took away* belongs to me.

這個句子是由下面兩個句子連接而來的：

$$\begin{cases} \textit{The book} \text{ belongs to me.}（主句）\\ \text{You took } \textit{it} \text{ away.}（從句） \end{cases}$$

而 the book 與 it 是指同一本書。

由從句變成主句裡面的關係子句，一共要經過三個步驟：

(1) 把從句裡面指同一個人或物的名詞用適當的**關係代名詞**（relative pronoun），

如 who, whom, whose, which, that 等來代替。例如：

she won first prize $\rightarrow$ *who* won first prize

you took *it* away $\rightarrow$ you took *that* away

(2) 把這個關係代名詞提前放在從句的句首。例如：

who won first prize $\rightarrow$ *who* won first prize

you took *that* away $\rightarrow$ *that* you took away

(3) 把整個從句放在主句裡面表示同一個人或物的名詞後面。例如：

$$\left.\begin{array}{l} \text{I know } \textit{the girl.}\\ \text{who won first prize} \end{array}\right\} \rightarrow$$

I know the girl *who won first prize.*

$$\left.\begin{array}{l} \textit{The book} \text{ belongs to me.}\\ \text{that you took away} \end{array}\right\} \rightarrow$$

The book *that you took away* belongs to me.

習　題　353

依照例句在關係子句前後加括弧，在被修飾的名詞下面畫橫線。

Examples:

　　　Here is the book (that you lent me).

1. These are the boys who work hard.

2. The boy who was lazy was punished.

3. This is the place where he lived.

4. Those whom the gods love die young.

5. The cat killed the rat that ate the corn.

6. I know the woman whose child was hurt.

7. They who live in glass houses should not throw stones.

8. The moment which is lost is lost for ever.

9. He has lost the watch you gave him.

10. The books which help you most are those which make you think most.

參考：由關係子句所修飾的名詞，總是放在關係子句的前面，因此文法上管它叫做「**前行語**」（antecedent）。

17-2. 關係代名詞 that

　　that 是關係代名詞中用途最廣的一種，不但可以代替任何名詞（人、物、動物、時間、場所、原因、理由、方法），而且所代替的名詞可能是主語、賓語、補語，甚至是動詞修飾語。

The doctor performs the operation.（主語，指「人」）

　　→ (I know) the doctor *that performs the operation.*

She bought *the dress*.（賓語，指「物」）

　　→ (We like) the dress *that she bought.*

The rat ate the corn.（主語，指「動物」）

　　→ (The cat killed) the rat *that ate the corn.*

I talked to *the woman*.（介詞賓語，指「人」）

　　→ (That's) the woman *that I talked to.*

We met *the man and the cattle*.（賓語，指「人」與「動物」）

　　→ The man and the cattle *that we met* (were going to the country fair).

You thought me *a fool*.（補語，指「人」）

　　→ (I'm not) the fool *that you thought me.*

She left here *at five o'clock*.（動詞修飾語，指「時間」）

　　→ (I forgot) the time *that she left here.*

He went *downtown*.（動詞修飾語，指「場所」）

　　→ (I know) the place *that he went.*

You came *to see her*.（動詞修飾語，指「理由」）

　　→ (Tell me) the reason *that you came.*

They travel *by train*.（動詞修飾語，指「方法」）

→ (How do you like) the way *that they travel*?

習　題　354

依照例句改寫下列各句。

Examples:

The doctor performs the operation.

→ *the doctor that performs the operation*

She bought *the dress*.

→ *the dress that she bought*

Wo went *the university*.

→ *the university that we went to*

1. I know *quite a few Americans*.

2. *The family* lives here.

3. She asked about *the book*.

4. *The pen* cost me ten dollars.

5. They are going to visit *the museum*.

6. *The doctor* was talking to a patient.

7. John went to see *the doctor*.

8. He gave *advice* to some people.

9. He gave advice to *some people*.

10. I come from *the country*.

11. She is working in *the laboratory*.

12. He gave *the money* to the clerk.

13. He gave the money to *the clerk*.

14. We elected *the man* our captain.

15. She looks like *the movie actress*.

17-3. 關係代名詞 who 與 whom

關係代名詞 who，用來代替表示人的名詞，而且只能代替當主語的名詞：

The man was drunk.（主語，指「人」）

→ The man *who was drunk* (had a bad accident).

A soldier had lost his arm.（主語，指「人」）

→ (I saw) a soldier *who had lost his arm*.

關係代名詞 whom, 是 who 的賓格 , 也是用來代替表示人的名詞，但是只能代替當動詞賓語或介詞賓語的名詞：

You know *the man*.（動詞賓語，指「人」）

→ The man *whom you know* (had a bad accident).

He is fond of *the girl*.（介詞賓語，指「人」）

→ (There comes) the girl *whom he is fond of*.

在口語英語中常用主格的 who 來代替賓格的 whom，或者把關係代名詞省掉：

The man (*who*) you know had a bad accident.

There comes the girl (*who*) he is fond of.

注意：我們只能省掉代替賓語或補語的關係代名詞，卻不能省掉代替主語的關係代名詞。

比較：

The man (that) was here is my uncle.（×）「that 在關係子句中當主語」

The man (that) you met is my uncle.（○）「that 在關係子句中當動詞賓語」

The man (that) you spoke to is my uncle.（○）「that 在關係子句中當介詞賓語」

He is no longer the man (that) he once was.（○）「that 在關係子句中當補語」

習 題 355

依照例句，把下列每對句子的第二個句子改為關係子句以後，放在第一個句子裡面。

Examples:

The lady has gone to London. ⎫
She was here yesterday. ⎭

　　→ *The lady who* (*that*) *was here yesterday has gone to London.*

The man has just left. ⎫
You want *him*. ⎭

　　→ *The man* (*that* / *who* (*m*)) *you want has just left.*

1. *Women* are to be admired. ⎫
   They work in hospitals. ⎭

2. *The doctor* is famous. ⎫
   She visited *him*. ⎭

3. The *girl* is my sister. ⎫
   You see *her* at the door. ⎭

4. *The people* are my parents. ⎫
   They are looking at that house. ⎭

5. *All the people* have disliked him. ⎫
   I have ever met *them*. ⎭

6. Who is *the girl*? ⎫
   She is sitting at the desk. ⎭

7. Where is *the student*? ⎫
   You sold your old dictionary to *him*. ⎭

8. *The man* is my English teacher. ⎫
   You spoke to *him* in the street. ⎭

9. Buy it back from *the man*. ⎫
   You sold it to *him*. ⎭

10. What was the name of *the girl*? ⎫
    She lost *the book*. ⎬
    You lent her *it*. ⎭

17-4. 關係代名詞 which

關係代名詞 which，用來代替表示人以外的名詞，包括表示動物與事物的名詞。
這個名詞，可能是主語，也可能是賓語。

The book is on the desk.（主語，指「物」）

→ The book *which is on the desk* (is mine).

The dog has long ears.（主語，指「動物」）

→ (I like) the dog *which has long ears*.

He bought the watch yesterday.（動詞賓語，指「物」）

→ (He lost) the watch *which he bought yesterday*.

She is fond of the cat.（動詞賓語，指「動物」）

→ (Is that) the cat *which she is fond of*?

這些句子裡面的 which 都可以拿 that 來代替。如果所代替的是賓語，還可以把
關係代名詞省掉：

The book *that* is on the desk is mine.

I like the dog *that* has long ears.

He lost the watch (*that*) he bought yesterday.

Is that the cat (*that*) she is fond of?

習 題 356

依照例句連接下列每對句子。

Examples:

The student comes from France.
I live with him.

→ *The student (that / who (m)) I live with comes from France.*

That's the university.
He teaches in it.

→ *That's the university (that / which) he teaches in.*

1. *The cigarette* is quite expensive.
   You are smoking *it*.

2. *The fish* was not good.
   I ate *it* yesterday.

3. *The doctor* is famous.
   She visited *him*.

4. *The music* is a Strauss waltz.
   The orchestra is playing *it*.

5. *The noise* is only our dogs fighting.
   You hear *it*.

6. I would like to see *the trees*.
   You picked these apples from *them*.

7. *The people* are coming to see you.
   You were living with *them* in New York.

8. Canyou remember *the person*?
   You took it from *him*.

9. That's the *knife and fork*.
   I eat with *them*.

10. What's *that music*?
    You are listening to *it*.

11. Here comes *the girl*.
    I am hiding from *her*.

12. Who is *the gentleman*?
    He is watching *the lady*.
    You spoke to *her* a moment ago.

習　題　357

依照例句改寫各句。

Examples:

Many of the people are poor.

    → *people many of whom are poor*

None of the material is very good.

    → *material none of which is very good*

1. Much of the food is cold.

2. Some of the classes met at night.

3. All of the coffee has sugar in it.

4. One of the five answers is completely wrong.

5. Most of the students are from China.

6. Neither of the two guests had a reservation.

7. Each of the members has to pay ten dollars.

8. Only a few of the many possibities are feasible.

17-5. 關係代名詞 whose

關係代名詞 whose 用來代替名詞（或代名詞）的所有格。這個名詞主要的是表示人的名詞，但是偶爾也可能是表示物或動物的名詞。注意，這個時候 whose 後面的名詞也要一起提前放在關係子句的句首：

The student's cousin is here.（指「人」）

    → (I know) the student *whose cousin is here.*

You bought *the man's* car.（指「人」）

    → (I met) the man *whose car you bought.*

The dog's ears are long.（指「動物」）

    → The dog *whose ears are long* (is my neighbor's).

The editor *of the newspaper* was fired.（指「物」）

    → (Have you read) the newspaper *whose editor was fired*?

The windows *of the house* are broken.（指「物」）

    → (Can you see) the house *whose windows are broken*?

The windows *of the house* are broken.

    → (Can you see) the house the windows *of which* are broken?

    → (Can you see) the house *of which* the windows are broken?

關係代名詞 whose，不能用 that 來代替，也不能省掉。

參考： 無生名詞的所有格，一般都避免用關係代名詞 whose 或 of which 來代替，而改用由 with 引導的介詞片語。比較：

> Can you see the house *whose windows / of which the windows* are broken?（欠通順）
>
> Can you see the house *with broken windows*?（較通順）

習 題 358

依照例句改寫下列各句。

Examples:

> The girl's father is a doctor.
>
> → *the girl whose father is a doctor*
>
> I never met girl's mother.
>
> → *the girl whose mother I never met*

1. The boy's brother is a policeman.

2. The girl's progress was remarkable.

3. The man's son is in the navy.

4. I will never forget these friends' faces.

5. We can't understand the man's English.

6. The hunter caught the fox's tail.

7. The university's faculty is mostly Chinese.

8. They aren't asking for the committee's advice.

9. We can't identify the woman's native language.

10. The company's employees are on strike for higher wages.

習 題 359

依照例句，把下列每對句子的第二個句子改成關係子句以後，放在第一個句子內。

Examples:

> There's *the lady*.
>
> *Her* purse has been stolen.

> *There's the lady whose purse has been stolen.*

1. *A child* is called an orphan.

   His parents are dead.

2. This is *the girl*.

   Her mother is president of the PTA.

3. That's *the man*.

   His daughter Betty is going to marry.

4. *The client* died.

   I was handling *his* stock.

5. *The man* is comingtotea.

   I always forget *his* name.

6. *The policeman* is at the door.

   You knocked off *his* helmet.

7. *The girl* has left the room.

   I was talking to *her* mother.

8. *A woman* is more obstinate than a man.

   Her mind is made up.

9. What's the name of *that man*?

   His wife has run away and left him.

10. *The boy* is the cleverest boy in the school.

    I showed you *his* work.

11. He went to *a university*.

    Its faculty is mostly Catholic.

12. *The house* is mine.

    In *its* windows there is a light.

17-6. 關係代名詞 when, where, why

關係代名詞 **when** 代替表示「時間」的名詞或副詞，因此常修飾 time, day, year 這一類的名詞：

They arrived *at three o'clock in the morning.*

→ (I know) the time *when they arrived.*

We left New York *ten days ago.*

→ (Do you remember) the day *when we left New York?*

關係代名詞 **where** 代替表示「場所」的名詞或副詞，因此常修飾 place, city 等名詞：

She lives *in the country.*

→ (Do you know) the place *where she lives?*

He went to *Chicago* with his wife.

→ (What was) the place *where he went with his wife?*

關係代名詞 **why** 代替表示「理由、原因或目的」的副詞，因此常修飾 reason, cause 等名詞：

You went back *to get your books.*

→ (Tell me) the reason *why you went back.*

She didn't come *because of illness.*

→ (That was) the reason *why she didn't come.*

在日常英語裡面關係代名詞 when, where, why 常用 that 來代替，或者乾脆省略而不用。

Do you remember the day (*that*) we left New York?

What was the place (*that*) he went with his wife?

Tell me the reason (*that*) you went back.

She prefers the way (*that*) they travel.

參考：除了 when 以外，after, before, since 等也常用來做表示時間的關係代名詞。

The day *after* I came was very beautiful.

The year *before* they got married he went to Europe.

The long lonesome period *since* we last met has depressed me very much.

習 題 360

依照例句改寫下列各句。

Examples:

She went away *at five o'clock*.

→ *the time* (*that* / *when*) *she went away*

They came *on Monday*.

→ *the day* (*that* / *when*) *she came*

He went *to Taipei*.

→ *the place* (*that* / *where*) *he went*

She came *to see me*.

→ *the reason* (*that* / *why*) *she came*

They went *by train*.

→ *the way* (*that*) *they went*

1. My father works *in the factory*.

2. We had an appointment *at three o'clock*.

3. They went home *by bus*.

4. I bought this dictionary *at the bookstore*.

5. They met each other *in 1951*.

6. He left for England *to attend the conference*.

7. A lot of people travel *in the summer*.

8. We paid a visit to our teacher *last Tuesday*.

9. The general was defeated *on the battlefield*.

10. I like to take a walk *in the morning*.

11. She put her necklace *in the jewel-box*.

12. He could not attend the meeting *because of illness*.

13. Our teacher explained the problem to me *patiently*.

14. She arrived home *quite late*.

15. He wrote his report *with care.*

習　題　361

依照例句，把下列每對句子的第二個句子改為關係子句以後，放在第一個句子裡面。

Examples:

That is *the place.*
He lives *there.*

　→ *That is the place (that / where) he lives.*

Do you know *the reason*?
She deserted him *for that reason.*

　→ *Do you know the reason (that / why) she deserted him?*

I am not satisfied with *the way.*
He did it *in that way.*

　→ *I am not satisfied with the way (that) he did it.*

The day was beautiful.
I came *after that day.*

　→ *The day before I came was beautiful.*

1. I cannot find *the place.*
   I lost it *there.*

2. *The hour* has not been decided.
   We leave *then.*

3. Tell us *the reason.*
   You did not come *for that reason.*

4. I met her *the year.*
   My father died *in that year.*

5. Is that *the house*?
   Bill was born *there.*

6. There is *no reason*.

   He should not be admitted *for that reason*.

7. There are *times*.

   Such things are necessary *then*.

8. I'll go *anywhere*.

   You want me go *there*.

9. We passed *the house*.

   The fire started *there*.

10. Those were the *days*.

    No one cared to be alive *then*.

11. *On the day* our car blew up.

    We started *before that day*.

12. *The year* was a momentous one.

    He enlisted *before that year*.

13. *The woods* were filled with mushrooms.

    We camp of *there*.

14. Brazil is *the place*.

    Most of the world's coffee comes from *there*.

15. *The reason* is now obvious.

    He moved *for that reason*.

16. Ten o'clock is *the time*.

    They take their coffee break *then*.

習 題 362

用關係代名詞 when, where, why 等改寫下列句子。

Examples:

That is the house *in which* he lives.

→ *That is the house where he lives.*

1. This is the office *in which* he works.

2. This is the reason *for which* I am angry.

3. Sunday is the day *on which* people go to church.

4. Is this the place *at which* we stopped to rest?

5. Do you remember the restarant *at which* we had dinner?

6. We visited the log house *in which* Lincoln was born.

7. There are times *at which* I despair of success.

8. This is the place *in which* the accident happened.

9. There is every reason *for which* you should be pleased.

10. I still miss the years *during which* we went to school together.

習　題　363

在下面的空白裡填關係代名詞 as, but 或 than。

1. Bees like the same odors _____ we do.

2. There is more money _____ is needed.

3. You are much taller _____ I was at your age.

4. There was no man _____ felt the terror.

5. He went away the same way _____ he had come.

6. You are as wise _____ wise can be.

7. The book is written in such easy English _____ beginners can understand.

8. There are few men _____ would risk all for such a prize.

9. There are as good fish in the sea _____ ever came put of it.

10. Such women _____ know Bob thought he was rich.

11. _____ was the custom, the young man bowed politely.

12. There is more _____ all of us can eat.

13. He was taken to a large arena, such _____ was popular during the period of Greece and Rome.

14. Not one of them has as much brains in his whole body _____ Bentley has in his little finger.

15. None of the engineers attended the meeting _____ was impressed by his demonstration.

參考：關係代名詞 as 常用在 such, the same, as 或 so 後面：

He was *such* a student *as* most teachers would be glad to have.

I am ready to accept *such* terms *as* are offered to me.

（比較：……*such* terms *as* they offered to me.）

He would never be *the same* man *as* he was before.

You are *as* wrong *as* can be.

He is *as* honest a man *as* ever breathed.

關係代名詞 as 還常用做 happen, be the case, be usual, be the custom 的主語：

The sea was frozen over, *as* frequently happens in those regions.

As was usual with him, he was late for school.

He comes to me when he is in need of money, *as* is very often the case.

關係代名詞 but（＝that … not）常用在表示否定的語詞（如 no, hardly, who is there … ?）後面：

There is *no* child *but* knows him.

= There is no child *that* does *not* know him.

= *Every* child knows him.

There is *hardly* a rule *but* has exceptions.

= There is hardly a rule *that* does *not* have exceptions.

= *Every* rule has exceptions.

Who is there but makes mistakes?

= There is *no* one *but* makes mistakes.

= *Everyone* makes mistakes.

關係代名詞 than 常用在「比較句」後面：

You have *more* money *than* I have.

I have already told you *more than* you ought to know.

Her services were *more* valuable *than* was supposed.

習　題　364

依照例句改寫下列各句。

Examples:

　　There is no one but knows it.

　　　→ *There is no one that does not know it.*

　　　→ *Everyone knows it.*

1. There is no child but knows him.

2. There was no boy but fell in love with her.

3. There is no work but he can criticize.

4. There is not a bird but does more harm than good.

5. There is no friend but he can find fault with.

6. There was not a soldier among them but hoped to get out alive.

17-7. 關係子句「限制的用法」與「連接的用法」

　　關係子句在性質上是一個形容詞子句，其功用在修飾前面的名詞。例如在下面的句子裡，關係子句 that was nearest to his house 修飾前面的名詞 the garage，即從眾多的修車廠裡面特地指出離他家最近的那一家修理廠來。

　　　He walked to the garage that was nearest to his house.
　　「他走到離家最近的修車廠。」

　　這種用法就叫做關係子句**限制的用法**（the restrictive use），因為這個時候關係子句的功用在修飾或限制前面的名詞。

　　另外有些關係子句，其功用並不在修飾前面的名詞，而在連接這個關係子句，以便接著繼續把話說下去。例如在下面的句子裡，我們已經知道他去的是最近的一家修車廠, 用不著再用關係子句來告訴我們究竟指的是那一家。所以這裡關係子句 which was a mile away 的主要目的是，補充說明或者順便提一提這家修車廠座落在一里遠的地方。

　　　He walked to the nearest garage, which was a mile away.
　　「他走到最近的一家修車廠，而這家修車廠離他家有一里之遠。」

這種用法就叫做關係子句**連接的用法**（the continuative use）。

「連接的關係子句」（continuative relative clause），在用法上與「限制的關係子句」（restrictive relative clause）有幾個不同的地方：

(1) 「限制的關係子句」前面的名詞是有定或無定的名詞；「連接的關係子句」前面的名詞是專指或泛指的名詞，而用「連接的關係子句」比用連詞連接兩個句子來得方便，因為不必把前面的名詞（或代名詞）再重覆一次。

比較：

He walked to the nearest garage,
$$\left\{\begin{array}{l} \textit{and the garage} \\ \textit{and it} \\ \textit{which} \end{array}\right\}$$
was three miles away.

The man (*that / whom*) *you met last night* is a music teacher.「你昨天晚上見到的那一個人是一位音樂老師。」（指某一個特定的人，限制的用法）

Mr. Lee, *whom you met last night*, is a music teacher.「李先生，你昨天晚上見過他，是一位音樂老師。」（李先生是專指，無需再加以指定，連接的用法）

The Mr. Lee (*that / whom*) *you met last night* is a music teacher.「你昨天晚上見到的那位李先生是一位音樂老師。」

（從幾位李先生中間指出特定的人，限制的用法）

The elephon (*that / which*) *you saw in the zoo* comes from Africa.「你在動物園看到的那一隻大象是從非洲來的。」（指特定的某隻象，限制的用法）

The elephant, which is an animal that never forgets, lives more than a hundred years.「象，據說是一種從來不會忘記的動物，可以活到一百多歲。」（泛指象的總類，連接的用法）

(2) 「限制的關係子句」可以用 that, who, whom, whose, which, when, where, why, how, as, but, than 等所有關係代名詞；「連接的關係子句」可以用 who, whom, whose, which, when, where 等，但是不能用 that, why, as, but, than 等：

Mme. Curie, *who discovered radium*, is one of the greatest women of our age.

The teacher in the next class *whose name I can never remember*, makes a lot of noise.

Boxing Day, *when Christmas boxes used to be given to servants*, is the day following

Christmas Day.

Stratford-on-Avon, *where Shakespeare was born*, is visited by thousands of tourists.

又代替賓語的 that, who(m), which 在「限制的關係子句」中可以省略，但在「連接的關係子句」中卻不能省略。比較：

> The girl you met last night is my best friend.（○）
>
> Miss Lee, you met last night, is my best friend.（×）

(3) 「限制的關係子句」的前後通常都不加逗號「,」；「連接的關係子句」的前後通常都要加逗號。比較：

His father, *who died twenty years ago*, was a professor of English.

He is a famous scientist, *about whom many books have been written*.

參考：

(4) 「限制的關係子句」與「連接的關係子句」有不同的念法：

His uncle who lives in Taipei is a doctor.

　= He has an uncle living in Taipei. This uncle is a doctor.

　　「有幾個舅舅，其中一個住在臺北的當醫生。（限制的用法）」

His uncle, who lives in Taipei, is a doctor.

　= His uncle is a doctor, and he lives in Taipei.

　　「只有一個舅舅，而他住在臺北。（連接的用法）」

(5) 「限制的關係子句」翻成中文的時候，關係子句要放在所修飾的名詞的前面；「連接的關係子句」翻成中文的時候，關係子句要放在所提及的名詞後面：

I like people *who always tell me the truth*.「我喜歡那些經常告訴我實話的人。」

Please believe me, *who always tell you the truth*.「請你相信我吧，我經常都告訴你實話呢。」

習 題 365

以適當的關係代名詞填入下面的空白裡。

1. My sister, _____ you met yesterday, wants to speak to you.

2. Her father, _____ has been to the United States, has just returned.

3. Swimming, _____ is a good sport, makes people strong.

4. Air, _____ we breathe, is made up of many gases.

5. Tom and Beth, _____ are playing in the garden, are very naughty children.

6. Oxford University, _____ is one of the oldest in the world, has many different colleges.

7. Grammar, _____ I dislike very much, is good for me.

8. Budapest, _____ is on the Danube, is a beautiful city.

9. George Washington, _____ became President of the United States, never told a lie.

10. The B.B.C., _____ is world-famous, spends millions of pounds every year.

11. My sister-in-law, _____ has been married for ten years, has just had her first baby.

12. In Norway, _____ is a Baltic country, you can see the midnight sun.

13. Love, _____ is a wonderful feeling, comes to everyone at some time in his life.

14. The import tax on mint, by _____ the country vastly increases their national income, is a very high one.

15. The Prime Minister of Kalama, to _____ I introduced you last week, is inordinately fond of his national drink.

習 題 366

依照例句改寫下列各句。

Examples:

It crashed into a bus-load of children, and they were all killed.

→ *It crashed into a bus-load of children, who were all killed.*

He bored a hole in my tooth, and it was very unpleasant.

→ *He bored a hole in my tooth, which was very unpleasant.*

1. They have four children, and all of them go to college.

2. He passed his examination with honors, and this made his parents very proud of him.

3. John went fishing last week-end, and that is one of the pleasantest ways of spending one's leisure.

4. I gave Mary a box of candies, and this pleased her very much.

5. He studied hard in his youth, and that contributed to his success in later life.

6. I saw two dwarfs at the circus, and neither of them was over three feet tall.

7. She was dropped when she was a baby, and that made her a permanent invalid.

8. We have two spare rooms upstairs, and neither of them has been used for years.

9. He came home drunk the other night, and that shocked the whole neighborhood.

10. My uncle built several houses, and they are none of them more than two miles from the station.

參考：關係代名詞 which 在「連接的用法」中，可以指前面的整個句子。比較：

John appeared with a dog *which surprised everybody*.

（= The dog surprised everybody.）

（which 指 a dog，「限制的用法」）

John appeared with a dog, *which surprised everybody*.

（= John's appearing with a dog surprised everybody.）

（which 指 John appeared with a dog，「連接的用法」）

關係代名詞 which 與 who 在「連接的用法」中，也可以指同位語。

The lectures are all given in Russian, *a language* (or *which language*) I never studied.

We stood silently before the warden, *the official who* (or *which official*) was in charge of the dormitory.

又注意，如果關係代名詞前面帶有「數量詞」（例如：all of, both of, some of, many of, one of），那麼通常都依照「連接的用法」。

He had five children, *all of whom died during the war*.

He has two sons, *both of whom are well-known doctors*.

習 題 367

依照例句改寫下列各句。

Examples:

Bob is in Taiwan now, because he wants to learn Chinese.

　　→ *Bob, who wants to learn Chinese, is in Taiwan now.*

The dictionary has been removed from the study room, although it was for everyone's use.

　　→ *The dictionary, which was for everyone's use, has been removed from the study room.*

Our neighbor is a piano teacher, and his wife teaches singing.

　　→ *Our neighbor, whose wife teaches singing, is a piano teacher.*

1. My mother teaches school, and she lives in Taichung.

2. Beth spends a lot on her clothes, because her father is rich.

3. Geometry seems a very dull subject, although I know nothing about it.

4. The king deserves his popularity, because his life has been devoted to his country.

5. My sister plans on becoming a nurse, although she faints at the sight of blood.

6. Her clothes are all beautiful, because they are made in Paris.

7. Chess is difficult to play, and it is a very old game.

8. Jane looked angry, because her pride was hurt.

9. We took a taxi to Kennedy Airport, because it was a few miles outside New York.

10. That land is now very valuable, although it was once a paddy field.

11. Switzerland is noted for its beautiful scenery, although it is a small country in Europe.

12. The chief of police takes care of the public safety, and his work is very important.

13. He met my mother, and he got the news of my marriage from her.

14. We cannot decide whether tomatoes are a fruit or a vegetable although we are all fond of them.

15. Our refrigerator was made in 1950, therefore its motor often stops.

參考：「連接的關係子句」都可以看做是由連詞 and, because, although, therefore 等）與句子變來的。變換的步驟是；(i) 把連詞省掉；(ii) 從後面的句子裡找出與前面句子裡的名詞指同一個人或物的名詞，並用適當的關係代名詞代替以後，提前放在關係子句的句首；(iii) 把整個關係子句放在前面句子裡的共指同一個人或物的名詞後面，並用逗號「,」把關係子句劃開。

習　題　368

依照例句改寫下列各句。

Examples:

At noon is the worst time to call him, because he rests then.

→ *At noon, when he rests, is the worst time to call him.*

They went to Boston, and they visited their relatives there.

→ *They went to Boston, where they visited their relatives.*

1. The best time to talk is at night, because we aren't busy then.

2. We went to Rome, and we stopped a week there.

3. At sunrise is too early to go swimming, because it is cold then.

4. They traveled together as far as Europe, and they separated there.

5. The nicest day in Mary's life was May 5, 1957, because she met Paul on that day.

6. The school library is the best place to study, because nobody will disturb you there.

參考：注意，關係詞 when 與 where 也有「連接的用法」。

習　題　369

依照例句改寫下列各句。

Examples:

If a student wants to get high grades, he should work hard.

→ *A student who wants to get high grades should work hard.*

If a water pipe leaks, it must be fixed.

→ *A water pipe that/which leaks must be fixed.*

1. If a teacher teaches well, he will be popular.

2. If a student comes to school late, he will be punished.

3. If a pen leaks, it should be repaired.

4. If a person is an original thinker, he will make a fine scientist.

5. If buildings are strong, they will last many years.

6. If a house is painted white, it is cooler in the summer.

7. If anyone reads fast, he can do well in school.

8. If people live in glass houses, they should not throw stones.

9. If an egg is spoiled, it can't be used for anything.

10. If a woman is in mourning, she often wears a black dress.

參考：有些關係子句在語意上等於一個條件句。例如，

A water pipe that leaks must be fixed.「漏水的水管必須修理。」

在語意上等於是

If a water pipe leaks, then it must be fixed.「如果水管漏水，必須修理。」

注意，這時候主語名詞都泛指某一類的人或物，而動詞都用現在單純式。

習 題 370

依照例句把下列每對句子用適當的關係代名詞連起來。

Examples:

Here comes *the men*. You dined with *him*.

→ *Here comes the man (that / whom) you dined with.*

→ *Here comes the man with whom you dined.*

These are *the things*. He is fond of *them*.

→ *These are the things (that / which) he is fond of.*

The courage was truly inspiring. He faced his enemy with *the courage*.

→ *The courage with which he faced his enemy was truly inspiring.*

I used to go to school with *George*. *He* is now mayor of this city.

→ *George, with whom I used to go to school, is now mayor of this city.*

1. That is *the house*. We have been invited to *the house*.

2. *The gentleman* is our school master. You trod on *his* foot.

3. *The building* is the Finance Ministry. I live opposite *it*.

4. *The spoon* was stolen from a hotel. He was eating the soup with *it*.

5. *The fountain* was built by the Romans. They are standing around *it*.

6. This is *the point*. I have never been beyond *it*.

7. *The pen* has a steel nib. I wrote the letter with *it*.

8. I appreciate *the kind words*. You have welcomed me with *kind words*.

9. *The dignity* greatly impressed the judge. He repudiated the charge with *dignity*.

10. The tree fell on to a party of *fishermen*. *All of them* were injured.

11. *St. John's Glacier* is only about 8,000 feet high. I've climbed beyond *it*.

12. He was not such *a coward*. We took him for *a coward*.

13. *The old man* has died. You were talking to me about *him* and told me to go and see *him*.

14. *Miss Taylor* has several *new friends*. *All of them* are artists. *Her father* is a millionaire.

參考：關係代名詞與介詞：

(1) 當關係代名詞 whom 是介詞賓語的時候，介詞可以放在關係代名詞的前面，也可以放在關係子句的句尾：

> the man *with whom* you dined（較文的說法）
> the man *who* (*m*) you dined with（口語的說法）

如果關係代名詞是 that，那麼介詞只能放在關係子句的句尾：

> the man *that* you dined *with*（○）
> the man *with that* you dined（×）

在日常英語裡，關係代名詞 that 常加以省略：

> the man you dined *with*

(2) 在下列情形中，介詞只能放在關係子句的後面。

  (a) 當關係代名詞被省略的時候：

> This is the house we have been invited *to*.

  (b) 當關係代名詞是 that, as 或 but 的時候：

> This is the very book *that* I am looking *for*.
>
> He was not such a coward *as* we took him *for*.
>
> There is no one but he can find *fault with*.

  (c) 當關係代名詞同時做兩個以上介詞的賓語的時候：

> What is the subject (*that*) you have seen an increasing interest *in* and controversy *over*?

(d) 當介詞與關係子句裡面的動詞或形容詞（如 think *of*, afraid *of*, fond *of*, delight *in*, come *across*, do *without*, laugh *at*, long *for*, wonder *at*, take care *of*, make use *of*) 形成固定的成語的時候：

We've done the best (*that*) we could think *of*.

These are all things (*that*) he is fond *of*.

(3) 在下列的情形，介詞常放在關係代名詞（whom, which）的前面。

(a) 「連接的關係子句」：

George, *with whom* I used to go to school, is now a well-known novelist.

(b) 關係代名詞前面有「數量詞」all, both, some, many, none, neither, one 等：

I have two friends, *both of whom* are on holiday at the moment.

(c) 介詞與關係代名詞 which 所代替的名詞形成一種固定的狀態副詞片語：

the courage *with which* he faced his enemy（表示狀態）

比較：the pen (*that / which*) he wrote with（表示工具）

(d) beyond, around, opposite, besides, than, as to, outside, except, during, considering 等介詞，一般都放在關係代名詞的前面：

the man *opposite whom* I'm sitting

the fountain *around which* they are standing

但是也有人把這些介詞放在關係子句的句尾：

the man (*that*) I'm sitting opposite

the fountain (*that*) they are standing around

習 題 371

依照例句改寫下列各句。

Examples:

They produce their food from *the water*.

→ *the water from which they produce their food*

1. Each obtains his food from *a piece of land*.

2. It's impossible to predict the outcome for *some countries*.

3. They derive all their income from *the cultivation of land*.

4. They're always competing among themselves for *the food*.

5. Productivity will increase through the use of *better fertilizer*.

6. Advances in *medical knowledge* will lengthen the average life span.

習　題　372

依照例句改寫下列各句。

Examples:

I know the person you're referring to.

→ *I know the person to whom you're referring.*

1. The flight they arrived on originated in San Francisco.

2. Is that the student you put the question to?

3. The station they broadcast the news over was WCBS.

4. The operator is the person they were able to obtain the information from.

5. Hsinchuang is the town you have to pass through to reach Taipei.

6. The person she places her trust in is not her father but her brother.

7. He needs a watch he can tell the day, the month and the year by.

8. The land reform the politician spoke about is nothing more than a dream.

習　題　373

用適當的關係代名詞填入下面的空白裡。能用 that 的地方，盡量填入 that；能省略的地方，盡量加以省略（用記號 '(that)' 來表示）。

1. Brazil is the country _____ produces the most coffee.

2. Coffee is the industry _____ Brazil developed.

3. Brazil is the country _____ people developed the coffee industry.

4. I can't understand people _____ don't put sugar in their coffee.

5. Do the people _____ you live with work in the city?

6. Latin America is the place _____ coffee originated.

7. Six o'clock is the time _____ we eat dinner.

8. That's the reason _____ I took up medicine in college.

9. The way _____ they use chopsticks are quite interesting.

10. The house in _____ they once lived is up for sale.

11. The house _____ they once lived in is up for sale.

12. The house, _____ they once lived, is up for sale.

13. The accident _____ they saw occurred at the corner of the street.

14. The accident, _____ they saw, cost the lives of three people.

15. The operator _____ they finally contacted supplied the information.

16. The operator, _____ they finally contacted, admitted that she eavesdropped the conversation.

17. The company, _____ employees are on strike, will even raise prices.

18. The *Times* is the paper _____ editorials I read.

19. The moment _____ he entered the room, everybody stopped talking.

20. He can break it with the same ease _____ you can break an egg.

21. She's not the woman _____ she was before she got married.

22. By the time _____ I told my mother, they had already left.

23. The people and the customs _____ I saw there seemed to be quite different from those of my country.

24. The number of mistakes _____ there are in this homework is simply astounding.

25. It was all _____ I could do to keep myself from laughing.

26. A welcome is extended to all _____ wish to come.

27. Who _____ saw her did not pity her?

28. Who am I _____ should object to their proposal?

29. He is the man _____ I believe can give you all the information you need.

30. He decided to marry the girl _____ I know he met only a few days ago and about _____ family background I think he knows almost nothing.

參考：關係代名詞 that 的用法與省略：

在日常英語裡遇有下列情形時常用關係代名詞 that。

(1) 在「限制的用法」中，除了表示人的主語用 who，所有格用 whose 以外，通常多用 that：

The boy *who* broke the window is called John Grey.

I know a girl *whose* father is a policeman.

The window *that* was broken by the boy has been repaired.

當動詞或介詞賓語用的關係代名詞 that，通常都加以省略：

The window (*that*) the boy broke has been repaired.

The boy (*that*) you spoke to broke the window.

(2) 表示人的補語常用 that，並且通常都加以省略：

He is not the man (*that*) he once was.

I'm not the fool (*that*) you thought me.

(3) 表示時間（time），場所（place），理由（reason），方式（way）的名詞後面，常用關係代名詞 that 並且通常都加以省略：

It happened the last *time* (*that*) we were together.

Take me to any *place* (*that*) you go.

Nobody knows the *reason* (*that*) he came here.

He did it in the *way* (*that*) I should have done it myself.

(4) 表示「存在」的 there is / are 後面的名詞常用關係代名詞 that 來代替，並且通常都加以省略：

It's the only one (*that*) there is in the shop.

He's one of the best men (*that*) there are in the world.

(5) 關係代名詞 who 在下列場合常用 that 來代替。

(a) 當前行語有最高級形容詞 the first, the last, the only, the same, the very, all, no 等修飾語的時候：

You are *the best* man *that* can do it.

He was *the first / last* guest *that* left.

He is *the only* student *that* knows the answer.

Was he *the same* person *that* attacked you?

There is *no* such person *that* lives in this house.

(b) 當句首有疑問詞 what, who 等的時候（以避免有 wh- 音的詞重覆兩次）：

What was the name of the girl *that* came here last night?

Who that understands music could say his playing was good?

(c) 在 much, little 的名詞用法後面常用關係代名詞 that：

There is not much (*that*) I can do to help you.

Little (*that*) he says makes sense.

(6) 下列情形時常用關係代名詞 who, which, when, where 等。

(a) 在「連接的用法」中不能用 that，只能用 who, which, when, where 等：

Julius Caesar, *who was* a powerful Roman general, came to Britain in 55 B.C.

The lark, *which* has a very sweet song, builds its nest on the ground.

They met each other in 1941, *when* the Second World War broke out.

(b) 在介詞後面只能用 whom 或 which, 不能用 that.

This was the knife *with which* I cut the rope.

(c) 在不定代名詞（如 anybody, everybody 等）的後面，who 與 that 都有人用；在 all, those 等代名詞的後面，如果表示人，多用 who，其他用 that：

Is there *anybody who / that* has his address?

The dog frightens *all who* come near the house.
That's *all* (*that*) I've got.

Those who are qualified must report to the office.
I would like to buy hats like *those that* are on the counter.

習 題 374

依照例句用適當的關係代名詞連接下列各句。

Examples:

You are the only *person*. I've met *him*. *He* could do it.

→ *You are the only person (that) I've met who could do it.*

This is the *paper*. I read *it* every day. And I find *it* so enjoyable.

→ *This is the paper (that) I read every day and which I find so enjoyable.*

1. These are *forms*. *They* occasionally occur. But *they* should not be taught.

2. *The best paly* is probably *King Lear*. Shakespeare wrote *it*. But I haven't read *it*.

3. He's the *person*. I meet *him* at the club every day. And I've invited *him* to dinner tonight.

4. It was the police *detective*. *He* told me to fetch the *rifle*. I had been practicing with *it*.

5. He's the best *man*. I can find *him*. *He* can mend it in an hour.

6. This is the *horse*. *It* kicked the *policeman*. I saw *him* trying to clear away the *crowd*. The *crowd* had collected to watch a *fight*. Two men had started the *fight*.

參考：在日常英語裡同時用兩個以上的關係代名詞修飾同一個名詞的時候，為了避免重覆，第一個常用 that，第二個常用 who 或 which。

習　題　375

以適當的關係詞填入下面的空白裡面。有兩個以上的解答的時候，把常用的關係詞放在前面；可以省略的關係詞放在括號裡。

Examples:

The boy (*that* / *who* (*m*)) Mary loved was an orphan.

She is the finest woman *that* / *who* ever lived.

1. Women _____ work in hospitals are to be admired.

2. The street _____ leads to the school is very wide.

3. The man _____ cut your hair did it very badly.

4. Was the hat _____ you were wearing yesterday very expensive?

5. The boy _____ threw that stone will be punished.

6. The ring _____ my mother gave me has three diamonds.

7. The man _____ you spoke to yesterday is coming to tea.

8. The book _____ I was reading last week was a detective story.

9. The picture _____ you were talking about has been sold.

10. Where is the man _____ sold me these sun-glasses?

11. I'm afraid that's all _____ I've got.

12. He's the only American _____ has swum across the river.

13. Any man _____ listens to you is a fool.

14. This is the very room _____ I first met my wife in.

15. All the people _____ I have ever met have disliked him.

16. Any paper _____ you read will give the same story.

17. A nation _____ citizens are cowards will perish.

18. No man _____ has common sense can believe it.

19. You may go to any place _____ you like.

20. "How can I possibly know" is the way _____ you should ask.

21. New Orleans is the place _____ you can see the French influence in America.

22. January is the month _____ you get the coldest weather in America.

23. Who is that man _____ is standing by the door?

24. He was the first man _____ came.

25. This is the best picture _____ I ever saw.

26. All _____ glitters is not gold.

27. Chauncey is the only student _____ is gifted with speech.

28. That is the very thing _____ I want.

29. Who _____ has ears cannot hear?

30. What is there _____ I do not know?

31. She is no longer the woman _____ she used to be.

32. I'm just the same _____ I was the day _____ I first met you.

33. I gave him the one _____ I wanted to keep, fool _____ I was.

34. It's all _____ there is to last us a week, _____ is not a very cheering thought, is it?

35. It'll be dark by the time _____ you get to the river, so I'm afraid you'll have to go back the same way _____ you came.

36. Put it down anywhere _____ you like and take anything else _____ you want _____ you can see.

37. So that's _____ you met at the party, is it? She's about the only friend of yours _____ I've met _____ I really like.

38. He played the piece, _____ was quite difficult, in the exact manner _____ I play it myself, but on an instrument _____ I wouldn't even accept as a gift.

17-8. 關係子句與其他名詞修飾語

在第 16 章（16-4）節裡我們曾經介紹了一些放在名詞後面的修飾語。它們是 (1) 場所副詞，(2)介詞片語，(3) 不定詞片語，(4)分詞片語，(5)形容詞片語，(6)同位語。其實，這些名詞修飾語都可以看做是由關係子句刪去關係代名詞與 Be 動詞而得來。

$$\boxed{\textbf{N that Be} \cdots} \quad \Rightarrow \quad \boxed{\textbf{N} \cdots}$$

the people *that are here* → the people *here*（場所副詞）

the garage *that is three miles away* →

　　the garage *three miles away*（場所副詞）

the girl *that is in the white car* →

　　the girl *in the white car*（介詞片語）

the machine *that is for washing clothes* →

　　the machine *for washing clothes*（介詞片語）

the boy *that is to send the message* →

　　the boy *to send the message*（不定詞片語）

the message *that is for the boy to send* →

　　the message *for the boy to send*（不定詞片語）

the baby *that is sleeping in the cradle* →

　　the baby *sleeping in the cradle*（現在分詞片語）

the man *that was standing at the gate* →

　　the man *standing at the gate*（現在分詞片語）

the cup *that was broken to pieces* →

　　the cup *broken to pieces*（過去分詞片語）

the students *that were killed in an accident* →

　　the students *killed in an accident*（過去分詞片語）

a soldier *that is afraid to die* →

　　a soldier *afraid to die*（形容詞片語）

the boy *that is old enough to know better* →

　　the boy *old enough to know better*（形容詞片語）

Joe Adams, *who is a good student,* →

John Adams, *a good student,*（同位語）

習 題 376

依照例句改寫下列各句。

Examples:

Is she the nurse who is visiting (the hospital)?

→ *Is she the nurse visiting the hospital?*

→ *Is she the visiting nurse?*

Is she the nurse who was trained (by the hospital)?

→ *Is she the nurse trained by the hospital?*

→ *Is she the trained nurse?*

1. They're scholars who are well known (to us).

2. Birds that are singing (in my garden) remind me that spring is here.

3. The income that is earned (abroad) amounts to two million dollars.

4. All visitors who tour (the art museum) are asked to sign the guest book.

5. All the guests who were invited (to the party) brought their presents.

6. All vehicles that drive (along the new highway) are required to pay a toll.

7. The table that is loaded (with books) belongs to the editor.

8. The young mother tenderly kissed the baby who was sleeping (in the cradle).

9. The candidates who were chosen (by the committee) include Mr. Lee.

10. People who are traveling (first-class) receive special privileges.

11. All the afternoon Jack was mourning over the effort that had been wasted (by us all).

12. Children who are growing (up in the city) need more exercise.

13. Skills that are acquired (through work) are very valuable.

14. I have thrown away the shoes that were worn out (with hiking).

15. He is one of the workers who have been laid off (by the factory).

習　題　**377**

依照例句改寫下列各句。

Examples:

He is a man who is nice to talk to.

→ *He is a man nice to talk to.*

→ *He is a nice man to talk to.*

1. She is a person who is good to know.
2. He is a man who is hard to convince.
3. That's a poem which is nice to remember.
4. Show me the instrument which is easiest to play.
5. She always knows a way to say it which is better.
6. Bob is the person who is most convenient to send.
7. We have some decisions which are hard to make.
8. Is that a course which is easy to pass?
9. That's a course which was impossible to do well in.
10. She's preparing all kinds of things which are wonderful to eat.

習　題　**378**

依照例句改寫下列各句。

Examples:

Do you know the man who's at the door?

→ *Do you know the man at the door?*

I have a brother who lives in Chicago.

→ *I have a brother living in Chicago.*

It's a custom that's a little hard to adopt.

→ *It's a custom a little hard to adopt.*

1. He'll catch another bus that's leaving in an hour.
2. You won't see a movie that's as good as that.

3. They gave me a question that was too hard to answer.

4. Mr. Lee, who is our chemistry teacher, speaks excellent German.

5. Who is the girl that's watering the flowers?

6. The boy who was bitten by a snake has been sent to the hospital.

7. These are advertisements that are designed to please housewives.

8. It turned out to be a day that was too hazy for pictures.

9. Students who want pencils please raise their hands.

10. Who does the new car that's over there belong to?

11. Bob, who was a good salesman, charmed them immediately.

12. Have you made a list of machines that need new parts?

13. Anyone who has finished his assignments may go home now.

14. You shouldn't have taken on activity that was as strenuous as that.

15. The teacher gave us a subject which was very easy to talk about.

16. I've never seen a movie that's as long as *Gone with the Wind*.

17. There is a job that's for you to do.

18. They need someone who is to take care of their children while they are away.

參考：通常不用「ing 式」的動詞，如 want, need, know, own 等，以及其完成式都
可以改成分詞片語來修飾名詞：

> students who want pencils → students *wanting* pencils

> anyone who has finished his assignments →

> anyone *having* finished his assignments

習 題 379

依照例句回答下列問句。

Examples:

> What's a machine that plays records?

>> *It's a record player.*

> What's a person that tells stories?

>> *He's a story filler.*

1. What's a machine that cools water?

2. What's a device that sharpens pencils?

3. What's a machine that wipes windshields?

4. What's a device that opens cans?

5. What's a device that throws flame?

6. What's a substance that kills weeds?

7. What's a device that distinguishes fire?

8. What's a person that reads minds?

9. What's a person that makes trouble?

10. What's a person that owns a home?

11. What's a person that inspects food?

12. What's a person that produces movies?

13. What's a person that collects garbage?

14. What's a person that plays the flute?

15. What's a person that operates an elevator?

習　題　380

依照例句回答下列問句。

Examples:

What's a eating place? → *It's a place for eating.*

What are striking workers? → *They're workers that are striking.*

What's a meeting place? → *It's a place of meeting.*

1. What's a living standard?

2. What's drinking water?

3. What are rising costs?

4. What's a coughing fit?

5. What's a pressing need?

6. What's wrapping paper?

7. What's a guessing game?

8. What's a frying pan?

9. What's an existing danger?

10. What's a revolving door?

11. What's chewing gum?

12. What's a turning point?

13. What's an inquiring mind?

14. What are parking privileges?

15. What are recording facilities?　　16. What's an acting career?

17. What's a working agreement?　　18. What's a penetrating analysis?

19. What's the teaching experience?　　20. What's a soothing ingredient?

習　題　381

依照例句回答下列問句。

Examples:

What's a sightseeing bus? → *It's a bus for seeing the sights.*

What's a self-starting motor? → *It's a motor that starts itself.*

What's a good qualifying candidate?

　　→ *It's a good candidate that qualifies.*

　　→ *It's a qualifying candidate that's good.*

Whats'a big advertising agency?

　　→ *It's an advertising agency that's big.*

　　→ *It's a big agency for advertising.*

1. What's a man-eating tiger?

2. What's an early-warning device?

3. What's a bullfighting arena?

4. What are ever-increasing costs?

5. What's a high living standard?

6. What's a perfect working agreement?

7. What's a very long-lasting effect?

8. What's a long tape-recording session?

9. What's a reliable self-winding clock?

10. What's a three-day speech-making tour?

11. What's a small eating capacity?

12. What's a hardworking beginning student?

習　題　382

依照例句回答下列問句。

Examples:

What's a company for mining gold?

　　It's a gold-mining company.

What's an operation that consumes time?

　　It's a time-consuming operation.

What's an operating cost that's high?

　　It's a high operating cost.

1. What's campaign for getting votes?

2. What's a display that catches the eye?

3. What's a withholding tax that's high?

4. What's a service for cashing checks?

5. What's an ingredient that works fast?

6. What's a mining company that's old?

7. What's an envelope that seals itself?

8. What are visiting hours that are short?

9. What's a hiding place that's good?

10. What are colonies that govern themselves?

11. What's a national society for watching birds?

12. What's a large organization for gathering news?

17-9.複合關係代名詞 what, whatever, whoever, whichever ,whenever, wherever, however

　　what「（所）…的（東西）」（＝'that which', 'the thing(s) that'）是一個比較特別的關係代名詞，因為它不修飾名詞，也就是說，它沒有前行語。傳統的文法書認為這種 what 實際上把前行語包合在內，因此叫做「複合關係代名詞」（compound relative pronoun）。

Take *what* you like.

He gave me *what* I wanted.

whatever「不管什麼，任何的（東西）」（= 'anything that', 'the thing that'）也是一個複合關係代名詞，與 what 一樣不能指「人」，只能指「物」：

You are welcome to *whatever* you want.

Whatever is worth doing at all is worth doing well.

whoever「不管誰，任何⋯的人」（= 'anyone who', 'the person who'), **who (m) ever**「不管⋯誰（受格），任何⋯的人」（= 'anyone whom', 'the person whom'）與 **whosever**「不管誰的」（= 'anyone whose', 'the person whose'），只能指「人」：

Whoever comes first may have it.

Sell it to *whomever* you like.

Return the letter to *whosever* address is on it.

whichever「不管那一個」（= 'any of those that', 'either of the two that', 'the one which'），「人」與「物」都可以指：

You had better see the girls yourself, and choose *whichever* suits you best.

Here are a watch and a camera. You may choose *whichever* you like.

whenever「無論什麼時候」（= 'anytime that', 'the time when'）指「時間」：

Whenever you come is the time to begin.

Whenever is convenient is fine with me.

wherever「無論什麼地方」（= 'anywhere that', 'the place where'）指「地方」：

Wherever he works is the only address she has.

He comes from Zambia, *wherever* that may be.

however「無論如何」（= 'anyway that', 'the way that'）指「方式」，「態度」或「程度」：

However they got there is a puzzle to me.

However you finished your job isn't important, so long as you have finished it.

Take *however* much you want.

參考：疑問詞 what 與關係詞 what 的用法與意義都不同。比較：

What he wants is the question. (= The question is: what does he want?)「問題
是他要什麼呢？」

What he wants is the question. (= The thing that he wants is the question. = He
wants the question.)「他要的是那個問題。」

同樣地，疑問詞 Who 與關係詞 whoever 的用法與意義也不同。比較：

Who he lives with isn't important. (The fact isn't important.)「他跟誰住在一
起（這個事實）並不重要。」

Whoever he lives with isn't important. (The person isn't important.)「不管跟
他住在一起的人是誰（這個人）並不重要。」

習　題　383

依照例句改寫下列各句。

Examples:

the person who succeeded → *whoever succeeded*

the person who (m) they asked → *who (m) ever they asked*

the thing that they did → *what / whatever they did*

the one which they chose → *whichever (one) they chose*

the time when they came → *whenever they came*

the place where they meet → *wherever they meet*

the way that they got there → *whatever way / however they got there*

1. the person who finishes first
2. the thing that happened
3. the one which costs most
4. the time that's convenient
5. the person who (m) he contacted
6. the place where they live now
7. the person who (m) it belongs to
8. the thing that bothered him
9. the time when he decided to come
10. the place where he used to live
11. the one which he likes a little more
12. the way that she finished her job

習 題 384

用關係代名詞改寫下列各句。

Examples:

> *Anyone who says so is liar.* → *whoever says so is a liar*

1. Our teacher will give a prize to *anyone who* writes well.

2. He will understand *anything that* you say.

3. I will invite *anyone who* is your friend.

4. Take *either of the two that* you want.

5. I know *the thing that* you want.

6. He spends *all that* he earns.

7. *Anyone who* comes will be welcome.

8. Give it to *anyone that* you like.

9. He will shoot *anyone that* comes near him.

10. He may choose *any of the three things that* he wants.

11. He flatters *any one whose* fatheris rich.

12. The police promised leniency to *anyone who* would confess.

13. *Anything that* he does is done well.

14. *The thing that* I think doesn't seem to matter.

15. I'll do *anything that* you tell me to.

習 題 385

用適當的關係詞填入下面的空白裡。

1. _____ he says is quite true.

2. _____ I get is at your disposal.

3. He quarrels with _____ he meets.

4. He drove out _____ came in.

5. He will take _____ comes his way.

6. He will take _____ you offer him.

7. He only laughed at _____ we said.

8. He will pay attention to _____ you may say.

9. Things are not _____ they seem.

10. This is _____ publishers would like us to read.

11. It is wrong _____ you are doing.

12. I insist on paying _____ it has cost.

13. He is not _____ he used to be.

14. She'll go with _____ of the boys asks her first.

15. My teacher has made me _____ I am.

16. From _____ I have seen of him, there is nothing peculiar about him.

17. You are welcome to _____ you want.

18. He is a good scholar; and, _____ is better, an excellent teacher.

19. She is _____ you call a "*new woman*".

20. The rules must be few, and, _____ is more important, they must be comprehensive.

習　題　386

依照例句改寫下列各句。

Examples:

Freedom of speech is imperative.

    → *What is imperative is freedom of speech.*

    → *Freedom of speech is what is imperative.*

It needs a little improvement.

    → *What it needs is a little improvement.*

    → *A little improvement is what it needs.*

They'll send an investigating committee.

    → *What they'll send is an investigating commitee.*

    → *What they'll do is (to) send an investigating committee.*

She finally called him.

    → *What she finally did was (to) call him.*

    → *What she did was finally (to) call him.*

I wanted to help him.

    → *What I wanted to do was help him.*

They want you to try.

    → *What they want you to do is try.*

    → *What they want is for you to try.*

He went out to buy cigarettes.

    → *What he went to do was buy cigarettes.*

    → *What he went out for was to buy cigarettes.*

1. His intelligence is really amazing.

2. She is looking for something to read on the train.

3. I want to know her name.

4. The missing diamond is in the box.

5. She writes to him every day.

6. She'll look at the display in the window.

7. We're returning her application by mail.

8. I tried to remind myself to do it.

9. A university has to have responsibility.

10. They wanted you to accept it.

11. They'll urge you to think twice.

12. Who he associates with isn't important.

13. What he had to say impressed me.

14. How you can have such a big argument amazes him.

15. They meant to ask a couple of questions.

16. She taught herself to speak English.

17. Where he comes from also came up in the discussion.

18. Their job is showing people around.

19. She ought to go over and over the whole thing.

20. When he gets here will determine when we can start.

21. They'll never find coffee as good as that.

22. They dressed to go out to a movie.

23. She slowed down for a left turn before reaching the intersection.

24. They expect to be able to keep up their growing business.

25. Why he likes to keep a record of all the people he ever met I just can't figure out.

26. I am certain that he will succeed.

27. He was afraid that you might object to the plan.

28. Mike is a doctor.

29. Jack wanted to be a hero.

30. Did you catch a rabbit by the ear?

參考：關係代名詞 what，有許多用例可以看做是由下列比較基本的句式加上 what 與 is 變出來的。

(1) 「主語 is 補語」⇒〔What is + 補語 is 主語〕⇒〔主語 is + what is + 補語〕

Freedom of speech is imperative.「言論的自由必不可缺少。」

→ *What is* imperative is freedom of speech.「必不可缺少的是言論的自由。」

→ Freedom of of speech is *what is* imperative.「言論的自由是必不可缺少的。」

(2) 「主語　及物動詞　賓語」⇒〔What + 主語　及物動詞 + is + 賓語〕→〔賓語 + is what + 主語　及物動詞〕

It needs a little improvement.「它需要一點改良。」

→ *What* it needs *is* a little improvement.「它（所）需要的是一點改良。」

→ A little improvement *is what* it needs.「一點改良是它所需要的。」

(3) 「主語　助動詞　及物動詞　賓語」⇒「what + 主語　助動詞 + do + is + (to) + 及物動詞　賓語」

They'll send an investigating committee.「他們要派一個調查（事實）的委員會。」

→ *What* they'll *do is* (*to*) send an investigating committee.「他們（所）要做的是派一個調查（事實）的委員會。」

I'm teaching him a lesson.

> → *What* I'm *doing is* teach*ing* him a lesson.

He's spoilt the whole thing.

> → *What he's done is* (*to*) spoil the whole thing.

> → *What he's done is spoilt the whole thing.*

(4) 「主語　及物動詞　賓語」⇒「What + 主語 + do + is + (to) + 及物動詞　賓語」

She finally called him.「她最後打了電話給他。」

> → *What* she finally *did was* (*to*) call him.「她最後（所）做的是打了電語給他。」

John ruined his suit.

> → *What* John *did was* (*to*) ruin his suit.

> → *What* John *did to* his suit *was* (*to*) ruin *it.*

注意，狀態副詞（如 finally）可以移到不定詞上面去。

> → *What* she *did was finally* (to) call him.

(5) 「主語　及物動詞 to 動詞…」⇒「What + 主語　及物動詞 + to do + is + 動詞…」

I wanted to help him.「我想幫助他。」

> → *What* I wanted *to do was* help him.「我（所）想做的是幫助他。」

(6) 「主語　及物動詞　賓語 to 動詞…」⇒「What + 主語　及物動詞　賓語 + to do + is + 動詞…」⇒「What + 主語　及物動詞 + is + for 賓語 + to　動詞」

They want you to try.「他們要你試一下。」

> → *What* they want you *to do is* try.「他們（所）要你做的是試一下。」

> → *What* they want *to do is for* you *to* try.「他們（所）要你做的是試一下。」

(7) 「主語　不及物動詞 to 動詞…」⇒「What + 主語　不及物動詞 + to do + is + 動詞…」⇒「What + 主語　不及物動詞 + for + is + to 動詞」

He went out to buy cigarettes.「他出去買香煙。」

> → *What* he went out to *do is* buy cigarettes.「他出去做的是買香煙。」

> → *What* he went out *for is to* buy cigarettes.「他出去的（目的）是為了買香煙。」

習 題 387

依照例句改寫下列句子。

Examples:

What they'll probably do is send an investigating committee.

→ *They'll probably send an investigating committee.*

1. What it will do is create a generation incapable of enjoying liberty.

2. What we do by silencing criticism is deny evidence of intellectual independence.

3. What it does is produce demoralization and eventual corruption.

4. What the search for subversives does is discourage independence of thought.

5. In order to get there on time what he has to do is leave before dawn.

6. What we want to know is where he gets all the time for speech-making.

7. What we'll do as soon as they all leave is havea bite.

8. What can upset me is what he says and does.

9. What's important is what his views are.

10. What's important is not what he says but what he does.

習 題 388

依照例句改寫下列各句。

Examples:

No matter when he comes, we have cakes for tea.

→ *Whenever he comes, we have cakes for tea.*

1. No matter where the singer goes, crowds welcome her.

2. No matter what happens, keep calm.

3. I'll discuss it with you no matter when you like to come.

4. No matter who you are, you don't belong here.

5. You are certainly right, no matter what others may say.

6. The car shouldn't be parked here, no matter whose car it is.

7. No matter how hard he tries, he'll never succeed.

8. No matter whom you'd like to get a letter of recommendation from, you should first ask for his permission.

9. No matter which measure you take, you are bound to offend some people.

10. No matter when she does an exercise she makes mistakes, no matter how hard she tries.

參考：帶有 -ever 的關係詞, 除了引導名詞子句以外，還可以引導表示「讓步」（concession）的副詞子句。這個時候，它們的含義等於 no matter（when / where / …）「無論（什麼時候 / 什麼地方 / …）」。

習 題 **389**

在下面的空白裡填 which, what, whatever, whichever。

1. I want a copy of *Pride and Prejudice*, _____ book we are to read next semester.

2. Take _____ measures you consider best.

3. Please take _____ one you want and bring it back whenever you like.

4. You should choose _____ book meets your requirements.

5. We traveled together as far as Paris, at _____ place we parted.

6. It is not known _____ course he will pursue.

7. I will approve _____ course you decide upon.

8. They stayed with me three weeks, during _____ time they drank all the wine I had.

9. I have lost _____ little confidence in him I ever had.

10. He will find difficulties _____ coursehe may take.

11. _____ orders he gives are obeyed.

12. I was told to go not by train but by bus, _____ advice I followed.

13. They robbed him of _____ little money he had.

14. I am glad to get these books, and I shall be grateful for _____ ones you may give me in the future.

15. The president visited the village, _____ fact made the people there very happy.

參考：

(1) 關係代名詞 which 在比較正式的文章裡常代替「限定詞」this, that, the 等：

> We arrived at eight.
> The party was in full swing at *that* time. $\Big\}$
>
> → We arrived at eight, at *which* time (= when) the party was in full swing.
>
> We could not find the lieutenant.
> The officer was to show us over the ship. $\Big\}$
>
> → We could not find the lieutenant, *which* officer (= who) was to show us over the ship.

(2) 「what + 名詞」表示「所…的名詞」 "such Noun as, the (that, those) Noun that"：

> Lend me *what books* (= such books as, those books that) you can spare
>
> I gave him *what little money* (= the little money that) I had.

(3) 「whatever + 名詞」表示「任何…的名詞」 "any Noun that" 或「不管什麼名詞」 "no matter what"：

> I'll pay *whatever price* (= any price that) is asked of me.
>
> *Whatever* (= no matter what) nonsense the newspapers print, some people always believe it.

(4) 「whichever + 名詞」表示「（有定事物中的）任何…的名詞」 "any Noun of those that" 或「不管那一個名詞」 "no matter which"：

> You may have *whichever apples* (= any apple(s) of those that) you choose.
>
> *Whichever* (= no matter which) one of us has got to pay for it, it won't be me.

習 題 390

以適當的關係詞填入下面的空白裡面。

1. Flies, _____ come mostly in the summer, carry disease.

2. The paint on the seat _____ you are sitting on is still wet.

3. The old gentleman _____ lives across the road has got married for the fifth time.

4. Julius Caesar, _____ was a great general, was also a writer.

5. This is the very room _____ I first met my wife in.

6. The girl _____ mother I was talking to has left the room.

7. I'm just the same _____ I was the day _____ I first met you.

8. It was a time _____ everyone was selling a property.

9. They wanted a spokesman _____ reputation was unblemished.

10. This is the scholar _____ was awarded the Nobel Prize for Chemistry.

11. Whiskey, _____ is very expensive, is the national drink of Scotland.

12. _____ you have invited is also my guest.

13. Here are a dozen books. You may choose _____ interests you.

14. Avoid such a man _____ will do you harm.

15. There are more guests _____ we have dreamed of.

16. _____ dog this is, get it out of my room.

17. I gave him more money _____ was necessary.

18. He went to bed late in the night, _____ is often the case.

19. The factory will take on as many workers _____ apply for a job.

20. There is no student _____ wants to get high grades.

21. Smoking, _____ is a bad habit, is nevertheless popular.

22. Take this bag, basket or _____ it is, and hang it up you can find room for it.

23. quickly I dry myself after a bath, I always catch _____ variety of cold there is going.

24. Eat _____ one you like and leave the rest for _____ comes in later.

25. _____ one of you children disturbs meagain, I shall punish severely _____ it may be. You always make a noise _____ I try to do any work.

第*18*章
形容詞與副詞的修飾語

18-1. 形容詞與副詞的修飾語

　　形容詞與副詞的主要功用分別是修飾名詞與動詞。另一方面，形容詞與副詞本身也可以用別的詞句來修飾。修飾形容詞與副詞的方式很多，但主要的有下列幾種：

(1) 加強詞

　　I am *very* glad.

　　The music was loud *enough*.

　　This book is *more* interesting *than that one*.

　　Tom is tall, but his brother is *still* taller.

　　He walked *too* fast.

(2) 表示程度的副詞

　　The two boxes are *slightly* different in size.

　　Joan sang a *remarkably* beautiful encore.

　　The experiment was *completely* successful.

(3) 不定詞

　　I am very glad *to see you*.

　　The music was loud enough *to be heard*.

　　He walked too fast *for me to catch up with*.

(4) 副詞子句

　　The music was loud enough *so that it could be heard*.

　　The music was so loud *that it could be heard three blocks away*.

　　He walked so fast *that I couldn't keep up with him*.

(5) 名詞（僅見於一些慣用語）

　　The grass is almost *knee* high.

　　Beauty is only *skin* deep.

His heart is *stone* cold.

(6) 形容詞與現在分詞（僅見於一些慣用語）

Hearing this, her face turned *deathly* pale.

Mr. Johnson was *crazy* drunk last night.

The weather was *biting* cold.

She was *dripping* wet in the rain.

習 題 391

依照例句在形容詞或副詞的修飾語下面畫線，在被修飾的形容詞或副詞上面加圈。

Examples:

He explained quite (clearly.)

That is just (long) enough.

I was so (tired) that I went to bed early.

1. The food here is pretty good.

2. An elephant is far larger than a horse.

3. He is much the best student in class.

4. I'm so glad you've come.

5. I'm awfully sorry that I hurt your feelings.

6. The patient is little better this morning.

7. Bob speaks Chinese remarkably well.

8. Jane is not old enough to get married.

9. She came too late to attend the meeting.

10. He was so careless as to forget the appointment.

11. She spoke so rapidly that I couldn't understand her.

12. Mary is beautiful, but she is not nearly tall enough.

18-2. 加強詞

　　形容詞與副詞最常見的修飾語是 very「很」，quite「相當」，too「太」等表示程度的**加強詞**（intensifiers）。加強詞除了 enough 以外，經常都放在所修飾的形容詞或副詞的前面。

Modifier（修飾語）	Headword（被修飾語）
Intensifier（加強詞）	Adj /Adv（形容詞 / 副詞）

very	quick / quickly
rather	slow / slowly
quite	easy / easily
somewhat	unhappy / unhappily
too	diligent / diligently

Adj / Adv（形容詞 / 副詞）	Intensifier（加強詞）
good / well	enough

加強詞，與一般的副詞不同，只能修飾形容詞或副詞，卻不能修飾動詞。

　　They were *very* kind.（○）

　　They spoke *very* kindly.（○）

　　They spoke *very*.（×）

　　又加強詞與形容詞和副詞不同，不能用 more 或 most 來表示比較級或最高級。

參考：下面是英語裡面常用的一些加強詞。

(1) 修飾「原級」形容詞或副詞的加強詞：

no「不」	a little「有點」
very「很」	too「太」
not very「不怎麼」	almost「差不多」
mighty「很，非常」	quite too「非常」
not so「沒有這麼」	just「恰 , 正」
awful(ly)「很，非常」	only too「非常」
not quite so「沒有這麼」	somewhat「多少有點」

real(ly)「真正，實在」	but too「非常」
none too「一點也不」	more or less「有幾分」
enough「夠」	too too「非常」
less「較不，更不」	quite「相當」
so「很」	rather「相當」
least「最不」	pretty「相當」
ever so「非常」	most「最」
more「更」	that「那麼」

(2) 修飾「比較級」形容詞或副詞的加強詞：

no「不」	a little (bit)「一點」
(very) much「…得很多」	not any「一點也不」
a good bit「…得多」	lots, a (whole) lot「…得很多」
little「毫不」	quite a bit「…得多」
a great / good deal「…得很多」	some「幾分，稍微」
yet「還要」	somewhat「多少有點」
still「還要」	rather「比較上還」
even「還要」	enough「夠」
(by) far「…得多，極」	far and away「…得多，非常」

(3) 修飾「最高級」形容詞或副詞的加強詞：

the very「最」	far the「最最」
much the「最」	by far the「最最」
far and away the「最」	

習題 392

把括弧裡面的「加強詞」放在句子中適當的位置。

1. The food is delicious. (quite)

2. The weather is hot. (too)

3. The suitcase is heavy. (rather)

4. She's a good speaker of Russian. (pretty)

5. This lesson is easy. (enough)

6. That was a silly thing to do. (rather)

7. It's a sudden change. (quite)

8. Two men came out carrying a large sofa. (very)

9. A child with a dirty face answered the door. (very)

10. It is nice of you. (awful)

11. It was thoughtless of him to forget the appointment. (rather)

12. His story sounded plausible until we examined it more carefully. (pretty)

13. The weather was cold, but we enjoyed our walk anyhow. (rather)

14. That's not a nice thing to say. (very)

15. He is not a gentleman. (quite)

16. You're fortunate to have come out of the accident without injury. (very)

17. This may sound outspoken, but I don't agree with anything you've said. (somewhat)

18. He is too clever for me. (far)

19. I can tell you something more interesting. (far)

20. She was prettier than her sister that she won the beauty contest. (enough)

21. The story is not very sensational. (so)

22. The story is more sensational. (rather)

23. His health seems a good bit better. (quite)

24. He is very strong. (indeed)

25. He is strong enough. (quite)

26. He is too clever to make such a mistake. (far)

27. He is the greatest poet living. (far and away)

28. His description was vague. (rather, too)

29. The rope is not strong. (quite, enough)

30. These apples are not better than the ones we bought last week. (quite, so, much)

參考：

(1) enough 放在「原級」形容詞或副詞的後面，「比較級」形容詞或副詞的前面。

$$\left\{\begin{array}{l}\text{It is good } \textit{enough} \text{ to be worth the money.} \\ \text{It is } \textit{enough} \text{ better to be worth the money.}\end{array}\right.$$

(2) indeed, still, by far 可以放在形容詞的前面，也可以放在形容詞的後面。

$$\left\{\begin{array}{l}\text{The music was } \textit{indeed} \text{ loud.} \\ \text{The music was loud } \textit{indeed.}\end{array}\right.$$

$$\left\{\begin{array}{l}\text{His brother is } \textit{still} \text{ taller.} \\ \text{His brother is taller } \textit{still.}\end{array}\right.$$

$$\left\{\begin{array}{l}\text{Paul is } \textit{by far} \text{ the best student in our class.} \\ \text{Paul is the best student in our class } \textit{by far.}\end{array}\right.$$

(3) little「一點也不 'not much, hardly at all'」含有否定的意味；a little「稍微 'rather, somewhat'」含有肯定的意思。比較：

$$\left\{\begin{array}{l}\text{He is } \textit{little} \text{ (= not much) better this morning.} \\ \text{He is } \textit{a little} \text{ (= somewhat) better this morning.}\end{array}\right.$$

not a little「不少，很 'considerably'」的意思與 quite a little 或 very much 相近。

He was not *a little* annoyed when he heard the news.

little 除了修飾形容詞與副詞以外，還可以放在 know, think, imagine, realize, guess, dream 等動詞前面表示「毫不，一點也不 'not at all'」。

You *little* know how much I suffered during your absence.

He *little* dreamed that the police were about to arrest him.

習 題 393

選出適當的「加強詞」。

1. This book is (very, much) too long.

2. This one is good, but that is (not so, a lot) better.

3. The show was (rather, far) amusing.

4. I find these oranges (too, much) sweet.

5. The young dancer is (quite, enough) skillful.

6. He is (by far, yet) the best student in the class.

7. This is (still, by far) the better of the two.

8. Would you make this belt (a little, just) tighter, please?

9. The estimate is not (enough, quite) precise.

10. His lecture was (most, far) profound.

11. She appears (a lot, pretty) more cheerful today.

12. This building was (a great deal, quite) more expensive.

13. I find this subject (enough, not a little bit) interesting.

14. I received (still, quite) a long letter from my father yesterday.

15. Diabetes is (by far, even) most frequent among overweight persons.

習　題　394

在下面的空白裡填 very, very much，或 much。

1. He is a _____ celebrated actor.

2. He has a _____ surprised look on his face.

3. He was _____ surprised to find only three men in the room.

4. He will be _____ pleased to see you.

5. After years of absence, he found his wife _____ changed.

6. The picture was _____ admired by those who came to see.

7. After two weeks' rest, his condition was _____ improved.

8. I hear a _____ exaggerated story.

9. The story has been _____ exaggerated by him.

10. He was _____ disappointed by her absence.

11. He went home alone, _____ disappointed.

12. While in Princeton, he was _____ influenced by one of his professors.

13. The doctor says she is _____ the same as yesterday.

14. He used the _____ same words.

15. He studies _____ harder than his brother.

16. He is _____ the best student in his class.

17. He is the _____ best student in his class.

18. He explained the lesson _____ clearly.

19. He explained it ＿＿＿＿＿ more clearly than my former teacher.

20. This is ＿＿＿＿＿ better than that. It is ＿＿＿＿＿ the better of the two.

參考：very 與 much 用法：

(1) 形容詞或副詞的「原級」用 very，「比較級」與「最高級」用 much。

> He is a *very* good student.
>
> He is a *much* better student.
>
> He is *much* the best student.

比較：He is the *very* best student.（這裡的 very 當形容詞用）

(2) 由「現在分詞」（V-ing）轉來的形容詞用 very，由「過去分詞」（V-en）轉來的形容詞用 much。

> The book is *very* interesting / amusing.
>
> The author is (very) *much* honored / obliged.

但是 tired, pleased, surprised, amused, frightened, astonished, disturbed 等形容詞前面常有人用 very。

> He seems very *tired / pleased / surprised,* etc.

(3) the same, like「像」，different, afraid, alike, alive, ahead, awake, asleep, ashamed 等字前面常用（very）much。

> They look *very much* the same.
>
> She is *very much* like her mother.
>
> The twins look *very much* alike.
>
> She is *very much* afraid of her father.
>
> The fish we caught is still *very much* alive.
>
> He is *much* ahead of his fellow classmates.
>
> His second book is *much* different from his first.

(4) much 可以用 very 去修飾，但是 very 不能用 much 來修飾。

> I am *very* much honored.

(5) 過去分詞修飾名詞的時候，常用 very；不修飾名詞的時候常用（very）much。

> I hear a *very* exaggerated story.
>
> The story has been *very much* exaggerated by him.

習 題 395

把括弧裡的程度副詞放在句中適當的位置。

1. That entertainer is funny. (terribly)

2. He's not skillful. (exceedingly)

3. This way is safe. (hardly)

4. It's nice of you to help me. (awfully)

5. A child with a dirty face answered the door. (extremely)

6. She is qualified for the job. (highly)

7. I can see well from here. (fairly)

8. The boy is clever. (remarkably)

9. Her sister is beautiful. (exceptionally)

10. She's overjoyed to hear of you. (simply)

11. The hall was packed with audience. (literally)

12. The Americans are deficient in the sense of proportion. (sadly)

13. The sales have been increased. (noticeably)

14. His risk is greater. (considerably)

15. His health has been improved. (markedly)

16. Your work is the best. (incomparably)

17. His load is heavier. (decidedly)

18. My responsibility is lighter.(appreciably)

19. She sang a fast encore. (surprisingly)

20. She is fond of music. (immensely)

21. She was wounded. (only slightly)

22. It is evident that he will not come today. (indisputably)

23. It was an amusing film. (highly)

24. They are appreciative of your offer. (deeply)

25. He's a well-to-do farmer, and prosperous. (relatively)

26. He speaks English well. (remarkably)

27. A large house was placed at our disposal. (moderately)

28. He is often cross. (dreadfully)

29. He is a miserable man. (uncommonly)

30. They are very poor-poor. (miserably)

31. She is very ill-ill. (hopelessly)

32. It was very cold-cold. (piercingly)

33. He was pleased. (highly)

34. This is better than that. (greatly)

35. He is more diligent than he was last year. (considerably)

36. His character is opposed to mine. (diametrically)

37. Our work becomes difficult. (increasingly)

38. They are different from each other in education. (strikingly)

39. I was ignorant of what happened. (entirely)

40. We had plenty of coal, enough rice, but could get no vegetable. (barely)

習　題　396

選出適當的程度副詞。

1. He is (slightly, fairly) deaf.

2. We are (remarkably, extremely) eager to learn how the story begins.

3. John is (barely, extraordinarily) tall enough for the team.

4. We were at the back of the hall but could see and hear (awfully, fairly) well.

5. He has a (moderately, greatly) large income.

6. His grammar is (simply, greatly) terrible.

7. That is (barely, totally) possible.

8. Jane was (totally, perfectly) happy about the result.

9. The project was (wholly, utterly) successful.

10. His calculation is (exceedingly, absolutely) wrong.

參考：

(1) hardly, scarcely 表示 "almost not"「幾乎不」，含有否定的意義；barely 表示 "only

just"「剛剛，勉強」，否定的意義沒有那麼強烈。

> That is *hardly* / *scarcely* possible. (= almost impossible)

> It's *hardly* / *scarcely* right. (= almost not right)

> He has *barely* enough money to live on. (= only just)

比較：He can *hardly* / *scarcely* support his family.「幾乎無法維持他的家」

> He can *barely* support his family.「勉強能夠維持他的家」

(2) entirely, completely, wholly, perfectly 表示「完全」，好壞兩方面的意義都可以用；totally, utterly 也表示「完全」，但是多半用在壞的意義。

> *entirely* (*completely*, *wholly*, *perfectly*) successful / useless

> *totally* (utterly) useless / wrong

習 題 397

　　在下面的空白裡填入 fairly 或 rather。

1. The room looks _____ clean.

2. The food was _____ badly cooked.

3. The bread is _____ stale.

4. I know him _____ well.

5. Your homework whs _____ good this week.

6. The train was _____ crowded this morning.

7. I'm afraid the soup is _____ cold.

8. I hope this exercise will be _____ easy.

9. It is _____ difficult to learn new things when you are old.

10. I'm afraid he is _____ stupid, and won't understand what you mean.

參考：fairly「相當」多半用在好的意義，rather「相當」多半用在壞的意義。

> {
> He is *fairly* well.
> He is *rather* ill.
> }

> {
> She is *fairly* tall for her age.（說話的人贊許她長得高）
> She is *rather* tall for her age.（說話的人嫌她長得太高了些）
> }

習 題 398

把括弧裡面的副詞放在句子中適當的位置。

1. Look ahead. (straight)

2. He lives beyond the sea. (far)

3. It was under your nose. (right)

4. It is beyond my power. (far)

5. The smoke rose up. (straight)

6. I turned to find him behind. (right)

7. He always looks ahead into the future. (far)

8. Don't stand in the middle of the road. (right)

9. The school was away from our home. (three miles)

10. I have known him since he was a boy. (ever)

11. Boys play ball because it is fun. (simply)

12. These are fresh and sound tomatoes from the vine. (right)

13. The bank is beyond the post office. (three blocks)

14. You are away from home. (a long way)

15. The island is off the coast. (a little way)

16. He lives beyond this space. (three doors)

17. Harry is beyond his brother in Latin. (far)

18. He went to Paris without stopping anywhere. (straight)

19. He asks for a price beyond what I can pay. (far)

20. As soon as I spoke of money, he went out. (straight)

21. He fell ill after you left. (three days)

22. He arrived after I left. (immediately)

23. He went from school into his father's business. (straight)

24. On his beginning to speak, everyone was silent. (immediately)

25. He promised to name his cabinet after the election. (as soon … as possible)

參考：有些詞副可以修飾介詞片語，副詞子句，或助詞。

Our house is *very much* like theirs.

She is *well* over fifty.

We had received the notice *long* before his arrival.

I've known him *ever* since he was a child.

Just as I was coming here, I met your brother.

He failed *simply* because he was lazy.

Go *right* back.

He was very *far* ahead.

Keep *straight* on.

18-3. 形容詞的比較級與最高級

　　英語的形容詞可以用不同的詞尾變化（-er, -est），或加「加強詞」more、most 來表示不同的程度或等級。沒有詞尾變化或不加 more、most 的形容詞叫做**原級**（positive degree）。例如：

　　　　small, brave, important, beautiful

加詞尾 -er 或「加強詞」more 的形容詞叫做**比較級**（comparative degree）。例如：

　　　　small*er*, brav*er*, *more* important, *more* beautiful

加詞尾 -est 或「加強詞」most 的形容詞叫做**最高級**（superlative degree）。例如：

　　　　small*est*, brav*est*, *most* important, *most* beautiful

This is a *small* house.

This is a *smaller* house than that one.

This is the *smallest* house in town.

Your work is very *important*.

Your work is much *more important* than mine.

Your work is the *most important* of all.

參考：

(1) 單音節形容詞的比較級，在形容詞後面加詞尾 -er；最高級在形容詞後面加詞尾 -est；

small	small*er*	small*est*
young	young*er*	young*est*
brave	brav*er*	brav*est*
big	bigg*er*	bigg*est*
thin	thin*ner*	thin*nest*

（短母音＋子音字）

dry	dr*ier*	dr*iest*

（子音字＋y）

　　但是下列單音節形容詞的比較級與最高級常用 more 與 most 來表示：wrong, right, free, full, just。

　　He is *more wrong* than I.

(2) 兩音節的形容詞的比較級與最高級, 通常在形容詞前面加 more 或 most:

useful	*more* useful	*most* useful
fluent	*more* fluent	*most* fluent
selfish	*more* selfish	*most* selfish

　　但是如果兩音節形容詞的詞尾是 -y, -ly, -le, -er, -ere, -ow, -some, 或者如果兩音節形容詞的重音落在第二音節的話，常加詞尾 -er, -est：

happy	happ*ier*	happ*iest*
lively	livel*ier*	livel*iest*
gentle	gentl*er*	gentl*est*
clever	cleverer	clever*est*
severe	sever*er*	sever*est*
narrow	narrow*er*	narrow*est*
handsome	handsom*er*	handsom*est*
common	common*er*	common*est*
polite	polit*er*	polit*est*

(3) 三音節以上的形容詞，比較級加 more，最高級加 most：

important	*more* important	*most* important
beautiful	*more* beautiful	*most* beautiful
diligent	*more* diligent	*most* diligent

有詞尾 -ing 或 -ed 的形容詞，不管音節長短，都用 more 與 most 來表示比較級與最高級：

trying	*more* trying	*most* trying
hurt	*more* hurt	*most* hurt
bored	*more* bored	*most* bored
interesting	*more* interesting	*most* interesting
frightened	*more* frightened	*most* frightened

(4) 有些形容詞有不規則的比較級與最高級，必須一一記住：

bad, ill	*worse*	*worst*
good	*better*	*best*
little	*less, lesser*	*least*
much, many	*more*	*most*
old	*older, elder*	*oldest, eldest*
late	*later, latter*	*latest, last*
far	*farther, further*	*farthest, furtherst*
		(or *farthermost, furthermost*)

18-4. 副詞的比較級與最高級

副詞，跟形容詞一樣，也可以比較。

John works *hard / diligently*.

John works *harder / more diligently* than Bob.

John works *hardest / most diligently* in class.

副詞的比較級與最高級通常都根據下列的原則。

(1) 沒有詞尾 -ly 的副詞（如 hard, fast, late, early, slow, quick, loud 等），加詞尾 -er 或 -est：

fast	fast*er*	fast*est*
early	earli*er*	earli*est*
loud	loud*er*	loud*est*

(2) 有詞尾 -ly 的副詞，加 more 或 most：

beautifully	*more* beautifully	*most* beautifully
efficiently	*more* efficiently	*most* efficiently
loudly	*more* loudly	*most* loudly

(3) 有些副詞有不規則的比較級與最高級：

well	better	best
badly	worse	worst
much	more	most
little	less	least
far	farther, further	farthest, furthest
late	later	latest, last

習 題 399

把括號裡面的形容詞或副詞改為適當的形式（原級、比較級、最高級）填入空白中。

1. He must be very _____ of his success. (sure)

2. I'm finding mathematics a lot _____ now. (easy)

3. His marks are much _____ this year. (good)

4. Her sister is lots _____. (intelligent)

5. The dinner is almost _____. (ready)

6. The traffic seems a little _____, doesn't it? (bad)

7. His lecture was most _____. (profound)

8. I'd like it a little bit _____. (salty)

9. You can never be too _____. (careful)

10. We will discuss no _____ today. (far)

11. This machine was a great deal _____. (expensive)

12. This exercise is quite a bit _____. (difficult)

13. She is a good bit _____ today. (good)

14. Bob is barely _____ enough for the basketball team. (tall)

15. You're much too _____ in your judgment. (severe)

16. The song has become quite _____ in recent months. (popular)

17. This is the very _____ fashion. (late)

18. Jane is five feet seven inches, but her sister is a bit _____. (short)

19. They were so tired that they could go no _____. (far)

20. I will see you _____. (late)

21. When did you _____ see him? (late)

22. These are the very _____ improvements we have. (late)

23. He got _____ and _____ into debt. (far)

24. He is the _____ man I wanted to see. (late)

25. Mr. Green has said that his _____ novel will be his _____. (late)

18-5. 形容詞與副詞的比較

(1) **用原級做比較**：as + 原級形容詞、副詞 + as

　　當我們就兩個人或物比較某些性質或態度的時候，如果這兩個人或物有相同或相似的地方，就可以用「as + 原級 + as」來表示比較：

$$\left.\begin{array}{l} \text{I am tall.} \\ \text{You are as tall.} \end{array}\right\} \rightarrow$$

　　You are *as tall as* I (am). 「你跟我一樣高。」

$$\left.\begin{array}{l} \text{You work hard.} \\ \text{He works as hard.} \end{array}\right\} \rightarrow$$

　　He works *as hard as* you (do). 「他跟你一樣努力工作。」

$$\left.\begin{array}{l} \text{This box is big.} \\ \text{That box is as big.} \end{array}\right\} \rightarrow$$

　　That box is *as big as* this one.「那個盒子跟這個盒子一樣大。」

$$\left.\begin{array}{l} \text{My car runs fast.} \\ \text{Your car runs as fast.} \end{array}\right\} \rightarrow$$

　　Your car runs *as fast as* mine (does).「你的車子跟我的車子跑得一樣快。」

　　有時候，我們還可以就同一個人或物，比較其兩種不同的性質。

例如：

She sings well.
She dances as well. } →

She dances *as well as* she sings.「她跳舞跳得跟唱歌唱得一樣好。」

She is intelligent.
She is attractive. } →

She is *as attractive as* she is intelligent.「她俏美一如她聰明。」

也可以就不同的兩個人或物，比較其不同的性質。例如：

She has money.
He has influence. } →

He has *as much* influence *as* she has money.「他有勢力正如她有錢。」

原級比較句的否定式可以用「not as … as …」，也可以用「not so … as …」：

I am tall.
You are not as tall. } →

You are *not as / so tall as* I (am).「你沒有我那麼高。」

You work hard.
He does not work as hard. } →

He does *not* work *as / so hard as* you (do).「他沒有你那麼努力工作。」

(2) **用比較級做比較**：比較級形容詞、副詞 + than

　　如果所比較的兩個人或物，其中一個比另外一個「更怎麼樣」或「還要怎麼樣」的時候，就用「比較級 + than」來表示：

I am tall.
You are taller. } →

You are *taller than* I (am).「你比我還要高。」

You work hard.
He works harder. } →

He works *harder than* you (do).「他比你更努力工作。」

This book is interesting.
That book is more interesting. } →

That book is *more interesting than* this one (is).

「那一本書比這本書還要有趣。」

She spoke clearly.
He spoke more clearly. } →

He spoke *more clearly than* she (did).「他講得比她還要清楚。」

I had a big lunch yesterday.
I had a bigger lunch today. } →

I had a *bigger* lunch *than* (I did) yesterday.

「我吃的午餐比昨天（吃）的還要豐盛得多。」

He was not hurt.
He was frightened. } →

He was *more frightened than* hurt.

「他沒有受什麼傷，倒是受驚不少。」

The car is comfortable.
The car is more expensive. } →

The car is *more expensive than* (it is) comfortable.

「這部車雖然舒服但是太貴了。」

She has money.
He has more influence. } →

He has *more influence than* she has monev.

「他的勢力比她的錢來得有力。」

如果所比較的兩個人或物中，一個「不如」另外一個，那麼就可以用 less 來表示：

This book is interesting.
That book is less interesting. →

That book is *less interesting than this one*.

「那一本書不如這一本書有趣。」

She made progress.
He made less progress. } →

He made *less progress than* she (did).「他的進步不如她。」

She spoke clearly.
He spoke less clearly. } →

He spoke *less clearly than* she (did).「他講得不如她清楚。」

(3) **用最高級做比較**：the + 最高級形容詞、副詞 + in / among / of

　　如果某一個人或物超過一般同類而「最怎麼樣」的時候，就用「the + 最高級」
來表示：

He is *the tallest* student *in* the class.（in + 單數集合名詞）

　　「他是班裡面個子最高的學生。」

She is *the prettiest among* my classmates.（among + 複數普通名詞）

　　「她是我的同學裡面最漂亮的。」

Iron is *the most useful of* all metals.（of + all + 複數名詞）

　　「鐵是所有金屬裡面最有用的（一種）。」

Henry was *the bravest of* the five men.（of + 數詞 + 複數名詞）

　　「亨利是五個人裡面最勇敢的（一個）。」

最高級副詞前面的 the, 通常都加省略：

Jack worked (*the*) *hardest* of all of them.

Mary spoke (*the*) *least clearly*.

　　注意，比較級形容詞或副詞只能用來比較兩個人或物；三個以上的人或物就用
最高級形容詞或副詞。比較：

{ Bob is *the shorter* of the two boys.
Jane is *the shortest* of the three girls.

{ He spoke *the more clearly* of the two.
He spoke (*the*) *most clearly* of all.

習　題　400

依照例句改寫下列各句。

Examples:

This line as long as that one.

　　→ *This line is the same length as that one.*

1. John is as tall as Bob.

2. Jane is not as heavy as Alice.

3. The camera is as expensive as the typewriter.

4. Your coat is not as large as mine.

5. The station is as far as the post office.

6. This book is as thick as that one.

7. This piece of wood is as hard as that one.

8. Mr. Higgins is as old as Mrs. Higgins.

參考：原級比較句，除了用「as + 形容詞 + as」的方式表示以外，也可以用「the same + 名詞（如 color, size, age, length, width, depth, weight, height, thickness, type, kind, style, price, speed, quality, distance 等）+ as」來表示。

比較：

My pencil is *as long as* yours.
My pencil is *the same length as* yours.

This dictionary is *as thick as* that one.
This dictionary is *the same thickness as* that one.

This hat is *as large as* that one.
This hat is *the same size as* that one.

習 題 401

依照例句完成下列各句。

Examples:

　　　Mr. Smith ⋯ twice ⋯ heavy ⋯ Mrs. Smith.

　　　　→ *Mr. Smith is twice as heavy as Mrs. Smith.*

　　　　→ *Mr. Smith is twice heavier than Mrs. Smith.*

1. The church ⋯ twice ⋯ old ⋯ the school

2. The steak ⋯ half ⋯ big ⋯ the plate

3. Bob worked ⋯ three times ⋯ hard ⋯ his brother

4. Jane ⋯ ten times ⋯ charming ⋯ Anne

5. The movie … not half … good … the one we saw last week

參考：倍數可以用「half / twice / three times, etc. ＋ as ＋原級形容詞、副詞＋as」或

「twice / three times, etc. ＋比較級形容詞、副詞＋than」的方式表示：

This box is *half as large as* that one.

⎰ Mr. Smith is *twice as heavy as* Mrs. Smith.
⎱ Mr. Smith is *twice heavier than* Mrs. Smith.

⎰ My car can run *three times as fast as* yours.
⎱ My car can run *three times faster* than yours.

習　題　402

依照例句改寫下列各句。

Examples:

（過去式）

I looked at the letter as carefully as I could.

⇄ I looked at the letter as carefully as possible.

1. Come as soon as you can.

2. Paul will try as hard as he can.

3. I tried to explain the problem as patiently as possible.

4. He said he would come here as quickly as he could.

5. Mary promised to stay there as long as possible.

6. The boy shouted as loudly as he could.

7. Mr. Lee treated his servant as kindly as possible.

8. Get as much firewood as possible.

參考：「as 原級 as possible」與「as 原級 as one can」都表示「盡可能怎麼樣」。

習　題　403

依照例句，用 the same, (a)like 或 different 改寫下列各句。

Examples:

He's seventeen years old, and she is too.

→ *He's the same age as she is.*

    → His age is the same as hers.

    → They're the same age.

He's eighteen, but she's twenty eight.

    → His age is different from hers.

    → They're different ages.

    → Their ages are different.

He works hard, and she does too.

    → He's like her.

    → They're alike.

1. Your hotel is the Hilton, and mine is too.

2. He comes from France, and she does too.

3. His nationality is Chinese, but hers is Japanese.

4. He doesn't practice, but he should, and you don't either.

5. I had my training at this school, and he had his here too.

6. He saves his money, and she does too.

7. Your analysis was difficult to understand, but mine wasn't.

8. His job is to show people around the building, and hers is too.

9. You are too stubborn for anybody to change your mind, and he is too.

10. His great ambition is to become a college professor, but hers is to join the government.

參考：the same 表示「相同」，(a)like 表示「相似」，different 表示「相異」。

習　題　404

選出適當的形容詞填入空白裡面：blind, busy, clear, deaf, dull, free, happy, hard, helpless, light, nervous, old, poor, quiet, strong。

1. I am as _____ as a bee.

2. He was as _____ as a king.

3. I was as _____ as a babe.

4. He was as _____ as a bird.

5. Our bread is usually as _____ as a rock.

6. Her voice was as _____ as a bell.

7. She was as _____ as a mouse.

8. The conversation was as _____ as dishwater.

9. He is as _____ as a church mouse.

10. Her gait was as _____ as a feather.

11. The custom is as _____ as the hills.

12. She was as _____ as a cat.

13. The young man was as _____ as an ox.

14. The old man was as _____ as a post.

15. The poor child was as _____ as a bat.

參考：英語，與中文一樣，常用原級比較句來表示「直喻」或「明喻」。例如：

　　　　as brave as a lion「勇猛如獅」

　　　　as free as a bird「自由如鳥」

　　　　as cruel as a tiger「殘暴如虎」

　　　　as light as a feather「輕如羽毛」

　　　　as fair as a lily「美如百合」

　　　　as black as ink「黑如墨水」

　　　　as strong as an ox「壯如公牛」

　　　　as clear as crystal「透明如水晶」

注意，許多美國人常把第一個 as 省去：

　　　John was (*as*) quick as a wink.

習　題　405

　　在下面的空裡面填 as 或 like。

1. She ran _____ a deer.

2. Candy is sweet _____ sugar.

3. Her coat looks _____ mine.

4. They eat _____ pigs.

5. The little girl is pretty _____ a picture.

6. She's _____ proud _____ a peacock.

7. He thinks _____ a computer.

8. They think the same _____ we do.

9. She always talks _____ a fool.

10. He always talks _____ if he were a millionaire.

11. I am _____ hungry _____ a wolf.

12. I worked all day _____ a horse.

參考：英語，除了原級比較句以外，還可以用 like 引導的介詞片語表示明喻。

例如：

run like a deer「奔跑如鹿」

work like a horse「工作如（牛）馬」

creep like a snail「爬行如蝸牛」

eat like a pig「貪吃如豬」

sing like a bird「歌唱如小鳥」

live like a king「生活如王（侯）」

習　題　406

依照例句完成下列各句。

Examples:

It ⋯ an animal ⋯ a cat.

→ *It was an animal like a cat.*

→ *It was a catlike animal.*

The tower ⋯ high ⋯ the sky.

→ *The tower was as high as the sky.*

→ *The tower was sky-high.*

1. It ⋯ a stone ⋯ a diamond.　　2. His hand ⋯ cold ⋯ ice.

3. It ⋯ a substance ⋯ chalk.　　4. Her skin ⋯ white ⋯ snow.

5. The night ⋯ black ⋯ pitch.　　6. He lived ⋯ a life ⋯ like a dream.

7. We enjoyed … the atmosphere … like that of home.

8. His intention … clear … crystal.

參考： It was a catlike animal. = It was an animal like a cat.

「那是一隻類似貓的動物。」

The tower was sky-high. = The tower was as high as the sky.

= The tower was very high. 「那座塔有天空那麼高。」

The knife was razor sharp. The knife was as sharp as a razor.

= The knife was very sharp. 「這把刀，銳如剃刀。」

習　題　407

依照例句改寫下列各句。

Examples:

The four-foot board wasn't long enough. It had to be five feet.

→ *It was one foot (too) short.*

They gave him ten, but he only needed five.

→ *He had five too many.*

1. It was a ten-foot pole, but he needed only five feet.

2. He had five glasses, but he needed only four.

3. It was 9:30, but his watch said 9:15.

4. Drivers can get licenses at 17, but he's only 15.

5. His temperature should be 98.6, but it's 100.6.

6. She wears a size 32, but they gave her a 34.

7. Thirty-one cents is enough postage for one ounce, but the letter weighs two ounces.

8. He agreed to come at 8:00, but he actually didn't get here till 8:30.

9. The speed limit is 50 miles per hour, but the police caught him at 65.

10. She needs four eggs for the recipe, but she only has two.

參考： 英語裡的「不足」或「過多」常用「too＋形容詞、副詞」來表示：

He gave me one book *too few*.

You said it once *too often*.

I paid her two dollars *too many*.

They arrived five minutes *too late / early*.

但是在 short, fast, slow 之前，常省去 too:

The board is *one foot* (*too*) *short*.

His watch was *ten minutes fast / slow*.

習　題　408

依照例句改寫下列各句。

Examples:

　　　She teaches here four days a week.

　　　　→ *She teaches here as often as four days a week.*

　　　The building has twenty stories.

　　　　→ *It's as high as twenty stories.*

　　　　→ *It's twenty stories high.*

　1. He calls home three times a week.

　2. The fisherman is 96 of age.

　3. She was born in 1890.

　4. We waited for them from 2:00 to 2:30.

　5. The concert lasted from 8:30 to 10:30.

　6. The airline weighed our luggage in at fifty pounds.

　7. They were able to drive from here to the next town.

　8. The top of the mountain is four miles above sea level.

　9. The thermometer on the porch reads nineteen degrees.

10. We usually order three or four dozen at a time.

參考：「as … as＋數量詞」表示「達…」或「…之多」。

　　　The building is *as high as twenty stories*.「建築物高達二十層樓。」

　　　The movie was *as long as three hours*.「電影演了三個鐘頭之久。」

　　　I had to travel *as far as 300 miles*.「我得旅行三百英里之遠。」

注意，數量詞可以放在形容詞 high, long 與 old 的前面，

The building is *twenty stories high*.

The movie was *three hours long*.

The fisherman is *96 years old*.

但是不能放在其他形容詞（如 heavy, many, much）的前面，也不能放在副詞的前面。比較：

- The letter was *as heavy as five ounces*.（○）
- The letter was *five ounces heavy*.（×）

- The movie lasted *as long as three hours*.（○）
- The movie lasted *three hours long*.（×）

習 題 409

依照例句用原級連接下列每對句子。

Examples:

Jane is charming.

Anne is as charming.

→ *Anne is as charming as Jane (is)*.

Jane is charming.

Anne is not as charming.

→ *Anne is not as / so charming as Jane (is)*.

1. Mathematics is difficult.
   Chemistry is as difficult.

2. The customers are pleased.
   The salesman is as pleased.

3. Your father is tall.
   Your mother is not as tall.

4. Your brother looked happy.
   You didn't look as happy.

5. She has many books.
   He has as many books.

6. He has power.
   Does he have as much money?

7. Our former secretary was competent.
   Miss King is as competent.

8. You studied hard then.
   Do you study as hard now?

9. The writer must be well-informed.
   The editor must be as well-informed.

10. The first string played well.
    Did the second string play as well?

11. He drove dangerously yesterday.
He drives as dangerously today.

12. Mr. Jones made money rapidly.
Mr. King made money as rapidly.

13. Mr. Jones made money rapidly.
Mrs. Jones spent money as rapidly.

14. Bob plays football brilliantly.
Jim palys basketball as brilliantly.

15. His son is very naughty.
Mr. Fogg is very severe.

16. You take many courses now.
Did you take many courses last semester?

習 題 410

依照例句用比較級連接下列每對句子。

Examples:

A pineapple is sweet.
A mango is sweeter.

　→ *A mango is sweeter than a pineapple.*

We think John drives fast.
John drives faster.

　→ *John drives faster than we think he does.*

1. Gold is useful.
Iron is more useful.

2. Cowper is a good poet.
Wordsworth is a better poet.

3. The streets of Hsinchu are wide.
The streets of Taipei are wider.

4. John looks well.
Bob looks better.

5. Alice behaved badly.
Betty behaved worse.

6. Mr. Jacobson is eccentric.
Mrs. Jacobson is more eccentric.

7. John bought a comfortable car.
I bought a more comfortable car.

8. I drove dangerously yesterday.
I drive more dangerously today.

9. My neighbor bought a comfortable car.
I bought a less comfortable car.

10. His teacher writes good prose.
He writes better prose.

11. Bill has a big car.
John has a bigger car.

12. George is a dull man.
I know a duller man.

13. That house is solidly built.
This house is more solidly built.

14. My neighbor has a big car.
The car is bigger.

15. John sold a big car.
John bought a bigger car.

16. I bought a big car in Chicago.
I bought a bigger car in New York.

17. He made some progress.
She made more progress.

18. It is easy to go by train.
It is easier to go by bus.

19. He can handle just so many customers.
He has more customers than that.

20. Mary is angry.
Mary is not sad.

21. They have quite a bit of enthusiasm.
They don't have much ability.

22. It's very easy for him to ask questions.
It's not very easy for him to answer them.

23. It's very easy for him to ask questions.
It's not very easy for her to ask them.

24. It's very easy for him to answer questions.
It's not very easy for her to ask them.

25. My neighbor expected me to buy a big car.
I bought a bigger car.

習　題　411

依照例句改寫下列各句。

Examples:

Buicks are more comfortable than economical.

→ *Buicks are more comfortable than they are economical.*

Buicks are more comfortable than Fords.

→ *Buicks are more comfortable than Fords are.*

1. Bob has more enthusiasm than intelligence.

2. Bob has more enthusiasm than Jack.

3. TV is more interesting than the radio.

4. TV is more entertaining than educational.

5. Cats are more of a pleasure than a nuisance.

6. Cats are more of a pleasure than dogs.

7. New York City has more Puerto Ricans than San Juan.

8. New York City has more Puerto Ricans than Creeks.

9. Driving across the country is more interesting than convenient.

10. Driving across the country is more interesting than flying across.

參考：比較句可以就同一性質比較兩個不同的事物，也可以就同一個事物比較同的

性質。比較：

> Buicks are more comfortable than Fords (are).
>
> 「別克牌的汽車比福特牌的汽車還要舒服。」
>
> Buicks are more comfortable than (they are) economical.
>
> 「別克牌的汽車雖然很舒服但是價錢並不便宜。」

習　題　412

依照例句改寫下列各句。

Examples:

That's as heavy as the letter was.

→ *The letter was no heavier than that.*

They traveled no further than one hundred miles.

→ *One hundred miles is as far as they traveled.*

1. That's as thick as the book is.

2. I have no more than ten friends.

3. That's as big as the room was.

4. He can pay no more than one hundred dollars.

5. That was as quickly as I could go.

6. They played chess no longer than 20 hours.

7. That was as much as we could compromise.

8. The car runs no faster than 60 miles an hour.

9. That is as far as I can go along with you.

10. He can read no more quickly than 1000 words a minute.

參考：我們可以用形容詞、副詞的原級與比較級表達同樣的意思。比較：

$\begin{cases} \text{That's as heavy as the letter was.「信只有那麼重。」} \\ \text{The letter was no heavier than that.} \end{cases}$

$\begin{cases} \text{That was as quickly as I could go.「我只能走得那麼快。」} \\ \text{I could go no more quickly than that.} \end{cases}$

習 題 413

把括號裡面的形容詞或副詞改為適當的形式（比較級或最高級）。

1. How is your sister today? Is she (good)?

2. Bob is the (tall) of the two.

3. Jane is the (good) friend I have.

4. It was the (proud) moment of his life.

5. The public is the (good) judge.

6. Silver is (light) than gold.

7. Name the (large) city in the world.

8. August here is (hot) than any other month.

9. There is no animal (ferocious) than a tiger.

10. Who is the (intelligent) boy in the class?

11. Iron is the (useful) of all metals.

12. This is the (interesting) book I ever read.

13. This is the (high) price I can take.

14. The piano was knocked down to the (high) bidder.

15. A panda is one of the (rare) animals.

16. He was the (generous) of men.

17. She smiled her (sweet) smile.

18. Kaohsiung is the second (large) city in Taiwan.

19. I take only the (gentle) of exercise.

20. His description was of the (vague).

21. He breathed his (late).

22. Bob is the third (good) player on our team.

習　題　414

依照例句改寫下列各句。

Examples:

>　If you are happier, you look younger.
>
>　　*→ The happier you are, the younger you look.*
>
>　As we stayed there longer, we like the place better.
>
>　　*→ The longer we stayed there, the better we liked the place.*

1. If you work harder, you make more money.

2. If you get here sooner, we will be able to start out sooner.

3. As you go higher, the scenery will be better.

4. As he read more, he understood less.

5. As I heard more about it, I became more anxious.

6. As we stayed there longer, we liked the place less.

7. As he makes more money, he wants more.

8. If a man is more learned, he is usually more modest.

9. If we get there sooner, we are more likely to get seats.

10. If you travel to more places, you find out more about the world.

參考：我們可以前後用兩個比較級來表達「越…就越…」的意思：

>　*The happier* you are, *the younger* you look.
>
>　　「你越快樂看起來就越年輕。」
>
>　*The longer* we stayed there, the better we liked the place.
>
>　　「我們在那裡待得越久，就越喜歡那一個地方。」
>
>　*The better* the job, *the higher* the pay. 「工作越好，待遇越高。」
>
>　*The sooner, the better.* 「越早越好。」

注意，這個時候比較級前面都要加上 the。

習 題 415

依照例句用不同級的形容詞或副詞改寫下列各句。

Examples:

The Times is the most powerful newspaper in England.

→ *The Times is more powerful than any other newspaper in England.*

→ *No other newspaper in England is as powerful as the Times.*

He is as wise as Solomon.

→ *Solomon was not wiser than he* (*is*).

→ *Solomom was no wiser than he* (*is*).

1. Lead is heavier than any other metal.

2. I know him quite as well as you do.

3. No man was as strong as David.

4. *Sakuntala* is the best drama in Sanskrit.

5. Shakespeare is greater than any other English poet.

6. The tiger is the most ferocious of all animals.

7. Iron is more useful than all the other metals.

8. The pen is mightier than the sword.

9. Very few boys are as diligent as Charles.

10. John came earlier than any other student.

參考：我們常常可以用不同級的形容詞或副詞表達同樣的意思。比較：

Jack is *the smartest* boy in class.

Jack is *smarter than* any other boy in class.

Jack is *as smart as* any other boy in class.

No other boy in class is *as smart as* Jack.

He speaks *least clearly* of all.

He speaks *less clearly than* others.

He does not speak *as clearly as* others.

習　題　416

依照例句改寫下列各句。

Examples:

I've been to a place which is better than this.

→ *I've been to a place better than this.*

→ *I've been to a better place than this.*

I know a girl who is more beautiful than Mary.

→ *I know a girl more beautiful than Mary.*

→ *I know a more beautiful girl than Mary.*

He's a man who is hard to convince.

→ *He's a man hard to convince.*

→ *He's a hard man to convince.*

1. Tell me a story that is better than this.
2. I don't know a boy who is braver than Tom.
3. We've seen a school library that is much bigger than this.
4. I never read a book that was more exciting than *the Treasure Island*.
5. Did you ever meet a person who was more careless than our brother?
6. You won't find a camera that is less expensive than this one.
7. Could you give me a book which is easier to understand?
8. He always knows a way to say it which is better.
9. Charles is the person who is most convenient to send our mail to.
10. She's preparing all kinds of things which are wonderful to eat.

參考：帶有「than …」的比較級形容詞可以出現在名詞之前，也可以出現在名詞之後。比較：

> I've been to a place *better* than this.
> I've been to a *better* place than this.「我去過比這裡更好的地方。」

同樣地，帶有「不定詞 (to V …)」的原級、比較級、最高級形容詞也可以出現在名詞之前與後。例如：

$$\left\{ \begin{array}{l} \text{Bob is a man} \left\{ \begin{array}{l} \textit{hard} \\ \textit{harder} \\ \textit{(the) hardest} \end{array} \right\} \text{to convince.} \\[2em] \text{Bob is} \left\{ \begin{array}{l} \textit{a hard} \\ \textit{a harder} \\ \textit{the hardest} \end{array} \right\} \text{man to covince.} \end{array} \right.$$

「Bob 是一個很難 / 較難 / 最難使他信服的人。」

習 題 417

依照例句改寫下列各句。

Examples:

It's harder to convince him than Bill.

→ *He's a harder man to convince than Bill.*

→ *He's a harder man than Bill to convince.*

1. It's easier to learn English than Russian.

2. It's harder to pronounce this word than that.

3. It's more interesting to study this lesson than the other.

4. It's more convenient to send John than the others.

5. It's more difficult to deal with these problems than the previous ones.

6. It's better to ask Mr. Hill for help than Mr. Tower.

7. It's more economical to keep Fords than Buicks.

8. It's more comfortable to drive in Buicks than Fords.

參考：修飾名詞的比較級形容詞如果帶有「不定詞」與「than …」，那麼可以有幾種不同的說法。例如：

He's a man who is harder to convince than Bill.

→ *He's a man harder to convince than Bill.*

（形容詞在名詞之後）

→ *He's a harder man to convince than Bill.*

（形容詞在名詞之前，不定詞在 than 之前）

→ *He's a harder man than Bill to convince.*

（形容詞在名詞之前，不定詞在 than 之後）

同樣地，帶有「不定詞」與「關係子句」的最高級形容詞也可以有幾種不同的說法。例如：

He's a man that I know is the hardest to convince.

→ *He's the hardest man that I know to convince.*

→ *He's the hardest man to* convince that I know.

習　題　418

按照中文完成下列各句。

1. Come as _____ as _____. 「盡可能早一點來。」

2. Read as _____ _____ as you _____. 「盡可能多讀一點書。」

3. You don't come _____ _____ _____ you used _____. 「你不像以前那麼常來。」

4. This book is as _____ as _____.
   「這一本書跟任何書一樣的好。＝這一本書很好。」

5. She is as _____ _____ _____ as _____. 「她依舊待我好。」

6. I am as _____ as _____ _____. 「我非常的快樂。」

7. He is as _____ as _____. 「他跟死了一樣。＝他就快要死了。」

8. He didn't so _____ as _____ me to sit down. 「他甚至於沒有請我坐下。」

9. He left _____ so _____ as _____ good-bye. 「他連再見都沒有說就走掉了。」

10. It is as _____ your _____ as _____. 「你和我都有責任。」

11. He gave a look as _____ as _____ say, "Mind your own business!" 「他裝出了好像要說『用不著你來管閒事』似的面孔。」

12. He cannot _____ _____ as _____ his own name. 「他連自己的名字都寫不來。」

13. He is not _____ _____ a scholar _____ a writer. 「他與其說是學者不如說是文人。」

14. He has as _____ _____ as you do.「他有你的兩倍多。」

15. The red dress is _____ _____ _____ the blue coat. = The red dress is the _____ _____ _____ the blue coat. = The red dress costs _____ _____ _____ the blue coat.「紅衣服與藍大衣一樣地貴。」

16. The history book isn't _____ _____ _____ the geography book.

= The history book isn't the _____ _____ _____ the geography book.

= The history book is _____ _____ the geography book.

= The geography book is _____ _____ the history book.

「歷史書沒有地理書那麼厚。」

習　題　419

按照中文完成下列各句。

1. He has _____ books _____ he can _____.「他的書多得讀不完。」

2. She worked hard _____ _____ _____.「她比以前越發用功。」

3. That is _____ _____ _____.「那是太多了。」

4. I can _____ eat _____.「我再也吃不下了。」

5. She was _____ _____ pleased.「她非常高興。」

6. I went _____ _____ a _____.「我走了一哩多路。」

7. He is _____ _____ than _____.= He is frightened _____ hurt.「他嚇得厲害，傷倒不重。」

8. I met her _____ _____ _____ years _____.「我十幾年前見到她。」

9. _____ _____ five came last night.「昨天晚上僅僅來了五個人。」

10. There are _____ _____ _____ (= at _____) five guests.「最多只有五位客人。」

11. He is _____ _____ _____ a puppet.「他只不過是一個傀儡。」

12. He is _____ _____ _____ god _____ we are.「他跟我們一樣不是神。」

13. I am _____ _____ mad _____ (= _____ little mad _____) you.「你既不瘋，我也不狂。」

14. I am ＿＿＿＿ ＿＿＿＿ mad ＿＿＿＿ (= ＿＿＿＿ so mad ＿＿＿＿) you.
「我（雖瘋但）沒有你那麼瘋。」

15. He's ＿＿＿＿ ＿＿＿＿ ＿＿＿＿ to read Chiness ＿＿＿＿ ＿＿＿＿ ＿＿＿＿.
「他跟我都不懂中文。」

16. I can ＿＿＿＿ ＿＿＿＿ do that ＿＿＿＿ ＿＿＿＿. = I can ＿＿＿＿ do that
＿＿＿＿ ＿＿＿＿ than ＿＿＿＿. = I can ＿＿＿＿ do that ＿＿＿＿ I cannot fly.
「我不會做那個（就如我不會飛一樣）。」

17. He earns ＿＿＿＿ ＿＿＿＿ ＿＿＿＿ (= ＿＿＿＿ much ＿＿＿＿) five
thousand dollars a week.「他每週賺五千元之多。」

18. He owns ＿＿＿＿ ＿＿＿＿ ＿＿＿＿ (= at ＿＿＿＿) two hundred acres of
land.「他擁有至少兩百英畝的土地。」

19. He, ＿＿＿＿ ＿＿＿＿ ＿＿＿＿ (= ＿＿＿＿ well ＿＿＿＿) you, is one of
my best friends.「他跟你一樣是我最好的朋友之一。」

20. He is ＿＿＿＿ ＿＿＿＿ clever ＿＿＿＿ his brother.「他跟他的兄弟一樣聰
明。」

21. That's ＿＿＿＿ ＿＿＿＿ more ＿＿＿＿ a shilling.「那不過值一先令。」

22. That's ＿＿＿＿ ＿＿＿＿ ＿＿＿＿ robbery!「那差不多等於搶劫！」

23. He's ＿＿＿＿ ＿＿＿＿ ＿＿＿＿ a common thief!「他比一個慣賊好不了多
少！」

24. ＿＿＿＿ is ＿＿＿＿ ＿＿＿＿ ＿＿＿＿ robbery ＿＿＿＿ ask ＿＿＿＿ a high
peice.「要求這樣高的價錢簡直與搶劫無異。」

25. Most people are ＿＿＿＿ or ＿＿＿＿ selfish.「大多數的人多少有點自私。」

26. The crowd is growing ＿＿＿＿ ＿＿＿＿ ＿＿＿＿.「人羣越來越大。」

27. The story got ＿＿＿＿ ＿＿＿＿ ＿＿＿＿ ＿＿＿＿.「故事越來越有趣。」

28. He became ＿＿＿＿ ＿＿＿＿ ＿＿＿＿ ＿＿＿＿ in mathematics.「他對於數學
越來越不感興趣。」

29. It is ＿＿＿＿ grey ＿＿＿＿ brown. = It is grey ＿＿＿＿ ＿＿＿＿ brown.「它
是灰色而不是褐色。」

30. She is _____ shy _____ unsociable. = She is shy _____ _____ unsociable. = She is _____ _____ _____ unsociable _____ shy.「她是怕羞，並不是不愛交際。」

31. _____ _____ I know him, _____ _____ I like him.「我越是認識他，越是喜歡他。」

32. _____ _____ _____ he spent on it, _____ _____ _____ he got.「他所費的時間越多，所得到的結果越少。」

33. I love him _____ _____ _____ _____ he has faults.「就因為他有缺點，我更加喜愛他。」

34. He likes to study English _____ _____ _____ _____ its difficulties.「就因為難，他更加喜歡英語。」

35. I do _____ like him _____ _____ _____ _____ he has faults.「我並不因為他有缺點而不喜歡他。」

36. She did _____ love him _____ _____ _____ _____ his mistakes.「她對於他的愛不因為他的過錯而稍減。」

37. He has faults, but I love him _____ _____ _____.「他有缺點，但是我仍舊愛他。」

38. I never think of it, _____ _____ _____ say it.「我想都沒有想到它，更不用說說到它了。」

39. I was _____ _____ surprised _____ I had been warned.「因為有人預先警告我，我沒有怎麼驚訝。」

40. There are _____ _____ nor _____ _____ ten persons in the room.「屋子裡正好有十個人，不多也不少。」

習 題 420

按照中文完成下列各句。

1. He is the _____ best student in town.「他是鎮裡最好的學生。」

2. He is the best _____ man (*or* the best man _____) for the job.「他是最適合這件工作的人。」

3. The worst _____ thing (*or* the worst thing _____) has happened.「再糟糕也沒有的事情發生了。」

4. The Yellow River is _____ _____ _____ river in China.「黃河是中國的第二大河。」

5. Jack is _____ _____ _____ student _____ our class.「傑克是班上個子第三高的學生。」

6. That is the _____ I can do.「我只能做到那樣。」

7. You should _____ the most _____ your time. = You should _____ the _____ use _____ your time.「你應該充分利用你的時間。」

8. You _____ _____ keep silent. = You can't do _____ than _____ silent.「你最好不要開口。」

9. There is _____ the _____ wind today.「今天一點風也沒有。」

10. I am not _____ the _____ (= at all) afraid to die.「我一點也不怕死。」

11. _____ _____ I can do is lend you a little money.「至少我能借一點錢給你。」

12. The _____ said the _____.「話說得越少越好。」

13. She speaks _____ eloquently than he. = She doesn't speak _____ _____ _____ he. = He speaks _____ _____ _____ she.「她說話不如他有口才。」

14. Taipei is _____ _____ _____ in Taiwan.= Taipei is _____ any _____ _____ in Taiwan = _____ other _____ is _____ _____ _____ Taipei.「臺北是臺灣最大的都市。」

15. Joe plays tennis _____ _____ in the family. (a) = Joe plays tennis _____ _____ _____ _____ other members in the family. (b) = No _____ _____ in the family plays tennis _____ _____ _____ Joe. (c) = The _____ _____ in the family play tennis _____ _____ _____ Joe. (d) = Joe spends _____ _____ on tennis _____ _____ _____ member in the family. (e) = No _____ _____ in the family spends _____ _____ _____ on tennis _____ Joe.

(f) = The _____ _____ in the family spend _____ _____ on tennis __
_____ Joe.「Joe 比家裡任何人都常打網球。」

**18-6. too＋形容詞、副詞＋不定詞；形容詞、副詞＋enough＋不定詞；so＋形容詞、
副詞＋as＋不定詞**

形容詞與副詞，也可以用「加強詞」too, enough, so⋯as 與不定詞來修飾：

John is *too* young *to go to school*.

「約翰年紀太小，還不能上學。」

That question is *too* hard *for me to answer*.

「那個問題太難，我不會回答。」

She got up *too* late *to catch the first train*.

「她起得太晚，沒有趕上第一班火車。」

You are old *enough to know better*.

「你年紀夠大了，應該更懂事一點。」

That question is easy *enough for me to answer*.

「那個題目很容易，我能回答。」

He knows China well *enough to answer your questions*.

「他對中國很了解，可以回答你的問題。」

I was *so* careless *as to take the wrong train*.

「我不小心所以搭錯了火車。」

He worked *so* hard *as to succeed at last*.

「他工作很努力，終於成功了。」

Come *so* early *as to be in plenty of time*.

「為要使時間從容一點早點來吧。」

這些句子都可以看做是由兩個句子合成而來。第一個句子是主句，第二個句子
是從句；從句要變成「不定詞子句」以後，才能加接到主句。

(1) too 表示「太」或「過分」，因此含有否定的意思：

John is too young.　⎫
He cannot go to school.　⎬　→
　　　　　　　　　　　⎭

　　John is too young *to go to school*.

That question is too hard.　⎫
I can't answer it.　　　　　⎬　→
　　　　　　　　　　　　　⎭

　　That question is too hard *for me to answer*.

She got up too late.　　　　　　　⎫
She couldn't catch the first tarin.　⎬　→
　　　　　　　　　　　　　　　　⎭

　　She got up too late *to catch the first train*.

(2) enough 表示「夠」或「足夠」，因此含有肯定的意思：

You are old enough.　　　⎫
You should know better.　⎬　→
　　　　　　　　　　　⎭

　　You are old enough *to know better*.

That question is easy enough.　⎫
I can answer it.　　　　　　　⎬　→
　　　　　　　　　　　　　　⎭

　　That question is easy enough *for me to answer*.

He knows China well enough.　　⎫
He can answer your questions.　⎬　→
　　　　　　　　　　　　　　⎭

　　He knows China well enough *to answer your questions*.

(3) 「so＋形容詞、副詞＋as」後面的「不定詞子句」表示「結果」或「目的」：

I was so careless.　　　⎫
I took the wrong train.　⎬　→
　　　　　　　　　　　⎭

　　I was so careless *as to take the wrong train*.（表示結果）

He worked so hard.　　⎫
He succeeded at last.　⎬　→
　　　　　　　　　　⎭

　　He worked so hard *as to succeed at last*.（表示結果）

Come early.　　　　　　　　　　⎫
You will be in plenty of time.　　⎬　→
　　　　　　　　　　　　　　　⎭

　　Come so early *as to be in plenty of time*.（表示目的）

習 題 421

依照例句，用 too … to, … enough to 或 so…as to 連接下列每對句子。

Examples:

This soup is too hot.
I can't drink it.

This soup is too hot for me to drink.

This soup is too hot to drink.

This soup is warm enough.
You can drink it.

This soup is warm enough for you to drink.

This soup is warm enough to drink.

John was so careless.
John broke the glass.

John was so careless as to break the glass.

1. John is tall enough.
   John can reach the ceiling.

2. The story is easy enough.
   You can understand it.

3. Jack is too short.
   Jack can't play on the team.

4. Dick was so excited.
   Dick started shouting.

5. He ran too quickly.
   I could not catch him.

6. The battery is strong enough.
   The battery can last forty-eight hours.

7. She is not so weak.
   She will give up her plan.

8. She is still too young.
   She can't marry you.

9. She is still too young.
   You can't marry her.

10. Dick is clever enough.
    Dick can solve any problem.

11. This problem is simple enough.
    Dick can solve it.

12. She is too good a wife.
    Tom cannot leave her.

13. It is too dangerous a job.
    He won't have anything to do with it.

14. It's too late.
    We can't go to the movies.

15. The weather is warm enough.
    You should be outside. }

16. He has enough time.
    He'll give an interview. }

17. She has too little time.
    She won't play bridge this evening. }

18. I am not confident enough.
    I will give a speech in public. }

19. Do you know him well enough?
    You are able to borrow money from him. }

20. We were so fortunate.
    We were in London for the Coronation. }

習　題　422

依照例句改寫下列各句。

Examples:

> a movie that good → *that good a movie*
>
> a book as good as that → *as good a book as that*
>
> a box too heavy for me to lift → *too heavy a box for me to lift*
>
> the finest doctor available → *the finest available doctor*
>
> waves ten feet high → *ten-foot-high waves*

1. a situation that bad
2. a movie so good
3. the best solution possible
4. a canyon five miles wide
5. a person taller than Mr. Taylor
6. a person rather nice to talk to
7. a story so unbelievable
8. a subject very easy to talk about
9. a man good enough for us to send to the United States
10. a movie as long as *Gone with the Wind*
11. the worst situation imaginable
12. an employee more cooperative than Miss Ford
13. a possibility too horrible to think about
14. a development that important
15. a movie as good as that

16. a day too hazy for pictures   17. a boy ten years old

18. a day too important for us to forget

19. a book as good as any that I ever read

20. a document important enough to require immediate attention

參考：

(1) 修飾原級形容詞的「加強詞」as, so, too, that 可以連同後面的形容詞移到名詞前面來。

注意，這個時候「冠詞」a(n) 放在形容詞後面。例如：

> a movie *so good* → *so good* a movie
>
> a movie *that good* → *that good* movie
>
> a movie *as good* as that → *as good* a movie as that
>
> a movie *too good* to miss → *too good* a movie to miss

比較　　a movie *good enough* far us to see

> → a *good enough* movie for us to see

(2) 修飾最高級形容詞的「加強詞」available, possible, imaginable, conceivable 可以出現在名詞的後面，也可以出現在去詞的前面。例如：

> the best teacher *available* → the best *available* teacher
>
> the worst situation *conceivable* → the worst *conceivable* situation

(3) 「數量詞」與形容詞可以出現在名詞的後面，也可以出現在名詞的前面。出現在名詞前面的時候，「數量詞」與形容詞常用「連號」 '-' 連起來，複數「量詞」要改為單數形。

比較：　　a baby *one month old* → a *one-month-old* baby

> a boy *five years old* → a *five-year-old* boy

18-7. so + 形容詞、副詞 + that- 子句

形容詞與副詞，還可以用 so 與「that- 子句」來修飾：

> The weather is *so* hot *that we don't want to go out*.
>
> 「天氣太熱了，我們不想出去。」

The exercise is *so* easy *that you can finish it in ten minutes*.

　　「習題很容易，你十分鐘就可以做完了。」

He worked *so* hard *that he finally succeeded*.

　　「他很努力工作，終於成功了。」

She spoke *so* quickly *that I couldn't understand her*.

　　「她講得太快，我沒有辦法了解她。」

　　這些句子也是由兩個句子合成而來的。第一個句子是主句，表示「理由」；第二個句子是從句，表示「結果」。從句要變成「that- 子句」以後才能加接到主句。

The weather is so hot.

We don't want to go out.　　}　→

　　The weather is so hot *that* we don't want to go out.

The exercise is so easy.

You can finish it in ten minutes.　　}　→

　　The exercise is so easy *that* you can finish it in ten minutes.

He worked so hard.

He finally succeeded.　　}　→

　　He worked so hard *that* he finally succeeded.

She spoke so quickly.

I couldn't understand her.　　}　→

　　She spoke so quickly *that* I couldn't understand her.

參考：有時候 so 可以直接修飾動詞。

He *so* handled the matter { *that* he won over his opponents. / *as to* win over his opponents.

　　「他籠絡住反對派把事情處理好了。」

習　題　423

　　依照例句，用 so … that 連接下列每對句子。

Examples:

> The soup was so hot.
> I couldn't drink it.

> → *The soup was so hot that I couldn't drink it.*

1. John is so nice.

   Everybody likes him.

2. The lecture was so long.

   The audience grew impatient.

3. I was so shocked.

   I didn't know what to say.

4. She was so clever.

   She solved all the problems at once.

5. His story was so funny.

   I couldn't help laughing.

6. She was so foolish.

   She believed everything he told her.

7. He was such a good runner.

   I couldn't catch him.

8. He ran so quickly.

   I couldn't catch him.

9. He was so crazy.

   He tried to jump down from the top of the house.

10. He worries so much about his financial position.

    He can't sleep at night.

習　題　424

依照例句，用 so … that 或 such … that 連接下列每對句子。

Examples:

He is poor.
He has nothing to give to others. $\Big\} \rightarrow$

He is so poor that he has nothing to give to others.

This is an interesting story.
I'd like to read it. $\Big\} \rightarrow$

This is such an interesting story that I'd like to read it.

1. She is nice.
   Everybody likes her.

2. She is a nice girl.
   Everybody likes her.

3. The room is big.
   We can have a party here.

4. It is a big room.
   All your family can live in it.

5. The news is good.
   We can hardly believe it.

6. The dress is old.
   I can't wear it any longer.

7. Yesterday was a hot day.
   We stayed home.

8. Alice has a good voice.
   She should study singing.

9. The weather is hot.
   I don't feel like going out.

10. I had a severe headache.
    I couldn't sleep all night.

參考：如果 so 出現在「a(n) + 形容詞 + 名詞」的前面，那麼形容詞要移到 a(n) 的前面，或 so 要用 such 來代替。比較：

> This book is *so interesting that* I can't stop reading it.
>
> This is *so interesting a book that* I can't stop reading it.
>
> This is *such an interesting book that* I can't stop reading it.

並比較下列用法：

> He was *so angry that* we were all frightened.
> His *anger* was *such that* we were all frightened.

> She loves her dog *so much* that she let it sleep in her bed.
> She loves her dog, *so much so that* (=to such an extent that)
>   she let it sleep in her bed.

習 題 425

填入適當的語詞，使左右兩邊的句子表示同樣的意思。

1. He is _____ tall _____ be can touch the ceiling. = He is tall _____ touch the ceiling.

2. He said he was _____ thirsty _____ he could drink a well dry. = He said he was thirsty _____ _____ drink a well dry.

3. He's not very good, so I can't marry him. = He is not good _____ _____ _____ to marry.

4. The current was so strong that he couldn't swim against it. = The current was _____ strong _____ _____ _____ swim against.

5. You're so young that you don't know about such things yet. = You're _____ _____ _____ know about such things yet.

6. The photograph was so clear that you could see every detail of the background. = The photograph was _____ _____ _____ _____ _____ see every detail of the background.

7. The path was so slippery that we couldn't walk along it. = The path was _____ _____ _____ _____ _____ walk along.

8. We were so lucky that we caught the first train. = We were _____ _____ _____ _____ catch the first train.

9. He was _____ fortunate _____ to succeed. = He was fortunate _____ to succeed.

10. The light is so dim that it can't be used for close work. = The light is _____ _____ _____ _____ _____ for close work.

11. He is quite well, and can go out again now.= He is _____ _____ _____ go out again now.

12. Mr. Chase is too fat to tie up his own shoes. = Mr.Chase is _____ _____ _____ he _____ tie up his own shoes.

13. An elephant's trunk is strong enough to hold a log of wood. = An elephant's trunk is
   _____ _____ _____ he _____ lift a log of wood.

14. I hope he is not so weak as to yield. =I hope he is not _____ _____ _____
   he _____ yield.

15. He ran too quickly for me to catch. = He was _____ _____ that I
   _____ catch _____ . =He ran _____ _____ that I _____ catch
   _____ . = He was _____ a good _____ that I _____ catch him.

參考：比較下面的句子。注意，在主句中已經出現的名詞要從不定詞子句中省略：

$$\begin{cases} \text{The box is } so \text{ heavy } that \text{ I cannot lift } it. \\ \text{The box is } too \text{ heavy } for \text{ me } to \text{ lift.} \end{cases}$$

$$\begin{cases} \text{The room is } so \text{ big } that \text{ we can live in } it. \\ \text{The room is big } enough \, for \text{ us } to \text{ live in.} \end{cases}$$

$$\begin{cases} \text{I was } so \text{ careless } that \text{ I forgot the appointment.} \\ \text{I was } so \text{ careless } as \, to \text{ forget the appointment.} \end{cases}$$

18-8. 帶有字尾 -ly 與不帶字尾 -ly 的副詞

有些副詞（如 fast, early, late, hard, loud, quick, slow 等）不帶字尾 -ly，因此形式上與形容詞相同。比較：

$$\begin{cases} \text{My watch is } fast. \\ \text{Don't speak so } fast. \end{cases}$$

$$\begin{cases} \text{You are } early. \\ \text{Don't come too } early. \end{cases}$$

$$\begin{cases} \text{He was } late \text{ for dinner.} \\ \text{He got here five minutes } late. \end{cases}$$

$$\begin{cases} \text{He is a } hard \text{ worker.} \\ \text{He works very } hard. \end{cases}$$

$$\begin{cases} \text{He has a } loud \text{ voice.} \\ \text{He laughs too } loud. \end{cases}$$

$\begin{cases} \text{He is a } slow \text{ walker.} \\ \text{Go } slow \text{ through the village.} \end{cases}$

$\begin{cases} \text{He has a } quick \text{ temper.} \\ \text{Run as } quick \text{ as you can.} \end{cases}$

這種不帶字尾 -ly 的副詞與帶有字尾 -ly 的副詞，無論意義與用法都不同：

$\begin{cases} \text{He works very } hard. \text{ (= diligently)「努力」} \\ \text{I can } hardly \text{ believe my eyes. (= scarcely)「幾乎不」} \end{cases}$

$\begin{cases} \text{He got up } late \text{ this morning.「晚」} \\ \text{It hasn't rained } lately. \text{ (= recently)「最近」} \end{cases}$

$\begin{cases} \text{He went } direct \text{ to the station. (= in a straight line)「直，逕」} \\ \text{People are } directly \text{ affected by the taxes. (= in a direct manner)「直接」} \\ \text{He went } directly \text{ after breakfast. (= immediately)「立即」} \end{cases}$

$\begin{cases} \text{Open your mouth } wide. \text{ / The window was } wide \text{ open.「大（開）」} \\ \text{The houses were } widely \text{ scattered. / He has traveled } widely.\text{「廣，遠」} \end{cases}$

$\begin{cases} \text{He tried to come } near.\text{「近」} \\ \text{He is } nearly \text{ as tall as I. (= almost)「差不多」} \end{cases}$

$\begin{cases} \text{Stay } close \text{ to me. (= near)「近」} \\ \text{Watch what I do } closely. \text{ (= carefully)「仔細」} \end{cases}$

$\begin{cases} \text{He guessed } wrong.\text{「錯」} \\ \text{We were } wrongly \text{ informed.「錯誤地」} \end{cases}$

$\begin{cases} \text{He guessed } right.\text{「對」} \\ \text{He } rightly \text{ guessed that } \cdots \text{「正確地」} \end{cases}$

$\begin{cases} \text{He spoke loud and } clear.\text{「清楚」} \\ \text{The bullet went } clear \text{ through the door. (= completely)「完全」} \\ \text{He is } clearly \text{ wrong.「顯然」} \\ \text{You must } clearly \text{ understand } \cdots \text{「清楚地」} \end{cases}$

$\begin{cases} \text{He was } dead \text{ drunk. (= completely)「完全」} \\ \text{The meeting is } deadly \text{ dull. (= extremely)「非常」} \end{cases}$

{
Go *slow*.「慢（多與 go, run, speak 等用在命令或勸告）」

He drove *slowly* along the street.「慢慢地」
}

{
Hold it *tight*. / Keep your mouth *tight* shut.「緊（閉）」

We were *tightly* packed in the bus.「緊密地，滿滿地」

（比較：We were packed *tight*.）
}

{
He always plays *fair*.「光明正大地」

We all treat him *fairly*.「公平地」

The weather is *fairly* good. (= moderately)「相當」
}

{
The ship loomed *large*.「大」

This was *largely* due to … (= to a great extent)「主要地」
}

{
The sea was running *high*.「高」

The story was *highly* amusing. (= greatly)「非，常」

Japan is *highly* industrialized.「高度地」

He *thinks* (/ *speaks*) *highly of* you.「尊重 / 激賞」
}

{
We are *most* concerned for their happiness.「非常」

Houses, are *mostly* built of brick and stone. (= for the most part)「多半」
}

{
He has *just* gone out.「剛剛」

He was *justly* punished.「公正地」
}

{
He appeared at six o'clock *sharp*. (= punctually)「準」

Look sharp! (= be quick)「趕快！當心！」

He never spoke *sharply* to me.「嚴厲地」

He turned *sharply* to the left. (= suddenly)「突然」
}

{
The problem was *pretty* easy.「相當」

She is dressed *prettily*. (= in a pleasing manner)「漂亮地」
}

{
He stood *firm* in the presence of danger.「穩，牢」

Fix the post *firmly* in the ground.「牢固地」

I *firmly* believe that …「堅定地」
}

$$\left\{\begin{array}{l} \text{He is } \textit{sound} \text{ asleep.「酣（睡）」}\\ \text{He is sleeping } \textit{soundly}.\text{「酣（睡）」}\\ \text{He always argues } \textit{soundly}.\text{「穩健地」} \end{array}\right.$$

$$\left\{\begin{array}{l} \textit{Sure enough}.\text{「果然，當然」}\\ \text{Work slowly but } \textit{surely}.\text{「確實地」} \end{array}\right.$$

$$\left\{\begin{array}{l} \text{He fell } \textit{flat} \text{ on the ground.「直挺挺地」}\\ \text{He told me } \textit{flat} \text{ that } \cdots \text{ (= positively)「明白地，斷然」}\\ \text{The suggestions were } \textit{flatly} \text{ opposed. / He } \textit{flatly} \text{ refused to join us.「斷然地，}\\ \quad \text{直截了當地」} \end{array}\right.$$

注意，帶有字尾 -ly 的副詞多半用在動詞、過去分詞，或形容詞的前面。

習　題　426

按照句意選出正確的副詞。

1. I had to speak _____ to him. (firm, firmly)

2. He holds _____ to his beliefs. (firm, firmly)

3. I will be there _____ .(direct, directly)

4. He tried _____ to succeed. (hard, hardly)

5. I could _____ understand him. (hard, hardly)

6. He was looking _____ at me. (direct, directly)

7. This train goes _____ to Keelung. (direct, directly)

8. Bob works _____ day and night. (hard, hardly)

9. _____ anybody believes that. (hard, hardly)

10. Take it _____ . (easy, easily)

11. You can do it _____ . (easy, easily)

12. That is _____ to be wondered at. (hard, hardly)

13. She looked _____ at the picture. (hard, hardly)

14. The shells seemed to be coming _____ towards us. (direct, directly)

15. I'll be with you _____ . (direct, directly)

16. It was _____ kind of you. (mighty, mightily)

17. You can _____ expect me to lend you money. (hard, hardly)

18. People living in the suburbs were _____ hit by the bus and train strikes. (hard, hardly)

19. He came _____ to London. (direct, directly)

20. He spoke very_____ of her. (high, highly)

21. We _____ ever go tothe theater. (hard, hardly)

22. Watch that man_____; he's a thief. (close, closely)

23. He was standing _____ to the door. (close, closely)

24. He resembles his father very _____. (close, closly)

25. You are _____ in the wrong. (clear, clearly)

26. Can you see _____ from here? (clear, clearly)

27. You should keep _____ of that fellow. (clear, clearly)

28. He turned _____ left. (sharp, sharply)

29. He turned _____ to the left. (sharp, sharply)

30. He called _____ for help. (loud, loudly)

31. You did _____ to apologize. (right, rightly)

32. Their views are _____ apart. (wide, widely)

33. His name was _____ known. (wide, widely)

34. The shot went _____. (wide, widely)

35. The children sat with their hands _____ clasped. (tight, tightly)

36. I haven't seen him _____. (late, lately)

37. It is _____ a matter of conjecture. (large, largely)

38. He was _____ beaten at tennis. (sound, soundly)

39. I said it would be, and _____ enough it is. (sure, surely)

40. He _____ refused to join us. (flat, flatly)

參考：一般說來, 不帶字尾 -ly 的副詞在語義上比較接近形容詞原來的含義，帶字尾 -ly 的副詞常用於引伸或比喻的意義。比較：

> The sea was running *high*. 「高」
> The story was *highly* amusing. 「非常」

> The ship loomed *large*.「大」
> It is *largely* a matter of conjecture.「主要地」

出現在現在分詞（V-ing）或過去分詞（V-en）前面的副詞，通常都用帶字尾 -ly 的副詞，例如：

His argument is *hardly* convincing.

The play was *highly* entertaining.

We were *wrongly* informed.

His name was *widely* known.

出現在動詞前面的副詞，通常也限於帶字尾 -ly 的副詞，例如：

He *flatly* refused to join us.

We *hardly* even go to the theater.

He *rightly* guessed that …

第*19*章
動詞的修飾語：介詞片語

19-1. 動詞的修飾語：介詞片語與副詞子句

英語的動詞可以用幾種不同的方法來加以修飾。在第八章裡我們曾經學到用副詞來修飾動詞。除了副詞以外，介詞片詞與副詞子句是最常見的動詞修飾語。比較下面的動詞修飾語。

(1) 表示「狀態」的修飾語

I wrote *carefully*.（副詞）

I wrote *with care*.（介詞片語）

I wrote *as I had never written before*.（副詞子句）

(2) 表示「場所」的修飾語

The house stands *there*.（副詞）

The house stands *on the street corner*.（介詞片語）

The house stands *where the two roads meet*.（副詞子句）

(3) 表示「時間」的修飾語

She played the piano *then*.（副詞）

She played the piano *in the morning*.（介詞片語）

She played the piano *when she had time*.（副詞子句）

(4) 表示「頻度」的修飾語

They saw each other *often*.（副詞）

They saw each other *from time to time*.（介詞片語）

They saw each other *whenever they had time*.（副詞子句）

習 題 427

在動詞修飾語下面劃橫線，並注出種類（副詞、介詞片語、副詞子句）。

Examples:

> She sang beautifully.（副詞）
>
> He sadly left the room with no money in his pocket.（副詞，介詞片語）
>
> They had already left before you arrived.（副詞，副詞子句）

1. I wrote the letter in English.

2. She left the room suddenly during the conference.

3. He hadn't yet eaten lunch when you came.

4. It was carefully planned by several experts.

5. The chairman often came with his secretary in the morning.

6. You had better go to the station as soon as you finish the work.

7. He cannot do it successfully unless he follows the directions.

8. The mother walked quietly into the room because the baby was sleeping.

9. We have always lived here since we moved to this city.

10. Come here early with your friend tomorrow morning if you want to see the manager.

19.2 介詞片語

介詞片語（prepositional phrase）由介詞（preposition）與後面的名詞組而成。據文法家的估計，英語介詞的數目共達三百多個，但是最常用的介詞卻只有九個 —— at, by, for, from, in, of, on, to, with。這九個主要的介詞在使用次數上佔所有英語介詞的百分之九十二。可是每一個介詞都有好幾種意義與用法，因此非把這些意義與用法一一了解與練習不可。在下面的幾節裡，我們把英語的介詞依照用途分成八類，詳細加以討論。

(1) 時間（when?）

> The baseball game will start *at 2:30 p.m.*

(2) 期間（how long?）

> We have learned English *for more than four years.*

(3) 場所（where?）

> Mr. Brown is sitting *in a leather chair.*

(4) 方向、運動（to where? to whom? 等）

They went *to the park*.

We spoke *to them*.

(5) 距離（how far?）

We walked for *many and many a mile*.

(6) 方法、狀態（how?）

He shaves *with an electric razor*.

(7) 原因、理由、動機、目的（why?）

We lost ourselves *through not knowing the way*.

(8) 其他（結果，伴隨，除外，代替，反對，關於，按照，條件等）

習　題　428

依照例句把下列各句改為「wh- 問句」。

Examples:

She wrote the letter *with care*.

→ *How did she write the letter?*

He has lived there *for three years*.

→ *How long has he lived there?*

1. They took a walk *in the park* in the morning.

2. *In summer* they like to sit under the tree.

3. They learned the poem *by heart*.

4. We are fighting *for liberty*.

5. Most city dwellers go to work *by bus*.

6. She hung the picture *on the wall*.

7. The ship is sailing *toward the coast*.

8. The car is running *at 60 miles an hour*.

9. She was trembling *with cold*.

10. He got the job *out of luck*.

19-3. 表示「時間」的介詞片語

(a) **in**「在…（時候）」：

~ the morning (afternoon, evening, night, daytime); ~ the spring (summer, etc.); ~ January (February, ect.); ~ (the year) 1968 (500 B.C. etc.); ~ (the) future; ~ the past; ~ one's life; ~ time: ~ the hour; etc.

(b) **on**「在…（時候）」，**before**「在…以前」，**after**「在…以後」，**by**「（最遲）在…以前」("not later than")：

~ Sunday (Monday, etc.); ~ January 1 (the first of January); ~ Sunday morning (a cold morning); ~ Thanks-giving (Day) (New Year's Eve, Labour's Day); ~ time; ~ this (that) occasion; ~ the hour; etc.

(c) **at**「在…（時候）」，**before**「在…以前」，**after**「在…以後」，by「（最遲）在…以前」：

~ six o'clock (half past ten, etc.); ~ noon (midday, midnight, night); ~ dawn (sunrise, daybreak, sunset), ~ Christmas (time) (Easter, the New Year, etc.); ~ breakfast (lunch supper) (time); ~ this (that) time, ~ (the) present (time); ~ the right (wrong, same) time; etc.

(d) **in**「在…以後 (= "at the end of")」：

~ an hour (week, month, year, etc.); ~ a few (two, three) minutes (hours, days, weeks); ~ an (two) hour's (week's) time; etc.

(e) **during**「在…期間」：

~ the vacation; ~ the war; ~ one's absence / stay / visit; ~ the meal; ~ the past three days; etc.

(f) **around, about**「大約在…（時候）」：

~ six o'clock (midnight, the 15th, the year 1875, etc.)

(g) **ahead of**「比…早」；**behind**「比…晚」：

~ time; ~ schedule, etc.

(h) **to, till, of, before**「（…點）差（…分）」：

a quarter ~ twelve, etc.

(i) **past, after**「（…點）過（…分）」：

five (minutes) ∼ one, etc.

(j) **toward (s)**「將近」：

∼ noon (evening, 6 o'clock, the end of the 15th century, etc.)

(k) **near**「將近」：

∼ 10 o'clock (the end of the month, Christmas, etc.)

(l) **within, inside of**「在 … 之內」：

He will be back ∼ a week.

(m) **by**：

∼ day「白天裡 "during the day"」；∼ night「夜晚裡 "during the night"」.

(n) **for**：

∼ the first (second, last) time；∼ the present「目前」；∼ the time being「權且，暫時」.

(o) **at the beginning of**「在 … 之初」；**at the end of**「在 … 之末」；**in the middle of**「在 … 之中」：

∼ the week (month, year, etc.)

(p) **on**「一俟 … 」：

They greeted us *on* our arrival. (= when we arrived)

(q) **with**「與 … 同時」：

Farmers rise *with* the sun. (= at the same time as)

With these words, he left the room.

參考：

(1) **at** 表示「在某一點時間 'a point of time'」；**in** 表示「在某一段較長的時間內 'an extended period of time'」；**on** 表示「在某一個特定的時間 'a particular day, morning, night or evening'」。比較：

Thay came $\begin{cases} at \text{ 2 o'clock.} \\ in \text{ the morning / May / summer / 1972.} \\ on \text{ Tuesday / July 9 / a cold morning.} \end{cases}$

(2) **in** 表示「在一段時間內 'not beyond'」或「（未來）過了一段時間以後 'at the end of'」；**within** 表示「在一段時間內」。

> Can you finish it *in / within* an hour?「一個鐘頭之內」
>
> We'll come back *in* a week.「一週以後，未來」
>
> We came back *after* a week.「一週以後，過去」

(3) **before** 表示「在 … 以前 'earlier than'」；**after** 表示「在 … 以後 'later than'」；**by** 表示「最遲在 … 以前 'not later than'」。

> Call me again *before / after* 10 o'clock.
>
> Try to be here *by* 2 o'clock.

(4) **after** 與 **past** 表示「（幾點）過（幾分）」；**before, to, till, of** 表示「（幾點）差（幾分）」。

> It's five (minutes) $\begin{cases} \textit{after / past} \\ \textit{Before / to / till / of} \end{cases}$ twelve.

(5) **ahead of** 表示「比（預定的時間）早」；**behind** 表示「比（預定的時間）晚」。

> The train is ten minutes $\begin{cases} \textit{ahead of} \\ \textit{behind} \end{cases}$ the schedule.

(6) **around** 與 **about** 表示「大約在 … 時候，… 前後」；**toward(s)** 與 **near** 表示「將近 … 時候」。

> I'll pick you up *around / about* 8 o'clock.
>
> It happened *toward* (*s*) / *near* the end of the century.

(7) **in** 表示「在某一個期間內的某一個時間」，**during**「在某一期間內的整個時間」，二者都用在 absence, illness, lifetime, reign 等名詞的前面。比較：

Who will take your place *during* your absence?（整個請假期間）

Someone called *in* your absence.（在請假期聞內發生了一件事情）

Many things happened *during* your absence.（在請假期間內發生了好幾件事情）

　　in 又表示「在通常，一般的時間」；**during** 表示「在某一個特定的時間」。

比較：

People go to Florida *in* winter.（通常，一般的「冬天」）

I went to Florida *during* the winter.(某一個特定的「冬天」）

(8) 在節日前面一般用 **at**，但是如果注重日期即可以用 **on**。

We send greeting-cards *at* Christmas (time).

We visited them on Christmas (Day).

(9) **on time** 表示「準時，exactly at an appointed time'」；**in time** 表示「及時，before an appointed time, with time to spare'」，後面常跟著不定詞或介詞 for 帶頭的片語。比較：

(Were you late for your appointment?)

No, I was on *time*.

No, I reached the office *in time* to have a cup of coffee before my appointment.

Did you get up this morning *in time for* breakfast?

習 題 429

在空白裡填入 in, at 或 on。如果不需要介詞，就打一個叉號（×）。

1. _____Sunday		2. _____the evening	
3. _____night		4. _____next Sunday	
5. _____December 7		6. _____December	
7. _____the spring		8. _____1941	
9. _____the summer		10. _____Saturday	
11. _____last Saturday		12. _____noon	
13. _____the morning		14. _____3 o'clock	
15. _____sunrise		16. _____midnight	
17. _____the right time		18. _____the past	
19. _____the present time		20. _____May 5, 1957	
21. _____present		22. _____the hour	
23. _____an hour		24. _____the daytime	
25. _____10 minutes to 6		26. _____Christinas	
27. _____future		28. _____breakfast	
29. _____moment		30. _____a moment	

31. _____ any-time   32. _____ the age of 8

33. _____ New Years Eve   34. _____ the near future

35. _____ a cold morning   36. _____ any minute

37. _____ the same time   38. _____ a month

39. _____ this month   40. _____ the end of the year

習 題 430

在空白裡填入 at, in 或 on。

1. I knew that his birthday was _____ July, but I had forgotten that it was_____

   July 10.

2. Swallows come _____ spring and leave us _____ fall.

3. He is generally at home _____ the morning, except _____ Sunday morning.

4. We started _____ sunrise and arrived _____ midnight.

5. The owl sleeps _____ the daytime, and comes out to seek for food _____

   night.

6. I leave _____ the end of next month, _____ July 31.

7. The sun shines _____ day, and the moon _____ night.

8. He was generally drunk _____ the evening, and that was the case _____ the

   present occasion.

19-4. 表示「期間」的介詞片語

(a) **for**「…（之久）」：

~ an hour (week, month); ~ two or three (several, a few, many) minutes (seconds,

hours, days) ~ some (a long, a short) time (while); ~ ever (good, life); etc.

(b) **from … to (till, until)**「從 … 到 … 」：

~ morning (dawn, birth, etc.) ~ night (dusk, death, etc.); ~ Sunday (January,

one o'clock, 1960, etc.); ~ Saturday (June, six o'clock, 1965, etc.); etc.

(c) **till, until, up to**「（一直）到 … 」：

~ tomorrow (morning, etc.); ~ next Sunday (week, etc.); ~ January the first

(1970,etc.); ～ now (then, death, etc.); etc.

(d) **from**「從 … （起）」：

　　～ early this morning; ～ the (very) beginning; ～ the (very) first; ～ childhood (a child); ～ now on (forth, onward); ～ that time onward; ～ time (day) to time (day).

(e) **over**「過 … 」：

　　stay ～ the night (the weekend, Wednesday the holiday, chrishtmas, etc.)

(f) **since**「自從 … （到現在）」：

　　～ yesterday (morning,etc.); ～ last (night, week, etc.); ～ May (1930, etc.); etc.

(g) **(all) through, throughout**「在 … 整個期間」：

　　～ the night (the summer, the year, the war, one's life), etc.

(h) **from … through**「從 … 到（包括後面的時間）」：

　　～ June ～ (=up to and including) September.

參考：

(1) **for** 一般表示「不特定的期間」；**during** 表示「特定的期間」。

　　　We waited *for* a week / two weeks / several months.

　　　I hope to see you some time *during* the week / the summer / the vacation.

　　　for 表示「（從頭到尾）整個期間」；**during** 可能表示「斷斷續續在那個期間」。

比較：

　　He was in Japan $\begin{cases} \textit{for} \text{ the month of May.「整個五月都在日本」} \\ \textit{during} \text{ May.「不一定整個五月都在日本」} \end{cases}$

　　$\begin{cases} \text{They are staying at the lake } \textit{for} \text{ the summer.} \\ \text{It rained a great deal } \textit{during} \text{ the summer.} \end{cases}$

　　We haven't seen him $\begin{Bmatrix} \textit{for} \\ \textit{during} \end{Bmatrix}$ the past week.

during：又可能表示「每天這個時間」；**for** 卻沒有這種含義。

　　The maid is here $\begin{cases} \textit{for} \text{ the day. (=only today)} \\ \textit{during} \text{ the day. (=every day)} \end{cases}$

(2) **since** 表示「自從 … 到現在，'from then till now'」，前面常用現在完成（進行）式；**from** 表示「從」，不受時式的限制。

He has been studying *since* this morning.

I have not seen him *since* last summer.

He studied *from* six till nine.

I will work harder *from* now on.

比較：

I have known him $\begin{cases} \textit{since} \text{ his childhood.} \\ \textit{from} \text{ a child.} \end{cases}$

(3) **till** 與 **until** 表示「直到」，只能與「持續性的動詞」合用。比較：

$\begin{cases} \text{He studied / waited / slept / stayed } \textit{until} \text{ nine o'clock.} \\ \text{He came / went / left / rose } \textit{at} \text{ nine oclock.} \end{cases}$

not … **till** / **until** 可與「瞬間性動詞」合用，表示「到 … 才」。比較：

$\begin{cases} \text{He did} \textit{n't} \text{ study } \textit{till} / \textit{until} \text{ nine o'clock.} \\ \quad（持續性動詞「他讀書沒有讀到九點鐘。」） \\ \text{He did} \textit{n't} \text{ come } \textit{till} / \textit{until} \text{ nine o'clock.} \\ \quad（瞬間性動詞「他到了九點鐘才來。」） \end{cases}$

(4) **(all) through**「在 … 整個期間」，強調「從頭到尾，from the beginning to the end'」；**over**「過」表示「過了這個期間以後還要 'through and till after」。比較：

$\begin{cases} \text{Will the fuel last } \textit{through} \text{ the winter?} \\ \quad「這些燃料夠不夠整個冬天之用？」 \\ \text{Will these apples keep } \textit{over} \text{ the winter?} \\ \quad「這些蘋果能不能過冬？」 \end{cases}$

習 題 431

在空白裡填入 for, during 或 since。

1. They stayed _____ six months in the United States.

2. We played tennis _____ a couple of hours.

3. Did he have a good time _____ his trip?

4. I asked them to come and stay _____ a weekend.

5. They have been visiting us _____ Sunday.

6. _____ the day, you can telephone her at the office.

7. Mrs. Hill has lived in the same house _____ 1952.

8. Everybody is busy _____ the Christmas season.

9. He hasn't been feeling well _____ last night.

10. We've been working in the garden _____ lunch time.

習　題　432

在空白裡填入 at, in, on, from 或 since。

1. School begins _____ eight.

2. He has been learning English _____ last year.

3. He studied nothing else _____ that time on.

4. I have known him _____ our school days.

5. I have known him _____ a schoolboy.

6. The school year begins _____ the first of September.

7. Our acquaintance started _____ our school-days.

8. Their acquaintance dated _____ their school-days.

9. He has been a lucky man _____ the day he started business.

10. He was a lucky man _____ the day he started business.

習　題　433

在空白裡填入 in, during, through 或 throughout。

1. Did anyone call me _____ my absence?

2. He works hard all _____ the day.

3. He is always at work _____ the day.

4. I need someone to take my place _____ my absence.

5. We saw him several times _____ our trip South.

6. People go to Florida _____ winter.

7. I went to Florida _____ the winter.

8. They have met many people _____ the two years they have been in London.

9. You can borrow money from the bank _____ time of need.

10. The firemen worked _____ the night in an effort to control the fire.

習 題 434

在空白裡填入 at, before, by, towards 或 till (until)。

1. I am usually tired _____ the end of the day.

2. He became a Christian _____ the end of his life.

3. She will stay here _____ the end of this month.

4. The work must be finished _____ the end of next week.

5. She wants to see her teacher _____ writing the letter.

6. Will my new suit be ready _____ Saturday?

7. _____ evening the breeze died away.

8. I intend to stay here _____ next month.

9. _____ the time helpcame, he was already dead.

10. I shall not be back _____ the end of this month.

習 題 435

在空白裡填入適當的時間介詞。

1. Tom will be back _____ Wednesday. (no later than Wednesday)

2. Tom will be back _____ Wednesday. (approximately Wednesday)

3. Tom will be back _____ Wednesday. (exactly Wednesday)

4. He will stay here _____ Wednesday.

5. I haven't seen him _____ last Wednesday.

6. The ice won't melt _____ spring.

7. Good-bye _____ tomorrow.

8. I was tired _____ dancing so much.

9. All _____ the year, he hoped for a promotion.

10. Come here _____ a minute, please.

11. I want to get to class _____ time to talk with the teacher before it begins.

12. We're usually at work _____ the daytime, but we're almost always home _____ night.

13. He promised to come _____ noon but I don't know whether to expect him _____ time.

14. We are getting that job finished little _____ little.

15. _____ the end, they were glad they had waited.

16. It seemed incredible that the storm could continue with such force day _____ day.

17. The child's mother told him that she was busy, but would read to him _____ a while.

18. All _____ a sudden, we heard a terrible crash.

19. School begins _____ nine a.m. and ends _____ four p.m.

20. The examination commences _____ September 19.

21. We started _____ the following morning.

22. I like to go fishing _____ an afternoon like this.

23. _____ returning home, I took supper. (as soon as I returned home)

24. I will finish it _____ a week. (in shorter than a week)

25. I will be there _____ five. (not later than)

26. We have known him _____ a child.

27. _____ this (= so saying) he left the room.

28. _____ today everything will be changed.

29. Everything has changed _____ that day.

30. I have been studying English _____ five years.

31. Where are you going _____ the summer?

32. Thousands of lives were lost _____ the war.

33. He didn't arrive until late _____ the afternoon.

34. I'll wait here for him _____ three o'clock.

35. I'll read it _____ my leisure.

36. _____ inquiry, I found I was mistaken.

37. _____ my father's death, I went to live with my uncle.

38. He is always _____ time with his payment.

39. We began _____ the stroke of the clock.

40. All was changed _____ a year.

習　題　436

用下面的介詞片語代替下列各句的斜體部分。

from now on	for the time being
in no time	after all
after a while	all at once
once in a while	in a (little) while
all of a sudden	at length
at once	at the moment
once and for all	from time to time
on the spur of the moment	

1. Please be prompt *from the present on*.

2. We can use this tool *temporarily*.

3. Another bus will come by *soon*.

4. Janet makes a mistake only *now and then*.

5. I'll go with you soon, but I'm busy *right now*.

6. While we were talking, *suddenly* Mary screamed.

7. He visits his uncle in Tainan *now and then*.

8. Paul did not consider his action very carefully. He did it *without planning to*.

9. If you go by plane, you can get from Taipei to Tainan *in very little time*.

10. At first they seemed to get along very well, but *after some time* they started quarreling.

11. *Suddenly* he realized that he had left his briefcase in the taxi.

12. She told him to leave the room *right away*.

13. *Definitely*, I tell you I will not do it.

14. Tab hesitated about going, but he went *finally*.

15. It has turned out to be a nice day *nevertheless*.

參考：下面是一些常用的表示時間的介詞片語。

day after day：「　成　天，　天　天，　每　天 "one day after another; daily; continually"」

　　That man asks me for a job *day after day*.

day by day：「成天，天天，每天 "gradually; a little more every day"」

　　Day by day I am getting older.

first of all：「首先 "before anything else"」

　　When you make coffee, *first of all* wash the pot.

at first：「起初 "in the beginning"」

　　At first I was nervous, but in a few minutes I felt relaxed.

at last：「最後，終於 "finally in the end"」

　　At last I understand what you mean.

after a while：「過了一會兒 "after an interval of time"」

　　I'll see you *after a while*.

all at once: all of a sudden：「忽然，突然 "suddenld, unexpectedly"」

　　At first I couldn't remember his name, and then *all of a sudden* I thought of it.

at length：「終於，好不容易才 "after some time"」

　　At length, the little town grew into a city.

at once：「立刻，馬上 "quickly, immediately"」

　　He told the child to come at once.

at the moment：「目前 "now"」

　　At the moment, we don't need anything from the grocery store.

before long：「不久 "soon"」

　　Summer will come *before long*.

for the time being：「權且，暫時 "for the present, temporarily"」

　　They're living in an apartment *for the time being*, but they hope to buy a house
　　　　next year.

from now on：「從今而後 "beginning now and continuing into the future"」

Jack has just had his twenty-first birthday. *From now on*, he isconsidered an adult.

from time to time：「時時 "intermittently, occasionally"」

Jim comes to Washington *from time to time*.

in a (little) while：「不久 "soon"」

Dinner will be ready *in a little while*.

in no time (flat)：「立刻 "quickly, in a short time"」

Don't worry. We won't be late. I'll get dressed *in no time (flat)*.

on the spur of the moment：「因一時高興或衝動；當場，即席 "spontaneously; without advance planning"」

They decided, *on the spur of the moment*, to go to the movies.

once and for all：「限此一次，斷然 "this time and not again, for the very last time (often said in anger and annoyance)"」

I told him, *once and for all*, that I wasn't interested in another insurance policy.

once in a while / way：「偶爾，間或 "intermittently, occasionally"」

They like to go to a dance *once in a while*.

in the course of：「在 … 之中 "during, within"」

In the course of our discussion, somebody mentioned his name.

I shall be back *in the course* of two or three days.

in due / good time, in due course：「在適當的時候，終究 "at the proper time, eventually"」

Don't get impatient. I'll talk with you *in due course*.

in the end：「終歸 "finally, ultimately"」

You will regret doing that *in the end*.

in the beginning：「起初，當初 "at first, within the first part of something"」

In the beginning, I did not understand geometry, but later on it became clear.

in time of：「當 … 之時 "in a period of"」

Life becomes difficult *in time of* war.

at times; at other times：「有時候，時時 "now and then, once in a while"」

At times I get very angry at Dan. *At other times* he seems very likable.

time after time：「一再 "again and again, repeatedly"」

I have asked him *time after time* not to bring his dog in.

in the meantime / meanwhile：「在那當中」

Bob will arrive tonight. *In the meantime* you should get his room ready.

after all：「終歸，到底 "considering everything; in spite of everything"」

The day turned out fine *after all*.

They did win; so you were right *after all*.

習　題　437

從括號裡的介詞片語中把不適當的劃去。

1. My teacher asked me to do it (since last night, on the spur of the moment, at once).

2. We'll go swimming (at, on, for, through) the weekend.

3. Mary played the piano (around, during, through) the day.

4. It is still warm here (behind, during, in) the fall.

5. We have learned English (for, since) three years.

6. I expect to hear from her (by, before, at) Sunday night.

7. He will be at home (until, in, on) Wednesday.

8. We always go swimming (since, for, during) the summer.

9. They will be in the United States (through, since, until) June.

10. I went to see him (once in a while, before long, from time to time).

11. The mayor can certainly come here (after, before, by, on) three o'clock.

12. I'd like to visit France (during, in, at) May.

13. The plane will take off (about, behind, around) seven o'clock.

14. (Day after day, At last, At Christmas) the war broke out.

15. They see each other (once in a while, in no time, from time to time).

16. I'm sure we'll get there (ahead of time, on schedule, for the time being).

17. If you keep practicing, your ability will improve (little by little, in the end, once and for all).

18. Charles started working for the company, and (in no time, before long, from time to time) he received two promotions.

19. (All at once, All of a sudden, At the moment) a blue station wagon came speeding around the corner.

20. The physics classes are meeting in the biology lab (for the time being, at the moment, once in a while).

19-5. 表示場所的介詞片語

(a) **at**「在（某一點場所）」：

He is ～ the dentist's. He stays ～ home.

She is standing. ～ the door.

(b) **on**「在 … 上面（與面接觸）」：

The lamp is ～ my desk. The picture is ～ the wall.

He sat ～ a bench.

The house stands ～ the coast. They live ～ a farm.

(c) **in**「在 … 裡面」：

The papers are ～ the desk drawer. He is swimming ～ the pool.

We Iiye ～ an apartment. He is studying at an university ～ the United States.

(d) **under**「在 … 下面」：

The ball of string was ～ the table. He lay down ～ a tree.

(e) **over**「在 … 上面」：

The sky is ～ our heads. He warmed his hands ～ the fire.

(f) **off**「不在 … 上面，離開」：

The lid is ～ the pan. The book fell ～ the table. Their hourse is ～ the main road.

(g) **across**「在 … 對面」：

The post office is ～ the street. Mr. and Mrs. Brown live ～ the street from us.

(h) **around**「在 … 周圍」：

She has a scarf 〜 her neck. Take your arm from 〜 my waist.

(i) **about, around**「在 … 附近」：

He gathered his family 〜 him.

I dropped my key somewhere 〜 here.

(j) **between**「在 … 中間」：

The bank is 〜 the hotel and the hospital. Tom is sitting 〜 Dick and Peter

(k) **among**「在 … 中間」：

There is one apple 〜 the bananas. Mary was standing 〜 the other girls.

(l) **throughout, all over**「在 … 到處」：

There was a drought 〜 the country.

(m) **above**「在 … 上面」：

The sun is rising 〜 the horizon. Look at the flag 〜 the building.

(n) **below**「在 … 下面」：

The sun is sinking 〜 the horizon.

Some of the land in Holland is actually 〜 sea level.

(o) **beneath, underneath**「在 … 下面（常與面接觸）」：

The surface of the earth is 〜 our feet.

He placed a pillow 〜 my head.

(p) **inside**「在 … 裡面」；**outside**「在 … 外面」：

The bird was 〜 its cage. The children were playing 〜 the house.

(q) **beside**「在 … 旁邊」，**by**「在 … 近旁」，**next to**「在 … 隔壁」：

Susan is standing 〜 Charles.

(r) **near**「在 … 附近」，**close to**「靠近」：

The bank is 〜 the post office.

(s) **behind, in back of**〔美式〕，**at the back of**〔英式〕「在 … 後面」：

The bicycle is 〜 the car.

(t) **in front of, ahead of**「在 … 前面」：

The car is 〜 the bicycle.

He stood *in front of* the door.（停止的）

He was running *ahead of* us.（運動的）

(u) **along**「沿著 …」：

We walked ～ the road. They planted flowers ～ the path.

(v) **beyond**「在 … 的那一邊；越過 …」：

Their house is ～ that hill. We walked several miles ～ your house.

(w) **against**「靠著 …」：

The book is ～ the wall. The bicycle is leaning ～ the garage.

(x) **from**「離開 …」：

The school is a long way ～ our house. Is the bank far ～ the grocery store?

(y) **aboard, on board**「在 …（船、車、飛機）上」：

He has never been ～ a ship. He went home ～ a train.

(z) **alongside**「靠著 …（船、碼頭）的旁邊」：

The ship lies ～ the pier. The boats came ～ the ship.

參考：

(1) **on** 表示「在 … 上面」，而且有「直接與面接觸」的意思，如：

The book is *on* the desk.

over 表示「在 … 正上面」，沒有「與面接觸」的意思，如：

The ceiling is *over* our heads.

above 表示「在 … 上」或「比 … 高」，沒有 **on**「直接與面接觸」的意思，也沒有 over「垂直的在上面」的意思，如：

The sun rose *above* the horizon.

The airplane is flying *above* the clouds.

beneath 與 **underneath** 表示「在 … 下面」，與 on 相對，如：

The earth is *beneath* / *underneath* our feet.

under 表示「在正下面」，與 over 相對，如：

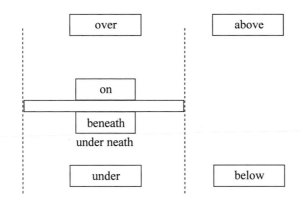

The ball is *under* the chair.

It is shady *under* the trees.

below 表示「在 … 下」或「比 … 低」，與 above 相對，如：

The sun set *below* the horizon.

Write your name *below* the line.

in 表示「在 … 裡面」；**by** 與 **beside** 表示「在 … 旁邊」；**near** 表示「（在）靠近 … （的地方）」；**against** 表示「靠著」；比較：

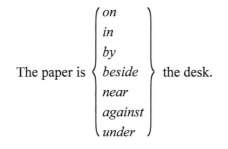

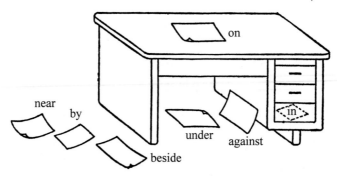

(2) **on** 表示「與面接觸」；**off** 表示「與面離開」。

The shade is $\begin{Bmatrix} on \\ off \end{Bmatrix}$ the lamp.

 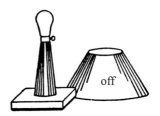

(3) **on** 表示「在 … 上面」；**over** 表示「遮在 … 上面」，有「覆蓋」的意思。

$\begin{Bmatrix} \text{The dish is } on \\ \text{The cloth is } over \end{Bmatrix}$ the table.

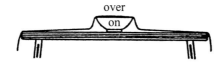

(4) **in** 表示「在比較大的地方（如國家、省、市）」；**at** 表示「在比較小的地方（如家、旅館）」。

I have been living $\begin{Bmatrix} in \text{ Taipei / Taiwan / China / the country} \\ at \text{ home / a hotel / Mucha （木柵）} \end{Bmatrix}$

for years.

on 表示「在 … 島」或「在 … 路」。比較：

They have been working $\begin{Bmatrix} in \text{ Taiwan.（省名）} \\ on \text{ Taiwan.（島嶼）} \end{Bmatrix}$

He lives $\begin{Bmatrix} in\ at \text{ No. 79, Mintsu Road.（門牌號碼）} \\ on \text{ Mintsu Road.（路名）} \end{Bmatrix}$

on 表示「與 … 接近」；**to** 表示「在 … 方向」；**off** 表示「在海上離 … 不遠的地方」。比較：

Tibet is *in* the south of Asia.

India is *on* the south of China.

Pakistan is *to* the south of China.

Ceylon is *off* the south of India.

(5) **in** 與 **inside** 表示「在 … 裡面」；**outside** 表示「在 … 外面」；**on (the) top**

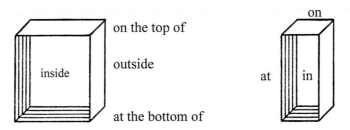

of 表示「在 … 的頂端」；**at the bottom of** 表示「在 … 的底部」。

(6) **in front of** 表示「在 … 前面」；**ahead of** 也表示「在 … 前面」，但是通常指運動中的事物；**behind, in back of, at the back of** 表示「在 … 後面」。

Jack is $\left\{\begin{array}{l}\text{standing } \textit{in front of}\\ \text{running } \textit{ahead of}\end{array}\right\}$ George.

There is a house *behind* / *in back of* / *at the back of* the house.

(7) **across** 表示「在 … 對面」；**beyond** 表示「在 … （邊遠的）那一邊」。

The bank is *across* the street.

My home town is far *beyond* the sea.

over 與 **across** 表示「橫過」；**all over** 與 **throughout** 表示「在 … 到處」。

There is a bridge *over* / *across* the river.

There is a drought *all over* / *throughout* the country.

(8) **around** 表示「在 … 的四周，圍繞 … 」；**about** 表示「在 … 附近」。

$\left\{\begin{array}{l}\text{She wore a necklace } \textit{around} \text{ her neck.}\\ \text{Her hair hung } \textit{about} \text{ her neck.}\end{array}\right.$

The children gathered $\left\{\begin{array}{l}\textit{around}\\ \textit{about}\end{array}\right\}$ the teacher.

(9) **between** 表示「在（二者之）間」；**among** 表示「在（三者以上之）間」。

He stood $\begin{cases} \textit{between} \text{ the } \textit{walls}. \\ \textit{among} \text{ the trees}. \end{cases}$

among 表示「在（同類事物之）間」；**amid (st)** 表示「在（異類事物之）間」。

I knew I was $\begin{cases} \textit{among} \text{ friends}. \\ \textit{amidst} \text{ enemies}. \end{cases}$

He was found $\begin{cases} \textit{among} \text{ the dead. (= He was dead.)} \\ \textit{amidst} \text{ the dead. (= He was alive.)} \end{cases}$

(10)**aboard** 與 **on board** 表示「在（船、飛機、火車）上面」

They went *aboard* the ship.

You'd better get *aboard* the train. It's about to leave.

alongside 表示「沿着或靠着（船、碼頭的）旁邊」；**alongside of** 表示「在 … 的旁邊，與 … 並排」。

The tug drew up *alongside* the freighter.

A car parked *alongside of* the curb.

The son fought *alongside of* his father.

習 題 438

在空白裡面填入 at, in 或 on。

1. New York is one of the greatest cities _____ the world.

2. It is _____ the state of New York.

3. I was born _____ Nanking _____ China.

4. The mailbox is _____ the corner.

5. The boy stood _____ a corner of the room.

6. _____ the road I met an old friend of mine.

7. I pass his house _____ my way to school.

8. I bought this book _____ a store _____ Taipei.

9. Sir Walter Scott, when a boy, attended the High School _____ Edinburgh _____ Scotland.

10. I frequently meet her _____ a friend's house.

11. Some children are playing _____ the street.

12. Is he _____ home? Is he _____ the house? No, he is _____ the garden.

13. Bob and I live _____ the same street.

14. How beautiful is the moonlight _____ the lake!

15. He lives _____ San Francisco. He lives _____ Green Street. He lives _____ 1236 Green Street.

16. I'll meet you _____ the information desk _____ the lobby of the hotel.

17. Tom is _____ breakfast now. Jack is still _____ bed.

18. Don't walk _____ the street. Walk _____ the sidewalk.

19. John was sitting _____ the sofa _____ the living room.

20. I go to work _____ the bus, but I like to travel _____ a train.

習　題　439

在空白裡面填入 above, below, over, under, on 或 beneath (underneath)。

1. Is the lamp _____ （上）the table? No, it hang _____ the table.

2. The beard grows _____ the chin. The moustache grows _____ the lip.

3. The sun has just sunk _____ the horizon.

4. He has a scar _____ his forehead, right _____ his left eye.

5. We lay down _____ a tree and took a rest.

6. Look at those flies _____ the ceiling.

7. Put the teapot _____ the fire.

8. The thick carpet made no noise _____ our feet.

9. How long can you remain _____ water?

10. I managed to keep my head _____ water.

11. The mother bent _____ the child and wept.

12. He wore a pair of spectacles _____ his nose.

13. They pulled their hats _____ their eyes, and sat moody and silent.

14. A tree spreads its branches _____ the roof.

15. They took the poor child from _____ （下）the fallen house.

16. Put a stamp _____ the envelope.

17. Put a pad _____ the rug.

18. The temperature is just _____（上）freezing.

19. The water is deepest _____（下）the bridge.

20. They wear a sort of turban _____ their heads.

21. He put a ring _____ her finger.

22. The water came _____（上）my mouth.

23. He wore a long coat that reached _____（下）his knees.

24. The door was locked, so I shoved the letter _____（下）the door.

25. Your score on the examination is well _____（上）average.

習 題 440

在空白裡填入 between, among, amid (st), inside 或 outside。

1. Martha is sitting _____ George and Jim

2. The letter is somewhere _____ these papers.

3. These plants should be kept _____（內）the house.

4. The chairs were left _____（外）the house all night.

5. They built a hut _____ the woods.

6. The books are _____ the book ends.

7. Mary was standing _____ the other girls.

8. _____ the books on the table was a small one bound in beautiful red leather.

9. I saw him _____ the crowd.

10. Hsinchu is situated _____ Taichung and Taipei.

11. His boy could not be found _____ the dead.

12. The money was concealed _____ the leaves of a book.

13. This paper has a large circulation _____ students.

14. It is raining. Don't go _____ the house.

15. He has always lived in China; he has never been the _____ country.

習　題　441

依照例句用不同的介詞把下面的句子改為相反的意義。

Examples:

Don't go inside the house.

→ *Don't go outside tke house.*

1. The tiger was *outside* the cage.

2. The car was running *ahead of* ours.

3. Our apartment is directly *over* yours.

4. The bicycle is *in front of* thecar.

5. He was standing *behind* me inthe cafeteria line.

6. Tell the servant to leave the suitcase *at the top of* the stairs.

7. What is there in the cabinet *under* the sink?

8. The temperature is now *below* freezing point.

9. The weight of the car is *above* two tons.

10. You will find the word *at the bottom of* the page.

習　題　442

在空白裡填入 before, behind, after, ahead of, in front of 或 in back of。

1. We were sitting ＿＿＿＿（後）you at the movies last night.

2. You'll find the newspaper ＿＿＿＿（前）the door.

3. The car was parked ＿＿＿＿（前）the house.

4. He was standing ＿＿＿＿（前）me in the line at the bank.

5. There is a grocery store ＿＿＿＿（後）the bank.

6. The dog trotted ＿＿＿＿ its master.

7. The dog ran ＿＿＿＿ the fox.

8. Shut the door ＿＿＿＿ you.

9. Put a question mark ＿＿＿＿ each question.

10. Never speak ill of a man ＿＿＿＿ his back.

參考：下面是一些常用的表示場所的介詞片語。

in the first place: "initially, as the primary reason"「第一」:

Why did you choose to come to this country *in the first place*?

in place of "instead of"「以代替」:

The teacher gave me a new exercise book *in place of* the old one I had just completed.

in (the) face of: "in the presence of, threatened by; despite"「在 ⋯ 前面，面臨；不顧」:

A coward retreats *in face of* danger.

Why do you insist on marrying her *in the face of* such opposition from your family?

in the presence of: "before"「在 ⋯ 前面」:

Mr. Buck signed the contract *in the presence of* witnesses.

by the side of: "close to; compared with"「在 ⋯ 的旁邊；與 ⋯ 比較」:

He is sitting *by the side of* the road.

She looked small *by the side of* her husband.

19-6. 表示「方向」與「運動」的介詞片語

(a) **to**：

① 「向，對（人或物）」

He pointed *to* the door.

I spoke (replied, turned, listened, wrote, called, shouted, etc.) *to* him.

② 「到（地方）」

He went (walked, returned, hurried, rushed, flew, etc.) *to* the place.

(b) **for**：「往（目的地）」

He left (started, departed, sailed, made, took off, set out, headed, was bound, etc.) *for* Japan last month.

(c) **toward(s)**：「朝（方向）」

He moved *towards* the door.

(d) **into**「進（裡面）」，**out of**「從 … 出」：

He went (ran, rushed, walked, stepped, etc.) $\begin{Bmatrix} into \\ out\ of \end{Bmatrix}$ the room.

(e) **up, down**：

① 「（垂直地）往 … 上 / 下」

go (come, run, etc.) ～ a hill (a ladder, the stairs, etc.); row (sail, etc.) ～ the stream (river, etc.); climb (go, etc.) ～ a tree (the mountain etc.).

② 「（水平地）往 … 過來（過去）」

go (come, run, walk, etc.) ～ the street (road, etc.)

(f) **on, onto**「到 … 上面」；**off, away from**「由 … 離開」

The cat jumped $\begin{Bmatrix} onto\ /\ on \\ off\ /\ away\ from \end{Bmatrix}$ the table.

(g) **across**：「從這一邊（端）到那一邊（端）」

go (walk, run, etc.) ～ the street (road, etc.); swim (row, get, etc.) ～ the river; drive ～ the town.

(h) **along**：「沿著」

walk (swim, sail, etc.) ～ the road (river, coast, etc.)

(i) **around, round**：

① 「繞著」

walk ～ the pond, dance ～ the fire, move ～ the sun.

② 「這裡那裡到處」

walk ～ the town (park, block, etc.); travel (roam, etc.) ～ the country.

③ 「迴避」

Drive *around* that big rock. Don't drive over it.

(j) **about**：「這裡那裡到處」

We walked *about* the town.

(k) **over**：「越過」

jump ～ the ditch (wall, etc.); go ～ the bridge.

(l) **through**：

   ① 「穿過」

    pass (go, etc.) 〜 a gate (door, window, tunnel, etc.); walk (drive, etc.) 〜 the park (town, etc.)

   ② 「遍及 "all over"」

    He traveled *through* / *all over* the country.

(m) **by, past**：「經過」

    A man passed *by* me.

    He ran *past* me.

(n) **at**：「對著」

    aim (fire, shoot, point, throw, etc.) 〜 something; look (gaze,stare, glare, wink, etc.) 〜 someone; laugh (smile, sneer, jeer, jest, frown) 〜 someone.

(o) **after**：「追趕」

    The police man ran *after* the thief.

參考：

(1) **up**「上」；**down**「下」；**around**「繞著」；**about**「這裡那裡到處」；**across**「越過」；**through**「穿過」；**onto**「到…上面」；**off, away from**「離開」。

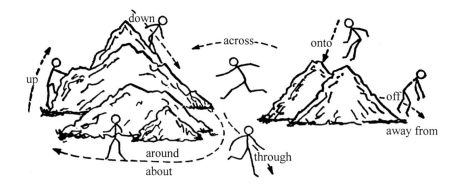

(2) **to** 含有「（最後）到達」的意思；**toward (s)** 只表示方向，不含到達的意思。
比較：

$$He \begin{Bmatrix} walked\ to \\ moved\ toward\ (s) \end{Bmatrix} the\ door.$$

(3) **to** 表示「方向」；**at** 表示「瞄準的目標」。比較：

$$He\ threw\ a \begin{Bmatrix} coin\ to \\ stone\ at \end{Bmatrix} the\ beggar.$$

(4) **by** 與 **past** 都表示「經過」，但是 **past** 常含有「很快地經過」的意思。比較：

> He walked *by* me without speaking.
>
> He walked *past* the house.
>
> He hurried *past* me without stopping to speak.

(5) **across** 表示「從一邊到另一邊」；**through** 表示「穿過」。

He swam *across* the river.

He bore a hole *through* the plank.

(6) **behind** 表示「在後面」；**after** 表示「在後面追趕」。比較：

$$Dick\ is\ running \begin{Bmatrix} behind \\ after \end{Bmatrix} George.$$

(7) **around** 與 **round** 可以通用，有「圍繞」、「環繞」、「繞過轉角」、「到處」
等意思。

They were sitting (*a*)*round* the table.（「圍繞」，位置）

The earth moves (*a*)*round* the sun.（「環繞」，運動）

He walked (*a*)*round* the corner.（「轉彎」）

She showed us (*a*)*round* the house.（「到處」）

(8) **into**「進」與 **out of**「出」在口語美語中常用 **in** 與 **out** 來代替。

He dived *in* (*to*) the swimming pool.

She looked *out* (*of*) the window.

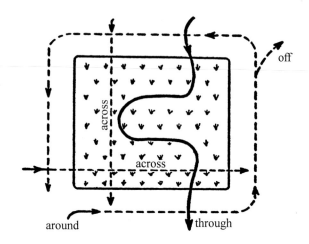

習 題 443

在空白裡填入 into, out of, inside, outside, in 或 at。

1. I walked _____（進）the room and sat down by the fireplace.

2. They ran_____（出）the burning building.

3. Jim dived _____ the swimming pool.

4. Hearing a shriek, I ran _____ the street.

5. He rushed _____ the house _____ the street.

6. The man drew his pistol _____ his pocket.

7. Pour the tea _____ the cup, and put some sugar _____ it.

8. Tobacco was introduced _____ Japan by the Portuguese.

9. I saw the shadow of a man standing _____（外）the window.

10. I never go to such places; I have never been _____ a theater.

習 題 444

在空白裡填入 along, across, beyond, through 或 over。

1. They live _____ the street from us.

2. We made our way _____ the crowd.

3. Flowers are growing _____ the road.

4. Their house is _____ that hill.

5. I once passed _____ that town.

6. This ship has sailed _____ the Pacific.

7. I noticed the plants that were growing _____ the stream.

8. His house is out in the country, several miles _____ the city limits.

9. Instead of going around by the road, I took a short cut _____ the field.

10. A bridge has been thrown _____ the river.

11. People were standing _____ the bridge, watching the river.

12. Is the house this side the bridge? No, it is a little way _____ the bridge.

習　題　445

在空白裡填入 around, about 或 against。

1. Let's take a walk _____ the block.

2. The boys stood _____ their teacher.

3. Men have sailed _____ the world.

4. The bookcases are _____ the wall.

5. He wore a handkerchief _____ his neck.

6. He was leaning _____ the wall.

7. I like to see happy faces _____ me.

8. Books and papers are lying _____ the room.

9. He lives _____ the corner.

10. Tie a rope _____ the post.

習　題　446

在空白裡填入 to, for 或 toward(s)。

1. He threw the book _____ the floor.

2. My brother has left _____ Taipei.

3. She stretched her hands _____ heaven.

4. The ship sails _____ Hong Kong on Friday.

5. As it was growing dark, we started _____ home.

6. I saw a man coming _____ me.

7. The house looks _____ the east.

8. They decided to move _____ the north.

9. Look _____ your right. You'll see it just left of the church.

10. He shut the door _____ my face.

習　題　447

在空白裡填入 in, on, to 或 of。

1. The sun rises _____ the east and sets _____ the west.

2. We were surrounded _____ every side.

3. We're living _____ the south now.

4. My hometown is south _____ Chicago.

5. The bank is _____ the left side of the street.

6. The little lake is _____ the east of the big lake.

7. We ran _____ the direction of the voice.

8. Yünnan lies _____ the south of China.

9. India lies _____ the south of China.

10. The Philippines lie _____ the south of Taiwan.

習　題　448

在空白裡填入 by, beside, to, near 或 past。

1. Sit _____ the fire and warm yourself.

2. I found my mother sitting _____ my bed.

3. The girl stood _____ her mother.

4. He passed _____ me without noticing me.

5. A bullet whistled _____ me.

6. The napkin is placed _____ the plate.

7. I sat reading _____ the window.

8. The house is close _____ the post office.

9. Who was the man that ran _____ you?

10. It is somewhere _____ Taipei.

習　題　449

用不同的介詞把下面的句子改為相反的義意。

1. The car drove *into* town in the middle of the night.

2. She walked slowly *toward* the door.

3. They walked *down* the street ringing merrily.

4. Suddenly the cat jumped *off* the table.

5. They sailed *up* theriver in a boat.

6. He came *to* Taipei *from* Tainan.

7. They have always wanted to move *out of* the city.

8. Bob was afraid of going *down* the ladder.

9. This is a letter *from* Jack *to* his girl friend Betty.

10. He was startled when the car moved rapidly *away from* him.

習　題　450

從括號裡面的介詞中把不適當的劃去。

1. They drove (about, at, around) Taipei City.

2. We drove (via, on, toward) Hsinchu.

3. The train went (up, across, over) the bridge.

4. We hurried (across, on top of, down) the street.

5. He walked (off, through, across) the room hurriedly.

6. He ran (down, into, from) the library.

7. They took a walk (onto, around, across, through) the park.

8. I am usually (in, at, on) church on Sunddy.

9. The ball rolled (through, around, off) the table.

10. The boat is sailing (above, through, across) the river.

11. His house is (in the middle of, near, ahead of) town.

12. The boy threw the stone (at, through, up) the window.

13. They saw her go (into, out of, onto) the restaurant.

14. The children ran (through, down, at) the street shouting.

15. The boy is lying (under, to, near) the tree.

16. Did the plane fly (over, around, off) the town?

17. Won't you come and sit (beside, by, at) me?

18. The stranger went (up, about, down) the stairs.

19. The monument is (beyond, in, at the top of) the hill.

20. Dick jumped (over, onto, down) the bicycle.

21. They were playing (into, in, inside) the house.

22. Please take that book (from, among, off) the shelf.

23. I can't find any shirts (into, at the bottom of, inside) my dresser drawer.

24. They finally decided to put the new train tracks (close to, to, beyond) the old ones.

25. The man entered the building (on, at, by) the front door.

習 題 451

在空白裡填入適當的介詞。

1. Are you going _____ the concert tomorrow?

2. They live _____ the same roof.

3. He passed _____ me without speaking to me.

4. In giving dates, we usually place the month _____ the day.

5. She spread a blanket _____ the grass.

6. The ball hit me _____ the head.

7. He turned his back _____ me.

8. Take the road _____ the right, and take the first turn _____ your left.

9. He sat _____ the table and began to eat.

10. The railway station is _____ the other side of the river.

11. The river flows _____ the bridge.

12. The soldiers marched _____ the town.

13. I put my book _____ the drawer.

14. Mexico lies _____ the south of America.

15. A river runs _____ the city.

16. The bank is close _____ the grocery store.

17. Is the bank far _____ the post office?

18. Is your car parked next _____ the curb?

19. Would you mind stopping _____ the bakery for some bread _____ your way home?

20. We walked _____ the town looking at all the sights.

21. Don't go _____ the street in the middle of the block.

22. It is harder to run _____ the stairs than to run _____ them.

23. Enter _____ the north gate.

24. The dog jumped _____ the man's throat.

25. The boy threw a rock _____ the bird.

26. Students cannot smoke _____ school bounds.

27. We walked several miles _____ your house.

28. He made a sandwich by putting a piece of cheese _____ two pieces of bread.

29. Mr. Kelly is usually _____ work _____ the daytime and _____ home _____ the evening.

30. They are _____ Rome now. I believe they are staying _____ the Majestic Hotel.

31. He go _____ his car and drove _____ the street.

32. I told the children to play _____ the sidewalk and not to go _____ the street.

33. I can't find the book. It must be _____ the shelf.

34. It would not be safe to let the lion get _____ his cage.

35. Jean was not _____ class yesterday. I think she was sick.

36. It gets very cold here _____ winter. In fact, it'shardly ever _____ freezing.

37. The boys left their bicycles leaning _____ the wall.

38. Her hair hung _____ her neck.

39. The earth moves _____ the sun.

40. He bored a hole _____ the wall.

41. His fame spread _____ all lands.

42. He is _____ his enemies.

43. He is _____ his friends.

44. We went _____ the river _____ a boat.

45. The Thames flows _____ the city of London.

46. London is situated _____ the Thames.

47. We lost sight of him _____ trees.

48. We lost sight of him _____ the wood.

49. I constantly thought of the home I had left _____ me.

50. We sailed _____ and _____ the river.

51. I was not allowed to enter, so I had to wait _____ the gate.

52. He came in _____ a secret door.

53. There was a hole _____ the ground.

54. I found a nail stuck _____ the tire.

55. Write _____ every other line.

56. There was a pillow _____ his head.

57. We trod on something _____ our feet.

58. The dog was _____ the chain.

59. The road leads _____ Tainan.

40. There are many stars _____ the sky.

19-7. 表示「路程」與「距離」的介詞片語

(a) **for**：表示經過若干路程，如果直接在動詞後面即可以省略。

　　We walked (*for*) three miles.

　　The road is lined with trees *for* ten miles.

(b) **from**：表示起點「從」

a mile (ten miles, a long way, etc.) ∼ here (there, etc.)

(c) **from … to …**：表示起點與終點「從 … 到 … 」

We walked (rode, drove, etc.) *from* the City Hall *to* the station.

(d) **as far as**：「一直到某一地點」

We walked *as far as* Fourteenth Street.

(e) **off**：「離開（道路、海岸等）」

a little way ∼ the road; three miles ∼ the coast (the seashore).

(f) **in the distance**：「在（遙）遠的地方」

A ship could be seen *in the distance*. (= far away)

at a distance, at some distance：「在離一段距離的地方」

The picture looks better *at a distance*. (= when placed not too near)

at a distance of (ten miles)：「在（十哩）外」

The explosion may be heard *at a distance of* ten miles.

習 題 452

在空白裡填 for, from, off, in 或 at。

1. We drove on _____ miles without meeting anyone.

2. We saw a ship _____ the distance.

3. He lives a little way _____ here.

4. He lives _____ some distance from my house.

5. We went together _____ a short distance, and then parted company.

6. A gun may be heard _____ a distance of twenty miles.

7. The ship sank three miles _____ the east coast of Africa.

8. Washington is two hundred and fifty miles _____ New York.

9. He is known to everybody _____ ten miles around.

10. The battle was fought _____ the mouth of the river.

19-8. 表示「方法」或「狀態」的介詞片語

(a) **by**：

(1) 交通與電訊工具等（注意名詞前面不加冠詞）

He came *by* plane (car, bus, train, streetcar, subway, boat, ship, foot, etc.)

It arrived *by* airmail (regular mail, express (mail), messenger, air, land, water, etc.).

They kept in touch *by* telephone (phone, radio, letter, etc.).

He earns his living *by* hard work.

learn 〜 heart (experience, ear); know 〜 sight (name, face); get 〜 force (persuasion); 〜 hook or 〜 crook「用種種方法 ‘ 〜 one means or another’」etc.

(2) 與抽象名詞連用，表示狀態「 … 地」

We met quite *by* chance.

〜 luck, 〜 good fortune, 〜 mistake, 〜 accident, 〜 turns,「輪流」〜 fits (and starts)「一陣陣地，不規則地」，〜 leaps and bounds「極迅速地」, etc.

(3) 表示行為者「被」

He was killed *by* his enemy with a pistol.

(b) **on**：交通工具，糧食等

He is going *on* foot (a bicycle, horseback, camelback, tiptoe, a train, a bus, a ship, etc.).

They live *on rice* (bread, a small income, etc.).

live (feed, dine, feast, subsist, prey, etc.) 〜 some food; talk with someone 〜 / over the telephone, listen to the news 〜 / over the radio, see a program 〜 / over TV.

(c) **with**：

(1) 「用（工具）」，相反詞是 without

He wrote it *with* apencil (pen, ball pen, etc.).

He was killed *with* a knife (sword, pistol, gun, etc.).

(2) 與抽象形容詞轉來的名詞連用，表示態度「⋯ 地」

They spoke French *with* fluency.

～ calmness, ～ emotion, ～ difficulty, ～ ease, ～ interest, ～ pleasure, ～ satisfaction, ～ wonder, ～ haste, ～ care, ～ diligence, ～ one's head down, ～ tears streaming down one's face, ～ all speed, etc.

He answered *without* hesitation.

The dog attacked her *without* warning.

(d) **in**：

(1) 材料，聲音，文字等

He wrote it *in* pencil (ink, etc.).

write ～ English, lecture ～ Chinese, speak ～ a low voice (tone), paint ～ water-colors (oils), work ～ metals, cast ～ silver, carve ～ wood, embroider ～ gold, etc.

(2) 與抽象名詞連用，表示情況「⋯ 地」

They wished to die *in* peace.

～ sorrow, ～ joy, ～ anger, ～ earnest, ～ jest, ～ fun, ～ play, ～ haste, ～ a hurry, ～ good (ill) humor, ～ high (low) spirits, ～ danger, ～ debt, ～ need, ～ misfortune, ～ adversity, ～ good (poor) health, ～ private, ～ secret, ～ public, ～ general, ～ particular, ～ detail, ～ full, etc.

(e) **like**：表示相似「像」

He walks *like* an at hlete.

He speaks English *like* an American.

His singing sounds *like* an animal howling.

(f) **as**：表示身份「以 ⋯ 資格或地位」

He works (acts, serves) *as* a waiter.

She was famous (known, well-known) *as* an actress.

(g) **through**: 表示中間人或媒介「透過」

He spoke *through an* interpreter.

I learned of the position *through* a newspaper advertisement.

(h) **by, by way of, via**:「經過」

Leave *by* the rear door, please.

We went to New York *by way of* Baltimore.

This plane goes to Tokyo *via* Okinawa.

(i) **by means of, by virtue of, by dint of, by force of**:「用 … 手段，靠」

He gained his supremacy *by means of* bribery.

The actor achieved his fame *by virtue of* his skill.

The boy got through college *by dint of* sheer determination.

Hard things are made easy *by force of* habit.

習　題　453

在空白裡填入 by, in 或 on。

1. Did Mr. Brown go to Washington { ＿＿＿ car / ＿＿＿ a car } ?

2. Do you come to school { ＿＿＿ bus / ＿＿＿ a bus } ?

3. Mary went to Taipei { ＿＿＿ train / ＿＿＿ a train } .

4. The Darwins made the trip { ＿＿＿ plane / ＿＿＿ a plane } .

5. Tony came to New York { ＿＿＿ ship / ＿＿＿ a ship } .

6. He traveled { ＿＿＿ bicycle / ＿＿＿ a bicycle } the whole way.

7. I will let you know my decision ＿＿＿ telephone.

8. Did you see Harry ＿＿＿ television last night?

9. The two expeditions kept in touch ＿＿＿ radio.

10. I heard news _____ the radio this morning.

11. American teen-agers talk _____ the phone a lot.

12. Some day it will be possible to send news around the world _____ television.

習 題 454

在空白裡填入 by, with, in 或 on。

1. The bridge was carried away _____ a flood.

2. She was stabbed _____ a knife.

3. He stirred his coffee _____ a spoon.

4. The ship is lighted throughout _____ electricity.

5. Can you read _____ the light of the moon?

6. Is it true that he is living _____ charity?

7. The lecture was given _____ German.

8. The figure is carved _____ marble.

9. He spoke _____ a low tone of voice.

10. The steam-engine was invented _____ James Watt.

11. He opened the door _____ a key.

12. He painted her pictures _____ oils.

13. The silk-worm feeds _____ the leaves of the mulberry.

14. He marked his place _____ a bookmark.

15. He addressed us _____ these words.

16. Your house won't be struck _____ lightning if you put up lightning rods.

17. They spoke _____ whispers, so I could not catch a word of what they said.

18. I thought the portrait was done _____ charcoal, but he said it was done _____ ink.

19. You cannot write it _____ a ball pen; it must be written _____ ink.

20. I know them _____ sight, but not _____ name.

習 題 455

在空白裡填入 by, in, with 或 like。

1. He succeeded _____ sheer luck.

2. He eyed the spinach _____ distaste.

3. She walks _____ a dancer.

4. He looked at us _____ surprise.

5. He retired from his job _____ reluctance.

6. That noise sounded _____ a firecracker.

7. She lives her life _____ satisfaction, even _____ pleasure.

8. I found him at home _____ good luck.

9. She acted _____ a spoiled child.

10. He spoke more _____ sorrow than anger.

11. I would do you a favor _____ pleasure.

12. It looks _____ spring today.

13. They reached the summit _____ great difficulty.

14. He eats _____ a pig.

15. I have learned _____ experience the miseries of being _____ debt.

16. He is usually very idle, and studies only _____ fits and starts.

17. We greet the opening flowers of spring _____ joy.

18. He looked on _____ his hands in his pockets.

19. I will explain it _____ full later on.

20. Somehow, he managed to do the boring job _____ enthusiasm.

習 題 456

依照例句把副詞改為介詞片語。

Examples:

He accomplished it easily. → He accomplished it *with ease*.

1. He speaks English fluently.

2. He improves very rapidly.

3. The sailor marched off triumphantly.

4. She took up the child tenderly.

5. She spoke calmly.

習　題　457

依照例句用 with 連接下列每一對句子。

Examples:

> She looked in my face.
> Her tears were streaming down her face. $\Bigg\}$ →
>
> She looked in my face *with her tears streaming down her face.*

1. They were running.
   Their ears were erect.

2. The dog ran away.
   His tail was between his legs.

3. She followed her guide.
   Her head was down.

4. He was sitting on the steps.
   His back was against the wall.

5. He was seated on the bench.
   His arms were resting on his knees.

6. She sat there.
   Her eyes were fixed on the ground.

7. I lay down to sleep.
   A heavy weight had been removed from my mind.

8. The servant found Sir Isaac Newton standing before the fire.
   The egg was in his hand.
   His watch was boiling in the saucepan.

習 題 458

依照例句改寫下列各句。

Examples:

They got there; they took the plane.

→ *They got there by (taking the) plane.*

He opened the door; he didn't use a key.

→ *He opened the door without (using) a key.*

She taught her students; she used a blackboard.

→ *She taught her students with a blackboard.*

1. He learned English; he listened to the radio.

2. She cannot manage; she doesn't have servants.

3. I reached his family; I telephoned.

4. She left for the States; she didn't telephone.

5. He cannot eat; he uses chopsticks.

6. I can tell his feelings; I look at his face.

7. They got to work; they rode the subway.

8. I can't teach; I don't use a blackboard.

9. He ended his story; he laughed.

10. They attacked; they didn't give any warning.

11. She returned her application; she sent it through the mail.

12. He left the office; he didn't promise anything.

參考：

(1) by 表示「手段」，可以與動名詞連用，形成狀態副詞。

How did he succeed? He succeeded *by working hard*.「靠努力」

by 又可以表示「交通或電信工具」。這個時候，從面的名詞常省去冠詞。

How did they communicate? They communicate *by radio*.「用無線電」

(2) with 表示「手段、工具」或「態度」；只能與名詞連用，不能與動名詞連用。

How do you see? We see *with our eyes*.「用眼睛」

How did she kill the man? She killed him *with a knife*. 「用小刀」

How did he answer? He answered *with a smile*. 「（面）帶笑容地」

(3) without 表示「沒有」或「不用」；可以與動名詞連用，也可以與名詞連用。

How did she answer? She answered *without* $\begin{cases} smiling. \\ a\ smile. \end{cases}$ 「（面）無笑容地」

習 題 459

依照例句改寫下列各句。

Examples:

He drove carefully. → *He drove with care.*

She drove carelessly. → *She drove without care.*

1. They spoke proudly.	2. She passed easily.
3. He didn't act honorably.	4. You did it honestly.
5. I contribute regularly.	6. The soprano sang beautifully.
7. He didn't study diligently.	8. She fought furiously.

9. They listened to the girl sympathetically.

10. They didn't work enthusiastically.

11. He tried hopelessly.

12. She talked very charmingly.

參考：with 與 without 可以與抽象名詞 joy, pleasure, force, patience, caution, care, pride, ease, difficulty, honor 等連用，形成一個表示狀態的副詞片語：

The teacher explained to the students *with patience* (= patiently).

He proceeded *with caution* (= cautiously).

She talked *with a lot of charm* (= very charmingly).

19-9. 表示「原因、理由」或「動機、目的」的介詞片語

(a) **from**：

① 表示直接的原因「由於」

I was much fatigued *from* having worked all day long.

　　　　～ this (that) cause.

② 表示一般的動機「由於」

He worked hard *from* a desire to please his parents.

∼ a motive (desire, necessity, consideration, sense of duty, etc.)

(b) **through**：表示間接的或偶然的原因「由於，因為」

I got into difficulty *through* helping him.

∼ fault (neglect, negligence, carelessness, etc.)

(c) **for**：

① 表示理由「由於 … 理由，因為」

I am angry with you *for* doing such a thing.

∼ this (that, etc.) reason; ∼ fear (lack, want, etc.) of.

② 表示目的「為了 …（目的）」

We went to the park *for* a walk.

∼ the purpose of, ∼ the sake of, ∼ the good of, ∼ the welfare of, ∼ the benefit of, etc.

(d) **out of**：表示特殊的動機

He said it *out of* pity.

∼ curiosity (pity, charity, generosity, politeness, mischief, impatience, spite, etc.)

(e) **with**：表示內在的理由而顯露在外表者「由於，因為」

He trembled *with* fear.

∼ fear (envy, joy, grief, rage, passion, cold, weakness, success, etc.)

(f) **because of**：「因為」

I couldn't come *because of* the rain.

due to：「為了」，常用在 be 動詞後面。

The accident was *due to* careless driving.

owing to：「為了」

He had to change jobs *owing to* the high cost of living.

on account of：「由於 …（理由）」，「因為 …（緣故）」

I couldn't go *on account of* the storm.

on the grounds of：「以 … 為理由」

Mrs. Brown got a divorce *on the grounds* of desertion.

by reason of：「憑 … 的理由」，「為了」

The speaker was absent *by reason of* illness.

in consequence of：「由於 …（的結果）」，「因為 …（的緣故）」

He was dismissed *in consequence of* his bad conduct.

(g) **with the intention of**：「以 … 為目的」，「打算」

He did it *with the intention of* bringing you into trouble.

with the view of：「以 … 為目的」，「希望 … 而」

I did it *with the view of* saving you trouble.

with a view to (V-ing)：「以 … 為目的」，「希望 … 而」

They went there *with a view to* discovering the truth.

with an eye to (V-ing)：「指望著」「為 … 打算才」

She studied *with an eye to* gaining a scholarship.

in hopes of：「希望著」，「期待者」

They came *in hopes of* getting some money.

in order to (V)：「為 … 起見」

They came *in order to* get some money.

on purpose to (V)：「為了故意使」

He said it *on purpose to* annoy me.

習　題　460

在空白裡填入表示原因、理由的介詞 from, through 或 for。

1. We lost ourselves _____ not knowing the way.

2. The boy was punished _____ stealing.

3. I have succeeded _____ your help.

4. I cannot see anything _____ the fog.

5. It happened _____ no fault of mine.

6. He could not go abroad _____ want of money.

7. He died _____ some unknown cause.

8. The boys ran away _____ fear.

9. We trembled _____ his safety.

10. He lost his place _____ neglect of duty.

11. The school was not opened _____ lack of funds.

12. Smoking becomes a necessity _____ habit.

13. I refused his offer _____ various reasons.

14. I got into trouble _____ helping him.

15. What can be his reason _____ doing such a thing?

16. You were studying when I came, so I went away _____ fear of disturbing you.

17. The workman died _____ the explosion.

18. He was rewarded _____ saving the girl's life.

19. It was all _____ your being late that we missed the train.

20. Men often succeed _____ failure.

習 題 461

在空白裡填入表示「原因，理由，動機，目的」的介詞：from, for, out of, through, with。

1. I went to see it _____ curiosity.

2. They obey only _____ fear.

3. Mr. Brown stayed home _____ consideration for his wife.

4. He works hard _____ a desire to earn his own living.

5. The woman refused _____ pride.

6. He became rich _____ hard work.

7. Mr.Bruce won't go _____ fear of making his wife angry.

8. I do not read _____ amusement.

9. I spare him _____ pity for his children.

10. John did this _____ a sense of duty.

11. He stole the money _____ his children, not _____ himself.

習　題　462

在空白裡填入適當的介詞。

1. _____ the sake _____ saving a few dollars, Tom walks to work.

2. He traveled _____ the benefit _____ his health.

3. Owing _____ the high cost of living, Mr. Brownell had to change jobs.

4. The project was undertaken _____ the purpose _____ housing poor people.

5. I went there _____ a view _____ visiting the exhibition.

6. He got up early _____ order to catch the first train.

7. _____ the good _____ the country we all ought to vote.

8. He cannot come to the meeting _____ account _____ illness.

9. They hate him because _____ his power and riches.

10. He has succeeded _____ dint _____ perseverance, energy and hard work.

11. Thanks _____ his care, we are safe, sound and happy.

12. They won the day, but only _____ virtue _____ hard fighting.

13. I did it _____ the view _____ saving your trouble.

14. We live _____ hopes _____ better fortune next time.

15. I came here _____ purpose to see you.

16. She bought it _____ he intention _____ selling it again.

17. A party was given _____ honor _____ Dr. Hill.

18. What did you say _____ answer _____ her question?

19. We finally found the house _____ the help _____ a map.

20. They are going to erect a monument _____ memory _____ the dead.

21. _____ consequence _____ his bad conduct he was dismissed.

22. The speaker was absent _____ reason _____ illness.

23. Mrs. Bryant thanked the speaker _____ behalf _____ the members.

24. I came here _____ the object _____ seeing you.

25. I am giving him Chinese lessons _____ exchange _____ English lessons.

26. _____ lack _____ something else to do, we went to the movies.

27. Thoughts are expressed _____ means _____ speech.

28. The houses were falling to pieces _____ want _____ care and a little paint.

29. John left New York and went to San Francisco _____ way Chicago.

30. They obey _____ fear _____ being punished.

31. The change in the rules was made _____ the interest _____ students with little money.

32. Most things can be made easy _____ force _____ habit.

33. He spoke _____ support _____ the plan.

34. They didn't give him heavy work _____ consideration _____ his youth.

35. He worked for weeks _____ behalf _____ the Community Chest.

36. I must say, _____ justice _____ him, that he has kept his word.

37. The young man wrote a poem _____ praise _____ his sweetheart.

38. What did you say _____ reply _____ the boy's question?

39. The group went _____ search _____ the lost child.

40. His failure was due _____ his laziness.

41. He was granted a pension _____ reward _____ his services.

42. Business is neglected owing _____ the excitement caused _____ the election.

習　題　463

依照例句把表示「原因 ‧ 理由」的副詞子句改成由 because of 或 on account of 帶頭的介詞片語。

Examples:

They didn't buy the house because the price was too high.

→ *They didn't buy the house because of / on account of the high price.*

He was upset because he lost the watch.

→ *He was upset because of / on account of his losing the watch.*

1. He was tired because the hour was late.

2. She was unhappy because she received a poor grade.

3. They didn't buy the house because its rooms were small.

4. He couldn't sleep because you were talking loudly outside.

5. He felt depressed because he was having personal problems.

6. I was worried because you did not arrive in time.

7. I have trouble walking because I have had a bad fall.

8. He got into trouble because we didn't warn him in advance.

9. She had trouble getting to see the play because the demand for tickets was great.

10. I couldn't hear what you said because there was noise in the room.

19-10. 其他介詞片語

(1)「結果」：**into, in, to**

Poverty led him *into* stealing.

That affair ended (resulted) *in* his dismissal.

Ideological rifts eventually led *to* military hostility.

broken (fallen, crushed, smashed, etc.) ～ pieces; burnt ～ ashes, reduced ～ ruins, fight ～ the last man.

(2)「伴隨」：**with, together with, along with, in company with, in conjunction with**「跟」，「和」，「連同」

Mary went *with* her mother to do some shopping.

brought my umbrella *with* me.

I am selling the house, *together with* the furniture.

Bob and John asked me to walk *along with* them.

I traveled in Europe *in company with* my uncle.

He opened a store *in conjunction with* his relative.

without 表示與 **with** 相反的意思。

Mary's mother went shopping *without* her.

He came to the office *without* his briefcase.

Betty went to the movies *without* telling her mother.

(3) 「除外」：**besides**, **in addition to**, **as well as**「除了 … 外（還有）」

Besides his salary, he has a large income.

Besides going to the movies, Mary ate her dinner at a restaurant.

Margaret is studying French *in addition to* German.

In addition to swimming, he likes tennis.

Henry *as well as* Tom is going with us.

Betty is working *as well as* going to school.

(4) 「除外」：**except**, **but**, **other than**, **with the exception of**, **save**「除了 … 以外」；常與 all, no, none, no one, nothing (-body, -where), everything (-body, -one, -where), anything (-body, -one, -where)，或含有否定意味的問句連用。

Except his salary, he has no regular income.

We all went *except* Tom.

We saw nothing *except* sea.

No one *but* a fool would do such a thing.

Who *but* a fool would do such a thing?

None *other than* my parents can help me.

How *else* can we come than on foot?

All is lost *save* honor.

There was not a sound *save* that from time to time a bird called.

(5) 「代替」：**instead of**, **in place of**, **rather than**「代替」，「不 … 而 … 」

He decided to have tea *instead of* coffee for breakfast.

Instead of going to the movies, Mary stayed home.

Why don't you use my book *in place of* the one you lost?

Rather than wait(ing) up for her husband, she went to bed early.

(6) 「反對」：**despite**, **notwithstanding**, **in spite of**, **regardless of**「不管」，「不顧」

Despite his age (= although he is old), he still enjoys skiing.

He kept on working *in spite of* his illness (= although he was ill).

We started, *notwithstanding* the rain.

They bought the jewels *regardless of* cost.

for all, **after all**, **with all** 表示「儘管 'in spite of all'」

For all (or *After all*) his efforts, he failed.

For all (or *With all*) his money, he was not happy.

(7) 「**關於**」：**about** 與 **of**「有關」，常用在 speak, tell, talk, hear, learn, know, think, dream, write, read 等動詞後面。

Before we hire a secretary, we want to know something *about* her background and
　　experience.

比較：

> Have you heard *of* any such person?「聽人提起」
>
> Have you heard *about* anything about him?「聽人談論」

> He spoke *of* you. (= He mentioned you.)「他提到你。」
>
> He spoke *about* you. (= He said something about you.)
>
> 　「他說了些有關你的話。」

> I didn't think *of* it. (= It didn't occur to me.)
>
> 　「我沒有想到這件事。」
>
> I haven't thought *about* it. (= I haven't considered it.)
>
> 　「我沒有考慮這件事。」

On 表示「（與）有關（的問題）"on the subject of"」，常用在 speak, lecture, debate, touch, decide, agree, reflect, comment, congratulate 等動詞後面。

The lecturer spoke *on* Poe yesterday.

They have agreed *on* a plan.

I want to congratulate you *on* your promotion.

concerning, **respecting**, **regarding** 是比較正式的用語。

He said nothing $\begin{cases} about \\ concerning \\ respecting \\ regarding \end{cases}$ the matter.

considering 表示「以 … 而論 "taking into account of, when you think about"」。

He is very strong and well, *considering* his age.

as for 表示「至於 "speaking of"」，常用在句首；**as to, as regards, as concerns** 表示「關於 "concerning"」，句首、句中都可以用。

As for me, I am quite satisfied. You had better leave.

As for your friend, you'd better take him with you. I don't know anything *as to* the others.

Now, *as regards* money what is to be done?

其他表示「關於」的介詞有 **with / in respect to, in respect of, with / in regard to, with / in relation to, with / in reference to, in connection with** 等

(8) 「**按照**」：**according to, in accordance with** 「依照」，「根據」

He will be punished *according to* the seriousness of his crime.

According to the newspapers, the strike will be settled tomorrow.

In accordance with custom, they bowed to their teacher.

You must play the game *in accordance with* the rules.

(9) 「**條件**」：**incase of, in the event of** 「萬一（有）」，「以防」

That extinguisher is to beused *in case of* fire.

All his property will go to charities *in the event of* his death.

習 題 464

在空白填入 with, without, besides, except, instead of 或 in spite of。

1. _____ his salary, he has no regular income.

2. _____ his salary, he has a large income.

3. We cannot live _____ air.

4. Why don't you come _____ us?

5. I would do anything _____ that.

6. _____ you there may be some who have seen a whale.

7. All of them went _____ myself. (= All and myself)

8. All went _____ myself. (= All, but not myself)

9. I went by train _____ by plane.

10. They drove for hours _____ stopping.

11. They went swimming, _____ the rain.

12. Take your umbrella _____ you.

13. _____ studying, he was just smoking.

14. They were happy _____ being poor.

15. He cannot see _____ his glasses.

16. I will go _____ you

17. _____ swimming and sailing, he enjoys fighting.

18. There was another visitor _____ me.

19. I can't do it _____ your help.

20. We succeeded _____ all difficulties.

習　題　465

在空白裡填入適當的介詞。

1. According _____ the papers, our export increases every year.

2. A cold climate, together _____ rocky soil, makes this country poor.

3. I want something to eat along _____ noodles.

4. _____ addition _____ Chinese we have to study a second foreign language.

5. _____ the exception _____ Harry, all the boys were anxious to go.

6. Betty is working _____ well _____ going to school.

7. He came _____ company _____ a group of boys.

8. We use chopsticks _____ place _____ knives and forks.

9. _____ all you say, I still like him.

10. _____ all his wealth, he is not a happy man.

11. _____ all his labors, he failed.

12. We have good news _____ respect _____ your promotion.

13. _____ regard _____ your last question, I will make this statement.

14. Regardless _____ what you say, I am going.

15. I have nothing to say _____ reference _____ that incident.

16. You will study vocabulary _____ connection _____ reading.

17. This sound occurs _____ conjunction _____ other sounds.

18. _____ regards money, I have enough.

19. You must play the game _____ accordance _____ the rules.

20. We must plan _____ relation _____ the future.

習 題 466

把括號裡面不適當的介詞（片語）劃去。

1. He decided to learn English (*instead of, besides, except*) French.

2. She got a red coat (*in spite of, in additionto, instead of*) a black one.

3. He gave the money to the poor (*according to, in accordance with, in respect to*) his father's wish.

4. They study geography (*together with, as well as, concerning*) history.

5. (*Despite, Regardless of, Except*) what you say, I still feel doubtful.

6. We must work and rest (*with, according to*) schedules.

7. They showed great anxiety (*concerning, as to, with*) their retired allowance.

8. She went (*together with, along with, without, about*) her sister to visit her aunt.

9. (*For all, With all, After all*) his wealth, he was unhappy.

10. (*For all, In spite of, In respect to*) his efforts, he failed.

11. Please go downtown (*except, without*) me.

12. George was determined to finish school (*despite, according to, inspite of*) his father's opposition.

13. We know little (*concerning, about, with*) her except that her family is very rich.

14. Why don't you use my book (*in place of, regardless of, instead of*) the one you lost?

15. Now, (*as to, as regards, as well as*) money what is to be done?

16. He bought it (*notwithstanding, despite, as for*) the high price.

17. They said nothing (*as to, as for, concerning*) wages.

18. (*Instead of, According to, Because of*) that magazine article, the government official

is thinking of resigning.

19. He has nothing (*except*, *despite*, *but*) his salary to depend on.

20. We have good news (*concerning*, *in respect to*, *despite*) your promotion.

習　題　467

在空白裡填入適當的介詞，使上下兩個句子表達相同的意思。

1. If there is no health, happiness is impossible.

= _____ health, happiness is impossible.

2. Though he was sick, he finished the job.

= He finished the job _____ being sick.

3. He is working indoors; he should be out playing instead.

= He should be out playing _____ working indoors.

4. John went to the movies; he ate at a restaurant besides.

= _____ going to the movies, John ate at a restaurant.

5. The moment she heard the news, she cried out.

= _____ hearing the news, she cried out.

6. A girl who has long hair came to see you while you were away.

= A girl _____ long hair came to see you while you were away.

7. He went away and did not say good-bye.

= He went away _____ saving good-bye.

8. Whenever he speaks English, he makes mistakes.

= He cannot speak English _____ making mistakes.

9. They never meet but they quarrel.

= They never meet _____ quarreling.

10. None but my friends are willing to help me.

= None other _____ my friends are willing to help me.

習　題　468

把介詞片語與意義相近的副詞連起來。

1. in fact	(a) especially
2. at last	(b) accidentally
3. at once	(c) easily
4. without warning	(d) actually
5. at times	(e) certainly
6. by chance	(f) immediately
7. above all	(g) suddenly
8. with ease	(h) finally
9. for good	(i) occasionally
10. for sure	(j) permanently

習　題　469

依照例句把表示「讓步」的副詞子句改成由 in spite of 或 despite 帶頭的介詞片語。

Examples:

Although it was raining, they went to the party.

　　→ *In spite of / Despite the rain, they went to the party.*

Even though it was crowded, I found a seat.

　　→ *In spite of / Despite the crowd, I found a seat.*

Although they were late, they went to the party.

　　→ *In spite of / Despite being late, they went to the party.*

Even though I called him, he didn't stop to talk to me.

　　→ *In spite of / Despite my calling him, he didn't stop to talk to me.*

1. Although she had a bad cold, she went to class.

2. Even though it was high-priced, he bought the car.

3. Although I came late, I found a seat.

4. Even though he was rude, I tried to be agreeable.

5. Though their uniforms were warm, the soldiers shivered in the snow.

6. Even though his parents disapproved, he took the job.

7. Although he seldom studies, he gets good grades.

8. Though I mentioned it several times, he couldn't remember my name.

9. Even though she showed some skill, she was an unsatisfactory secretary.

10. Although she doesn't have the necessary skills, she wants asecretarial job.

11. Even though he had just read the book, he couldn't remember the names of the characters.

12. Although it was a late hour, they went on talking.

13. Though he expressed his love for her, she refused to marry him.

14. Although the weather was unbearably hot, they played tennis all afternoon.

15. Even though he has never been to Japan, he speaks very fluent Japanese.

習 題 470

依照例句把表示「條件」的副詞子句改成由 in case of 帶頭的介詞片語。

Examples:

　　　　If you are in difficulty, please dial this number.

　　　　　→ *In case of difficulty, please dial this number.*

　　　　I'll give you a key in case you get back first.

　　　　　→ *I'll give you a key in case of your getting back first.*

1. If it rains, they can't go.

2. You must consult a doctor in case you fall ill.

3. Take warm clothes in case the weather is cold.

4. In case a fire breaks out, ring the alarm bell.

5. Give us a call in case you have a motor trouble.

6. I had better bring the umbrella with me in case the weather turns bad.

7. Take this medicine three times a day if you have a bad cold.

8. Promptly notify the police in case a sudden emergency arises.

9. In case he arrives before I get back, please ask him to wait.

10. Please forward my mail to the following address if I am away.

第20章
動詞的修飾語：副詞子句

20-1. 副詞子句

副詞子句（adverbial clause）由**從屬連詞**（subordinator），如 when, whenever, while, as, before, after, until, till, since, once, now that, as soon as, where, wherever, as far as, as if, as though, in that, so that, so … that, such … that, that, in order that, lest, because, in, as much as, if, unless, in case, provided (that), so longas, although, though, even though, even if, whereas, whoever, whomever, whatever, whichever, however 等與句子合成。

Adverbial Clause（副詞子句）	
Subordinator （從屬連詞）	Sentence （句子）
when	I entered
before	it struck eight
so that	he could see better
if	he comes
though	it was raining

副詞子句最主要的功用是修飾動詞（組），例如：

He arrived *before it struck eight*.

He pushed his way to the front *so that he could see better*.

I will tell him *if he comes*.

She went there *though it was raining*.

差不多所有的副詞子句都可以出現在句尾與句首兩個位置。比較：

⎧ He was reading *when I entered*.
⎨
⎩ *When I entered*, he was reading.

$$\begin{cases} \text{I will tell him } \textit{if he comes.} \\ \textit{If he comes,} \text{ I will tell him.} \end{cases}$$

有時候，還可以出現在句中的位置。比較：

$$\begin{cases} \text{We didn't dream that anyone would object } \textit{until John spoke.} \\ \text{We didn't dream, } \textit{until John spoke,} \text{ that anyone would object.} \end{cases}$$

$$\begin{cases} \textit{Whereas you merely dislike him,} \text{ I hate him.} \\ \text{I hate, } \textit{whereas you merely dislike,} \text{ him.} \end{cases}$$

放在句首或句中的副詞子句通常都是修飾整個主要子句，因此要用逗號「,」劃開。

習　題　471

在副詞子句下面劃線，在從屬連詞上面加圈。

Examples:

I'll be busy shopping (until) the store closes at six.

1. He read the newspaper while he was eating breakfast.

2. We called off the picnic because it was raining.

3. Even though it was snowing very hard, we went to school.

4. You said you were coming so I expected you.

5. Since John's answers were incomplete, he received a poor grade.

6. I came downstairs as soon as I found out the guests had arrived.

7. I've been wearing glasses ever since I entered the high school.

8. I often meet him on the bus in the morning if I'm not late.

9. He occasionally makes mistakes when he speaks English with his friends.

10. Whenever he wants to talk to his friends, he goes to school early.

習　題　472

依照例句完成下列問句。

Examples:

I take a walk ⋯ (frequently, after breakfast, if I have the time)

→ *I frequently take a walk after breakfast if I have the time.*

1. I went to the ball games … (always,　with my brother,　before he went in the army)

2. He accepted our offer … (happily,　without hesitation,　when we suggested it)

3. I make mistakes … (seldom,　in spelling,　if I'm careful)

4. He will speak English … (soon,　fluently,　if he studies his lessons carefully)

5. The mother walked … (quietly,　into the room,　because the baby was sleeping)

6. Get up … (early,　tomorrow morning,　if you don't want to miss the train)

7. The temperature dropped … (quickly,　to 30 degrees,　as soon as the wind changed)

8. I'll help you … (gladly,　with your homework,　whenever I have time)

9. Have you been absent … (ever,　from class,　because you were sick)

10. He entertains us … (willingly,　with his violin,　whenever we ask him to do so)

20-2. 表示「時間」的副詞子句：when?

　　跟介詞一樣，副詞子句可以根據所表達的意思，分成表示「時間」、「場所」、「狀態」、「原因」、「目的」、「結果」、「程度」、「條件」、「讓步」等幾類。表示「時間」的從屬連詞主要的有下列幾種：

(1) **when**：

　(a) 「… 的時候 "at the moment that,　during the time that"」

　　　注意，when 帶頭的副詞子句裡面常用動詞的單純式。

　　　It was raining *when we started*.

　　　It was raining *when we were out*.

　(b) 「每次 … 總是 "on any occasion that,　whenever"」

　　　It is cold *when it snows*.

　(c) 「那時 "and just then"」

　　　We were about to start, *when it began to rain*.

(2) **while**：「當 … 的時候 "during the time that,　as long as"」

　　　注意，*while* 帶頭的副詞子句裡面動詞常用進行式。

　　　He had an accident *while I was coming here*.

　　　While I was speaking,　he said nothing.

(3) **as**：

(a) 「正當 … 的時候 "when, at the same time that"」

注意，as 帶頭的副詞子句裡面動詞的單純式、進行式都可以用。

As I looked up, I saw a man looking at me.

The train arrived *just as* (= at the very moment that) *the clock struck six.*

(b) 「正在 … 的時候，一面 … 一面 … "while, during the same time that"；隨 "according as"」

I met him *as I was coming here.*

As we grow older, we know better.

(4) **whenever**：

(a) 「每次 … 總是，隨時 "every time that; as often as"」

注意，whenever 帶頭的副詞子句裡面動詞常用單純式。

Whenever he comes, he brings me something.

I hope you will come and play *whenever you feel inclined.*

(b) 「無論甚麼時候 "at whatever time, no matter when"」

I will see him *whenever he likes to come.*

(5) **before**：「在 … 以前 "earlier than the time that"」

注意，before 帶頭的副詞子句裡面，動詞常用單純式：主句的動詞，單純式、完成式都可以用。

He (had) died *before I was born.*

I must finish my work *before I go home.*

(6) **after**：「在 … 以後 "at a time that follows"」

注意，after 帶頭的副詞子句裡面，動詞可用完成式、也可以用單純式；主句的動詞常用單純式。

I left *after he (had) arrived.*

After her husband died, she had to earn her own living.

(7) **until, till**：

(a) 「（一直）到」"upto the time that"

Wait *till I come.*

He gambled *until he had lost all his money*.

(b) **not … until / tll**:「到 … 才 "only when"」

People do *not* know the blessing of health *till they lose it*.

(= People know the blessing of health only when they lose it.)

It was *not until he warned me* that I became aware of danger.

(= I became aware of danger only when he warned me.)

(8) **since**：「自從 "from the time that, after the time that"」

注意，since 帶頭的副詞子句裡面，動詞常用過去單純式；主句的動詞常用現在完成（進行）式。

What have you been doing *since I last saw you*?

He has been home only once ever *since he went* to New York.

(9) **now (that)**:「如今，既然，因為 … 已經 "since, as, considering that"」，含有「時間」與「理由」兩種含義。

Now that winter has come, we had better repair the furnace.

Now (that) you are well again, you can travel.

(10) **once**：「一旦 "from the moment that, as soon as"」

Most boys like to swim, *once they have learned how*.

(11) **as soon as**：「一 … 就 " the moment (/ minute / instant) that"」

As soon as he comes back, I will tell him.

He started *as soon as* he received the news.

Get out *as soon as* you have finished it.

(12) **no sooner … than**:「一就 …"immediately after … "」

注意，no sooner 常與完成式動詞合用，而 than 後面的動詞即用單純式。又如果 no sooner 出現在句首，主語與動詞要倒序。

He (had) *no sooner* arrived *than* he fell sick.

No sooner had he arrived *than* he fell sick.

No sooner did he appear *than* all were silent.

(13) $\begin{Bmatrix} \textbf{scarcely} \\ \textbf{hardly} \end{Bmatrix}$ $\begin{Bmatrix} \textbf{when} \\ \textbf{before} \end{Bmatrix}$ ：「一 … 就 … "immediately after … ,　no sooner … than"」

注意，scarcely 和 hardly 與完成式動詞合用，而 when 與 before 後面的動詞即用單純式。又當 scarcely 與 hardly 出現在句首的時候，主語與動詞要倒序。

He had *scarcely* escaped *when* he was recaptured.

I had *hardly* reached there *when* it began to rain.

I had *hardly* spoken to him *before* he was gone.

Scarcely had he gone out *when* it began to rain.

(14) **as long as**：「只要 "during the time that,　all through the time that"」

He stayed in Paris *as long as* he had money.

I shall never forget that supper *as long as* I live.

(15) **as often as**：「盡（可能）常，每次 "as frequently as"」

He comes *as often as* he can.

They will call you *as frequently as* they can.

(16) **時間語詞**（that): **the time (that)**：「當 … 的時候 "when,　while"」

The time (*that*) I was in Japan,　I saw many interesting things.

by the time (that)：「到了 … 的時候（已經）」

By the time (*that*) we got there,　all the other guests had left.

By the time (*that*) you get back,　the dinner will be ready.

the year (that),　the month (that)：「當 … 那一年」，「當 … 那一月」

I bought it *the year* (*that*) I was in Europe.

I met her *the month* (*that*) I was travelng in Japan.

the night (that),　the day (that)：「當 … 那一晚」，「當 … 那一天」

He fell ill the *night* (*that*) we went to France.

The day (*that*) she was missing,　he was there.

the moment (that),　the minute (that),　the instant (that)：「一 … 就 … "as soon as"」

The moment (*that*) she saw him,　she shouted "Bob"!

I hurried off *the minute* (that) school was over.

every time (that), **any time (that)**, **each time (that)**：「每次 … 總是 "whenever"」

Every time (*that*) he appears, her face brightens up.

Come and see us *any time* (*that*) you are in town.

Each time (*that*) he came, he brought children some candies.

the last time (that), **the next time (that)**：「當上／下一次 … 的時候」

The last time (*that*) you were here, you promised to take me to the zoo.

The next time (*that*) you come, we must have an evening together.

(17) **directly**, **immediately**, **instantly**：「一 … 就 … "as soon as"」

Directly I had done it, I knew I had made a mistake.

Let me know *directly* he comes.

Immediately (or *instantly*) the button is pressed, the mine explodes.

(18) **never … but (that)** … ：「每 … 就，一 … 就 … "never … that … not"」

He *never* passes a lady on the street *but* he tips his hat politely.

(= He never passes a lady that he does not tip off his hat politely.

= Whenever he passes a lady, he tips off his hat politely.)

It *never* rains *but* it pours.

(= Every time it rains, it pours.

= It never rains without pouring.)

習　題　473

在空白裡填入 when, while 或 as。有的答案可能不只一個。

1. I was taking a bath _____ the light went out.

2. The light went out _____ I was taking a bath.

3. I will see you _____ I return.

4. I studied nothing but English _____ I was in the country.

5. Please drop in _____ you have time.

6. I read the book _____ I went along.

7. Strike _____ the iron is hot.

8. I met him _____ I was coming here.

9. He trembled _____ he spoke.

10. A dog wags his tail _____ pleased.

11. Just _____ he was speaking, everyone listened attentively.

12. _____ I arrived at Taipei, I at once went to my friend's house.

習　題　474

在空白裡填入 before, after 或 whenever。有的答案可能不只一個。

1. Look _____ you leap.

2. _____ I finished my task, I went home.

3. She weeps _____ she hears such a story.

4. You may come _____ you like.

5. I'll do it now _____ I forget it.

6. I will go _____ I please.

7. _____ he left college, he went to the United States for higher studies.

8. It was some _____ time he saw me (= he didn't see me for some time).

9. It was not long _____ I saw my mistake (= I saw my mistake before long).

10. It was a long time _____ he could speak (= he couldn't speak for a long time).

習　題　475

在空白裡填入 until / till, since 或 now (that)。

1. Wait _____ the rain becomes lighter.

2. I have been studying nothing but English _____ I came here.

3. _____ you mention it, I do remember.

4. _____ our father is dead, we must try to help ourselves.

5. How long is it _____ we last saw each other?

6. _____ I am older, I have changed my mind.

7. It is three years _____ I came here.

8. Three years have passed _____ I came here.

9. It was not _____ he told me that I noticed.

10. This is the tenth day _____ I wrote to him.

習　題　476

在空白裡填入 now, once, dirctly, the moment, as soon as, as (so) long as, no sooner … than 或 scarcely (hardly) … before (when)。有的答案可能不止一個。

1. I came _____ _____ _____ I heard of it.

2. _____ you show any fear, he will attack you.

3. Stay _____ _____ _____ you like.

4. The fly bad _____ _____ hit the water _____ a huge trout snapped at it.

5. _____ a beast of prey has licked blood, it longs for it for ever.

6. _____ I uttered these words, there was a dead silence.

7. I had _____ done it _____ I regretted it.

8. You are safe enough, _____ you are outside the gate.

9. _____ I come to think of it, I suppose you are right.

10. He had _____ _____ seen it _____ he started back home.

11. _____ you are here, you'd better stay.

12. I waited for you _____ _____ _____ I could.

13. _____ you are a big boy, you must behave better.

14. _____ the motor warms up, the grinding noise will fade out.

15. _____ _____ _____ I live, I will help you.

16. _____ _____ _____ I entered the room, the bell rang.

17. _____ _____ had I left the house _____ it began to rain.

18. You will not succeed, _____ _____ _____ you do not work in earnest.

19. I will stay _____ _____ _____ I can.

20. _____ had I sat down _____ the telephone rang again.

習　題　477

在空白裡填入 the moment, the time, the year, the day。

1. He turned pale ＿＿＿＿＿ ＿＿＿＿＿ he saw her.

2. By ＿＿＿＿＿ ＿＿＿＿＿ we reached the house, it was dark.

3. ＿＿＿＿＿ ＿＿＿＿＿ I opened my eyes I saw him looking at me.

4. ＿＿＿＿＿ ＿＿＿＿＿ I was in London, I went to a concert at the Albert Hall.

5. I met her ＿＿＿＿＿ ＿＿＿＿＿ my uncle Bill died.

6. By ＿＿＿＿＿ ＿＿＿＿＿ you have finished, it'll be too late.

7. It happened ＿＿＿＿＿ last ＿＿＿＿＿ we were together.

8. He died ＿＿＿＿＿ very ＿＿＿＿＿ you arrived.

習　題　478

在空白裡填入適當的「時間」連詞。

1. ＿＿＿＿＿ she comes, tell him to wait.

2. We got the lawn planted ＿＿＿＿＿ the rains came.

3. Don't open the door ＿＿＿＿＿ the rain stops.

4. The terrified lad ran ＿＿＿＿＿ he was exhausted.

5. You are safe enough, ＿＿＿＿＿ you are outside the gate.

6. Just ＿＿＿＿＿ he was passing, she looked out of the window.

7. She telephoned ＿＿＿＿＿ ＿＿＿＿＿ ＿＿＿＿＿ she could.

8. ＿＿＿＿＿ I come to think of it, he be haved rather strangely.

9. He stayed in Tokyo ＿＿＿＿＿ ＿＿＿＿＿ ＿＿＿＿＿ he had money.

10. ＿＿＿＿＿ ＿＿＿＿＿ ＿＿＿＿＿ she saw him, she shouted "Charles"!

11. We can't go over the pass ＿＿＿＿＿ the sun has melted the ice.

12. ＿＿＿＿＿ he had lost his wife, he settled in France.

13. You can't stop ＿＿＿＿＿ you have started.

14. Be calm, ＿＿＿＿＿ you show any fear, the dog will attack you.

15. Good bye ＿＿＿＿＿ I see you next.

16. Not a day went by ＿＿＿＿＿ some new accident happened.

17. It seemed scarcely a week ＿＿＿＿＿ he had been there last.

18. The words were _____ out of his mouth _____ a man appeared at the door of the room.

19. _____ has a foreigner set foot in the United States _____ they ask him what he thinks of the country.

20. The children never played _____ _____ a quarrel followed.

習 題 479

依照例句把下列每對句子中的一個句子改成「ing 式」以後，與另外一個句子連起來。

Examples:

We were driving in the country. ⎫
We admired the view. ⎭ (while)

→ *While we were driving in the country, we admired the view.*

→ *While driving in the country, we admired the view.*

He left college. ⎫
Then he went to America for further studies. ⎭ (after)

→ *After he left college, he went to America for further studies.*

→ *After leaving college, he went to America for further studies.*

1. John was running for the train. ⎫
   He got out of breath. ⎭ (while)

2. I did all I could. ⎫
   I calmly awaited the result. ⎭ (after)

3. I will ask you some questions. ⎫
   Then I will give my answer. ⎭ (before)

4. I'm studying. ⎫
   I like to play the radio. ⎭ (while)

5. He made a great effort. ⎫
   He at last finished his task. ⎭ (after)

6. I must finish this book. 〕
   Then I will read that one. 〕 (before)

7. Alice was getting dressed. 〕
   She kept looking at the clock. 〕 (while)

8. Bob finished his homework. 〕
   Then he went out to play. 〕 (after)

9. I left school. 〕
   Then I began to study German. 〕 (after)

10. Betty was lying in bed. 〕
    She thought about her vacation. 〕 (while)

參考：「時間」副詞子句的主語，如果與主句的主語相同，而且述語中含有 Be 動詞與名詞、形容詞、分詞、介詞片語的話，可以連同後面的 Be 動詞一起省去。比較：

When I was a boy, I looked at such things differently.

　　→ *When a boy*, I looked at such things differently.

When he was young, he loved music.

　　→ *When young*, he loved music.

Do not read while you are eating.

　　→ Do not read *while eating*.

John, don't speak until you are spoken to.

　　→ John, don't speak *until spoken to*.

When you are in doubt, look up the dictionary.

　　→ *When in doubt*, look up the dictionary.

「時間」副詞子句有時候也可以改寫成介詞片語或分詞片語。比較；

While I was going downtown, I met an old friend.

　　→ { *In going downtown* / *Going downtown* }, I met an old friend.

They would die before they yield.

　　→ They would die *before yielding*.

After I had finished my work, I went to bed.

$$\rightarrow \left\{ \begin{array}{l} \textit{After having finished my work} \\ \textit{Having finished my work} \end{array} \right\} , \text{ I went to bed.}$$

As soon as she saw him, she shouted "Bob"!

$$\rightarrow \left\{ \begin{array}{l} \textit{On seeing him} \\ \textit{Seeing him} \end{array} \right\} , \text{ she shouted "Bob"!}$$

習　題　480

在空白裡填入適當的字使前後兩個句子表達相同的意思。

1. _____ the bell rang, we had not finished our work.

   = The bell rang _____ we had finished our work.

2. We'd like you to pay this bill as soon as it is convenient.

   = We'd like you to pay this bill as _____ as _____ .

3. While he was in the hospital, Henry crocheted a bedspread.

   = _____ _____ _____ _____ ,Henry crocheted a bedspread.

4. After we visited in New York, we went on to Washington.

   = _____ _____ in New York, we went on to Washington.

5. When he was asked his opinion, he remained silent.

   = _____ _____ his opinion, he remained silent.

6. Wait there till you are called for.

   = Wait there till _____ _____ .

7. He had an accident while he was on his way home.

   = He had an accident _____ _____ _____ _____ _____ .

8. I had no sooner seen the lightning _____ I heard a clap of thunder.

   = Scarcely _____ _____ _____ seen the lightning _____ I heard a clap

   of thunder.

9. _____ I see that ship, I am astonished at its bulk.

   = _____ time I see that ship, I am astonished at its bulk.

   = _____ I never see that ship I am astonished at its bulk.

10. He had _____ sooner seen me _____ he left the room.

　　= He left the room _____ soon _____ he saw me.

　　= _____ _____ he saw me he left the room.

11. He never passed anybody on the street but he greeted him.

　　= He never passed anybody on the street _____ he _____ not _____ him.

　　= _____ he passed _____, he greeted him.

　　= He never passed anybody _____ _____ him.

12. No leader worth of the name ever existed but he was an optimist.

　　= _____ leader worthy of the name _____ ever existed was an optimist.

13. He studied English while he was a child.

　　= He studied English _____ _____ _____.

14. Experience is seldom thrown away altogether when it is dearly bought.

　　= Experience, _____ _____ _____, is seldom thrown away altogether.

20-4. 表示「場所」的副詞子句：where?

　　表示「場所」的從屬連詞有下列幾種：

(1) **where**：「在 / 到 … 的地方 "in, at, or to the place where"」

　　　　We must camp *where* we can get water.

　　　　Let him go *where* he likes.

　　　　Where there is no rain, farming is difficult or impossible.

　　　　Where there is life, there is hope.

(2) **wherever, wheresoever**：「無論何處 "in, at, or to any place; no matter where"」

　　　　I will follow you *wherever* you go.

　　　　You must find him, *wherever* he is.

　　　　Wheresoever (Wherever) we looked, we saw miseries.

(3) **everywhere (that), anywhere (that)**：「無論甚麼地方 wher-ever」

　　　　The stores were closed *everywhere* we went.

　　　　I'll go *anywhere* you want me to.

　　　　She is the spirit of the company *everywhere* (*that*) she goes.

習 題 481

在空白裡填入 where, wherever, anywhere (that) 或 everywhere (that)。有的答案可能不只一個。

1. We live _____ the road crosses the river.

2. He is welcomed _____ he goes.

3. _____ you go, I'm following you.

4. He lay _____ the grass was thickest.

5. Go back (to) _____ you came from.

6. _____ he goes, he is sure to find friends.

7. _____ there's plenty of sun and rain, the fields are green.

8. _____ there's little or no rain, you don't find green fields.

9. _____ there is a will, there is a way.

10. Go _____ you like; I don't mind.

20-4. 表示「狀態」的副詞子句：how?

表示「狀態」的從屬連詞主要的有下列幾種：

(1) **as**：「照、如、隨 "in the way that, in the same manner as"」

Do *as* you are told.

He came early, *as* he had been asked (to do).

She treated her husband *as* she would treat a servant.

as 後面的主語（如例句中的 it）常省略：

Do *as* (it) seems best.

You will proceed *as* (it) follows.

(2) **as if, as though**：「恰像 … 一樣，彷彿 "as would be the case if"」，動詞常用過去式。

He talks *as if* he knew everything.

He looks *as though* he were tired.

She looks *as though* she had been very ill.

It looks *as if* it would rain.

口語英語裡常有人用 like 來代替 as 或 as if, as though。

Do it *like* (= as) I told you.

It looks *like* (= as though) it would rain.

(3) **in the way / manner (that)**：「照 / 依 … 的方式」

You can do it *in the way* (*that*) you think best.

She tried to conduct the business *in the manner* (*that*) her father used to do.

They strove to escape *in what* (*ever*) *manner* they might.

(4) **as it is**：「但事實上 "really, in reality"」，用在句首。

As it is, I can't pay you.

We hoped things would get better, but *as it is* they are getting worse.

as it is, **as it stands**：「照原來樣子，照事實 "without change"」，用在句尾。

Leave it *as it is* (or *as it stands*).

as it were, **so to speak**：「可謂，好比 "as one might say, if I may use such an expression"」

He became, *as it were*, a kind of hero, from a strange land.

Mr. Power is, *so to speak*, a walking dictionary.

習　題　482

在空白裡填入 as, as if (though) 或 the way (that)。

1. Do _____ you think best.

2. It looks _____ _____ we should lose the game.

3. He does not speak _____ the other people do.

4. He must do _____ I told him to do.

5. She looked at the toad _____ _____ it were poisonous.

6. They trim the roses just _____ _____ their mother used to trim them.

7. She plays with him _____ a cat (plays) with a mouse.

8. I felt _____ _____ I hadn't long to live.

9. The law, _____ it stands at present, is severe on the author.

10. I treat her _____ tenderly _____ _____ she were my daughter.

習 題 483

在空白裡填入適當的字使前後兩個句子表達相同的意思。

1. She lay down on the sofa as though she were tired.

= She lay down on the sofa _____ _____ _____.

2. He behaved as if he were crazed.

= He behaved _____ _____ _____.

3. He looked round as if he were in search of something.

= He looked round as if _____ _____ in search of something.

4. He treats his wife as though she were a child.

= He treats his wife _____ a child.

5. He spoke as though he were thoroughly frightened.

= He spoke _____ _____ _____ _____.

6. He lowered his head as if he were to ask my forgiveness.

= He lowtred his head _____ _____ _____ _____ my forgiveness.

參考：「狀態」副詞子句中的主語，如果與主句的主語相同，常可省去。比較：

She hurriedly left the room *as though she were angry.*

→ She hurriedly left the room *as though angry.*

He raised his hand *as though he would command silence.*

→ He raised his hand *as though to command silence.*

Men here *as they are elsewhere* like dance and music.

→ Men here *as elsewhere* like dance and music.

20-5. 表示「原因、理由」的副詞子句：why?

表示「原因」與「理由」的從屬連詞有下列幾種：

(1) **because**：「因為 "for the reason that"」

We stayed at home *because* it rained.

It's true *because* I say it's true.

It is because he has neglected his duties *that* he must be punished.

not that … but (because) … , not because … but because … 「不是因為 … 而是因為」

I am provoked at your children, *not that* they didn't behave well *but because* they
　left us too early.

I declined the invitation, *not because* I did not want to go, *but because* I had no
　time.

the reason (why) … is that (在口語中也用 because)

The reason (why) he was absent was *that / because* he was ill.

(2) **since**：「既然 "as, seeing that, because"」

Since you say so, I suppose it's true.

Since we have no money, we can't buy it.

(3) **as**：「因為 … 所以 "since, because"」

As it is getting dark, let's go home now.

I went straight off to bed, *as* I had to rise at six the next day.

(4) **in that**：「因為 "because"」，（較文的說法）

Alice disappointed her mother *in that* she didn't write very often.

He made a great mistake *in that* he didn't act promptly.

(5) **now (that)**「如今，因為 … 已經 "since, as"」

Now that you are a big boy, you must behave better.

(6) **inasmuch as**：「鑒於，因為 " since, because, seeing that"」

Inasmuch as you wish to, you may go.

參考：引導表示「原因、理由」的副詞子句的還有 considering (that), seeing (that),
　　　for the reason that, by reason that, on the ground that 等。

習　題　484

在空白裡填 because, since, as 或 that。有時候可能有兩個以上的答案。

1. He was angry, _____ no one spoke to him.

2. _____ You have nothing else to do, why not remain with me?

3. I saw that I had said something wrong _____ they all laughed.

4. _____ you are not ready, we must go without you.

5. _____ you are not ready, we must go on.

6. Seeing _____ it's raining, you had better stay indoors.

7. Did you go on _____ he was not ready, or for another reason?

8. _____ there is no help, let us try to bear it as best we may.

9. Now _____ we're here, we may as well see the sights.

10. Some peopleeat not _____ they are hungry, but for the pleasure of it.

參考：because 帶頭的子句，表示對方聽話的人所未知的原因或理由，因此常放在句尾：

> I didn't come *because* I was very sick.

as 帶頭的子句，表示說話與聽話的人所共知的原因或理由，常放在句首。

> *As* he is working hard, he is likely to succeed.

> *As* the train does not come till 5:30, we have plenty of time.

注意，這些句子都可以改寫成由「對等連詞」so 所連接的句子：

> He is working hard, *so* he is likely to succeed.

> The train does not come till 5:30, *so* we have plenty of time.

since 帶頭的子句，表示為對方聽話的人所熟知的原因或理由，常放在句首。

> *Since* I don't have much money, I can't buy it.

> *Since* you say so, I suppose it is true.

習 題 485

依照例句把表示「原因、理由」的副詞子句改寫成分詞片語。

Examples:

> As he was poor, he could not afford to buy books. →

> *Being poor, he could not afford to buy books.*

> As the rain had ruined her hat, she had to buy a new one. →

> *The rain having ruined her hat, she had to buy a new one.*

1. As he was a careless fellow, he forgot all about it.

2. As it was very stormy, she stayed home.

3. As I had nothing to do, I went swimming.

4. As she was a shy little thing, she said nothing.

5. As I did not receive any letter, I wrote to him again.

6. As she is a good girl, she is liked by all.

7. As it was Sunday, we did not go to school.

8. As I had read the book, I could answer the question.

9. As there was no taxi, we had to walk.

10. As he didn't know what to do, the boy started crying.

11. As he had finished his exercise, he put away his books.

12. As the fog was very dense, the plane was forced to alight.

13. As night came on, we went home.

14. The tiger is renowned through all the countryside because he is so cunning and ferocious.

15. As there was no expense connected with the plan, it was quickly adopted.

參考：表示「原因、理由」的副詞子句常可以簡化為分詞片語。

　　　As he was poor, he could not afford to buy books.

　　　　→ *Being poor,* he could not afford to buy books.

　　　As we had run for an hour, we were almost exhausted.

　　　　→ *Having run for an hour,* we were almost exhausted.

注意，上面兩個句子裡，子句的主語與主句的主語相同。

　　　As there was nothing to do, we went home.

　　　　→ *There being nothing to do,* we went home.

　　　As the weather was fine, we went outfora walk.

　　　　→ *The weather being fine,* we wentoutfor a walk.

注意，上面兩個句子裡，子句的主語與主句的主語不同。

習　題　486

在空白裡填入適當的字使前後兩個句子表達相同的意思。

1. The poor man is to be pitied because he's friendless.

   = _____ _____, the poor man is to be pitied.

2. As I felt the house shake, I ran out into the garden.

   = _____ the house shake, I ran out into the garden.

3. I have learned by experience the misery of being in debt, so I will never borrow money if I can help it.

   = _____ _____ by experience the misery of being in debt, I will never borrow money if I can help it.

4. Stoutly the two swimmers strove, as they knew nothing of the danger from the shark.

   = Stoutly the two swimmers strove, _____ nothing of the danger from the shark.

5. Since the case has been decided, further defense is useless.

   = _____ _____ _____ _____ _____, further defense is useless.

6. She is a bit lonesome because her husband was so much away.

   = She is a bit lonesome _____ her husband _____ _____ _____.

7. We did not express any opinion because he was present.

   = We did not express any opinion _____ of _____ _____.

8. As this book is written in simple English, it is suitable for beginners.

   = This book, (_____) in _____ simple English, is suitable for beginners.

9. Mr. Lee was unable to come because he had been asked to lecture in Taipei.

   = _____ _____ asked to lecture in Taipei, Me. Lee was unable to come.

10. As you speak in that way about the neighbors, they must have annoyed you very much.

    = The neighbors must have annoyed you very much _____ you _____ speak in that way about them.

20-6. 表示「目的」的副詞子句 : for what?

表示「目的」的從屬連詞有下列幾種；而表示「目的」的副詞子句裡面常用 may, might, can, could, should 等助動詞。

(1) **that** :「為了（要），以便 "to the end that, with the purpose that"」

Work *that* you may succeed.

He ran fast *that* he might not be late.

(2) **so that**：「為了（要），以便」

I gave him the book *so that* he might study the subject at home.

Let the dog loose *so that* it can have a run.

(3) **in order that**：「為了（要），以便」

I explained the matter *in order that* he might understand my wishes.

I did that *in order that* everyone should be satisfied.

(4) **lest**：「為了怕，免得，以免 "for fear that, so that … not"」

注意，lest 後面的動詞常用（should）動詞原形。

Be careful *lest* you fail.

Lest he (should) disturb his father, he kept very quiet.

There was danger *lest* (= that) the plan be known.

(5) **for fear (that / lest)**：「唯恐，以防 "lest"」

He is working hard *for fear* (*that*) he should fail.

We dared not move *for fear* the enemy might see us.

For fear lest I should mispronounce some words, I read very slowly.

參考：引導表示「目的」的副詞子句的還有 with the purpose that, for the purpose that, to the end that, in the hope that 等。在口語英語中也常用 so。例如：

He put a new lock on *so* no one would steal his boat.

Let us be silent — *so* we may hear the whisper of the god.

習　題　487

在空白裡填入 that, so that, in order that, lest 或 for fear (that)。

1. Be careful _____ you fall from that tree.

2. We hid it carefully _____ _____ no one should see it.

3. He fled _____ he should be killed.

4. He raised his hand _____ _____ _____ the bus might stop.

5. She turned away _____ he should see her tears.

6. He wrote down the number, _____ _____ he should forget it.

7. She starved herself _____ her children might be fed.

8. Jack slammed the door _____ _____ his mother would know he was home.

9. We pushed our way to the front of the hall _____ _____ we could see the speaker.

10. Jane took off her shoes and tiptoed into the house, _____ her mother should waken.

11. He worked himself to death, _____ _____ _____ his wife might live in luxury.

12. We had to be very careful _____ the news should become known too early.

13. Better chain up the dog _____ _____ he bites.

14. Thirty copies of the book were bought _____ _____ each boy in the class should have one.

15. _____ the plan be discovered, we should take some precautions.

習　題　488

依照例句把下列各句表示「目的」的不定詞片語改為副詞子句。

Examples:

　　I've come here to have a talk with you.

　　　→ *I've come here that (so that, in order that) I may have a talk with you.*

1. She has gone to the United States to study social work.

2. The car is waiting to take you to the station.

3. He labored day and night to improve the condition of the people.

4. I shall go on working late today so as to be free tomorrow.

5. Children go to school to learn things.

6. He stood up so as to see better.

7. They came here in order to study English.

8. He works hard so as to keep his family in comfort.

9. She saved the money for her daughter to go abroad.

10. The teacher explained the passage again and again for every student to understand.

習　題　489

在空白裡填入適當的字使前後兩個句子表達同樣的意思。

1. I stood aside so that she might enter.

   = I stood aside _____ her _____ enter.

2. He brought some papers in order that I should sign them.

   = He brought some papers for _____ to _____.

3. The announcement was put up on the notice-board so that everyone could see it.

   = The announcement was put up on the notice-board _____ _____ _____

   _____.

4. They died so that we might live in safety.

   = They died _____ _____ _____ _____ in safety.

5. I did that in order that everyone should be satisfied.

   = I did that _____ _____ _____ _____ _____.

6. The maid has gone so that she can bring in some coal.

   = The maid has gone _____ _____ _____ bring in some coal.

7. School was closed early in order that the children might get home ahead of time.

   = School was closed early _____ _____ _____ the children _____ get
   home ahead of time.

8. He is working hard so that he should not fail.

   = He is working hard _____ _____ _____ _____ fail.

9. She is baking some biscuits so that you can eat them.

   = She is baking some biscuits _____ _____ _____ _____.

10. I will have everything ready so that I will not keep you waiting.

    = I will have everything ready _____ _____ _____ _____ keep you
    waiting.

參考：表示「目的」的副詞子句常可以改寫成不定詞片語。比較：

Mary went downtown *that she might see her aunt.*

→ Mary went downtown *to see her aunt.*

The boy pulled at his mother *that she might take notice of him.*

→ The boy pulled at his mother *for her to take notice of him.*

I am going early *so that I may get a good seat.*

→ I am going early *so as to get a good seat.*

John works hard *in order that his brother may go to college.*

→ John works hard *in order for his brother to go to college.*

表示「目的」的副詞子句有時候也可以改寫成介詞片語。比較：

We use a hammer that *we can knock in nails.*

→ We use a hammer *for knocking in nails.*

We planted a hedge *so that we can prevent the cattle from straying.*

→ We planted a hedge *for preventing the cattle from straying.*

20-7. 表示「結果」的副詞子句

表示「結果」的從屬連詞有下列幾種。與表示「目的」的副詞子句不同者，表示「結果」的副詞子句通常都不用 may, might, should 等助動詞。

(1) **so that**：「因此，所以 "with the result that, consequently"」

He worries about his examination all day, *so that* he can't sleep at night.

It rained hard *so that* I didn't bother to water the lawn.

(2) **so … that**：「因為很 … 所以 … ， … 得 … "to such a degree or extent that"」

He was *so* quick *that* I couldn't catch him. (*so* + Adj)

He ran *so* quickly *that* I couldn't catch him. (*so* + Adj-ly)

He was *so* good a runner *that* I couldn't catch him. (*so* + Adj + *a* (*n*) + N)

He *so* likes science *that* he has made up his mind to be a scientist. (*so* + V)

(3) **such … that**：「因為很 … 所以」

He was *such* a good runner *that* I couldn't catch him. (*such* + *a* (*n*) + Adj + N)

He has always lived *such* a life *that* he cannot expect sympathy now. (*such* + *a* (*n*) + N)

His anger was *such that* nobody dared to speak to him.

(4) **so … but that**：「因為很 … 所以不 … "so … that … not"」

　　　No one is *so* old *but that* he may learn.

　　　　=No one is *so* old *that* he may *not* learn.

　　　　(=A man may learn, however old he may be.)

參考：在非正式的口語英語中, 連詞 that 常加以省略。

　　　　　She sat directly before me *so* (*that*) I could not see the expression on her face.

　　　　　It was *so* hot (*that*) I couldn't sleep.

在口語英語中，副詞子句也常移到句首。

　　　　　I couldn't sleep, it was *so* hot.

　　　　　He couldn't speak, he was *so* angry.

習　題　490

　　　在空白裡面填入 so, such 或 that。

1. I was _____ tired _____ I could hardly stand.

2. His bravery was _____ _____ it astonished all his friends.

3. He spoke _____ well _____ he convinced everybody of his innocence.

4. It's _____ noisy no one can study.

5. I was _____ happy _____ I could dance all night.

6. Bob slammed the door _____ _____ he awakened his mother.

7. Mary has _____ a good voice _____ she should study singing.

8. Yesterday was _____ a hot day _____ we stayed at home.

9. The weather was _____ hot _____ we stayed at home.

10. I had _____ a bad headache _____ I couldn't sleep all night.

11. The burglar wore gloves, _____ _____ there were no finger prints to find.

12. Philip is _____ a poor preacher _____ he would drive away anyone from church.

13. All precautions have been taken, _____ _____ we may expect to succeed.

14. He worries _____ much about his financial position _____ he can't sleep at night.

15. His anger was _____ _____ we were frightened.

習　題　491

用 so … that 或 such … that 連接下列每對句子。

1. He became nervous.
   He could barely speak.

2. He speaks good English.
   We can understand him easily.

3. He had much intelligence.
   We admired him.

4. He spoke many languages.
   He could travel anywhere.

5. I was hungry.
   I could eat an ox.

6. He walked slowly.
   He hardly moved.

7. It is a long address.
   I can't remember it.

8. The story is short.
   You can read it in an hour.

9. Bob has a good memory.
   He can remember all the names.

10. The teacher gave many assignments.
    We were always busy.

習　題　492

依照例句把下列各句裡面的副詞子句改寫成不定詞片語。

Examples:

He is *so tall that he can reach the ceiling.*

　→ *He is tall enough to reach the ceiling.*

The book is *so easy that you can understand it.*

　→ *The book is easy enough for you to understand.*

I was so excited that I couldn't sleep.

　→ *I was too excited to sleep.*

It's *so small that you can't see it.*

　→ *It's too small for you to see.*

He was *so fortunate that he escaped.*

　→ *He was so fortunate as to escape.*

1. I was so much distressed that I could not speak.

2. The days were so hot that we could not go outdoors.

3. He was so proud that he would not learn.

4. He ran so quickly that I could not catch him.

5. The book is so easy that we can understand it.

6. The weather is so warm that we can go out to play.

7. I was so stupid that I believed his story.

8. The problem was so difficult that none of us could solve it.

9. The car is so cheap that everybody can buy it.

10. We were so fortunate that we arrived there just in time.

11. It is never so late that one cannot mend.

12. He is not so proud that he will not work for bread.

13. He is so clever that I cannot keep pace with him.

14. His success was so unexpected that it aroused suspicion.

15. The artificial flowers are so skillfully made that they cannot be distinguished from the natural flowers.

16. He spoke in such a low voice that he could not be heard from the other end of the room.

習 題 493

把下列各句表示「結果」的不定詞片語改寫成副詞子句。

1. He speaks too fast to be understood.

2. The tree is too high for me to climb.

3. I hope he will not be so weak as to yield.

4. The news is too good to be true.

5. You are tall enough to hang the picture.

6. The book is easy enough for us to understand.

7. The bed is big enough for both of us to sleep in.

8. He is too fond of spending money to become rich.

9. Do you know him well enough to be able to borrow money from him?

10. You're not so foolish as to believe all you read in the newspapers, I hope.

11. Yesterday was too cold a day for us to go swimming.

12. It was too bad a story to be liked by children.

13. He is not such a fool as to do that.

14. His bravery was such as to astonish the world.

15. When a straight line meets another so as to make the adjacent angles equal to each other, it's called a perpendicular.

20-8. 表示「條件」的副詞子句

表示「條件」的從屬連詞主要的有下列幾種。

(1) **if**（ … **then** … ）：「如果 …（那麼）」

I'll drop in *if* I have time.

If it is time, we had better go.

If you are tired, *then* you had better go to bed.

(2) **unless**：「除非 "if … not"」

Don't come *unless* I call.

Unless it rains, I must go there tomorrow.

(3) **suppose (that)**, **supposing (that)**, **say**：「假定」，後面常跟著問句。

Suppose your father saw you, what would he say?

Supposing he can't come, who will do the work?

Say you were in his place, would you do it?

(4) **provided (that)**, **providing (that)**：「倘若，以 … 為條件 " if, on condition that"」，條件的含義比 if 還要強。

I don't mind lending you the money *provided* (*that*) you pay it back within a month.

He says he'll accept the post *provided* (*that*) the salary is satisfactory.

I will come *providing* (*that*) I have time.

(5) **on condition (that)**：「以 … 為條件」

I will do it *on condition that* you help me.

He was allowed to live in the house rent-free *on condition that* he kept it in repair.

(6) **in case (that)**, **in the event that**：「如果，萬一；以防 "if it should happen that; lest, as a precaution against"」

    In case he arrives before I get back, please ask him to wait.

    You'd better take an umbrella *in case* it rains.

(7) **so / as long as**, **so far as**：「如果，只要 "on condition that, provided that"」

    So long as it is done, it doesn't matter how.

    You may borrow the book *so long as* you keep it clean.

    So far as the weather remains settled, we will start tomorrow.

(8) **so (that)**：「如果，只要 "on condition that"」

    You may go where you like *so (that)* you are back by dinner time.

    So (that) it is done, it doesn't matter who did it.

習　題　494

依照例句把下列每對句子用 if 和 unless 連起來。

Examples:

    The weather is good. ⎫
    We'll go to the lake. ⎭

      → *If the weather is good, we'll go to the lake.*

      → *Unless the weather is good, we won't go to the lake.*

    The weather is bad. ⎫
    We can't go to the lake. ⎭

      → *If the weather is bad, we can't go to the lake.*

      → *Unless the weather is bad, we can go to the lake.*

    He doesn't work hard. ⎫
    He won't succeed. ⎭

      → *If he doesn't work hard, he won't succeed.*

      → *Unless he works hard, he won't succeed.*

1. We have nine players.
   We can start a baseball team.

2. You tell me what your trouble is.
   I can help you.

3. Bob studies hard.
   He will get a scholarship.

4. There is a sudden frost.
   The flowers won't bloom.

5. You don't have an appointment.
   You can't see the doctor.

6. You don't ask him.
   He won't tell you the answer.

7. The tires are properly inflated.
   The car will drive well.

8. A nation is not free.
   It can't be strong.

9. You don't keep your promises.
   You'll lose your friends.

10. We advertise in the newspaper.
    We will sell a lot of merchandise.

習 題 495

在空白裡填入 if 或 unless。

1. She'll come _____ you ring the bell.

2. He won't come _____ you ring the bell.

3. _____ you send a telegram now, he'll get it this evening.

4. _____ you don'tring the bell, the servant won't come.

5. _____ you ring the bell, the servant won't come.

6. _____ you ring the bell, the servant will come.

7. He wouldn't have waited _____ you had been late.

8. _____ my watch hadn't been slow, I shouldn't have been late.

9. I shall go there tomorrow _____ I am too busy.

10. The baby seldom cries _____ he is tired.

習 題 496

依照例句先把下列各句改寫成含有 if 的句子，然後設法把句子中的 if 省去。

Examples:

Bill didn't get up on time, so he didn't catch the train.

> → *If Bill had got up on time, he would have caught the train.*

> → *Had Bill got up on time, he would have caught the train.*

I am not with him, so I can't help him.

> → *If I were with hint, I could help him.*

> → *Were I with him, I could help him.*

1. Jack got up on time, so he caught the bus.

2. Today is not a holiday, so you cannot go to the beach.

3. Alice didn't have a cold, so she went to school.

4. I am not accepted, so I won't go to the university.

5. I didn't know you were hungry, so I didn't offer you dinner.

6. There isn't enough money for a car, so I will buy a scooter.

7. He didn't have enough money, so he didn't buy a car.

8. The dog was tied up, so it didn't bite you.

9. I had something to do, so I didn't come yesterday.

10. He stopped the train in time, so there were no casualties.

參考：在比較正式的英語裡常把條件句中的假設式助動詞 *were, should, could, might* 移到句首來代替 if。

> *Were it* (= If it were) not for his idleness, he would be a good student.
>
> *Should* he (=If he should) call, tell him I am not at home.
>
> *Had* I (=If I had) but taken your advice, all this misery might have been avoided.
>
> *Could / might I* (=If I could/might) see it once more, all my desires would be fulfilled.

習 題 497

在空白裡填入 if, unless, suppose, supposing, provided (that), on condition that, in case (that), so long as。

1. S＿＿＿＿e it rains, what shall we do?

2. I shall come here tomorrow ＿＿＿＿ I am too busy.

3. _____ he should call, tell him I am not at home.

4. You had better be ready _____ _____ he comes.

5. I should not mind so much, _____ I was not bo busy.

6. I'll scream _____ you let me go.

7. I do not care _____ _____ _____ you are happy.

8. Take warm clothes _____ _____ the weather is cold.

9. We'll have plenty of sandwiches, p_____ that no uninvited guests turn up.

10. I shall do it _____ you tell me not to.

11. Where can you hide, even s_____ g you are able to escape from the police?

12. Peter will keep his mouth shut, p_____ he knows what he's supposed to.

13. I don't mind lending him the book _____ _____ _____ he returns it to me before the end of this month.

14. He declared himself willing to try, p_____ _____ he was given a free hand.

15. Come next week _____ you hear to the contrary.

16. P_____ that the weather keeps like this, the farmers have no need to worry about the crops.

17. _____ he has done the work to my satisfaction, I shall not pay him for it.

18. We'll get to Taipei tonight, _____ _____ _____ we don't have tire trouble.

19. _____ you follow the printed directions, the set will not fit properly together.

20. You can borrow the book _____ _____ _____ you return it by the weekend.

習 題 498

在空白裡填入適當的字使前後兩個句子表達相同的意思。

1. If anything should happen to me, give this envelope to my brother.

   = _____ anything _____ to me, give this envelope to my brother.

2. If it were mine, I would call the vet.

   = _____ it _____ , I would call the vet.

3. If I had known it was going to rain, I'd have closed the window.

　　= _____ I _____ it was going to rain, I'd have closed the window.

4. But for the bay Mrs. Brown could get a position in the bank business.

　　= _____ it _____ for the boy, Mrs. Brown could get a position in the business.

5. I shall not go if you do not come with me.

　　= I shall not go, _____ you come with me.

6. But that he is sick, he would be here today.

　　= _____ he _____ _____ sick, he would be here today.

7. Take care of the pence, and the pounds will take care of themselves.

　　= _____ _____ take care of the pence, _____ the pounds will take care of themselves.

8. Aren't you anxious to make money? Then buy these shares.

　　= Buy these shares, _____ _____ _____ anxious to make money.

9. If he wins the battle, he will bromoted.

　　= _____ the battle, he will be promoted.

10. There are few, if there is any.

　　= There are few, _____ _____.

11. Come at once, if you cannot come sooner.

　　= Come at once, _____ _____ _____.

12. He seldom, if he ever does, goes to church.

　　= He seldom, _____ _____, goes to church.

13. A tiger cannot be tamed unless it is caught young.

　　= A tiger cannot be tamed _____ _____ _____.

14. If we wish to master a language, we must constantly practice it.

　　= _____ _____ a language, we must constantly practice it.

15. A tiger can be tamed if it is caught young.

　　= A tiger can be tamed _____ _____ _____.

16. If you turn to the right, you will find the house you want.

　　= _____ _____ _____ _____, you will find the house you want.

17. He is very smart, if we consider his age.

    = He is very smart, _____ his age.

    = He is very smart, his age _____ _____.

18. They are, if I may use the expression, grown-up boys.

    = They are, _____ _____ _____, grown-up boys.

參考：由 if 或 unless 帶頭的條件子句，如果子句裡面的主語與主句裡面的主語相同，常可以與後面的 Be 動詞一起省去。比較：

If he had been born in better times, he woud have become a great scholar.

　　→ (*If*) *born in better times,* he would have become a great scholar.

He will do it *if he is properly approached.*

　　→ He will do it *if properly approached.*

The child is never peevish *unless he is sick.*

　　→ The child is never peevish *unless sick.*

虛詞的 it 與 there，也常可以與後面的 Be 動詞一起省去。例如：

Come tomorrow *if it is possible.*

　　→ Come tomorrow *if possible.*

We wondered what answer, *if there was any,* he would give us.

　　→ We wondered what answer, *if any,* he would give us.

表示條件的副詞子句又常可以簡化成不定詞或分詞片語。比較：

He must be very busy, *if he is not able even to write.*

　　→ He must be very busy, *not to be able even to write.*

If I am to be frank with you, I do not care much for your project.

　　→ *To be frank with you,* I do not care much for your project.

If you do your best, you will succeed.

　　→ *Doing your best,* you will succeed.

If conditions are favorable, he might succeed.

　　→ *Conditions being favorable,* he might succeed.

If weather permits, I will come.

　　→ *Weather permitting,* I will come.

20-9. 表示「讓步」與「對照」的副詞子句

表示「讓步」與「對照」的從屬連詞主要的有下列幾種。

(1) **although**, **though**：「雖然 "in spite of the fact that"」

(*Al*) *though* it was cold, he didn't light the fire.

I will do my best (*al*) *though* I cannot say I am very smart.

注意，(al)though 可以與 yet 或 still 連用，但是不能與 but 合用。比較：

$\begin{cases} \textit{Although} \text{ he hates me, } \textit{yet} \text{ I will do it.（○）} \\ \textit{Though} \text{ it was raining, } \textit{still} \text{ he went there.（○）} \\ \textit{Though} \text{ he hates me, } \textit{but} \text{ I will do it. （×）} \end{cases}$

(2) **even though**, **even if**：「即使，縱然」

We will go *even if* it rains.

The men managed to survive, *even though* they were without water three days.

(3) **while**, **whereas**：「雖然 "while on the contrary, although"」

Some men are rich *while* others are poor.

While some people like fat meat, others hate it.

Whereas he had numerous enemies, his brother was loved by everyone.

(4) {**Adj**, **N**, **Adv**, **V**} **though** / **as** / **that**：「雖然 "even though"」，使用在較為正式的英語中。

Poor *though* / *as* he is (= Even though he is poor), he is honest.

Idiot *though* / *as* he was (= Even though he was *an* idiot),

his parents loved him.（注意，名詞前面的冠詞要省略）

Much *though* / *as* I admire his courage (= Even though I admire his courage very much), I don't think he acted wisely.

Try *as* / *though* I might (= Even though I tried very hard), I could not lift the stone.

美式英語裡也有人用 **as** … **as**：

As poor *as* he is, he is honest.

Get up *as* early *as* he may, he will find the room ready.

(5) **V wh-word may** (**might**) / **will** (**would**), **etc.**：「無論 …」，正式英語。

Go where he will (= Wherever he may go)，he is sure to find people who speak English.

Say what I would (= Whatever I said)，he refused to go.

Come what may (= Whatever may come)，we must remain cheerful.

(6) **no matter wh-word，wh-word-ever**：「無論 … ，不管 …」，後面常用助動詞 may 以表示可能性。

$\left\{\begin{array}{l}\textit{No matter who}\\ \textit{Whoever}\end{array}\right\}$ you may be，I'm deeply grateful to you.

I'm going to take the day off，$\left\{\begin{array}{l}\textit{no matter what}\\ \textit{whatever}\end{array}\right\}$ the boss says.

$\left\{\begin{array}{l}\textit{No matter how}\\ \textit{However}\end{array}\right\}$ annoying his behavior may be，we cannot get rid of him.

$\left\{\begin{array}{l}\textit{No matter how}\\ \textit{However}\end{array}\right\}$ hard he studied，he could not conquer the fourth grade.

(7) **whether … or …**："in either case"「不管 …（是否）…」

Whether she is sick *or* well，she is always cheerful.

Whether he succeeds *or* fails，we shall have to do our part.

Whether you like it *or no*(*t*)，you'll have to do it.

Whether I go alone，*or whether* he goes with me，the result will be the same.

(8) **for all** (**that**)：「儘管，雖然如此 "though，in spite of all"」

For all (*that*) he seems to dislike me，I still like him.

For all you say (= Whatever you may say to the contrary)，I still like him.

參考：表示「讓步」與「對照」的從屬連詞還有 *in spite of the fact that，despite that，notwithstanding* (*that*)，*granting* (*that*)，*granted* (*that*)，*admitting that，assuming that，albeit*（古字）等。

習 題 **499**

依照例句把下列每對句子用 no matter 與「wh- 詞」或「wh-ever 詞」連起來。

Examples:

It doesn't matter who told you this.
It was a lie.

→ *No matter who told you this, it was a lie.*

→ *Whoever told you this, it was a lie.*

1. It doesn't matter what is bothering you.
   Don't think about it any more.
2. It doesn't matter where George goes.
   He gets along well with people.
3. It doesn't matter how strong the enemy are.
   We will drive them out of the country.
4. It doesn't matter what you find within this room.
   It is for sale.
5. It doesn't matter whose book this is.
   You must return it to him at once.
6. It doesn't matter what orders he gives.
   They must be obeyed.
7. It doesn't matter who cooked it.
   I would like to eat some.
8. It doesn't matter when I call on him.
   He is always busy.
9. It didn't matter what I did.
   No one paid any attention.
10. It doesn't matter how much she practices.
    She will never be a pianist.
11. It doesn't matter which boy broke the glasses.
    He must pay for them.
12. It doesn't matter which one you took.
    You should give it back to George.

習 題 500

在空白裡填入 whoever, whatever, whichever, whenever, wherever 或 however。

1. Eat _____ one you like and leave the others for _____ comes in later.
2. I'll come _____ I can, and I'll bring _____ you like with me.
3. _____ the weather, we go hiking at the weekend with _____ likes to join with us.
4. _____ she does an exercise she makes mistakes, _____ hard she tries.
5. _____ it is you've found, you must give it back to _____ it belongs to.
6. Never mind, I'll give it back to John or Henry—or _____ it belongs to.
7. _____ one of you children disturbs me again, I shall punish severel, _____ it may be. You always make a noise _____ I try to do my work.
8. Of course you can dance with _____ you like, but don't expect me to introduce you to the glamorous Laura, Lorna, or _____ her name is.
9. _____ has time this afternoon, will he please clear out books, clothes, or _____ there is in the closet?
10. _____ travels will find there's no place like home, _____ he may go, _____ humble it may be, there will be a yearning in his heart _____ he thinks of it.

習 題 501

在空內裡填入 (al)though (… still, yet), even though / if, while / whereas, as, whether, notwithstanding 或 for all (that)。

1. _____ they are brothers, they never write to each other.
2. He went out, _____ I stayed at home.
3. _____ sick or well, she is always cruel.
4. _____ he was poor, he was quite generous to his needy friends.
5. Some children like school, _____ others do not.
6. I shan't mind _____ _____ he doesn't come.

7. _____ we help him or not, he will fail.

8. I have remained poor, _____ my brother has made a fortune.

9. _____ he answers or not, I shall go on distrusting him.

10. N_____g there was need for haste, he still delayed.

11. I am sorry about our quarrel; you began it, _____.

12. Jack was happy, _____ broke.

13. Tired _____ he was, Bob resolved to finish the job that night.

14. Deep _____ her sympathy was, she still had no words to offer.

15. He had always imagined his cousin to be a captain, _____ he was only a sergeant.

習　題　502

在空白裡填入適當的字，使前後兩個句子表達相同的意思。

1. However often I tried, I could not find the answer.

    = _____ _____ how often I tried, I could not find the answer.

2. Although he has a car, he often uses buses and trains.

    = He has a car, _____ he often uses buses and trains.

3. Whatever you may say, I shall trust to my own judgement.

    = _____ _____ you will, I shall still trust to my own judgement.

4. However often you ring, no one will answer.

    = _____ you ring again and _____, no one will answer.

5. Although I tried very hard, I couldn't manage it.

    = _____ _____ I tried, I couldn't manage it.

6. Whatever faults he may have, meanness is not one of them.

    = _____ he _____ has some faults, meanness was not one of them.

7. Try as you will, you won't make it.

    = _____ hard you _____ try, you won't make it.

8. No matter what I did, no one paid any attention.

    = _____ I did, no one paid any attention.

9. Rich as he is, I don't envy him.

    = I don't envy him _____ he is rich.

10. Although he is wealthy, he is not happy.

    = _____ _____ his _____ he is not happy.

11. Though he is very learned, heis a mean man.

    = _____ _____ his _____ he is a mean man.

12. Whether she is calm or worried, she is always restrained in her feeling.

    = _____ _____ _____, she is always restrained in her feeling.

13. Vagabond or no vagabond, he is a human being and deserves pity.

    = _____ _____ _____ _____ vagabond or no vagabond, he is a human being and deserves pity.

14. Laugh as much as you like, I will stick to my plan.

    = _____ _____ laugh as much as you like, _____ I will stick to my plan.

15. Though she is a woman, she carries on with her father's business.

    = _____ _____ she is, she carries on with her father's business.

16. He is young, but he is able.

    = Young _____ _____ _____, he is able.

17. Though he didn't tell me what he had done, I knew it.

    = He didn't tell me what he had done, but I knew it, _____.

18. Well, I'll come, whether the weather is rainy or wet.

    = Well, I'll come, _____ _____ _____.

19. Notwithstanding it is raining, I must go.

    = It is raining; I must go, _____.

20. For all you say about him, I still like him.

    = _____ _____ you will about him, I still like him.

參考：表示「讓步」的副詞子句裡的主語，如果與主句裡的主語相同，常可以連同後面的 Be 動詞一起省略。比較：

    He is better, *though he is not cured yet.*

      → He is better, *though not aired yet.*

Whether she is well or sick, she is always cheerful.

→ (*Whether*) *well or sick,* she is always cheerful.

表示「讓步」的副詞子句常可以改用介詞片語 (for all …，with all …，after all … 等) 來表達同樣的意思。例如：

Though he is very learned, he is a mean man.

→ *For all his learning,* he is a mean man.

Even though conditions were quite unfavorable, he would succeed.

→ *Even with conditions quite unfavorable,* he would succeed.

though, notwithstanding, for all that 常出現在句尾：

He is very rich. He has made his money quite dishonestly, *though*.

（比較：*Though* he is very rich, he has made his money quite dishonestly.）

It is raining; I must go, *notwithstanding*.

（比較：I must go *notwithstanding that* it is raining.）

He seems to dislike me, but I like him *for all that*.

（比較：*For all that* he seems to dislike me, I still like him.）

20-10. 表示「例外」、「比例」、「限制」、「程度」、「手段」的副詞子句

(1) 表示「例外」的副詞子句

a. except that，excepting that，except for the fact that：

「除 … 外，只是」

It's a very satisfactory hat, *except that* it doesn't fit me.

The account is correct *excepting that* the carriage is omitted.

Not much is known of his boyhood *except for the fact that* he received a good education.

b. but that：「要不是 "if … not"」，常表示「不可能的假設」，因此主句要用假設法動詞 (但是副詞子句仍用直說法動詞)。

She would have fallen *but that* I caught her (= if I hadn't caught her).

I'd come with you *but that* I'm so busy (= if I were not so busy).

c. beyond that，save that，saving that，only that：「除 … 外，只是」

I can say no more *beyond that* you have made me very unhappy.

There was not a sound *save / saving that* from time to time a bird called.

I know almost nothing about him, *only that* he is a young lawyer.

(2) 表示「比例」的副詞子句

a. as：「隨，照 "according as"」

As I grew richer, I became more ambitious.

One advances in modesty *as* one advances in knowledge.

Men will reap *as* they sow.

b. as …, so …：「像 … 那樣」，後面的主語與動詞常倒序以加強語氣。

As a man lives, *so* he dies.

As two is to four, (*so*) eight is to sixteen.

As the eagle is king of birds, *so* is the lion king of beasts.

As you treat me, *so* will I treat you.

c. … .no more than …, … not … any more than：「A 不 … 正如 B 不 … "… not … just as … not …"」

A whale is *no more* a fish *than* a horse is.

= A whale is *not* a fish *any more than* a horse is.

= A whale is *not* a fish, *just as* a horse is *not* a fish.

He can *no more* swim *than* a pig can fly.

= He can *not* swim, *just* as a pig can *not* fly.

d. X is to Y $\begin{Bmatrix} \textbf{as} \\ \textbf{what} \end{Bmatrix}$ Z is to W：「X 之對於 Y 猶如 Z 之對於 W」

Air is to man *what / as* water is to fish.

Leaves are to the plant *what / as* lungs are to the animal.

e. the comparative（比較級）…, the comparative …（比較級）：「越 … 越 …」

The more he has, *the more* he wants.

The longer you work, *the more* you get.

The sooner, the better.

The more, the merrier.

f.　**according as**：「依照，根據，隨 "in proportion as"」

Things are often good or bad for us *according as* (= *according* to how) we look
at them.

You may go or stay, *according* as you decide (= *according* to your decision).

g.　**in proportion as**, **in degree as**：「按著 … 的比例，越 … 越 … 」

A man will not always succeed *in proportion as* he exerts himself (= *in
proportion to* his exertion).

His humid eyes seemed to look within *in degree as* they grew dim to things
without.

(3) 表示「限制」的副詞子句

a.　**so far as**, **as far as**, **in so far as**「儘，依 … 而言，就 … 的說 "to the extent
that"」

So / As far as I could see, they were all satisfied.

He is a good doctor, *so / as far as* I know (= to the best of my knowledge).

It is all right *as far as* that goes (= *as for* that).

So / As far as I am concerned (= *in so far* as it concerns me, *as for* me), I have
nothing to say.

b.　**as**：「就 … 而論 "as far as"」

It's not a bad price, *as* (*far as*) prices go these days.

(4) 表示「程度」的副詞子句

a.　**as … as**：與形容詞或副詞的「原級」合用。

Bring me *as many* flowers as you can find.

I had *as much as* I could bear.

I followed him with my eyes *as far as* I could.

This line is *as long* (= has the same length) *as* that line.

He speaks English *as easily as* (= with equal ease) he speaks Chinese.

b.　**not so … as**, **not as … as**：與形容詞或副詞的「原級」合用。

This line is *not so / as long as* (= shorter than) that line.

He *can't* speak English *as / so* easily as (= He speaks English with more difficulty than) he speaks Chinese.

c. **than**：與形容詞或副詞的「比較級」合用。

This line is *longer than* that line.

He speaks English *more easily than* he speaks Chinese.

He is *less* dependable *than* his brother.

d. **the superlative（最高級）（that）**：與形容詞或副詞的「最高級」合用。

She sang *the best* (*that*) she could (= *as well as* she could).

(5) 表示「手段」的副詞子句

by the fact that

You can recognize him *by the fact that* he limps badly

(= by his limping badly, by his bad limp).

習　題　503

在空白裡填入 except that 或 but that。

1. I am well _____ _____ I have a cold.

2. I'd come with you _____ _____ I am so busy.

3. It will do _____ _____ it is too long.

4. _____ _____ I saw it, I could not have believed it.

5. The suit is quite satisfactory, _____ _____ the sleeves are a little too long.

6. _____ _____ he is slightly deaf, he has preserved all his faculties.

7. _____ _____ he was shy, he would certainly have made his mark as a speaker.

8. _____ _____ I was prevented by my family, I would have gone to the United States.

參考：**except(ing) that** 及 **except(ing) for** 與直說法動詞合用；**but that** 及 **but for** 與假設法動詞合用。比較：

Your composition *is* good *except that* there are a few spelling mistakes (= *except for* a few spelling mistakes).

I *would have ruined but that* you helped me (= *but for* your help).

But that I have a family here (= *but for* my family here), I *would go* to the United States.

注意，雖然主句動詞用假設式，but that 帶頭的子句中不用假設式而用直說式。

beyond that 通常用在否定句中：

I know *nothing* about it *beyond that* you are somehow involved in the matter.

習 題 504

在空白裡填入 as, so, than, the, according as, so / as far as, in proportion as。

1. You will be paid ＿＿＿＿ ＿＿＿＿ you work.

2. That is all right, ＿＿＿＿ ＿＿＿＿ ＿＿＿＿ I am concerned.

3. ＿＿＿＿ bigger they come, ＿＿＿＿ harder they fall.

4. ＿＿＿＿ ＿＿＿＿ ＿＿＿＿ I know, he doesn't have much money.

5. You will be rewarded ＿＿＿＿ ＿＿＿＿ ＿＿＿＿ you succeed.

6. You will be praised or blamed ＿＿＿＿ ＿＿＿＿ your work is good or bad.

7. ＿＿＿＿ ＿＿＿＿ ＿＿＿＿ I can see, he cannot be more than thirty.

8. We see things differently ＿＿＿＿ ＿＿＿＿ we are rich or poor.

9. Take ＿＿＿＿ much ＿＿＿＿ you want.

10. It isn't ＿＿＿＿ easy ＿＿＿＿ you think.

11. ＿＿＿＿ some are rich, ＿＿＿＿ others are poor.

12. They were praised or scolded ＿＿＿＿ ＿＿＿＿ they had done their work.

13. The stone gets ＿＿＿＿ harder, ＿＿＿＿ longer it is exposed to the weather.

14. I am ＿＿＿＿ interested ＿＿＿＿ you are in the matter.

15. ＿＿＿＿ ＿＿＿＿ ＿＿＿＿ I know, he is beyond reproach.

16. ＿＿＿＿ the desert is like a sea, ＿＿＿＿ is the camel like a ship.

17. ＿＿＿＿ more I asserted my innocence, ＿＿＿＿ more they disbelieved me.

18. He is ＿＿＿＿ stupid ＿＿＿＿ he is crazy.

19. ＿＿＿＿ we grow older, we know better.

20. He said he would rather be poor ＿＿＿＿ get money in such a dishonest way.

21. You can no more fly from it _____ from your shadow.

22. _____ _____ _____ the structure of a government gives force to public

opinion, it is essential that public opinion should be enlightened.

習　題　505

在空白裡填入適當的字，使前後兩個句子表達相同的意思。

1. Men will reap as they sow.

   = _____ men sow, _____ _____ they reap.

2. As five is to three, so ten is to six.

   = _____ is to _____ _____ _____ is to _____ .

3. You will be paid according as you work.

   = You will be paid _____ _____ your _____ .

4. I'd go with you if I were not so busy.

   = I'd go with you but _____ I _____ so busy.

5. The essay is well written except that there are a few mistakes in the last paragraph.

   = The essay is well written _____ _____ a few mistakes in the lastparagraph.

6. But for your help, I should have failed.

   = _____ that _____ _____ me, I should have failed.

7. You are rewarded according _____ you have merits _____ demerits.

   = You are rewarded according _____ _____ merits and demerits.

8. We should live according as we have a big or small income.

   = We shoud live _____ _____ _____ _____ .

9. He will be rewarded in proportion to his success.

   = He will be rewarded in proportion _____ _____ _____ .

10. He may be dead for all I know.

    = He _____ dead _____ _____ _____ I know.

11. But for your unfortunate remark, the conference would not have ended in a fiasco.

    = But that _____ _____ an unfortunate remark, the conference would not have

    ended in a fiasco.

= _____ you _____ _____ made an unfortunate remark, the conference would not have ended in a fiasco.

12. The painting is perfect except that red and green are a little over-used.

= _____ _____ a little over-use _____ red and green, the painting is perfect.

13. I have never seen _____ big a diamond _____ this.

= This diamond is bigger _____ any _____ that I have ever seen.

= This is _____ _____ diamond that I have seen.

14. Though he was a whig, or perhaps, because he was a whig, he was one of the haughtiest men breathing.

= _____ _____ _____, or perhaps, _____ _____ _____ he was one of the haughtiest men in the world.

15. Though he was a mere boy, he offered to fight the giant.

= _____ spite _____ _____ a mere boy, he offered to fight the giant.

16. The Chinese, as they are compared with the Japanese, are more peace-loving by nature.

= The Chinese, _____ _____ _____ the Japanese, are more peace-loving by nature.

第*21*章
整句的修飾語

21-1. 整句修飾語

除了修飾名詞、形容詞、副詞、動詞的修飾語以外，還有修飾整個句子的修飾語。例如：

Fortunately, John has prepared his lessons.「幸虧，約翰準備好了他的功課。」在這一個句子裡，副詞 fortunately 所修飾的不是主語 John，也不是述語 has prepared his lessons，而是整個句子 John has prepared his lessons；因為這個句子的意思並不是 John was fortunate，也不是 John has prepared his lessons fortunately，而是 It was fortunate that John has prepared his lessons。有修飾整個句子的功用的修飾語，叫做「**整句修飾語**」（sentence modifier）。

可以修飾整個句子的修飾語很多，有副詞、介語片語、分詞片語、形容詞片語、名詞片語、關係子句、副詞子句等。注意，這些整句修飾語通常都是用逗號「,」劃開。

Obviously, she arrived home safely.（副詞）

At least, you could give me a hint.（介詞片語）

Walking across the street, he was hit by a car.（現在分詞片語）

Awakened by the noise, she could sleep no more.（過去分詞片語）

To understand Asia, one must begin by understanding China.（不定詞片語）

Angry at the delay, Jane refused to join the party.（形容詞片語）

A devout Christian from a child, Bod never drinks or smokes.（名詞片語）

Bob, *who is my best friend*, plays the piano beautifully.（關係子句）

When he left, we went to the airport to see him off.（副詞子句）

習　題　506

在「整句修飾語」下面劃橫線。

1. Unfortunately, he arrived too late.

2. Susan, feeling unwell, went to bed.

3. The boy, who was laughing, ran away.

4. According to the paper, it will rain.

5. The policeman chased the man, waving a big stick.

6. The vans having arrived, we were ready to move.

7. Rain or shine, he walked to school every morning.

8. The assistant, encouraged by the result, continued the experiment.

9. Father, anxious about Mother, picked up the telephone.

10. Whoever is elected, it makes no difference to me.

21-2. 修飾整句的副詞

修飾整句的副詞多半都出現在句首，而且多半都用逗號劃開。例如：

Apparently,　the man did not love his wife.

(= It was apparent that the man did not love his wife.)

Unluckily,　Sam did not arrive on time.

(= It was unlucky that Sam did not arrive on time.)

Certainly,　he will come.

(= It is certain that he will come.)

Most likely,　they would come by bus.

(= It is most likely that they would come by bus.)

有時候，也可能出現在句尾，

The man did not love his wife, *apparently*.

He will come, *certainly*.

They would come by bus, *most likely*.

或句中。

The man *apparently* did not come.

He *certainly* will come.

They would, *most likely*,　come by bus.

副詞做為動詞的修飾語或整句的修飾語，其用法與意義都不同。

試比較：

> *Interestingly*, he told the whole story.（整句修飾語）
>
> (= The fact that he told the whole story was interesting.)
>
> 「有趣的是他把整個事實都說了出來。」
>
> He told the whole story *interestingly*.（動詞修飾語）
>
> (= He told the whole story in an interesting manner.)
>
> 「他把整個故事講得很有趣。」

> *Happily*, he did not die.（整句修飾語）
>
> (= We are happy that he did not die.) 「好在他沒有死。」
>
> He did not die *happily*.（動詞修飾語）
>
> (= He died rather miserably.) 「他死得並不快活。」

參考：最常用的修飾整句的副詞

(1) 表示「推測」與「認定」的副詞：如 surely, certainly, assuredly, truly, undoubtedly, unquestionably, possibly, likely, reportedly, supposedly, admittedly, naturally, actually, clearly, apparently, obviously, similarly, precisely, specifically, indeed, perhaps, maybe 等。

(2) 表示「事態」的副詞：如 wisely, cleverly, sensibly, artfully, ingeniously, foolishly, shrewdly, childishly, tenderly, generously, prudently, graciously, heartlessly, (un)fortunately, (un)luckily, interestingly, curiously, surprisingly 等。

(3) 表示「列舉、說明」的副詞：如 firstly, secondly, thirdly, …, lastly; first, next, then, finally, last (of all) 等。

(4) 表示「時間」與「場所」的副詞：如 often, sometimes, usually, frequently, afterwards, later, before, now, then, previously, recently, lately, seldom, rarely, so far, soon(er) or late(r), by and by, now and then, there, here, inside, outside, nearby, below, above 等。

這些副詞通常都不用逗號劃開。

> *Sometimes* we had nothing but bread for breakfast.
>
> *There* we had a nice breakfast together.

習　題　**507**

依照例句把形容詞改成修飾整句的副詞。

Examples:

It is certain that he will do it.

→ *Certainly (,) he will do it.*

→ *He certainly will do it.*

→ *He will do it, certainly.*

1. It is unfortunate that things went from bad to worse.

2. It was unlucky that John did not arrive on time.

3. It was apparent that Mr. Dale did not love his wife.

4. It was obvious that Sam did not know what he was saying.

5. It is possible that he has misunderstood what I said.

6. It was natural that Bob did not agree to your plan.

7. It was interesting that no one found out their marriage until a month later.

8. It is reported that he has made a fortune in real estate business.

9. It was supposed that he did not like the idea very much.

10. It was admitted that he was the best player in school.

11. It is curious that he is willing to relinquish his control.

12. It is not surprising that the whole economy has collapsed.

21-3. 修飾整句的介詞片語

　　介詞片語具有副詞的功能，因此也可以用來修飾整句。出現在句首的介詞片語，特別是較長的介詞片語，通常都用逗號劃開。

　　At that moment (,) no one was there.

　　At the time of which we were speaking, no one was there.

如果介詞後面接的是「ing 式動詞」或動名詞，那麼經常都用逗號劃開。

　　On hearing the news, Mary burst into tears.

　　In looking for the missing boy, Frank fell into the river.

出現在句尾的介詞片語一般都不打逗號。

No one was there *at that moment*.

參考：最常用的修飾整句的介詞片語

(1) 表示「時間」的介詞片語：如 after a short time「稍後」，after a while.「過了一段時間以後」，at (long) last「終於」，since then「自從那時候起」，up to now「到現在為止」，up to this point「到目前為止」，down to the present「一直到現在為止」，to date「到今天」，till / until now「到現在為止」，from now on「從今而後」，before long「不久」，in no time「馬上，立刻」，at first「首先」，in the beginning「起初」，for the first time「首次」，for the last time「最後一次」，for the first and the last time「第一次也是最後一次」，at once「立刻」，all at once「突然」，without warning「猝然」，from time to time「時時」，from day today「天天」，at all times「始終」，at the same time「同時」，in the meantime / meanwhile「當其時」等。

(2) 表示「對照」的介詞片語：如 after all「到底，畢竟」，despite that「雖然如此」，for all that「儘管如此」，in contrast (to, with)「相對地」，by contrast「相對地」，on the contrary「相反地」，on the one hand「一方面」，on the other hand「另一方面」，in comparison (to, with)「較之」等。

(3) 表示「比較」的介詞片語：如 in a like manner「同樣地，'likewise'」，in the same way「同樣地」，by the same token「同樣地」，on the same account「同樣地」等。

(4) 表示「總結」的介詞片語：如 in brief「簡而言之」，in conclusion「統而言之」，in a word「一言以蔽之」，in short「簡言之」，in a nutshell「扼言之」等。

(5) 表示「列舉，說明」的介詞片：如 in the first place「首先」，in the next place「其次」，in the last place「最後」，for one thing「一則」，for another「二則」，for example / instance「例如」，in other words「換言之」，in fact「事實上，質言之」，as a matter of fact「事實上，質言之」，in particular「尤其是」等。

(6) 其他介詞片語：如 of course「當然」，as a result「結果」，for that reason「因此」，in addition「加之」等。

習 題　508

把介詞片語與意義相近的副詞連起來。

(b) 1. for the most part	a. finally
( ) 2. by the way	b. mostly
( ) 3. by degrees	c. especially
( ) 4. in (point of) fact	d. generally
( ) 5. as a rule	e. certainly
( ) 6. as a matter of fact	f. partly
( ) 7. on no account	g. anyway
( ) 8. at any cost	h. incidentally
( ) 9. to (some) extent	i. besides
( )10. in the end	j. simultaneously
( )11. without doubt	k. never
( )12. after all	l. nevertheless
( )13. above all	m. gradually
( )14. in addition	n. actually
( )15. in general	o. eventually
( )16. in any event / case	p. briefly
( )17. at (long) last	q. suddenly
( )18. at any rate / price	r. similarly
( )19. at the same time	s. very soon
( )20. of course	t. very likely
( )21. on no consideration / condition	
( )22. in a word	
( )23. in most cases	
( )24. for all that	
( )25. under no circumstances	
( )26. at all events / costs	

( )27. in particular

( )28. in all probability

( )29. in the long run

( )30. in short

( )31. by the same token

( )32. all at once

( )33. before long

( )34. in no time

( )35. in a like manner

21-4. 修飾整句的分詞片語

由「現代分詞」（V-ing）或「過去分詞」（V-en）帶頭的分詞片語也可以用來修飾整句。

修飾整句的分詞片語經常都要用逗號劃開。它們可能出現在句首：

Hoping for the best, Bill entered the teachers' office.（現在分詞片語）

Seen by Charles, Susan blushed with shame.（過去分詞片語）

也可能出現在句尾：

Bill entered the teachers' office, *hoping for the best.*

Susan blushed with shame, *seen by Charles.*

甚至也可能出現在句中：

Bill, *hoping for the best,* entered the teachers' office.

Susan, *seen by Charles,* blushed with shame.

這些帶有分詞片語的句子可以看做是由兩個句子連接與簡化而得來的。這兩個句子，一個表示「原因、理由」或「背景、事態」，另一個表示「結果」或「主要的敘述」。同時這兩個句子的主語必須相同。例如：

$\begin{cases} \textit{Bill} \text{ hoped for the best.} \\ \textit{Bill} \text{ entered the teachers' office.} \end{cases}$

$\begin{cases} \textit{Susan} \text{ was seen by Charles.} \\ \textit{Susan} \text{ blushed with shame.} \end{cases}$

　　把第一個句子的主語省略，動詞改為「ing 式」以後放在第二個句子的句首、句尾或句中，就變成了「現在分詞片語」。例如：

Subj（主語）	Pred（述語）
NP	V …

Bill　　　　　　　hoped for thebest.　　⇒

NP	VP

Bill　　　　　　　entered the teachers' office.

Sentence Modifier （整句修飾語）	Sentence （主句）
V-ing … ,	NP　　　VP

Hoping for the best,　　*Bill entered the teachers' office.*

再研究下面的例句：

The sailor *scanned* the horizon.
The sailor sighted a ship.　　⇒

　　Scanning the horizon, the sailor sighted a ship.（單純式）

Jane *was* a shy little thing.
Jane said nothing.　　⇒

　　(*Being*) a shy little thing, Jane said nothing.（Be 動詞與名詞組）

I *was* very tired.
I did not attend the meeting.　　⇒

　　(*Being*) very tired, I did not attend the meeting.（Be 動詞與形容詞）

We *did not want* to anger him.
We pretended to agree.　　⇒

　　Not wanting to anger him, we pretended to agree.（否定式）

The boys *had finished* their work.
The boys went out to play.　　⇒

　　Having finished their work, the boys went out to play.（完成式）

He *had not received* the notice.
He refused to move out. $\Big\}$ ⇒

Not having received the notice, he refused to move out.（否定完成式）

注意，分詞片語裡面的 being 通常都可以省略。省去 being 的結果，分詞片語在形式上就變成了名詞或形容詞片語。這些片語在功能上還是「整句修飾語」，因此可以出現在句首、句尾或句中。例如：

(*Being*) *a devout Christian from a child,* Bob never drinks or smokes.

Bob, *a devout Christian from a child,* never drinks or smokes.

Bob never drinks or smokes, *a devout Christian from a child.*

(*Being*) *angry at the delay,* Jane walked away.

Jane, *angry at the delay,* walked away.

Jane walked away, *angry at the delay.*

如果第一個句子的動詞是被動式，那麼這個句子就要變成「過去分詞片語」。例如：

Subj（主語）	Pred（述語）
NP	Be V-en …

Susan was seen by Charles.

NP	VP

$\Big\}$ ⇒

Susan blushed with shame.

Sentence Modifier （整句修飾語）	Sentence （主句）
V-en … ,	NP　　　VP

(*Being*) *seen by Charles, Susan blushed with shame.*

She was *awakened* by the noise.
She could sleep no longer. $\Big\}$ ⇒

Awakened by the noise, she could sleep no longer.

Mr. Allen *was elected* president by the members.
Mr. Allen promised reforms. $\Big\}$ ⇒

Elected president by the members, Mr. Allen promised reforms.

I was *forced* to tell all I knew.
I told them everything. ⎫⎬⎭ ⇒

Forced to tell all I knew, I told them everything.

參考：當「名詞修飾語」與「整句修飾語」的分詞片語，無論用法、意義、標點都不同。試比較：

⎧ The policeman chased the boy, *waving a big stick.*

　（揮棍子的是警員「整句修飾語」）

　The policeman chased the boy *waving a big stick.*

⎩（掉棍子的是小孩「名詞修飾語」）

⎧ *Waving a big stick,* the policeman chased the boy.

　（「整句修飾語」）

　The policeman chased the boy (*who was*) *waving a big stick.*

⎩（「名詞修飾語」）

習　題　509

依照例句把下列每對句子的第二個句子改為「修飾整句的分詞片語」。注意，分詞片語可以在句中不同的位置出現。

Examples:

Jane answered the question.
Jane smiled. ⎫⎬⎭

→ *Smiling, Jane answered the question.*

→ *Jane, smiling, answered the question.*

→ *Jane answered the question, smiling.*

1. John went to the barber shop.
   John needed a haircut. ⎫⎬⎭

2. Alice turned off the gas.
   Alice was alarmed. ⎫⎬⎭

3. The man ran into the street. ⎫
   The man heard the noise. ⎭

4. Betty sang another song. ⎫
   Betty was pleased by the compliment. ⎭

5. Susan didn't say anything. ⎫
   Susan knew nothing about it. ⎭

6. We might play cards. ⎫
   We have nothing better to do. ⎭

7. The principal smiled his approval. ⎫
   The principal was watching the play. ⎭

8. He made his way back to the plane. ⎫
   He walked and crawled. ⎭

參考：分詞片語的主語必須與主語相同，否則會犯了文法上的禁忌，形成所謂的「懸垂的分詞」（dangling participle）。比較：

⎧ *Scanning* the horizon, a ship was sighted.（×）「懸垂的分詞」
⎪　（不可能由無生命的「船（a ship）」去「審視水平線」。）
⎨ *Scanning* the horizon, the sailor sighted a ship.（○）
⎩　（「審視水平線」的是船上的「水手（the sailor）」。）

⎧ *Running* into the hole, I saw a mouse.（×）「懸垂的分詞」
⎪　（「跑進洞裡」的是「我（I）」。）
⎨ I saw a mouse *running* into the hole.（○）
⎩　（「跑進洞裡」的是「老鼠」。）

⎧ *Damaged*, the captain radioed for help.（×）「懸垂的分詞」
⎪　（「被損毀」的是「船長（the captain）」。）
⎨ *Damaged*, the ship radioed for help.（○）
⎩　（「被損毀」的是「船（the ship）」。）

$$\left\{\begin{array}{l}\text{By } \textit{playing} \text{ with matches, the house was burned down. (×)}\\\quad\text{「懸垂的動名詞」（「房子（the house）」不可能「玩火柴」。）}\\\text{By } \textit{playing} \text{ with matches, the child burned down the house. (○)}\\\quad\text{（「玩火柴」的是「小孩（the child）」。）}\end{array}\right.$$

習　題　510

　　依照例句把下列每對句子的第二個句子改為修飾整句的名詞或形容詞片語，然後放在你認為最適當的位置。

Examples:

He walked away. ⎱
He was indignant. ⎰

　　→ *Indignant, he walked away.*

Mrs. Wilson attended every meeting. ⎱
Mrs. Wilson was an active member of the society. ⎰

　　→ *An active member of the society, Mrs. Wilson attended every meeting.*

1. The child climbed onto the roof. ⎱
   The child was eager to help. ⎰

2. Mrs. Lee cooks every meal herself. ⎱
   Mrs. Lee is an excellent cook. ⎰

3. Susan went to bed early. ⎱
   Susan was very tired. ⎰

4. I didn't understand the difficulty. ⎱
   I was only a small boy at the time. ⎰

5. Jack picked up the telephone. ⎱
   Jack was anxious to know the result. ⎰

6. Mr. Pane lives alone in the hut. ⎱
   Mr. Pane is a forgotten man. ⎰

7. Julie just smiled and nodded. ⎱
   Julie was a shy little thing. ⎰

8. The boy set out to look for a fairy.

The boy was full of many strange ideas.

21-5. 獨立分詞片語

如果表示「原因、理由」或「背景、事態」的句子與表示「結果」或「主要敘述」的句子，有不同的主語，就可以變成另外一種分詞片語，傳統的文法書管它叫做「**獨立分詞片語**」（absolute participial phrase）。

It being cloudy, I took my umbrella with me.

The lesson finished, the teacher gave us some assignments.

這種分詞片語是保留第一個句子的主語，並把動詞改為「ing 式」以後得來的。例如：

It was cloudy.

I took my umbrella with me. ⇒

　It being cloudy, I took my umbrella with me.

The lesson was finished.

The teacher gave us some assignments. ⇒

　The lesson (*being*) *finished*, the teacher gave us some assignments.

Dinner was over.

We played tennis. ⇒

　Dinner (*being*) *over*, we played tennis.

There were no taxis.

I walked home. ⇒

　There being no taxis, I walked home.

「獨立片語」，與其他「整句修飾語」一樣，可以出現在句首、句尾或句中：

I took my umbrella with me, *it being cloudy*.

The teacher, *the lesson* (*being*) *finished*, gave us some assignments.

參考一：「獨立分詞」可以表示幾種不同的含義：

The teacher coming (= as soon as the teacher came), the students grew quiet. （時間）

— 374 —

We'll sail on Tuesday, *weather permitting* (= if weather permits us).（條件）

The car having escaped from the fire (= As the car had escaped from the fire), insurance was not paid.（原因、理由）

又「獨立分詞」是屬於比較文言的說法，因此在口語中常用子句來代替。例如：

It being cloudy I took my umbrella with me.

　⇒ *It was cloudy, so* I took my umbrella with me.

The lesson finished, the teacher gave us assignments.

　⇒ *As the lesson ivas finished,* the teacher gave us assignments.

參考二：如果「獨立分詞」的主語是指說這句話的人，那麼這個主語便常加以省略。

　例如：

Considering his age, Sam is a hearty old man.

　「就他的年齡而論（論的人是說話者）」

Judging from the weather report, it is going to rain.

　「根據氣象報告來判斷（判斷的人是說話者）」

Frankly speaking, he is not a great man.「坦白地說」

Taking everything into consideration, he lives a very happy life.「考慮各種因素」

　其他常用的「獨立分詞」有 supposing …「假定…」，assuming …「假設…」，admitting …「即令…」，granting …「姑認…」，continuing with …「繼續談」，talking about …「談到…」，speaking of …「提到」，generally speaking「一般說來」，strictly speaking「嚴格說來」等。

習　題　511

　依照例句把下列每對句子的第二個句子改寫成「獨立分詞片語」。有些獨立分詞片語，前面還可以加上介詞 with。

Examples:

　　We decided to stay home.

　　The day was cloudy.

　　→ *The day being cloudy, we decided to stay home.*

She fell on her knees.

Her hands were clasped.

> → (*With*) *her hands clasped, she fell on he knees.*

> → *She fell on her knees,* (*with*) *her hands clasped.*

1. We had a fine view of the city.

   The day was a very fine one.

2. He gave the watch to the boy.

   His hand trembled violently.

3. He was seated on the bench.

   His arms were rested on his knee.

4. No obstacle remained.

   They were reassured.

5. She looked in my face.

   Tears streamed down her face.

6. She handed the letter to me.

   Her eyes shone with joy.

7. The butler sounded the gong.

   The dinner was ready.

8. He told me he would never forget me.

   His voice shook with emotion.

9. He stood silent.

   His head was slightly to one side.

10. She said her prayers at home.

    Her heart was full of love and tenderness.

參考：表示「情態、背景」的獨立分詞片語可以冠介詞 with，改成表示狀態的介詞
片語。例如：

> *With tears streaming down her face,* she fell on her knees before him.

> She fell on her knees, *with tears streaming down her face.*

比較：

$$\left\{\begin{array}{l} \text{The man stood there, } \textit{hat (being) in hand and pipe (being) in mouth.} \\ \text{The man stood there, } \textit{with a hat in his hand and a pipe in his mouth.} \end{array}\right.$$

習　題　512

依照例句把下列各句改為含有（獨立）分詞片語的句子。

Examples:

When school was over, the students went home by twos and threes.

→ *School over, the students went home by twos and threes.*

As she was only a small girl at the time, Mary didn't understand the difficulty.

→ *Only a small girl at the time, Mary didn't understand the difficulty.*

1. As she was eager to please her parents, Mary prepared her lessons very carefully.

2. As the rain had stopped, we resumed our walk.

3. Alice, who was a shy little thing, said nothing.

4. I went to the show alone because my girl friend had stood me up.

5. If other things are equal, the simplest explanation is the best.

6. As I had not received the notice, I did not attend the meeting.

7. She smiled prettily and gave me her hand.

8. She did not know what to do, so she stood there smiling.

9. We saw no objection to going ahead, since everything was in order.

10. As the troops had been given their orders, there was nothing to do but wait.

11. Since what he wanted was power, he couldn't be tempted by money.

12. Mr. Douglas assigned the job to Paul, because Henry was already overburdened with work.

13. As there are no survivors, the exact causes which led to the accident will never be known.

14. Susan sat sewing in the garden, and her thoughts were easier than her fingers.

15. They were sitting in a loft library, where the walls were covered with books that stretched to the ceiling.

21-6. 修飾整句的不定詞片語

「不定詞片語」（to V …）可以用來修飾動詞以表示「目的」、「原因 · 理由」或「結果」。

(1) **表示「目的」的不定詞片語**：常出現在表示「運動」或「活動」的動詞，come、go、run、stop、get up、stand up、sit down、wait、work 等後面。

> Mary went downtown *to see her aunt*.
>
> He works hard *to earn a living*.
>
> We stopped *to have a rest*.
>
> They sent him *to investigate the matter*.

如果要強調「目的」的意思, 可以用 in order to 來代替 to:

> Mary went downtown *in order to* see her aunt.
>
> He works hard *in order to* earn a living.
>
> We stopped *in order to* have a rest.
>
> They sent him *in order to* investigate the matter.

這些表示「目的」的不定詞片語，都可以看做是由表示「目的」的副詞子句簡化而得來的。比較：

> Mary went downtown (*in order*) *that she might see her aunt*.
>
> ⇒　Mary went downtown (*in order*) *to see her aunt*.
>
> 　　（子句與主句的主語相同）
>
> John works hard (*in order*) *that his brother can go to college*.
>
> ⇒　John works hard (*in order*) *for his brother to go to college*.
>
> 　　（子句與主句的主詞不同）
>
> Bob got up early *so that he might catch the first train*.
>
> ⇒　Bob got up early *so as to catch the first train*.
>
> 　　（子句與主句的主語相同）

如果把這些不定詞片語移到句首，並且用逗號劃開，就成了修飾整句的不定詞片語：

> (*In order*) *for his brother to go to college,* John must work hard day and night.

To put an end to the argument, he stepped off the platform.

(= As he wanted to put an end to the argument, he stepped off the platform.)

To understand Asia, one must begin by understanding China.

(= If one wants to understand Asia, one must begin by understanding China.)

(2) **表示「原因‧理由」的不定詞片語**：常出現在表示「情緒」的動詞，如 weep、regret、grieve、smile、laugh、rejoice、blush、shudder、tremble 等後面。

I grieved *to hear of your failure.*

「我（因為）聽到你的失敗而傷心。」

She wept *to see her son in this condition.*

「看到兒子落到這種地步她哭了。」

這些「不定詞片語」也是由表示「原因‧理由‧時間」的副詞子句簡化而得來的。比較：

I grieved *when / because I heard of your failure.*

⇒　I grieved *to hear of your failure.*

She wept *when / because she saw her son in this condition.*

⇒　She wept *to see her son in this condition.*

(3) **表示「結果」的不定詞片語**：經常都出現在句尾。

He lived *to see his dream come true.*

「他活著見到自己的夢想實現了。」

He awoke *to find himself lying on the floor.*

「他醒來發現自己躺在地板上。」

I worked hard *only to fail at last.*

「他努力用功，結果反而失敗了。」

這些表示「結果」的不定詞片語也可以看做是由下面的句子簡化而得來的：

He lived *till he saw his dream come true.*

He awoke *and found himself lying on the floor.*

I worked hard *but failed at last.*

only to V⋯「結果反而，卻」，表示與預期相反的結果。比較：

I pushed the door *and* discovered that it was unlocked.

⇒ I pushed the door, *to discover that it was unlocked.*

I rushed to the door *but* discovered that it was locked.

⇒ I rushed to the door, *only to discover that it was locked.*

最後兩個句子的不定詞片語都用逗號隔開，因此也是「整句修飾語」。

參考：不定詞片語跟分詞片語一樣，也可以有「獨立片語」。「獨立不定詞片語」（absolute infinitive phrase）在語義上與主句有不同的主語。例如：

He proposed a picnic, *he to pay the tickets* and *I to provide the food.*

We divide it; *he to speak to the boys* and *I to the girls.*

如果「獨立不定詞」在語義上的主語是說這句話的人，那麼這個主語經常加以刪略。例如：

To tell the truth, he is not as clever as you may think.

To begin with, she is too young.

(= *in the first place*「第一，首則」)

It was rather an unsatisfactory dinner, *to say the least of it.*

(= *to put the case moderately*「（姑且不說其他）至少可以如此說」)

He can't speak English, *to say nothing of* Russian.

(= *not to mention, let alone, much less*「更不用說、何況」)

He is, *so to speak,* a grown-up boy.

(= *as it were*「可以說，可謂」)

To make matters worse, Sam fell off the bus.

(= *what is worse*「更糟的是」)

其他常用的「獨立不定詞」有：to start with「第一」，to sum up「總括言之」，to sum-marize「約略而言」，to conclude「簡而言之」，to be more specific「更明確地說」，to be frank (with you)「坦白說來」，to be honest「說實話」，to do one justice「對某人公平起見」，to use one's words「套某人的話說」，to crown all「加之，尤其是」，to return to the subject「言歸正傳」，to change the subject「改變一個話題」，so to say「可謂」，to make along story short「長話短說」等。

習　題　513

依照例句把下列每對句子的第二個句子改為表示「目的」的不定詞片語。

Examples:

> Mary went downtown.　⎫
> Mary might see her aunt.⎭
>
> → *Mary went downtown to see her aunt.*

1. We stopped.　⎫
   We might have a rest.⎭

2. He got up.　⎫
   He might answer the bell.⎭

3. They ran.　⎫
   They might help her.⎭

4. John went to the station.　⎫
   John might see his friend off.⎭

5. Bob studied hard.　⎫
   Bob might gain a prize.⎭

6. I am waiting.　⎫
   I may hear your explanation.⎭

7. Dick has called.　⎫
   Dick may see you.⎭

8. The fox jumped up.　⎫
   The fox might get the grapes.⎭

9. She cooked the dinner.　⎫
   You might eat the dinner.⎭

10. They are waiting.　⎫
    He may make the final decision.⎭

習　題　514

依照例句改寫下列各句。

Examples:

> He came for the books. (get)
>
> → *He came (in order) to get the books.*

1. They came for the concert. (attend)

2. They went for the radio program. (hear)

3. Bob went to the restaurant for lunch. (eat)

4. Betty bought the meat for sandwiches. (make)

5. Mary went to the kitchen for some matches. (get)

6. Susan went to the store for the coat. (buy)

7. George came here for a chair. (find)

8. Charles went to the barbershop for a haircut. (have)

9. Everybody works hard for a living. (earn)

10. I'm going to see Mr. Lee for some advice. (get)

習 題 515

依照例句把下列各句中表示「目的」的副詞子句改為不定詞片語。

Examples:

He went back to the classroom that he might get the books.

→ *He went back to the classroom to get the books.*

She walked lightly so that she would not disturb her husband.

→ *She walked lightly so as not to disturb her husband.*

1. Bob went to the bank in order that he might cash checks.

2. Mary went to the shoestore that she might buy a pair of shoes.

3. He got up early so that he might catch the first train.

4. They came here in order that they could study English.

5. We practice constantly so that We can learn to speak English.

6. Bob took a taxi in order that he would not miss the concert.

7. We hurried so that we would not be late.

8. Jack hurried through his work that he might catch the train.

9. He shouted at the top of his voice in order that he might be heard.

10. She saved the money that her daughter might go abroad.

11. The teacher explained that passage again and again in order that every student might understand it.

12. In order that everybody may understand it, write it in simple language.

習 題 516

依照例句把下列各句改為「wh- 問句」。

Examples:

He has to go out for …

→ *Why does he have to go out?*

→ *What does he have to go out for?*

I have to go out to …

→ *Why do you have to go out?*

→ *What do you have to go out for?*

1. She stepped outside for …

2. I'll drop over tomorrow to …

3. He needs to study for …

4. I asked a lot of questions to …

5. They're applying for a bank loan to …

6. They're applying to the local bank for …

參考：表示「目的」的介詞片語（for NP）與不定詞片語（to V…）都可以改成以
why 或 what … for 開頭的「wh- 問句」。比較：

He is stoppin $\begin{cases} \text{for lunch.} \\ \text{to have lunch.} \end{cases}$

⇒ Is he stopping $\begin{cases} \text{for lunch?} \\ \text{to have lunch?} \end{cases}$

⇒ $\begin{cases} \textit{What} \text{ is he stopping } \textit{for}? \\ \textit{Why} \text{ is he stopping?} \end{cases}$

習 題 517

依照例句把下列各句中表示「原因・理由」的副詞子句改為不定詞片語。

Examples:

She grieved because she saw him hurt.

→ *She grieved to see him hurt.*

1. She trembled when she saw the stranger come in.

2. I could not help laughing when I saw his funny face.

3. He shuddered when he thought of what might have happened to him.

4. They rejoiced when they heard the news of victory.

5. We all grieved when we heard the death of such a great and good man.

6. He wept when he heard the sad news.

7. She smiled when she saw her husband so happy.

8. I tremble when I think of the danger ahead of me.

9. The girl blushed because she heard her name called.

10. He did not bat an eyelid when he saw her come toward him.

習　題　518

依照例句把下列各句中表示「原因‧理由」的介詞片語改為不定詞片語。

Examples:

> She trembled at the sight of her master.
>
> → *She trembled to see her master.*
>
> She wept at the sound of his footsteps.
>
> → *She wept to hear his footsteps.*
>
> She shuddered at the thought of it.
>
> → *She shuddered to think of it.*

1. He trembled at the thought of being sent to prison.

2. He wondered at the sound of the steam-whistle.

3. She rejoiced at the sight of her son.

4. He shuddered at the sight of her friend's corpse.

5. She blushed at the thought of becoming Mrs. Hill.

習　題　519

依照例句把下半句改為表示「結果」的不定詞片語。

Examples:

> He awoke and found himself become famous.
>
> → *He awoke to find himself become famous.*

He lived till he was ninety.

　　→ *He lived to be ninety.*

1. She awoke and found the house on fire.

2. The poor man sank and never rose again.

3. I offered to assist him but was turned down.

4. Few people live until they are a hundred years old.

5. He did his best but failed again.

6. They grew up and became handsome lads.

7. The good old days have gone and will never return.

8. One day you will wake up and find your daughter is a woman.

9. They escaped the sword but were perished by famine.

10. He opened his eyes and found that he had rolled from the rock to the grass.

習 題　520

依照例句把下列各句的一部分改為「獨立不定詞片語」。

Examples:

　　John must work hard so that he may go to college.

　　　→ (*In order*) *to go to college, John must work hard.*

　　John must work hard so that his brother may go to college.

　　　→ (*In order*) *for his brother to go to college, John must work hard.*

1. We need more money so that our children can go to college.

2. Bob must study hard so that he may gain a prize.

3. We must buy more books so that everybody will have one.

4. We must realize that our time is limited so that we may use our time wisely.

5. You shouldn't speak too fast so that foreigners will understand your Chinese.

6. I must write the letter neatly so that my aunt can read it.

7. He struck his fist on the table so that he might emphasize his point.

8. She read the passage again and again so that she might understand thoroughly.

9. The story must be short and simple so that everybody will understand it.

10. We should practice constantly so that we can learn to speak English.

11. He went to see the manager again so that he could explain the situation more clearly.

12. A poem must be either realistic or humorous so that I will enjoy it.

參考：「獨立不定詞片語」中所刪略的主語必須與主句的主語相同，否則會形成所謂的「懸垂的不定詞」（dangling infinitive）。比較：

> *To get through college,* hard work is necessary.（×）
>
> 「懸垂的不定詞」
>
> *To get through college,* one must work hard.（○）
>
> 「大專畢業」的是「人（one）」，不是「勤勞（hard work）」。

21-7. 修飾整句的副詞子句

　　副詞子句，如前所述，可以放在動詞後面或句尾來修飾動詞。另一方面，副詞子句也可以放在句首或句中來修飾整個句子。修飾整句的副詞子句，通常都用逗號劃開。比較：

> They talked with careful courtesy *whenever they met.*「動詞修飾語」
>
> *Whenever they met,* they talked with careful courtesy.「整句修飾語」
>
> They talked, *whenever they met,* with careful courtesy.「整句修飾語」

「連接的關係子句」經常都用逗號劃開，也可以看做是一種「整句修飾語」。例如：

> Jane, *who had a bad cold,* didn't come.
>
> Mr. Green, *whom you met last night,* is a music teacher.
>
> She has lived as a nurse in English family, *which accounts for her acquaintance with English.*
>
> We traveled together as far as Paris, *where we departed.*

　　實際上，有許多「整句修飾語」都可以看做是由這種關係子句刪略關係代名詞（與 Be 動詞）而得來的。例如：

> Bill, *who hoped for the best,* entered the teachers'office.
>
> ⇒　Bill, *hoping for the best,* entered the teachers'office.
>
> ⇒　*Hoping for the best,* Bill entered the teachers'office.

Susan, *who was seen by Charles*, blushed with shame.

　⇒　Susan, *seen by Charles*, blushed with shame.

　⇒　*Seen by Charles*, Susan blushed with shame.

Jane, *who was angry at the delay*, walked away.

　⇒　Jane, *angry at the delay*, walked away.

　⇒　*Angry at the delay*, Jane walked away.

Bob, *who is a devout Christian*, never smokes.

　⇒　Bob, *a devout Christian*, never smokes.

　⇒　*A devout Christian*, Bob never smokes.

參考：「從屬連詞」although, though, whereas, while（＝whereas「雖然」），since（＝because「因為，既然」），provided（that）等所帶頭的副詞子句多半都做「整句修飾語」用。因此這些副詞子句，雖然出現在句尾，常用逗號劃開。例如：

He didn't light the fire, *although it was cold*.

Some people like fat meat, *whereas others hate it*.

She will go, *provided her friends can go also*.

We have to hurry, *since we are late*.

He went out, *while I stayed at home*.

　注意，副詞子句做「動詞修飾語」與「整句修飾語」，其意義、用法、標點都不同。比較：

Tom was working hard *because he had to take a make-up examination*.（用以回答 "Why was Tom working hard?"；「動詞修飾語」）

Tom was working hard, *because he had to take a make-up examination*.（用以回答 "What was Tom doing?"，because 之後的句子是說話者自己補上的：「整句修飾語」）

習　題　521

　依照例句用逗號把「整句修飾語」劃開。

Examples:

The rain over we went outdoors.

→ *The rain over, we went outdoors.*

1. Peter was happy until he got married with his wife.

2. Peter insulted left the room angrily.

3. It was as it were a case of excess irritation.

4. Mr. Benjamin unfortunately couldn't afford to buy a new car.

5. One should probably when in doubt say nothing.

6. To emphasize his point he jabbed me vigorously in the chest.

7. I knew when I heard the news that there was no more hope.

8. Jim Bob having gone ahead directed the operation.

9. The men by working double shifts got the job done in two weeks.

10. He knew nevertheless that there would be a trouble.

11. She guessed although there was little evidence that there was something fishy.

12. The last bus having gone they had to walk all the way home.

13. Johnson knowing what he had to do didn't hesitate.

14. Mr. Jackson decided after he saw what had happend to reorganize the company.

15. To the great surprise of everyone who was present Charles turned out to have a beautiful tenor voice.

習 題 522

依照例句把「連接的關係子句」改成「整句修飾語」。

Examples:

John, who needed a haircut, went to the barber shop.

→ *John, needing a haircut, went to the barber shop.*

→ *Needing a haircut, John went to the barber shop.*

1. Stephen, who was not very satisfied, asked one more question.

2. Mr. Wilson, who felt bad about it, apologized.

3. St. Isadore Cathedral, which was built in 1612, caved in.

4. The bay, who did not know anything about it, said nothing.

5. The man, who was getting out of the car, twisted his ankle.

6. The girl, who was forgotten by her friends, wandered off by herself.

7. The lady, who fainted from heat, collapsed on the sofa.

8. Chicago, which was determined to have the convention, made new concessions.

9. President Johnson, who knew what he had to do, didn't hesitate.

10. Miss Davis, who did not want to anger her, pretended to agree.

11. The suspect, who was confronted with the evidence, made a full confession.

12. The knave, who was smiling an ugly little smile, drew a knife from his pocket.

13. The captain, who had never been to the island before, addressed the natives in English.

14. The lawyer, who was aware that his client did not have a very good case, decided to bribe the judge.

15. George, who was a man willing to risk all to get what he wanted, did not hesitate for a moment.

第22章 句子的連接

22-1. 句子的連接

兩個或兩個以上的句子可以用各種**連詞**（conjunction）連成一個句子。例如：

The boy sang.
The girl danced. } → The boy sang *and* the girl danced.

It was late.
The guests had not arrived. } → It was late, *but* the guests had not arrived.

I went to the meeting.
I did not stay long. } → I went to the meeting; *however*, I did not stay long.

連詞，因為其用法上的不同，可以分為**對等連詞**，**句連詞**與**從屬連詞**。

習 題 523

在連詞下劃橫線。

Examples:

The boy and the girl threw the ball.

I wonder if my answer was correct.

1. Men and women are welcome.

2. The doctor warned him not to smoke or drink.

3. The violinist played brilliantly but dispassionately.

4. I'll pick you up at eight and get you back home by midnight.

5. After eating dinner and taking a long nap, he felt much better.

6. I don't know when he left town or why he wanted to do so.

7. He said that he was very tired and that he was going home to rest.

8. Mr. Black's speech, though he read it fervently, made no impression.

9. I want you to play because when you do, I feel relaxed.

10. If you like me, you will go away, and if you love me, you will stay away.

22-2. 對等連詞

　　對等連詞（coordinator）可以連接句子或子句，也可以連接句子的一部分——詞組或語詞。由對等連詞所連接的結構必須在語法上具有相同的地位：例如都是主語、賓語，或述語；都是名詞、動詞、形容詞、或副詞等。在所連接的句子裡重複出現的語詞通常多要刪略。例如：

The boy sang.
The girl sang. } → The boy ~~sang~~ and the girl sang. →

　　The boy and *the girl* sang.（連接主語名詞與主語名詞）

I saw the boy.
I saw the girl. } → I saw the boy and ~~I saw~~ the girl. →

　　I saw *the boy* and *the girl*.（連接賓語名詞與賓語名詞）

The boy sang.
The boy danced. } → The boy sang and ~~the boy~~ danced. →

　　The boy *sang* and *danced*.（連接動詞與動詞）

The boy was tired.
The boy was hungry. } → The boy was tired and ~~the boy~~ ~~was~~ hungry. →

　　The boy was *tired* and *hungry*.（連接形容詞與形容詞）

The girl typed quickly.
The girl typed correctly. } → The girl typed quickly and ~~the~~ ~~girl typed~~ correctly. →

　　The girl typed *quickly* and *correctly*.（連接副詞與副詞）

　　英語的主要對等連詞有：and「跟、並、而（且）」，or「或（者）」，but「但是，而」，yet「然而，而」，only「祗是，不過」，nor「也不」，for「因為」，so「所以」，even「甚至」，rather than「而不」，as well as「連同、也」等。

(1) 對等連詞 and、or、but、yet、only、nor、for、so 等可以連接兩個以上的句子。

　　I went to his house, *and* he came to mine.

　　You can keep it, *or* you can throw it away.

I thought I could go, *but* I can't.

He worked hard, *yet* he failed.

I would have gone, *only* you objected.

He can't do it, *nor* can you.

We can't go, *for* it is raining.

He is sick, *so* they are quiet.

這些對等連詞都放在所連接的句子與句子的中間，而且，通常都在對等連詞的前面打逗號。如果所連接的句子比較長，也可以用分號「；」。

The mail, which you had been waiting for since early dawn, had come; *but* there weren't and letters for you.

如果想特別強調後半句，也可以用句號。例如比較：

The mail had come, *but* there weren't any letters for you.

The mail had come. *But* there weren't any letters for you.

(2) 對等連詞 and、or、as well as 可以連接兩個以上的名詞、動詞、形容詞、副詞等。（注意，這個時候對等連詞的前面不需要用逗號。）

Dick *and / or / as well as* Jack will do it.

They sang *and / or / as well as* danced.

The boy was tired *and / or / as well as* hungry.

He did it quickly *and / or / as well as* accurately.

如果三個以上的結構用對等連詞連起來的話，通常在最後兩個結構之間用對等連詞，其他的地方只打逗號。例如：

They were singing, dancing, *and* telling jokes.

He is young, handsome, *and* very rich.

(3) 對等連詞 yet、even、rather than 可以連接兩個形容詞或副詞。

The boy was tired *yet* happy.

The girl was tired *even* exhausted.

They were surprised *rather than* excited.

He did it quickly *yet* sloppily.

She walked in slowly *even* dejectedly.

They did it quickly *rather than* accurately.

but (not), not 可以連接動詞、形容詞或副詞。

The boy sang *but* did*n't* dance.

He didn't sing *but* danced.

The girl was poor *but* happy.

She was poor *but not* miserable.

They did it quickly *but not* accurately.

He works for the city government, *not* the state government.

(4) 對等連詞 no less than 連接兩個名詞或代名詞。

Your friends, *no less than* I, will be glad to see you.

(5) 對等連詞 nor「也不」連接兩個句子。注意，這個時候第二個句子的主語與動詞要倒序。

Bill isn't very handsome, *nor* (= and neither) is his brother.

Paul can't speak French, *nor* (= and neither) can I.

John doesn't like to swim, *nor* (= and neither) does Dick.

習　題　524

用 and 連接並簡化下列每一對句子。

Examples:

This hair cream may be used by men.

This hair cream may be used by women.

　→ *This hair cream may be used by men and women.*

1. The old woman slipped.

The old woman fell on the pavement.

2. The thief moved quickly.

The thief moved quietly.

3. He walked into the house.

He walked up the stairs.

4. After dinner he went out for a ride.

After a long nap he went out for a ride.

5. His love for his father is most touching.

His respect for his father is most touching.

6. He professed his love for his king.

He professed his allegiance to his king.

7. I'll inform you if he comes.

I'll inform you when he comes.

8. We can succeed.

We will succeed.

9. Mistakes have been made in that office.

Mistakes will continue to be made in that office.

10. He has always contributed to that cause.

He will always contribute to that cause.

習 題 525

用括號裡面的對等連詞連接並簡化下列每一對句子。

1. The girl enjoyed the movie.

Her mother enjoyed the movie. (and)

2. You can keep it.

You can throw it away. (or)

3. We decided to leave at dawn.

We had many miles to ride. (for)

4. His mother was a peasant woman.

His father was a famous artist. (but)

5. Paul must have known it.

Bob must have known it. (or)

6. He was tired.

He was happy. (but)

7. He walked slow.

   He walked steadily. } (yet)

8. You will have to report this immediately.

   You will be in serious trouble with the police. } (or)

9. He has experience.

   He has knowledge. } (as well as)

10. You must tell the truth.

    You must say nothing. } (or)

11. They usually played chess in the evenings.

    They usually watched television in the evenings. } (or)

12. They couldn't find any firewood.

    They simply chopped up some of the furniture. } (so)

13. He looked everywhere for his keys.

    He looked everywhere for his wallet. } (and)

14. He gave me money.

    He gave me advice. } (as well as)

15. She was very pretty.

    She was rather hard to get along with. } (but)

16. None of the teachers knew what had happened.

    The students could not offer any explanation. } (nor)

17. He had excellent manners.

    Everybody distrusted him. } (yet)

18. My friends were betrayed.

    I was betrayed. } (as well as)

19. Mr. Lee is always busy.

    Mrs. Lee hasn't much free time. } (nor)

20. Children were tired and cross.

    Their parents were not in a much better humor. } (nor)

21. Does he sing?
    Does he dance? } (as well as)

22. I don't know when he left town.
    I don't know why he wanted to do so. } (or)

23. Anyone who doesn't like the new policy of this company
    is free to do so.
    Anyone who would like to resign is free to do so. } (and)

24. He married a woman who was very intelligent and charming.
    He married a woman who couldn't cook at all. } (but)

25. She left the white hat.
    She left the white dress. } (and)
    She left the black shoes.

26. He was contented.
    He was happy. } (and)
    He was wealthy.

27. He told me to shut up.
    He told me to mind my own business. } (and)
    He told me to leave him alone.

28. He gave her a ring.
    He gave her a diamond bracelet. } (and)
    He kissed her.

29. He owned a nice home.
    He rented a cabin at the beach. } (and)
    He was on the point of buying a new car.

30. He just wanted to loaf a little.
    He just wanted to do a little fishing. } (and)
    He just wanted to try to regain his strength.

習 題 526

依照例句用 and 或 but 連接並簡化下列每一對句子。

Examples:

They invited me to come again.
I'll come again.

→ *They invited me to come again, and I will.*

They invited me to come again.
I shouldn't come again.

→ *They invited me to come again, but I shouldn't.*

They tried to get me to sing a song.
I refused to sing a song.

→ *They tried to get me to sing a song, but I refused to.*

1. He should try.
   He will try.

2. I shouldn't be unhappy.
   I am unhappy.

3. I didn't expect to enjoy myself.
   I did enjoy myself.

4. They don't seem to be very happy.
   They aren't very happy.

5. He meant to write it down.
   He forgot to write it down.

6. We reminded them to pick us up.
   They picked us up.

7. You didn't give them an answer before.
   You'll have to give them an answer now.

8. He won't need to use his own money.
   He shouldn't have to use his own money.

9. She wants to take out a loan. ⎫
   They're allowing her to take out a loan. ⎭

10. I'm not trying to find out now. ⎫
    I will try to find out later. ⎭

習 題 527

依照例句用 but 或 or 連接並簡化下面的句子。

Examples:

> She smiled. ⎫
> She refused. ⎭ → *She smiled but refused.*

> (Maybe) five people camfe. ⎫
> (Maybe) six came. ⎭ → *Five or six people came.*

1. He can speak Russian. ⎫
   He can understand Russian. ⎭

2. It's cold outside. ⎫
   It's sunny. ⎭

3. Did you give him a ring? ⎫
   Did you write him a note? ⎭

4. It's on the floor. ⎫
   It's near the window ⎭

5. Do we meet again at seven? ⎫
   Do we meet again at eight? ⎭

6. I know Dick. ⎫
   I don't know Bob. ⎭

7. This restaurant serves cocktails. ⎫
   The one on the corner serves beer only. ⎭

8. Manuscripts are available at the library. ⎫
   Manuscripts are not available at the bookstore. ⎭

9. Are manuscripts available at the library?
   Are manuscripts available at the bookstore?

10. Did she say "yes"?
    Didn't she say "yes"?

習　題　528

在空白裡面填 and、but 或 or。

1. He was poor _____ miserable.

2. He was poor _____ happy.

3. He was poor _____ not miserable.

4. They usually eat here _____ in a restaurant.

5. Do we pay you _____ the cashier?

6. I had an egg, a piece of toast, _____ a cup of coffee.

7. Rare, medium, _____ well done for the steak?

8. It should be rare _____ not raw.

9. He slammed the door _____ walked away.

10. He's trying _____ failing.

11. It's on the floor _____ behind the door.

12. It's under the sofa _____ behind the television.

13. He went downtown _____ bought a new suit.

14. He went downtown _____ bought very little.

15. I know Jane _____ not Alice.

16. He's tired _____ hungry _____ very happy.

17. Where _____ when does he teach?

18. Are you ordering a cocktail, _____ do you want the menu?

19. It was snowing _____ that made the climb difficult.

20. You may come tomorrow _____ the day after.

21. You must come after ten o'clock _____ before noon.

22. John washed _____ dried his hands.

23. John washed his face _____ dried his hands.

24. He respected _____ loved his father.

25. He respected _____ feared his father.

參考：and, or 與 but 在用法上應該注意下列幾點：

(1) but 所連接的句子需要有兩點不同的地方；or 所連接的句子要有一點不同的地方；and 所連接的句子不必有不同的地方。試比較（問號「？」表示有問題的句子，星號「＊」表示不合語法的句子）：

John washed $\begin{cases} \text{and} \\ \text{or} \\ \text{?but} \end{cases}$ dried his hands.

John washed his face $\begin{cases} \text{and} \\ \text{or} \\ \text{but} \end{cases}$ dried his hands.

John washed $\begin{cases} \text{and} \\ \text{*or} \\ \text{*but} \end{cases}$ washed his face.

He had a green and yellow apple. （○）

He had a green but yellow apple. （×）

He had a green or a yellow apple. （○）

John and Mary arrived. （○）

John but Mary arrived. （×）

John but not Mary arrived. （○）

(2) but 所連接的語詞必須在語意上相對立。試比較：

He respected *but* feared his teacher. （○）

He understood *but* admired his teacher. （×）

I am an early riser *but* my wife is a late riser. （○）

I am forty-five *but* my wife is forty-three. （×）

and 沒有這種語意上的限制，因此用途最廣。例如：

He respected *and* feared his teacher.

He understood *and* admired his teacher.

I am an early riser *and* my wife is a late riser.

I am forty-five *and* my wife is forty-three.

唯一的例外是其中一個語詞含有否定語 not 的時候。這個時候只能用 but，不能用 and。試比較：

$$
\begin{cases}
\textit{Not} \text{ the method } \textit{but} \text{ the timing is questionable.（○）} \\
\textit{Not} \text{ the method } \textit{and} \text{ the timing is questionable.（×）}
\end{cases}
$$

and 與 or 可以連接介詞或助詞；but 沒有這種用法。比較：

They are *inside* $\left\{ \begin{array}{c} \text{and} \\ \text{or} \\ \text{*but} \end{array} \right\}$ outside the house.

They are jumping *up* $\left\{ \begin{array}{c} \text{and} \\ \text{or} \\ \text{*but} \end{array} \right\}$ *down* in the playground.

(3) and 與 but 可以與 too 合用；or 不能與 too 合用。試比較：

The glass broke $\left\{ \begin{array}{c} \textit{and} \\ \textit{but} \\ \textit{*or} \end{array} \right\}$ the bottle did *too*.

習　題　529

在下列的句子裡面補上逗號與對等連詞 and。有些句子可能不需要 and。

Examples:

They sighted chased caught it.

　→ *They sighted, chased, and, caught it.*

She is an old foolish unhappy woman.

　→ *She is an old, foolish, unhappy woman.*

1. The boys the girls the dogs chased the cat.

2. He should must will win the contest.

3. Mary is tall blond blue-eyed.

4. He is a tall dark handsome young man.

5. The boy who was here who left the note who disappeared was Bob Tower.

6. He walked out to the porch looked carefully around the garden and jumped.

7. Some books are to be tasted others to be swallowed some few to be chewed and digested.

8. I had an egg a piece of toast a glass of orange juice a cup of coffee.

9. Because he didn't care for the country because the beach had no appeal to him because the mountain always scared him he decided to travel during his vacation.

10. A huge celebration dinner was given for all the officers in the party for all those who had contributed sizable amounts of money to their campaign for all the party workers who had helped bring about their victory at the polls.

習 題 530

依照例句用 and 與 respectively 連接下列每一對句子。

Examples:

> The boy sang.
> The girl danced.
>
> → *The boy sang, and the girl danced.*
>
> → *The boy and the girl sang and danced, respectively.*

1. Bob laughed.
   Dick cried.

2. John loves Mary.
   Harry loves Alice.

3. Tom is six years old.
   Jack is eight years old.

4. He lives in Boston.
   She lives in Philadelphia.

5. A training college for men is to be built in Taipei.

A training college for women is to be built in Hsinchu.

6. John took a position in a bank.

Bob took a position in a school.

Dick took a position in a shipping firm.

參考：對等連詞 and 與 respectively「個別地、各自地」可以連接兩個不同的主語與述語。例如：

The boy *and* the girl sang and danced, *respectively*.

The boy *and* the girl, *respectively*, sang and danced.

「男孩唱了歌而女孩跳了舞。」

習　題　531

依照例句改寫下列各句：

Examples:

He talked. → *He talked and talked.*

We went on. → *We went on and on.*

1. I laughed.　　　　　　　　　2. He waited.

3. She read it over.　　　　　　4. We climbed down.

5. They argued for hours.

6. They went around to the top of the lighthouse.

7. Prices went up until nobody could afford to buy them.

8. I tried again to reach you.

9. Why do we have to go over the same material?

10. I hit him until he died.

參考：許多英語的動詞（特別是「持續動詞」）、助詞（如表示「繼續」的 on，表示「上、下」的 up 與 down, over, around 等）、副詞（如 again, through 等），可以用對等連詞 and 來重複，以表示這些動作或事態不斷地繼續、反復或加強。例如：

He *talked and talked*.「他講啊講啊地講個不停。」

I walked *on and on* for miles.「我繼續不斷地走了好幾英哩。」

He was soaked *through and through*.「他渾身都濕透了。」

習 題 532

依照例句用 and 或 but 連接並簡化下列各句。

Examples:

Bob likes apples. Mary likes oranges.

→ *Bob likes apples, and Mary, oranges.*

I tried to write a novel. My wife tried to write a play.

→ *I tried to write a novel, and my wife, a play.*

1. John hit the boy. Bill hit the girl.

2. My brother likes music. I like painting.

3. I have studied German. My sister has studied French.

4. Nancy told the story badly. Jane told the story marvelously.

5. Mr. White plans to go to North America. Mrs. White plans to go to South America.

6. Mr. Jones has decided to start for Japan on Monday. Mr. Johnson has decided to start for Japan on Tuesday.

參考：用 and 或 but 所連接的兩個句子，如果述語動詞一樣而賓語名詞、狀態副詞、時間副詞、處所副詞等不一樣，那麼第二個句子的述語動詞可以省略。例如：

Jack ate the apple, and Dick (*ate*) the orange.

Mr. Lin has been to America, but Mrs. Lin (*has been*) to Europe.

習 題 533

依照例句改寫下列各句。

Examples:

Bob and Dick met each other in Vietnam.

→ *Bob met Dick in Vietnam.*

Tom and Bill discussed business.

→ *Tom discussed business with Bill.*

A and B are similar. → *A is similar to B.*

A and B are the same. → *A is the same as B.*

1. Jane and Grace resemble each other.

2. Charles and Susan are married.

3. The president and the dean conferred on the matter.

4. This rope and that rope are equal in length.

5. This pencil and that one are different in color.

6. The sand and the loam are mixed.

7. John and Bill agree that Harry is an idiot.

8. The earth and the moon are identical in their chemical composition.

9. The secretary and the treasurer differed in their opinions.

10. The resemblance between John and Bill is very striking.

參考：英語有些動詞（如 meet, marry, mix, fight, talk, confer, discuss, agree, consult, differ, resemble 等）與形容詞（如 same, similar, equal, identical, different, parallel 等）必須以複數名詞為主語。試比較：

$$\left\{ \begin{array}{l} \text{Bob and Dick} \\ \text{They} \\ \text{The group} \end{array} \right\} \text{met in Vietnam.（○）}$$

Bob met in Vietnam.（×）

這些動詞與形容詞除了有「A and B 動詞 / 形容詞」的說法以外，還可以有「A 動詞 / 形容詞（介詞）B」的說法。例如：

$$\left\{ \begin{array}{l} \textit{Bob and Dick met} \\ \textit{Bob met Dick} \end{array} \right\} \text{in Vietnam.}$$

$$\left\{ \begin{array}{l} \textit{A and B are different.} \\ \textit{A is different from B.} \end{array} \right.$$

習　題　534

依照例句改寫下列各句。

Examples:

If you work hard, you will succeed.

→ *Work hard, and you will succeed.*

If you don't work hard, you will fail.

→ *Work hard, or you will fail.*

1. If you work hard, you will pass the examination.

2. If you don't hurry up, you will be late for the train.

3. If you go straight on, you will see a church.

4. If you don't put on your overcoat, you will catch a cold.

5. If you work well, you will be rewarded.

6. If you make one step, you will be a dead man.

參考：

(1) 在祈使句或含有祈使語氣的句子後面常用 and「那麼」與 or「否則，不然的話」
來表示可能的結果。

You must work hard, or you will fail the exam.

「努力用功，否則你會失敗。」

One more step, and you are a dead man.

「再跨一步，那麼你就要變成死人了（＝我就要「斃」你了）。」

(2) 表示「否則」的 or 可以用 else, otherwise 代替，也可以用 or else。

Hurry, *else* you will be late.

You must go there quickly, *or else* you will not be back in time.

Do what you are told; *otherwise* you will be punished.

(3) 表示「或者」的 or 後面可以用 rather「毋寧」、at least「至少」、better still「更
好」等。例如：

I fell in love, or *rather* I thought I was in love, with the girl next door.

Why don't you write us before you come here, or, *better still*, send us a telegram?

習 題 535

依照例句改寫下列各句。

Examples:

Neither the pen nor the pencil is on the desk.

　　→ *The pen is not on the desk. Nor is the pencil.*

I read neither novels nor poetry.

　　→ *I don't read novels. Nor do I read poetry.*

I didn't see it and you didn't, either.

　　→ *I didn't see it, (and) neither / nor did you.*

1. Bob eats neither meat nor fish.

2. She used neither sugar nor cream in her coffee.

3. He had neither cigarettes nor matches.

4. There is neither paper nor pencils in the desk.

5. Neither the hats nor the coats are in the closet.

6. Neither cash nor checks were available.

7. Jack has neither admitted nor denied it.

8. Tom neither saw us nor heard us call.

9. I don't know, and I don't care, either.

10. I have not gone there, and I will never go there, either.

11. I didn't see it, and nobody else see it.

12. He can't do it; I can't do it; you can't do it; and nobody can do it.

參考：對等連詞 nor 的用法與 (and) neither (= and … not … either) 的用法相似。

$$\text{The pen is not on the desk,} \begin{cases} \text{and the pencil isn't, either} \\ \text{(and) neither is the pencil} \\ \text{(and) nor is the pencil} \end{cases}.$$

$$\text{I didn't see it,} \begin{cases} \text{(and) neither} \\ \text{(and) nor} \end{cases} \text{did anybody else.}$$

（比較：= Not I, *nor* anybody else, saw it.

　　　　= *Neither* I *nor* anybody else saw it.）

習　題　536

從括號裡面選出適當的對等連詞。

1. He knew what he wanted, (and, but, so, or, for) he didn't know how to get it.

2. His speech was almost not intelligible, (so, and, yet, or, for) for some reasons they enjoyed it.

3. They were very tired, (so, and, but, or, for) they still had miles to ride.

4. His mother was the daughter of a New England minister, (but, and, so, or, for) his father had been a missionary in China.

5. The new city administration has been six months in office, (and, so, for, yet, or) not one of the promised reforms has been put into effect.

6. We decided to help Bob once more, (and, so, for, but, or) we loved him very much despite his faults.

7. Put on your overcoat, (and, so, for, but, or) you will catch cold.

8. Hurry up, (and, so, for, but, or) else you'll be late.

9. He did the work, (and, so, for, but, or) he did it well.

10. You doubt bis capacity, (and, so, for, but, or) with reason.

11. He felt no fear, (and, so, for, but, or) he was a brave man.

12. He was a brave man, (and, so, for, but, or) he didn't feel afraid.

13. We were getting a little worried, (so, yet, nor, and, for) none of us had heard from Father for three days.

14. Everything seemed to be all right, (so, yet, nor, and, for) she couldn't get rid of a vague feeling of nervousness.

15. He has to pay up by the afternoon, (so, yet, or, and, for) they will take away the furniture.

16. Keep well buttoned up, (so, yet, or, and, for) you will come down with pneumonia.

17. I did my best to reason with George. (So. Yet, And, Or, For) I felt it is my duty to tell him so.

18. The house was old, needed paint badly, (and, so, for, but, or) was in some ways a very good buy.

習　題　537

利用適當的對等連詞連接並簡化下列各句。

1. He's poor. He's happy.

2. You haven't got much time. I haven't got much time.

3. Don't sit at this table. Don't sit at any other table.

4. They didn't find her a seat. I found her a seat.

5. He handed her the money. He went out.

6. This phone is out of order. The other one is out of order.

7. Spain is in Europe. Portugal is in Europe.

8. The post office doesn't sell cigarettes. The bank doesn't sell cigarettes.

9. Arabic is a Semitic language. Turkish isn't a Semitic ianguage.

10. She thought for a moment. She didn't say anything at all.

11. You shouldn't leave him a big tip. They shouldn't leave him a big tip.

12. Is this table all right? Do you prefer another one?

13. We supposed it was morning. The roosters were making a lot of fuss.

14. He kept failing the examinations. He decided to withdraw from his physics class.

習　題　538

依照例句在應該念第一重音的音節上面加重音記號。

Examples:

> *Í can go, and Máry can, tóo.*
>
> *Máry didn't try, and Jáck didn't, éither.*
>
> *Hé saw it, but Mary dídn't.*
>
> *Máry is prettier than Hélen.*
>
> *Mary is préttier than Helen, but she isn't as intélligent.*
>
> *She was wearing a wóol sweater, not a cótton one.*
>
> *It is his sìster that I want to sée.*
>
> *Is he fifteen or síxteen?*

1. Bill saw the accident, and Jim did, too.

2. Mr. Jones quit smoking, and I did, too.

3. They couldn't get tickets, and we couldn't, either.

4. Mr. White isn't a doctor, and Mr. Black isn't, either.

5. Bill can swim, but Jim can't.

6. We weren't alarmed, but they were.

7. Jim doesn't like school, but his sister does.

8. This suitcase is lighter than that one.

9. This picture is as expensive as that one.

10. Our house is bigger than theirs, but theirs is prettier.

11. This chair is prettier than that one, but it isn't as comfortable.

12. Bobby is younger than Jim is, but he's a better player.

13. We work harder than they do, but we don't get as much done.

14. This book cost five dollars and this one three dollars.

15. This book cost five dollars and this one three pounds.

16. It's his wife that I don't like.

17. The one that I don't like is his wife.

18. It's his wife that's always nasty.

19. The one that's alway nasty is his wife.

20. It's a little sympathy that he wants.

21. What he wants is a little sympathy.

22. This isn't an easy book, but it's a good one.

23. Mary isn't a beautiful child, but she's very pretty.

24. He works for the city government, not the state government.

25. That isn't my favorite picture, but I like it very much.

26. I have three children, not four.

27. I've met Mr. White, but I've never met Mrs. White.

28. Is the letter in the desk, or on the desk?

29. Does John sit in front of Bill, or in back of him?

30. Is he getting in the taxi, or out of it?

31. Can you tell whether he's going up the hill, or coming down?

32. Is he for the proposal, or against it?

33. Is he walking toward the office, or away from it?

34. She is upstairs, not downstairs.

35. He is inside, not outside.

36. I told you to take your coat off, not put it on.

37. I asked you to turn the volume down, not turn it up.

38. I asked you to hang your coat up, not throw it on the floor.

39. (Does John always beat you at tennis?) He usually wins, but he doesn't always win.

40. (Is Mr. Jones thoughtful at home?) He's not always thoughtful, but he's usually thoughtful.

41. (Isn't Mrs. Jones a teacher at your school?) Yes, she is a teacher. But she isn't my teacher.

42. (Is that the best way to do it?) Well, it's a way to do it. But I'm not sure it's the best way.

43. (Didn't you find a lot of money?) I found some money, but not very much.

44. (Isn't that Mr. Johnson?) Well, it's a Mr. Johnson. But it isn't the Mr. Johnson. I mean his name is Johnson, but he isn't the famons Mr. Johnson.

45. (Isn't this the book you were looking for?) Well, it's a book, but it isn't the book.

46. (Do you know Mrs. Jones?) Well, I know a Mrs. Jones. But I don't know whether it's the same one.

47. (What do you think of George's point of view?) Well, it's a point of view. But it's not mine.

48. Is he eighteen or nineteen?

49. Did you say "sixty-seven" or "seventy-seven"?

50. Did you say "encouraged" or "discouraged"?

51. Do "dislike" and "unlike" have the same meaning?

52. Did you overestimate or underestimate?

53. I said malignancy, not malignity.

54. They were at once similar and dissimilar.

55. I said she was a French teacher, not a fresh teacher.

56. That happened both in revolutionary and postrevolutionary France.

參考：一般說來，英語的「第一重音（primary stress）」"′" 多落在句尾「實詞」（如名詞、動詞、形容詞、副詞）的重音節。例如：

> That's Mr. Whíte.
>
> Do you have a báseball?
>
> When did you arríve?
>
> This sweater is béautiful.
>
> They're leaving tomórrow.

如果句尾是「虛詞」如代名詞、介詞、連詞、冠詞與 here, there, now, yet, ago 等，「第一重音」就要移到前面一個實詞的重音節。例如：

> I want to sée it.
>
> I bought the bóok for him.

但是如果句中有兩個語詞在語意上是相對立的，那麼「第一重音」就落在這兩個語詞上，在語法上就叫做**對比重音**（contrastive stress）。

> Í can go and Máry can, too.
>
> Hé saw it, but Mary dídn't.
>
> This isn't an éasy book, but it's a góod one.
>
> Máry is prettier than Hélen.

虛詞如有「對比重音」，也要讀重音。例如冠詞 a 與 the 平常都讀輕音，但是有對比的時候就要分別讀〔é; éi〕和〔ði′; ði〕。

> Wéll, it's á book, but it isn't thé book.

有時候，讀「對比重音」的結果，字音都會改變。

Is he fifteen or síxteen?（比較：fiftéen, sixtéen）

Did you say "díscourage" or "éncourage"？（比較：discóurage, encóurage）

22-3. 成對對等連詞

有些對等連詞必須前後成對地使用，而叫做 **成 對 對 等 連 詞**（paired coordinator）。英語的主要成對對等連詞有 :both … and …，either … or …，neither … nor …，not … but …，more … than …，not only / just … but (also / too / as well)。

(1) either … or …「或者 … 或者」可以連接句子、名詞、動詞、形容詞或副詞。

    ⎧ *Either* he should do it himself, *or* he should let us do it.
    ⎩ He *either* should do it himself, *or* let us do it.

    He learns *either* French *or* German.

    They *either* sang *or* danced.

    She was *either* tired *or* hungry.

    You should do it *either* today *or* tomorrow.

(2) neither … nor …「既不 … 也不」可以連接句子、名詞、動詞、形容詞或副詞。
    注意，neither 出現在句首的時候，前面的句子的主語與動詞要倒序。

    ⎧ He was *neither* mad, and he was *nor* completely sane.
    ⎨ *Neither* was he mad, *nor* was he completely sane.
    ⎩ He was *neither* mad *nor* completely sane.

    He learns *neither* French *nor* German.

    They *neither* sang *nor* danced.

    She was *neither* tired *nor* hungry.

    You did it *neither* accurately *nor* quickly.

(3) not only / just … but (also / too / as well)「不但 … 而且（也）…」可以連接句子、
    名詞、動詞、形容詞或副詞。注意，not only 出現在句首的時候，前面的句子
    的主語與動詞也要倒序。

    ⎧ *Not only* was she rich, *but* she was wealthy *too*.
    ⎩ She was *not only* rich *but* wealthy *too*.

    He learns *not only* French *but also* German.

They *not only* sang *but also* danced.

She was *not only* tired *but also* hungry / *but* hungry *too*.

You did it *not only* accurately *but also* quickly / *but* quickly *as well*.

(4) both … and … 「… 與 … 都、又 … 又 …」與 not … but … 「不 … 而 …」可以連接名詞、動詞、形容詞與副詞。

Both John *and* Dick are studying English.

He learns *both* French *and* German.

They *both* sang *and* danced.

She was *both* tired *and* hungry.

You did it *both* accurately *and* quickly.

如果 and 後面帶有 alike 或 as well，both 就可以省略。

Gifts were distributed to (*both*) rich *and* poor *alike* / *as well*.

not … but … 的用例如下：

Not John *but* Dick is studying English.

He learns *not* French *but* German.

They did *not* sing *but* danced.

She was *not* tired *but* hungry.

You did it *not* accurately *but* quickly.

It is *not* what you say *but* what you do that counts.

(5) more … than … 「比 … 更 …」、less … than … 「比 … 更少 …」、not so much … as … 「與其說 … 不如說 …」等連接形容詞與副詞。

She was *more* tired *than* hungry.

You did it *more* quickly *than* accurately.

比較：

He is *less* hurt *than* frightened.

He is *not so much* hurt *as* frightened.

He is *more* frightened *than* hurt.

He is frightened *rather than* hurt.

習 題 539

用括號裡面的成對對等連詞連接並簡化下列每一對句子。

Examples:

Frank was not a liar. ⎫
Frank was not a thief. ⎭ (neither … nor …)

Frank was neither a liar nor a thief.

Neither was Frank a liar, nor was he a thief.

1. You must tell the truth. ⎫
   You must say nothing. ⎭ (either … or …)

2. He was thoughtless. ⎫
   He was insolent. ⎭ (not only … but also)

3. She forgot about the party. ⎫
   She didn't want to come. ⎭ (either … or)

4. Peter is lazy. ⎫
   Peter is careless. ⎭ (both … and …)

5. Paul works hard. ⎫
   Bob works hard. ⎭ (both … and …)

6. Jane did not like pork. ⎫
   Jane did not like beef. ⎭ (neither … nor …)

7. The girls were not at fault. ⎫
   The boys were at fault. ⎭ (not … but …)

8. Bob was mad. ⎫
   He was a very shrewd young man. ⎭ (either … or …)

9. Bob was not mad. ⎫
   He was not ignorant. ⎭ (neither … nor …)

10. Shakespeare wrote carelessly. ⎫
    We have corrupt texts of some of his plays. ⎭ (either … or …)

11. The old man cannot be trusted.
    His sons cannot be trusted. } (neither … nor …)

12. There were not six members.
    There was one. } (not … but …)

13. He came to the office late.
    He came to the office quite disheveled. } (not only … but also)

14. It turned out to be not an oil well.
    It turned out to be a very dry hole. } (not … but …)

15. Mom will fix dinner.
    Dad will take us out. } (either … or …)

16. The girls want new jobs.
    Their mother wants new jobs. } (both … and …)

17. Joe is coming to the party.
    Mary is coming to the party. } (both … and …)

18. She was a pretty girl.
    She was a good cook. } (both … and …)

19. Paul helped in the kitchen.
    Paul helped in the yard. } (both … and …)

20. The parents who disciplined the child are to blame.
    The grandparents who spoiled her are to blame. } (either … or …)

習 題 540

把空白裡面的動詞改為適當的時式。

1. Neither his father nor his mother (be) alive.

2. The great poet and novelist (be) dead.

3. Extravagances as well as parsimony (be) to be avoided.

4. A good and useful man (have) passed away.

5. Kindness as well as justice (be) to be our guide.

6. Every leaf and every flower (be) stripped off the tree.

7. To take pay and then not do work (be) dishonest.

8. The long and the short of the matter (be) this.

9. The cow as well as the horse (eat) grass.

10. One or the other of these fellows (have) stolen the watch.

11. Man's happiness or misery (be) in a great measure in his own hands.

12. Curry and chicken (be) my favorite dish.

13. Bread and butter (be) fattening.

14. Mr. Johnson or his employers (be) mistaken.

15. Iron as well as gold (be) found in China.

16. Jack, and not you, (have) won the prize.

17. Neither Bob nor I (be) willing to do that.

18. Not only you but also your brother (be) lazy.

19. Two and two (be) four.

20. Sugar and water (make) syrup.

參考：主語與動詞一致

　　當有兩個（或兩個以上的）主語用對等連詞連起來的時候，動詞的單數或複數常根據下面的通則來決定。

(1) 如果兩個主語都是複數，動詞也要用複數：

　　　　Neither the *men* nor the *women want* to go.

(2) 如果兩個主語用 and 連接，動詞要用複數：

　　　　Chinese *and* English *are* required subjects.

　　　　Both Joe *and* Mary *are* coming to the party.

　　但是下列例外的情形下，動詞仍要用單數。

(a) 兩個名詞均指一人，或兩個名詞合起來統指一物或一個概念的時候：

　　　　My old *friend* and *schoolmate*, Bob Turner, *is* going with me.

　　　　Curry and *rice is* my favorite food.（「咖哩飯」）

　　　　Bread and *milk is* his only food.（「麵包牛奶」視為一物）

(b) 名詞前面有數量詞 *each, every, no, many a* 等的時候：

　　　　Every boy and girl *is* ready.

Each day and *each* hour *brings its* duty.

No teacher and *no* student *was* present.

(3) 如果兩個主語用 *as well as*、*no less than* 或 not 連接的話，動詞要跟前面的主語一致。

My parents, as well as I, *were* glad to see her.

He, no less than you, *is* my good friend.

I, not my brother, *am* going to get married.

（較佳：I am going to get married, *not my brother*.）

注意，用 as well as, no less than, not 所連接的主語常用逗號劃開。

(4) 如果兩個主語用其他的連詞連接的話，動詞要跟後面的主語一致。

You or *he has* forgotten to turn off the gas.

（較佳：*You have* forgotten to turn off the gas, or *he has*.）

Either he or *you have* made a mistake.

（較佳：Either *he has* made a mistake, or *you have*.）

Neither you nor *I was* responsible for this.

（較佳：*You were* not responsible for this; neither *was I*.）

Not only you but *I am* disgusted.

There *were* present *not* six members, *but* one.

但是也有許多英美人士在 *or, either … or, neither … nor, not, as well as, every*（… *and*）所連接的主語後面用複數動詞。

Neither French nor German *is / are* required.

French *as well as* German *is / are* required.

Every boy and girl *are* coming.

22-4. 句連詞

英語中有些對等連詞祇能連接句子，但不能連接名詞、動詞、形容詞、副詞等，就叫做**句連詞**（sentence connector）。主要的句連詞有：

(1) 「因此、所以」：therefore, accordingly, consequently, hence, thus;

(2) 「並且、而且」：also, besides, furthermore, moreover, in addition;

(3) 「然而」：still, however, nevertheless, nonetheless;

(4) 其他：「同樣地」likewise, similarly；「否則」otherwise；「即是」that is, namely；「例如」for example, for instance；「另一方面，相反地」on the other hand, on the contrary；「確實」indeed；「事實上」actually, in fact, as a matter of fact 等。

　　句連詞多半用在較為正式的文章中。用句連詞所連接的句子常用「分號」";"劃開。例如：

　　　　I don't like him very much; *however*, I have to invite him.

　　　　Something had to be done immediately; *therefore* we formed a committee.

如果想特別強調後面的句子，也可用「句號」"•"劃開。例如：

　　　　I don't like him very much. *However*, I have to invite him.

　　　　Something had to be done immediately. *Therefore* we formed a committee.

　　有些句連詞（例如 therefore, accordingly, consequently, thus, however, nevertheless, nonetheless, likewise, similarly, namely, for example 等）還可以出現在句中，甚至可以出現在句尾：

　　　　I don't like him very much; I have to, *however*, invite him.

　　　　I don't like him very much; I have to invite him, *however*.

注意，出現在句尾的句連詞一定要用「逗號」","劃開。

參考：出現在句首與句中的句連詞是否應該用逗號劃開，似乎並沒有一定不變的原則。一般說來，在句首的位置出現的 consequently, accordingly, however, moreover, furthermore, besides, likewise, indeed 等句連詞後面打逗號的人較多；在 also, thus, therefore, hence, nevertheless, nonetheless 等句連詞後面打逗號的人較少。例如：

　　　　I don't like him very much; $\left\{ \begin{array}{l} \textit{however,} \\ \textit{nevertheless} \end{array} \right\}$ I have decided to invite him.

　　　　I don't like him; *moreover*, I don't care who knows it.

　　　　I don't like him; *therefore* I didn't invite him.

　　在句中的位置出現的句連詞前後用逗號劃開的機會較多，特別是出現在述語中間的句連詞。試比較：

I don't like him very much; I nevertheless have decided to invite him.
（出現在主語與述語中間）

I don't like him very much; I have decided, *nevertheless*, to invite him.
（出現在述語中間）

習 題 541

依照例句用括號裡面的句連詞連接下列每一對句子。注意，句連詞可能有幾種不同的位置。

Examples:

We didn't like him very much.
We had to invite him.
(however)

We didn't like him very much; however, we had to invite him.

We didn't like him very much; we had, however, to invite him.

We didn't like him very much; we had to invite him, however.

1. I'm too tired to go.
   It is too late.
   (besides)

2. The window was open.
   The whole place was open.
   (that is)

3. Do what you are told.
   You will be punished.
   (otherwise)

4. I see your point of view.
   I don't agree with you.
   (still)

5. I have noted his better behavior.
   I cannot change my decision.
   (nonetheless)

6. We have not yet reached a decision.
   Our opinion of your plan is favorable.
   (however)

7. He was the only candidate.
   He was elected.
   (therefore)

8. She was very tired.　⎫
   She kept on working.　⎬ (nevertheless)

9. I did not like the house.　⎫
   It was too high-priced.　⎬ (moreover)

10. He is the popular candidate.　⎫
    He will be elected.　⎬ (consequently)

11. She didn't like him very much.　⎫
    She decided to invite him.　⎬ (nevertheless)

12. He knew what he wanted.　⎫
    He didn't know how to get it.　⎬ (however)

13. I don't like skating.　⎫
    The ice is too thin.　⎬ (furthermore)

14. Her father had been active in politics.　⎫
    He had once run for governor.　⎬ (indeed)

15. He had never been out of Japan.　⎫
    He had never been twenty miles from Tokyo.　⎬ (in fact)

16. The coach was not on speaking terms with any of the players.　⎫
    Team morale was rather low.　⎬ (hence)

17. There seemed no chance of coming to an agreement.　⎫
    It was decided to break off negotiations.　⎬ (therefore)

18. The floods had damaged many ofthe railroad bridges.　⎫
    All trains were running late.　⎬ (accordingly)

19. Each attack left him weaker than the one before.　⎫
    He crept softly into the arms of death.　⎬ (thus)

20. France was fearful of Germany.　⎫
    She was bound by a treaty to come to the aid of Russia.　⎬ (besides)

22-5. 從屬連詞

　　從屬連詞（subordinator）與句連詞一樣，祇能連接句子，不能連接名詞、動詞、

形容詞。但句連詞是連接兩個對等句子，而從屬連詞則為引導從句把它連接到主句上面去。同時，由句連詞所連接的兩個句子有一定的前後次序；而由從屬連詞所引導的從句卻可以出現在主句之後，也可以出現在主句之前。試比較：

$$\begin{cases} \text{I asked her to stay, } \textit{for} \text{ I had something to tell her. （○）} \\ \textit{For} \text{ I had something to tell her, I asked her to stay.（×）} \end{cases}$$

$$\begin{cases} \text{I asked her to stay } \textit{because} \text{ I had something to tell her.（○）} \\ \textit{Because} \text{ I had something to tell her, I asked her to stay. （○）} \end{cases}$$

$$\begin{cases} \text{He went home } \textit{when he finished his job.} \\ \textit{When he finished his job,} \text{ he went home.} \end{cases}$$

注意：由從屬連詞所引導的從句出現在句尾的時候，通常都修飾述語動詞，因此不用逗號劃開；而出現在句首的時候，卻修飾整個句子，常用逗號劃開。

我們可以用下列的句式代表對等連詞、句連詞、從屬連詞三種連詞的不同用法。

S_1 : sentence 1

S_2 : sentence 2

(1) 對等連詞：

$$S_1 \begin{Bmatrix} , \\ ; \\ . \end{Bmatrix} \text{對等連詞 } S_2.$$

(2) 句連詞：

(i)　$S_1 \begin{Bmatrix} ; \\ . \end{Bmatrix} \text{句連詞 } S_2.$

(ii)　$S_1 \begin{Bmatrix} ; \\ . \end{Bmatrix} S \text{句連詞 } S_2.$

(iii)　$S_1 \begin{Bmatrix} ; \\ . \end{Bmatrix} S_2 \text{句連詞 } .$

(3) 從屬連詞：

(i)　S_1 從屬連詞 $S_2.$

(ii)　從屬連詞 $S_2, S_1.$

習 題　542

在空白裡面填入 for 或 because。

1. Boys play ball _____ it is fun.

2. _____ we are late we have to hurry.

3. He must be very tired, _____ he has been working all day long.

4. He felt no fear, _____ he was a brave man.

5. Some people eat not _____ they are hungry, but _____ the pleasure of it.

6. I went back not _____ of the rain but _____ I was tired.

7. He was glad to go; _____ the hostess had been especially good to him.

8. I went to see him _____ I had something to tell him.

9. I went to see him, _____ I had something to tell him.

10. Exuse me _____ not having answered your letter.

11. Excuse me _____ I have not answered your letter.

12. English is a very useful language. _____ it is now used in many parts of the world, and is much more used than any other language.

參考：關於 for 與 because 的用法有下列幾點要注意：

(1) for 是對等連詞，因此只能出現在句中，而前面則常打逗號、分號或句號；because 是從屬連詞，因此可以出現在句中，也可以出現在句首。

$$\text{We couldn't go} \left\{ \begin{array}{l} \text{, for} \\ \text{because} \end{array} \right\} \text{ it was raining.}$$

Because it was raining, we couldn't go.

(2) for 表示「理由」或「原因」，多用於較為正式的文章裡，because 表示「原因」，常用於非正式的口語（例如在 why ⋯ 的答句）裡。因此在表示「推測」或「結論」的句子後多用 for。

It must have rained, *for* the ground is wet.

He can't be very rich, *for* he has been borrowing money from me.

(3) 介詞 for 表示「理由」；介詞 because of 表示「原因」。

He was punished *for* stealing.

I did not go out *because of* rain.

Because of sickness she didn't go to school.

習　題　543

依照例句用括號裡面的連詞改寫下列各句。

Examples:

Mary didn't want to marry John, but she couldn't bear to hurt his feelings. (however)

→ *Mary didn't want to marry John; however, she couldn't bear to hurt his feelings.*

1. She was very pretty; however, she was rather hard to deal with. (but)

2. They were very tired and they still had miles to ride. (nevertheless)

3. There seemed no chance of coming to an agreement, so it was decided to break off negotiations. (therefore)

4. The outside temperature was around eighty, and it was rather muggy. (also)

5. The river was filled with crocodiles, and they seemed to be of a particularly vicious sort. (moreover)

6. The plan had certain weakness; we decided, nevertheless, to adopt it. (yet)

7. I heard my name on the loudspeaker; therefore I hurried to the information desk. (so)

8. France was fearful of Germany, and she was bound by a treaty to come to the aid of Russia. (besides)

9. Charles would not help; therefore Bob was angry. (because)

10. He had used no word that was not in the dictionary; nonetheless, he got an F on the paper. (although)

11. The army had to move fast because the Prime Minister's adherents were already gathering in the streets. (consequently)

12. Because it was hard to get books in America at that time, Franklin hit on the notion of a circulating library. (for)

13. John needed the job badly; he was anxious, therefore, to make a good impression. (because)

14. Bob wasn't much interested in the project; he was, nevertheless, determined to do his best. (though)

15. He guessed, although there was little evidence, that there was something fishy. (nevertheless)

習 題 解 答

習題 272 解答

1. I forgot that we don't have to go to school today.

2. I don't know that he is not coming.

3. I am sorry that I cannot go.

4. He is sure that he is right.

5. That you go there at once is necessary.

   It is necessary that you go there.

6. Is it true that he has left school?

7. It appeared that he didn't have enough money.

8. We agreed that we would see each other every week.

9. They consider it important that you got there in time

10. That he won the election was fortunate.

    It is fortunate that he won the election.

習題 273 解答

1. They expect that he will go.

   It is expected that he will go.

2. It amazes me that she speaks English so fluently.

   I am amazed that she speaks English so fluently.

3. Someone explained it to me that the project would never succeed.

   It was explained to me that the project would never succeed.

4. It bothered him that she never answered his letters.

   He was bothered that she never answered his letters.

5. You must never say that he was selfish.

   It mush never be said that he was selfish.

6. It amuses her that we eat with chopsticks.

   She is amused that we eat with chopsticks.

7. We thought that the examination would take place the next week.

   It was thought that the examination would take place the next week.

8. It annoyed his brother that he kept asking for more money.

   His brother was annoyed that he kept asking for more money.

9. They have decided that a new branch will be opened next year.

   It has been decided that a new branch will be opened next year.

10. It shocked their teacher that twenty students failed the course.

    Their teacher was shocked that twenty studeuts failed the course.

習題 274 解答

1. The thought that I would be on time pleased me.

   The thought pleased me that I would be on time.

2. The news that the enemy were near alarmed the citizens.

   The news alarmed the citizens that the enemy were near.

3. No one can deny the fact that fire burns.

4. The rumor that there will be a general election goes around.

   The rumor goes round that there will be a general election.

5. They did not pay attention to the advice that they should consider seriously.

6. The realization that he forgot all about his appointment embarrassed Bob.

   The realization embarrassed Bob that he forgot all about his appointment.

7. The suggestion that we reconsider the plan never came up.

   The suggestion never came up that we reconsider the plan.

8. We passed the.proposal that they adopt the resolution.

9. The information that the enemy were launching an attack was passed on to the commander in chief.

The information was passed on to the commander in chief that the enemy were lauching an attack.

10. The question whether we should contribute or not came up during the discussion.

The question came up during the discussion whether we should contribute or not.

習題 275 解答

1. I hope he won't fail.

2. I don't imagine he will pass.

3. I imagine he won't pass.

4. I learned that there wasn't enough time.

5. He didn't realize that time was getting short.

6. I didn't realize he couldn't hear very well.

7. He's sure he won't succeed.

8. He isn't sure he will succeed.

9. She found that you $\begin{cases} \text{didn't miss aythinng} \\ \text{missed nothing} \end{cases}$

10. I guess nobody told you that.

習題 276 解答

1. Yes, I think so.

No, I don't think so. No, I think not.

2. Yes, I believe so.

No, I don't believe so. No, I believe not.

3. Yes, I am afraid so.

No, I am afraid not.

4. Yes, I hope so.

No, I don't hope so. No, I hope not.

5. Yes, I guess so.

No, I don't guess so. No, I guess not.

6. Yes, I believe so.

No, I don't believe so. No, I believe not.

7. Yes, I think so.

No, I don't think so. No, I think not.

8. Yes, I am afraid so.

No, I am afraid not.

9. Yes, I guess so.

No, I don't guess so. No, I guess not.

10. Yes, I hope so.

No, I don't hope so. No, I hope not.

習題 277 解答

1. give	2. be	3. not go	4. had
5. were	6. get	7. not be	8. got, settled
9. paid	10. had not	11. not tell	12. be, not make

習題 278 解答

1. He forgot when he saw her last.

2. They don't care why she decided not to do it.

3. I don't know where he got that idea.

4. I wonder who paib the dill.

5. I don't know what is bothering him.

6. They can't figure out how he is going to accomplish it.

7. You can't imagine how many people attended the meeting.

8. We wonder how much she spent on her dresses.

習題 279 解答

1. We know who did it.

2. We know where she went.

3. We know when she left home.

4. We know how she left for America.

5. We know why she couldn't come.

6. We know who (m) she went down with.

7. We know what she wants to buy.

8. We know who (m) she wants to buy a present for.

9. We know who (m) she wants to go with her.

10. We know where she wants to go to buy a present.

11. I wonder how long they're going to stay when they get here.

12. I wonder when / how they're going to get where they're going.

習題 280 解答

1. She showed us which one she wanted.

2. Could you tell me who rang the bell?

3. I wonder when they left.

4. We'll discuss where the problem lies.

5. Nobody knew what happened.

6. 1 ask him why the idea isn't popular.

7. I'm not sure which one she wants.

8. Let's find out what the trouble is.

9. He explained to us how they brought down the government.

10. May I ask you what's the matter with you?

習題 281 解答

1. She follows what she likes.

2. Is that what he prefers?

3. This does not come up to what I have expected.

4. They paid no attention to what I warned.

5. Is that what they guaranteed?

6. What they threatened was never carried out.

7. She always makes good what she promises.

8. You failed to follow what he ordered.

9. He carries out what we decided.

10. Well discuss what you planned later.

習題 282 解答

1. Does he know where she comes from?

2. Is where she comes from a secret?

3. Did he say how he managed?

4. Is why he came a mystery?

5. Did she tell you who paid the bill?

6. Will when he arrives be an open question?

7. Do you know what's bothering him?

8. Is where he went that night a matter for investigation?

9. Do you always agree with what he says?

10. Is what he says usually interesting?

習題 283 解答

1. Did she remember where she put the book?

2. What did he guess you were going to buy?

3. Do you forget who will come tomorrow?

4. Who do you suppose has been elected captain?

5. Did Bob find out when / where the meeting would take place?

6. Who(m) does Jane believe her father will give a new watch to?

7. Did he discover how he could send the message?

8. Does she realize when / how she has to finish her job?

9. Who(m) do they think their teacher lives with?

10. Where do you suppose these scholars come from?

習題 284 解答

1. When was it (that) she left?

2. Who was it that made the plan?

3. Where was it (that) they saw each other?

4. What was it that finally occurred?

5. What was it (that) you are worried about?

6. Why was it (that) you didn't tell the truth?

7. Who was it that didn't know the answer?

8. Who is it (that) you are angry with?

9. What is it (that) he wants to be sent to the post office?

10. How is it (that) the government thinks it can reduce taxes?

習題 285 解答

1. Where it is he didn't say.

2. Where is it, I wonder?

3. Who the others were she didn't ask.

4. When he saw them last he can't remember.

5. Which one she is going to buy she won't tell.

6. How much does he really know about it, we wonder?

7. How she is going to accomplish it he can't imagine.

8. Why he would ever do anything like that I can't figure out.

9. Where are they going to stay when they get here, I wonder?

10. Who it was knocking at the door I didn't realize.

習題 286 解答

1. The important thing is for you to practice every day.

2. His plan is for his family to spend the vacation at the seaside.

3. Her duty is (for her) to look after the children.

4. The important thing is for her not to be late any more.

5. His job is (for him) to give advice to foreign students.

6. His orders are for me to remind her to be there.

7. His hobby is (for him) to collect stamps.

8. His advice is for you to take a couple of weeks off.

9. The important thing is for me to get there on time.

10. His favorite pastime is (for him) to make airplane models.

習題 287 解答

1. For a young boy to smoke isn't good.

   It isn't good for a young boy to smoke.

2. (For us) to learn difficult words is useless.

   It is useless (for us) to learn difficult words.

3. (For you) to learn how to use a word in more useful.

   It is more useful (for you) to learn how to use a word.

4. For Bob to tell the truth is right.

   It is right (for Bob) to tell the truth.

5. (For you) to practice English every day is important.

   It is important (for you) to practice English every day.

6. For my sister to invent a new machine is impossible.

   It is impossible for my sister to invent a new machine.

7. For John to pay in cash wasn't necessary.

   It wasn't necessary for John to pay in cash.

8. Is it possible for you to finish the job in a week?

9. Is it all right for me to take the book back?

10. Do you think it proper for me to wear white gloves?

習題 288 解答

1. Her job is to type letters.

   It is her job to type letters.

2. His idea was to leave early.

   It was his idea to leave early.

3. Their business is to supply everybody with enough paper.

   It is their business to supply everybody with enough paper.

4. It is nice to see you again.

5. My duty is to warn them all to stay away.

   It is my duty to warn them all to stay away.

6. It is wonderful to be home again.

7. It was a delight to hear from you again.

8. It was a great honor for him to receive the award.

9. It always makes me dizzy to climb up high.

   It was just bad luck to have failed the course.

習題 289 解答

1. For them to learn Chinese characters is difficult.

   It difficult (for them) to learn Chinese characters.

   Chinese characters are difficult (for them) to learn.

2. For Henry to win the first place is lucky.

   It is lucky for Henry to have won the first place.

   Henry is lucky to have won the first place.

3. For us to ask him for help was foolish.

   It was foolish (for us) to ask him for help.

   We were foolish to ask him for help.

4. For you to answer this question is much easier.

   It is much easier (for you) to answer this question.

This question is much easier (for you) to answer.

5. I thought it impossible (for her) to learn the whole lesson by heart.

6. For you to agree to such a proposal was crazy.

It was crazy (for you) to agree to such a proposal.

You were crazy to agree to such a proposal.

7. Is it hard for them to deal with this case?

Is this case hard for them to deal with?

8. Isn't it fortunate for Jane to have a lot of good friends?

Isn't Jane fortunate to have a lot of good friends?

9. They consider it wrong (for you) to always talk like that.

10. For us to watch the dying child was really painful.

It was really painful (for us) to watch the dying child.

The dying child was really painful (for us) to watch.

習題 290 解答

1. It was unwise of you to accept his offer.

How unwise (it was) of you to accept his offer!

2. It was stupid of her to make such a mistake.

How stupid (it was) of her to make such a mistake!

3. It was careless of me to leave my book in the train.

How careless (it was) of me to leave my book in the train!

4. It was naughty of Mary to pull the kitten's tail.

How naught (it was) of Mary to pull the kitten's tail!

5. It was foolish of Bob to lend money to Dick.

How foolish (it was) of Bob to lend money to Dick!

6. It was clever of the boys to answer the questions so quickly.

How clever (it was) of the boys to answer the questions so quickly!

7. It was wrong of you to put the blame on him.

How wrong (it was) of you to put the blame on him!

8. It was polite of Henry to offer his seat to his teacher.

   How polite (it was) of Henry to offer his seat to his teacher!

9. It was brave of him to go into the burning building to save the child!

   How brave (it was) of him to go into the burning building to save the child!

10. It is wicked of them to say such things behind my back.

   How wicked (it is) of them to say such things behind my back!

習題 291 解答

1. She is eager to attend the party.

2. I'm very pleased to see you.

3. He is anxious to have to pass the examination.

4. She was delighted to hear his success.

5. He was disappointed to hear that the game was over.

6. I am afraid to see to principal.

7. Jane was excited to hear the good news.

8. Tom was very quick to realize his advantage.

9. Bob was slow to understand his mistake.

10. Dick was cruel to beat his sister.

11. Peter was wicked to tell me a lie.

12. You were lucky to be born into a rich family.

13. Jim was naughty to embarrass me before my friends.

14. I was crazy to give him all my money.

15. She was curious to want to know who the man was.

16. You are free to choose to go or stay.

17. I am sorry to trouble you.

18. I am sorry to have troubled you.

習題 292 解答

1. We find him to be a coward.

   We find him a coward.

2. We prove her to be wrong.

   We prove her wrong.

3. I thought them to be my friends.

   I thought them my friends.

4. He declares himself President.

5. Everyone believes this dictionary to be very useful.

6. We understand them to be in love with each other.

7. You must admit the task to be difficult.

8. He denied this to have been the case.

習題 293 解答

1. They want the house (to be) clean.

2. He has pushed the door open.

3. They set the prisoner free.

4. She left her hat downstairs.

5. He likes to wear his hair long.

6. He plans to paint the wall green.

7. They keep the meat in the refrigerator.

8. We mistook her to be your secretary.

9. I always thought him (to be) my best friend.

10. He found his favorite vase broken to pieces.

習題 294 解答

1. He ordered them to keep away from the dog.

2. She encouraged you to try agam and again.

3. They asked him to leave at once.

4. We reminded you not to forget your appointment.

5. They will force you to tell them the truth.

6. She begged them not to be so hard on her.

7. He urged us not to make any more mistakes.

8. We invited them to have dinner with us.

9. We warned each of them not to expect any favors.

10. They instructed us all to report to the embassy.

習題 295 解答

1. I expected to stay home.

2. He told me to stay home.

3. I persuaded myself to stay home.

4. He hates to pay out money.

5. Do you really intend to take a job next semester?

6. I'll have to remind myself to keep the appointment.

7. We tried hard to help him (to) win the prize.

8. I train each one to support himself.

9. Each one trains himrself to protect the other.

10. She doesn't even know how to pronounce the word correctly.

習題 296 解答

1. The teacher told us to practice English every day.

2. She watched him walk across the street.

3. Let me help you (to) finish your work.

4. The child begged her not to tell his father.

5. She heard someone break a glass.

6. I felt the earth move.

7. The manager let the secretary leave earlier than usual.

8. The doctor forced the nurse work until midnight.

9. The janitor noticed the burglar sneak into the apartment.

10. The robber made the clerk open the safe.

習題 297 解答

1. She was asked to come in.

2. The boy was seen to hit the dog.

3. I was advised to start early.

4. He was made to take up medicine.

5. She has never been known to lose her temper.

6. He is rumored to have escaped to South America.

7. Was John heard to leave the room?

8. He is said to have a lot of money.

9. He is said to have had a lot of money.

10. He is believed to have made acquaintance with many artists.

習題 298 解答

1. He seems to be displeased (by something).

2. He expects to be contracted (by someone).

3. He continues to be annoyed (by something).

4. He likes to be respected by everyone.

5. He tends to be misunderstood by everyone.

6. He began to be liked by everyone.

7. He wants to be taught (by someone).

8. He asked to be believed by everyone.

9. He happened to have been seen (by somebody).

10. He requested to be listened to by everybody.

習題 299 解答

1. They trained him to be a dancer.

2. They said that he was a dancer.

3. They knew that she was a novelist.

4. They invited him to be a speaker.

5. They supposed that she was a typist.

6. They encouraged him to be a doctor.

7. They understood that she was a secretary.

8. They expected him to be an engineer.

9. They believed him to be a Christian.

    They believed that he was a Christian.

10. They found him to be a Muslin.

    They found that he was a Muslin.

習題 300 解答

1. She advised us to wait another semester.

2. I wish to get there in time.

3. We understand you to come from Germany.

4. I prefer you to take a taxi.

5. He asked you not to speak English.

6. He didn't ask you to speak English.

7. We found him a coward.

8. I thought him to be outside.

9. They know Paul to have been abroad.

10. We believed him (to be) innocent.

11. She declared herself Queen.

12. No one seemed to know what happened.

13. He happend to be out of work at that time.

14. We chanced to be out when she called.

15. This appears to be the only exception to the rule.

習題 301 解答

1. No, but I hope to.

2. No, but I have to.

3. No, but I expect to.

4. No, but I ought to.

5. No, but I want to.

6. No, but I'd liketo.

7. No, but he intends to.

8. No, but I'd like to.

9. No, but she hopes to.

10. No, but he plans to.

習題 302 解答

1. I wonder how to do it.

2. Please tell me which to take.

3. Can you tell me who to see?

4. Can you advise me which to buy?

5. They told the girl where to get tickets.

6. She doesn't know what dress to wear.

7. Tell me when to be there, and I'll not be late.

8. They were not sure which room to give you.

9. He can't decide whether to attend the party or not.

10. I don't really know who to recommend you to apply to.

習題 303 解答

1. Who did you remind to call me up?

2. Who encourged you to be patient?

3. Where is she allowing them to sit?

4. What did I advise her to do?

5. When did she expect you to get up?

6. Who(m) did you instruct her to contact?

7. What did they warn everybody not to forget?

8. When does he like us all to be there?

9. What did she tell her children not to do?

10. Who(m) are you telling them to bring many chairs to?

習題 304 解答

1. Collecting stamps is his hobby.

2. Making lots of money is his only interest.

3. Selling is his business.

4. His business is falling off.

5. His job is changing.

6. Changing money is his job.

7. Turning out automobiles is his business.

8. His factory is turning out automobiles.

9. His favorite pastime is becoming his occupation.

10. Getting together for an evening of bridge is his favorite pastime.

習題 305 解答

1. I have just finished writing my paper.

2. Do you mind my / me smoking a pipe?

3. He insisted on going there himself.

4. I believe in helping others.

5. He denied having seen him before.

6. Some people admit to saying "It's me".

7. He's counting on their being able to lend him some money.

8. She dreads his / him having another heart attack.

9. Your composition needs to be improved.

Your composition needs improving.

10. I'll get around to correcting your papers tomorrow.

11. I can't risk you(r) leaving me without knowing where you are going.

12. Can you imagine his / him marrying a girl with a temper like hers?

習題 306 解答

1. We are careful to say the right thing.

   We are careful about saying the right thing.

2. We were surprised to see you in town.

   We were surprised at seeing you in town.

3. He was lucky to win the election.

   He was lucky at winning the election.

4. I was ashamed to make a mistake.

   I was ashamed of making a mistake.

5. She is afraid to fail the examination.

   She is afraid of failing the examination.

6. They were annoyed to have to do it all over again.

   They were annoyed with having to do it all over again.

7. I'm glad to be taking this course.

   I'm glad about being taking this course.

8. Is she satisfied to have a chance to compete?

   Is she satisfied with having a chance to compete?

9. They are anxious to arrive home safely.

   They are anxious about arriving home safely.

10. I'm disappointed not to see you.

   I'm disappointed with not seeing you.

習題 307 解答

1. We watched the train leaving the station.

2. I found her working at her desk.

   She was found working at her desk.

3. He kept me waiting in the lobby.

   I was kept waiting in the lobby.

4. They heard a plane coming nearer and nearer.

   A plane was heard coming nearer and nearer.

5. I smell something burning in the kitchen.

6. They listened to the band playing the national anthem.

7. They caught him stealing apples from his garden.

   He was caught stealing apples from his garden.

8. The news left me wondering what would happen next.

   I was left wondering what would happen next.

9. His question set all of us thinking seriously.

10. I could feel my heart beating rapidly.

習題 308 解答

1. It took him three weeks to complete the experiment.

2. She spent the whole day looking up all the new words.

3. It took the teacher half an hour to explain the problem to us.

4. John had a good time watching TV.

5. It will take the committe almost a year to investigate the matter.

6. Do you have trouble studying English?

7. We had an excellent time working together on the project.

8. I spent a lot of money fixing (/ to fix) my radio.

9. They will have a hard time looking for a job.

10. Did you have any difficulty explainning the word to a foreign student?

習題 309 解答

1. That he passed the course was a surprise.

   It was a surprise that he passed the course.

   For him to pass the course was a surprise.

It was a surprise for him to pass the course.

His passing the course was a surprise.

2. That she is leaving so suddenly is unfortunate.

It is unfortunate that she is leaving so suddenly.

For her to leave so suddenly is unfortunate.

It is unfortunate for her to leave so suddenly.

Her leaving so suddenly is unfortouate.

3. That you are alone without companions seems sad.

It seems sad that you are alone without companions.

For you to be alone without companions seems sad.

It seems sad for you to be alone without companions.

Your being alone without companions seems sad.

4. That they came home safely was a miracle.

It was a miracle that they came home safely.

For them to come home safely was a miracle.

It was a miracle for them to come home safely.

Their coming home safely was a miracle.

5. That he was not able to remember her name was very odd.

It was very odd that he was not able to remember her name.

For him not to be able to remember her name was very odd.

It was very odd for him not to be able to remember her name.

His not being able to remember her name was very odd.

習題 310 解答

1. I asked him to practice every day.

2. I wish that he practiced every day.

3. I objected to his practicing every day.

4. I wouldn't pay for him to practice every day.

5. I'm surprised that he practices every day.

I'm surprised at his practicing every day.

6. I encouraged him to practice every day.

7. It wasn't good that he practices every day.

   It wasn't good for him to practice every day.

8. I helped him (to) practice every day.

9. I can't imagine his practicing every day.

10. I'm telling you that he practices every day.

11. I'd rather (that) he practiced every day.

12. I assume that he practices every day.

13. I made him practice every day.

14. I didn't mind his (/ him) practicing every day.

15. I'm aware that he practices every day.

    I'm aware of his practicing every day.

16. He looked as if he (had) practiced every day.

17. It's high time that he practiced every day.

18. Are you sure that he practices every day?

19. I'll have him practice every day.

20. Don't you appreciate his practicing every day?

    Don't you appreciate that he practices every day?

習題 311 解答

1. We're confident of his being able to play well.

   We're confident of his ability to play well.

2. He's used to their being inclined to drink a little.

   He's used to their inclination to drink a little.

3. I'm glad about her being eligible to vote.

   I'm glad about her eligibility to vote.

4. They're sure of my being qualified to register.

   They're sure of my qualification to register.

5. She's opposed to our being free to move around.

   She's opposed to our freedom to move around.

6. We're satisfied with his being ready to the exam.

   We're satisfied with his readiness to take the exam.

7. He's tired of their being unable to finish on time.

   He's tired of their inability to finish on time.

8. I'm sorry about her being ineligible to vote.

   I'm sorry about her being ineligibility to vote.

9. They're disappointed with our being unwilling to do more.

   They're disappointed with our unwillingness to do more.

10. I'm concerned about his being reluctant to see a doctor.

    I'm concerned about his reluctance to see a doctor.

習題 312 解答

1. No one knew about his decision to leave home.

2. He was angry at her failure to keep her promise.

3. I have heard about her intention of going abroad (/ to go abroad).

4. She was very pleased with their invitation of her to attend the party.

5. You broke your promise to lend him money.

6. Her refusal to marry her boss surprised nobody.

7. His hatred of attending parties is a well-known fact.

8. He ignored their threat of calling the police.

9. Everybody knows her liking for wearing jewels.

10. My advice to him to study harder was all in vain.

習題 313 解答

1. our demand that you investigate the matter

   our demand for you to investigate the matter

2. the requirement that he take the course without delay

the requirement for him to take the course without delay

the requirement of his taking the course without delay

3. the possibility that she arrives on time

the possibility for her to arrive on time

the possibility of her arriving on time

4. his order that she not sell the car

his order for her not to sell the car

5. the probability that he arrived here in 1960

the probability for him to arrive here in 1960

the probability of his arriving here in 1960

6. our proposal that he not be punished

our proposal for him not to be punished

7. George's claim that you were there with him

George's claim for you to be there with him

8. the certainty that tomorrow will be warm and sunny

the certainty for the weather to be warm and sunny

the certainty of its warm and sunny

9. our expectation that they would have a lot of things to think about

out expectation for them to have a lot of things to think about

10. the expert's announcement that the government's estimate was accurate

the expert's announcement for the government's estimate to be accurate

習題 314 解答

1. I regret John's agreeing to the proposal.

2. They're glad to hear Jane's winning first prize in the speech contest.

3. The girl's singing of the national anthem brought the audience to their feet.

4. I cannot understand his not being willing to go to college.

5. You must keep in mind the fact of her giving money to him.

6. Jane's sweet singing of "Annie Lawrie" delighted everybody.

7. She found his questioning of her motives very annoying.

8. Her boss's constant questioning of her motives annoyed her.

9. Do you know Jack's leaving the town suddenly?

10. Jack's sudden leaving of the town caught us by surprise.

習題 315 解答

1. We watch the trees **swaying** in the wind.

   We watch the trees **sway** in the wind.

2. Didn't Mrs. Brown make her children **obey**?

3. Did you listen to the man $\begin{cases} \textbf{speak} \\ \textbf{speaking} \end{cases}$?

4. We like $\begin{cases} \textbf{to see} \\ \textbf{seeing} \end{cases}$ young people $\begin{cases} \textbf{enjoy} \\ \textbf{enjoying} \end{cases}$ themselves.

5. He admitted **taking** the money.

6. We have decided not **to go**.

7. The club endeavored **to raise** five thousand dollars for charity.

8. I don't care **to see** him again.

9. They encouraged me **to study** abroad.

10. I promised him not **to tell** you.

11. I dread **thinking** about it. I dread **to think** about it.

12. They intend **to call** her tomorrow.

13. The traffic continued $\begin{cases} \textbf{to move} \\ \textbf{moving} \end{cases}$ slowly.

14. Imagine **his winning** the first prize!

    Imagine **him winning** the first prize!

15. We expect **them to leave** tonight.

16. The child begged me not **to go**.

17. They allow **us to smoke** here.

They allow **our smoking** here.

18. They don't allow **smoking** here.

19. Do they permit **us to camp** here?

　　Do they permit **our camping** here?

20. Do they permit **camping** here?

21. I can't bear $\begin{Bmatrix} \textbf{seeing} \\ \textbf{to see} \end{Bmatrix}$ her $\begin{Bmatrix} \textbf{crying} \\ \textbf{cry} \end{Bmatrix}$.

22. I can't stand $\begin{Bmatrix} \textbf{hearing} \\ \textbf{to hear} \end{Bmatrix}$ that again.

23. He neglected **to file** his income tax return.

　　He neglected **filing** his income tax return.

24. I remember **to write** to him every week.

　　I remember **writing** to him every week.

25. She prefers **to type** her own letters.

　　She prefers **typing** her own letters.

26. I saw him $\begin{Bmatrix} \textbf{help} \\ \textbf{helping} \end{Bmatrix}$ her $\begin{Bmatrix} \textbf{to cook} \\ \textbf{cook} \end{Bmatrix}$ the dinner.

27. We finally got **him to accept** the offer.

28. I advise **you to see** a lawyer.

29. I didn't mean **to (have) hurt** your feelings.

30. We dislike **to play** bridge tonight.

31. I plan **to take** French next year.

32. My mother objected to **going** there.

33. Are you used to **getting** up early?

34. I used to **buy** my clothes in Dixon's.

35. Paper is used to **make** a lot of things.

36. The butler took to **hiding** the dishes he broke.

37. I am accustomed to **working** late.

38. They are looking forward to **seeing** you.

39. Mr. Wilson has dedicated himself to **helping** the poor.

40. The teacher couldn't get around to **correcting** our papers.

41. Philip devotes all his money to **studying**.

42. They went on $\begin{Bmatrix} \textbf{talking} \\ \textbf{to talk} \end{Bmatrix}$ for hours.

43. Let's keep on **working** for a while.

44. You had better hold off **writing** the letter until tomorrow.

45. I put off **doing** my assignment until the last minute.

46. I don't feel like **going** out today.

47. I don't feel up to **talking** with anybody else now.

48. If you keep **your talking** up you will be sorry.

49. I have avoided **meeting** him so far.

50. He escaped **being hurt** in the accident.

51. I'm sorry that I missed **seeing** you.

52. Mr. Jackson considered **buying** a car.

53. The guard commanded **us to halt**.

54. Don't start $\begin{Bmatrix} \textbf{to refuse} \\ \textbf{refusing} \end{Bmatrix}$ to listen before I **have begun**.

55. Let me help you $\begin{Bmatrix} \textbf{get} \\ \textbf{to get} \end{Bmatrix}$ it right.

56. He was encouraged **to start** $\begin{Bmatrix} \textbf{to look} \\ \textbf{looking} \end{Bmatrix}$ **for a** job immediately.

57. We have decided **to allow** her **to do** as **she wishes**.

58. She heard him $\begin{Bmatrix} \textbf{say} \\ \textbf{saying} \end{Bmatrix}$ he wanted **to buy the house**.

59. I would love **to hear** that orchestra $\begin{Bmatrix} \textbf{play} \\ \textbf{playing} \end{Bmatrix}$.

60. The manager let us watch the actors $\begin{cases} \textbf{rehearse} \\ \textbf{rehearsing} \end{cases}$.

61. They promised **to help** me **(to) prepare** for the party.

62. We found the trip **to be** very dull andwe couldn't help **saying** so.

63. Can you **manage to finish packing** these parcels by yourself?

64. She endeavored **to arrange to come** early **to help (to) cut** the bread and butter.

65. Have you ever watched people $\begin{cases} \textbf{try} \\ \textbf{trying} \end{cases}$ **to catch** fish.

66. Try to **avoid offending** him.

67. Are you going **to keep** me **waiting** all day?

68. Do you remember $\begin{cases} \textbf{my} \\ \textbf{me} \end{cases}$ **returning** those books to the library?

69. My mother hates $\begin{cases} \textbf{my} \\ \textbf{me} \end{cases}$ **smoking** in the bathroom.

70. I dislike $\begin{cases} \textbf{your} \\ \textbf{you} \end{cases}$ **reminding** me continually of the things I ought to have done.

71. I always enjoy **watching** $\begin{cases} \textbf{him act} \\ \textbf{his acting} \end{cases}$ Shakespeare.

72. Do you mind $\begin{cases} \textbf{my} \\ \textbf{me} \end{cases}$ **closing** the window?

73. I can't risk $\begin{cases} \textbf{your} \\ \textbf{you} \end{cases}$ **leaving** me without **knowing** where you're going.

74. I don't think she will forgive $\begin{cases} \textbf{our} \\ \textbf{us} \end{cases}$ **eating** all the rest of the pipe.

75. I dread $\begin{cases} \textbf{his} \\ \textbf{him} \end{cases}$ **coming** back when I'm alone.

76. I advise you **to stop thinking** of **carrying** out such a dangerous plan.

77. Please excuse $\begin{Bmatrix} \textbf{my} \\ \textbf{me} \end{Bmatrix}$ **saying** so.

78. Would you mind **watching** the instructor $\begin{Bmatrix} \textbf{demonstrte} \\ \textbf{demonstrating} \end{Bmatrix}$ so as to learn **to swim** more quickly?

79. I beg you **to hesitate** before **deciding to accept** his proposal.

80. Could I trouble you **to arrange to travel** with my young brother?

81. She loves **powdering** her nose.

82. I'd like to **powder** my nose.

83. She told me how **to make** clothes **last** longer.

84. She forgot $\begin{Bmatrix} \textbf{to remind} \\ \textbf{reminding} \end{Bmatrix}$ you **to give** the servants orders **to prepare** for their arrival.

85. The witness was compelled **to swear to speak** the truth.

86. They took her **to be** a foreigner on **hearing** her $\begin{Bmatrix} \textbf{speak} \\ \textbf{speaking} \end{Bmatrix}$.

87. I beseech you **to persuade** her **to be** reasonable.

88. They noticed him $\begin{Bmatrix} \textbf{hesitating} \\ \textbf{hesnate} \end{Bmatrix}$ **to sign** the agreement.

89. Don't let me **find** you **day-dreaming** again.

90. They dislike $\begin{Bmatrix} \textbf{to be} \\ \textbf{being} \end{Bmatrix}$ **interrogated** while **trying to finish** a piece of work.

91. This loss went near to **ruining** him.

92. The army came near **obtaining** a complete victory.

習題 316 解答

1. That <u>pretty</u> **girl** is <u>John's</u> **sister**.

2. The **car** <u>outside</u> belongs to <u>my</u> **uncle**.

3. The **building** <u>with a red roof</u> is the <u>school</u> **library**.

4. That is a very <u>disappointing</u> **answer** indeed.

5. I have never seen a **girl** more beautiful than Mary.

6. The **hat** on the counter is different from the **one** on the shelf.

7. He gave me some **coffee** to drink.

8. The mother tenderly kissed the sleeping **baby**.

9. A **child** whose parents are dead is an orphan.

10. I don't know the **place** he lives.

習題 317 解答

1. a nêw máster（新的主人）

   a héad màster（中學或小學的校長）

2. a hîgh wáll（很高的牆）

   a brîck wáll（磚牆）

3. a bîg báll（很大的球）

   a cánnon bàll（礮彈）

4. an êvening páper（晚報）

   some whîte páper（一些白色的紙）

5. a bêautiful flówer（美麗的花朵）

   a gârden flówer（花園內的花）

   a gárden flòwer（適合於種在花園裏的花）

6. a strânge náme（奇怪的名字）

   a fámily nàme（姓）

7. a lông spóon（很長的湯匙）

   a sîlver spóon（由銀製成的湯匙）

8. an ôld lámp（舊油燈）

   a désk làmp（枱燈）

9. a spâre tícket（備用的車票）

   a retúrn tìcket（回程票）

10. ûseless fúrniture（沒有用的傢具）

    díning roòm fùrniture（餐廳用的傢具）

11. a sîngíng bírd（唱著歌的鳥）

 a réading roòm（閱覽室）

12. an Eñglish géntleman（英國籍的紳士）

 an Eñglish téacher（英國籍的老師）

 an Eñglish tèacher（教英文的老師）

習題 318 解答

1. She's a happy wife.

2. It's a very interesting story.

3. It was stolen money.

4. He's a returned hero.

5. It's a burning building.

6. It's a walking stick.

7. He's a retired general.

8. They're dormitory students.

9. It's a growing economy.

10. They're moaning patients.

11. She was a very much frightened girl.

12. He's an escaped convict.

13. They're failing students.

14. It's a settled matter.

15. It's running water.

16. It's writing paper.

17. He's a flying officer.

18. It's (They're) an angrily snouting mob.

19. They're newly arrived guests.

20. It's a surprisingly high price.

習題 319 解答

1. I gave an honest answer.

2. She makes regular contributions.

3. He does occasional odd jobs.

4. They suffered frequent defeats.

5. We need continual repair.

6. I'll do a careful analysis.

7. He offered enthusiastic advice.

8. He has his usual tea.

9. They held a peaceful demonstration.

10. I must have an immediate explanation.

習題 320 解答

1. The party was pleasing (to the guests).

   The guests were pleased (with the party).

2. The questions were confusing (to the students).

   The students were confused (by the question).

3. His long talk was tiring (to us).

   We were tired (of his long talk).

4. The children were amusing (to the parents).

   The parents were amused (by the children).

5. The concert was disappointing (to the audience).

   The audience was disappointed (in / by the concert).

6. The performer was fascinating (to the spectators).

   The spectators were fascinated (by the performer).

7. The horror movie was frightening (to the children).

   The children were frightened (by the horror movie).

8. The TV program was never boring (to him).

   He was never bored (by the TV program).

9. Yesterday's events were upsetting (to them).

   They were upset (about / over yesterday's events).

10. His argument was convincing (to everybody).

    Everybody was convinced (by his argument).

11. Her remarks are not interesting (to me).

    I'm not interested (in her remarks).

12. Were the results amazing (to you) ?

    Were you amazed (at the results) ?

習題 321 解答

1. dried   2. baked   3. lost   4. damaged

5. broiled	6. faded	7. constructed	8. finished
9. known	10. excited	11. buried	12. sparkling
13. whistling	14. proposed	15. startled	16. closed
17. waiting	18. reduced	19. typed, written	20. expected

習題 322 解答

1. It's a moving train. / The train is moving.

2. It was a very moving experience. / The experience was very moving.

3. It's a very striking resemblance. / The resemblance is very striking.

4. They're striking workers. / The workers are striking.

5. He's the commanding officer. / The officer commands.

6. He had a very commanding presence. / His presence is very commanding.

7. It was not a very convincing argument. / The argument was not very convincing.

8. Was it a very thrilling race? / Was the race very thrilling?

習題 323 解答

1. lamp shade	2. sailing boat	3. college student
4. lifeboat	5. apple tree	6. mailbox
7. desk lamp	8. teacup	9. traffic lights
10. shoe store	11. church bell	12. hat box
13. engagement ring	14. doorman	15. baseball game ticket
16. department store	17. ten-cent stamp	18. raincoat
19. salesman	20. moonlight	

習題 324 解答

1. this large college dormitory

2. those tall sophomore players

3. that photogenic girl swimmer

4. this enthusiastic senior counselor

5. George's blue wool necktie

6. her old leather shoes

7. his large hardwood desk   8. these cheap ballpoint pens

9. my portable student typewriter   10. our sturdy garden fence

習題 325 解答

1. It's a bôok about hístory. It's a hístory bòok.

2. It's smôke from cigaréttes. It's cigarétte smòke.

3. It was a cônference on disármament.

    It was a disármament cònference.

4. He's a mêmber of the fáculty. He is a fáculty mèmber.

5. It's a tîcket for móvies. It's a móvie ticket.

6. It's pôlish for shóes. It's shóe pòlish.

7. It's fûrniture for the living ròom. It's líving ròom fùrniture.

8. It was a môvie about wár. It was a wár mòvie.

9. It was a spêech on eléction. It was an eléction spèech.

10. They're lôans for stúdents. They're stúdent lòans.

習題 326 解答

1. It's an impôrtant mátter.   2. It's a búsiness màtter.

3. He's a pâtient mán.   4. He's a cíty mán.

5. They're wêalthy péople.   6. They're sôciety péople.

7. It's a tráffic pròblem.   8. It's an ûrgent próblem.

9. It's a lêngthy prógram.   10. It's a strông posítion.

習題 327 解答

1. sélling prìce   2. stánding roòm   3. exîsting dánger

4. líving stàndard   5. wrápping pàper   6. inqûiring mínd

7. líving còst   8. sléeping pìll   9. rîsing cósts

10. gúessing gàmes   11. bóiling poìnt   12. prínting bùsiness

13. párking plàce   14. spénding mòney   15. chéwing gùm

16. prêssing néed   17. revôlving dóor   18. decîding vóte

19. ácting carèer   20. invéstigating commìttee

習題 328 解答

1. the job of editing   2. a pan for frying

3. the side (that) opposes   4. a place of hiding.

5. privileges of voting   6. a cup for measuring

7. an agreement (that) works   8. the point of breaking

9. fluid for cleaning   10. facilities for recording

11. a current (that) shifts   12. heat (that) stifles

13. a machine for dictating   14. marks for identifying

15. power of purchasing   16. opinions (that) differ

17. remark (that) cuts   18. edge for cutting

19. a pain (that) grows   20. pains of growing

習題 329 解答

1. Fôlding cháir   2. Rócking chàir

3. Rîsing príces   4. Sélling prìces

5. Speêding cár   6. Rácing càr

7. Míning còmpany   8. Expânding cómpany

9. Prâcticing attórney   10. Prósecuting attòrney

11. Téaching expèrience   12. Înteresting expérience

習題 330 解答

1. They're fâst-môving cárs.

2. They're hâppy-lôoking stúdents.

3. They're hâbit-fôrming drúgs.

4. They're fâr-rêaching decísions.

5. They're bâd-smêlling éggs.

6. They're wîde-rânging refórms.

7. They're tâx-pâying cítizens.

8. It's fâst-wôrking médicine.

9. He's a bêer-drînking sérgeant.

10. They're fôrward-lôoking mén.

11. It's a têmpting smêlling róast.

12. They're lông-lâsting effécts.

13. It's a wônderful-sôunding párty.

14. It's a mân-eâting tíger.

15. They're âll-knôwing politícians.

16. They're lông-plâying récords.

17. It's an outgôing máil.

18. It's a tíme-consûming operátion.

19. He's a hîgh-rânking díplomat.

20. It's hêart-brêaking néws.

習題 331 解答

1. It's a van for moving furniture.

   It's a fúrniture-mòving vàn.

2. It's a society for watching birds.

   It's a bírd-wàtching socìety.

3. It's a committee for finding the facts.

   It's a fáct-finding commìttee.

4. It's a department for cleaning the streets.

   It's a stréet-cleàning depàrtment.

5. It's a campaign for getting the votes.

   It's a vóte-gètting campàign.

6. It's an apparatus for fighting fires.

   It's a fíre-fighting apparàtus.

7. It's time for cleaning the house.

It's hóuse-clèaning tìme.

8. It's an equipment for saving lives.

It's a lífe-sàving eqùipment.

9. It's a party for coming home.

It's a hóme-còming pàrty.

10. It's an expedition for climbing the mountain.

It's a móuntain-clìmbing expedìtion.

習題 332 解答

1. He's a well-dressed gentleman.

2. It was a hastily erected bridge.

3. It was a well-pitched ball.

4. It was a repeatedly bombed target.

5. She's a well-educated girl.

3. It was a perfectly planned party.

7. It was a brilliantly performed program.

8. It was an officially announced engagement.

9. It has been a long-established tradition.

10. It was a half-filled glass.

11. He was a seriously wounded soldier.

12. It was a badly damaged bridge.

習題 333 解答

1. They're worn-out shoes.

2. They're well-known scholars.

3. She's a self-educated woman.

4. It's hand-made furniture.

5. They're trouble-making gangs.

6. It is a moth-eaten rug.

7. They are laid-off workers.

8. They're well-educated citizens.

9. It's government-owned property.

10. He is a self-elected official.

11. It is a burned-out engine.

12. He's a self-employed businessman.

13. They're paid-for announcements.

14. It's city-operated transportation.

15. It's a student-organized demonstration.

16. He is a self-appointed spokesman.

17. It is a broken-down car.

18. It's a home-cooked meal.

19. It's an enemy-held territory.

20. They're chocolate-covered peanuts.

習題 334 解答

1. He is a boy with fair hair.

   He is a fair-haired boy.

2. It is a train with ten cars.

   It is a ten-car train.

3. He is a radical with a strong will.

   He is a strong-willed radical.

4. It is a shirt with short sleeves.

   It is a short-sleeved shirt.

5. It is an apartment with three rooms.

   It is a three-room apartment.

6. They are traditions with deep roots.

   They are deep-rooted (deeply-rooted) traditions.

7. It is a building with ten stories.

   It is a ten-story building.

8. He is a boy with many talents.

   He is a many-talented boy.

9. He is a man with a narrow mind.

   He is a narrow-minded man.

10. They are shoes with high heels.

    They are high-heeled shoes.

11. It is a jet with twin engines.

    It is a twin-engine jet.

12. It is an animal with four feet.

    It is a four-footed animal.

13. He is a scientist with a mind like a computer.

    He is a computer-minded scientist.

14. She is a woman with a mind on a career.

    She is a career-minded woman.

15. It is a pudding with a flavor like orange.

    It is an orange-flavored pudding.

習題 335 解答

1. a licensed driver

2. striped shirts

3. the helmeted police

4. a spirited discussion

5. a biased opinion

6. stringed instruments

7. a salaried employee

8. uniformed troops

9. a simple-minded housewife

10. a (strikingly) talented person

11. a long-legged athlete

12. a brilliantly gifted performer

13. a short tempered official

14. a clearly detailed photograph

15. a deeply / deep rooted tradition

16. a well-mannered student

習題 336 解答

1. He's (She's) a broad-minded parent.

2. It's a well-earned vacation.

3. She's (He's) a marvelously gifted performer.

4. He's a young licensed driver.

5. It's a wide-angled lens.

6. It's a fast-cooked meal.

7. It's a strongly biased opinion.

8. He's a well-intentioned person.

9. It's a broad-brimmed hat.

10. They're horn-rimmed glasses.

11. It's a three-cornered hat.

12. It's a three-room apartment.

習題 337 解答

1. has been burnt	2. is painted	3. has retired
4. is lying	5. is torn	6. has departed
7. are deeply moved	8. is well-educated	9. finds (the) facts

10. shatters ones nerves　　11. has two stories

12. has a broad mind　　13. has two edges

14. was born first　　15. keeps house

16. looks humble　　17. has been paid up

18. is turned up　　19. are made at home

20. are made in Japan　　21. worn-out

22. well-dressed　　23. heart-breaking

24. kind-hearted　　25. blue-eyed

26. weak-sighted　　27. well-furnished

28. thought-inspiring　　29. sulky-looking

30. slow-witted 　　　　 31. short-tempered

32. panic-stricken 　　　 33. labor-saving

34. high-ranking 　　　　 35. far-reaching

36. left-handed 　　　　 37. shabby-looking

38. Swiss-made 　　　　 39. good-for-nothing

40. long-looked-for

習題 338 解答

1. There were many rain clouds in the sky.

2. Mr. Smith bought a gray flannel suit yesterday.

3. That low wire fence must be removed.

4. The women wore their new evening dresses to the opera.

5. Let me see these two steel knives.

6. Jack wants to be a fóreign lànguage tèacher.

7. There are some other bad newspaper reports.

8. Any such childish pranks are unworthy of you.

9. We need much more white sand.

10. All the last three chapters are very important.

11. Both my studious Chinese roommates want to go.

12. I want no cold cheese sandwich.

13. All our friendly neighborhood dogs never bite.

14. Where can I get another huge glass ornament?

15. We need all the long copper wires.

16. Both her lovely engagement rings are expensive.

17. What are you going to do with all those fresh prairie flowers?

18. Half our new engineering students come from China.

19. This is a very valuable old gold watch.

20. I want to buy a long brown leather belt.

21. There is a high red brick wall around the house.

22. Where did you get these smart brown snakeskin shoes?

23. I've bought several large red pickling cabbages.

24. This is quite an attractive triangular green Cape-Colony stamp.

習題 339 解答

1. The library has several very easy English books.

2. Mrs. Miller has a very pretty green suit.

3. The church has some very old Spanish pictures.

4. I like those two blue silk dresses.

5. Her pretty black wool dress is at the cleaner's.

6. The parents select their two children's first names (The parents select their first two children's names).

7. These five new one-dollar bills are for you.

8. Her daughter's first two names are Mary Grant.

9. Our first six reading lessons are not difficult.

10. The teacher's two interesting afternoon classes are large.

11. That old blue evening dress is beautiful on her.

12. Several very good American radio programs are beginning this month.

習題 340 解答

1. Korea's proposal to the United Nations

   the Korean proposal to the United Nations

   the proposal to the United Nations by Korea

2. China's solution of (to. for) that problem

   the Chinese solution of (to, for) that problem

   the solution of that problem by China

3. France's application for membership

   the French application for membership

   the application for membership by France

4. Russia's belief in subverting unfriendly governments

   the Russian belief in subverting unfriendly governments

   the belief in subverting unfriendly governments by Russia

5. Germany's request to Japan to attack America

   the German request to Japan to attack America

   the request to Japan to attack America by Germany

6. France's attempt to determine the Algerian government

   the French attempt to determine the Algerian government

   the attempt to determine the Algerian government by France

7. Britain's realization that the Empire was doomed

   the British realization that the Empire was doomed

   the realization by Britain that the Empire was doomed

8. America's wish for Germany to attack Russia

   the American wish for Germany to attack Russia

   the wish for Germany to attack Russia by America

9. India's explosion of its first atomic bomb

   the Indian explosion of its first atomic bomb

   the explosion of the first atomic bomb by India

10. Spain's constant justification of itself

    the constant Spanish justification of itself

    the constant justification of itself by Spain

習題 341 解答

1. The branches overhead were laden with fruit.

2. The discussion yesterday was informal and lively.

3. The laundry outside is almost dry.

4. The party downstairs is very noisy.

5. The clouds above us were dark and threatening.

6. The road ahead was crowded with automobiles.

7. The noise during the party annoyed the neighbors.

8. She longed for her home town thousands of miles away.

9. The applause after the performance was loud and enthusiastic.

10. The refreshments (served by the hostess) following the dance were delicious.

習題 342 解答

1. The clock on the wall says 4:30.

   The wall clock says 4:30.

2. They live in a room in a dormitory.

   They live in a dormitory room.

3. He is looking for a job for the summer.

   He is looking for a summer job.

4. She bought a book about psychology.

   She bought a psychology book.

5. Don't forget to take the lunch in the box with you.

   Don't forget to take the lunch box with you.

6. She's expecting to get a check from the government today.

   She's expecting to get a government check today.

7. Where did you get the frame for the picture?

   Where did you get the picture frame?

8. She sang a song of love.

   She sang a love song.

9. They attended the conference on disarmament.

   They attended the disarmament conference.

10. Can I use your telephone to make a call out of town?

    Can I use your telephone to make an out-of-town call?

習題 343 解答

1. the cup with a broken handle

2. the boy without friends

3. the coat with three pockets

4. the clerk without a necktie

5. the baby without (any) clothes on (*or* the baby with no clothes on)

6. the poor orphans without a home

7. the woman with an angry look in her eyes

8. the man without a single penny with him

9. the soldier with a sword in his hand

10. the lady without a hat or a coat on

習題 344 解答

1. He's an honest man.

2. He's a doorman.

3. He's a man with sun-glasses.

4. He's a one-eyed man.

5. He's a garbage collector.

6. He's a businessman from Brazil.

7. He's a fat man with a moustache.

8. He's a thin man without a coat on.

9. He's a man in naval uniform.

10. He is a newspaperman from New York.

習題 345 解答

1. They are looking for the person missing from school.

   They are looking for the missing person.

2. Get me the water boiling on the stove.

   Get me the boiling water.

3. I can't hit the target moving so fast.

   I can't hit the moving target.

4. Men trained in mathematics can be engineers.

   Trained men can be engineers.

5. Did you hear the rumor spreading around the town?

   Did you hear the spreading rumor?

6. We are going to support the workers striking for higher salary.

   We are going to support the striking workers.

7. The packages insured by the sender get special handling.

   The insured packages get special handling.

8. It was unsale to enter the building damaged by fire.

   It was unsafe to enter the damaged building.

9. We went directly to the table reserved in our name.

   We went directly to the reserved table.

10. A student beginning his studies at this university must take no more than fifteen credits.

    A beginning student must take no more than fifteen credits.

習題 346 解答

1. That statement was stupid to make.

   That was a stupid statement to make.

2. That comparison wasn't hard to make.

   That wasn't a hard comparison to made.

3. George is (a) wonderful (person) to work with.

4. Those places were dangerous to explore.

   Those were dangerous places to explore.

5. She is (an) impossible (person) to argue with.

6. These offices are pleasant to work in.

   These are pleasant offices to work in.

7. Your analysis is funny to listen to.

   Yours is a funny analysis to listen to.

8. A Volkswagen is (an) economical (car) to drive.

9. Twenty-five dollars was a terrible price to pay.

Twenty-five dollars was a price terrible to pay.

10. "My Fair Lady" is a marvelous show to go to.

"My Fair Lady" is a show marvelous to go to.

習題 347 解答

1. He went to the bookstore on the campus.

2. Pass me the newspaper lying on the table.

3. We don't often see a movie as good as that.

4. Fines paid by students on overdue books are placed in the scholarship fund.

5. The secretaries working weekends get additional pay.

6. They attended the conference on public health.

7. A house as cheap as that is difficult to find.

8. You can buy your shirts at the shop opposite the post office.

9. Do you know the girl standing between Betty and Anne?

10. They sat down at the table reserved in their name.

習題 348 解答

1. Here comes **George**, your best friend.

2. **Mr. Smith**, the Secretary, read the minutes of the last meeting.

3. **The other**, Miss Thompson, is very beautiful.

4. It was **Sunday**, always a dull day in **London**.

5. **You** Germans admire Hitler, **we** *English* do not.

6. **These boys** were absent-namely, *Tom, Dick* and *Harry*.

7. There are many **Latin words** in present-day English, for example, ratio and bonus.

8. **They** were themselves busy that day.

9. **They** are neither of them very honest.

10. I have **three ambitions**, to live in peace, to have a few good friends, and to finish my

life-work successfully.

11. **The news** that her son had been killed was a great shock to her.

12. **It** occurred to me that it was a good opportunity.

習題 349 解答

1. We saw Hamlet, a play by Shakespeare.

2. Mr. Wilson, the oldest resident, moved away.

3. President Harding was called to Washington.

4. The motorcycle, a secondhand contraption, was in good shape.

5. We inspected his new car, a long sleek Humber.

6. "Trees", his favorite poem, was included in the new collection.

7. I felt what I always feel, a sense of frustration.

8. The dog, man's best friend, can be an infernal nuisance.

9. The idea that Alice is a thief is ridiculous.

10. The proposal that we send a telegram to the President was defeated.

習題 350 解答

1. The old man with the gray hair is a music professor.

2. The evening lecture on the life in the United States was very interesting.

3. The third examination question on the second page was difficult.

4. Those two steel knives in the drawer are sharp.

5. Here are some paper napkins for you to wash.

6. The young men wearing the uniforms are Egyptian army officers.

7. The thin boy in the blue sweater talking to the professor is John's cousin.

8. Do those new English magazines on the table in the hall belong to you?

習題 351 解答

1. sleepy	2. asleep	3. asleep	4. sleepy
5. content	6. contented	7. content	8. contented

9. older   10. elder   11. elderly   12. alive

13. live   14. alive   15. alive   16. lively

17. ashamed; shameful   18. fearful   19. afraid   20. alike

21. Like; like   22. likely   23. likely   24. likely

習題 352 解答

1. She is a poor typist.

2. He was a true poet.

3. The girl was a total stranger in the town.

4. She was his former wife.

5. He is your present friend.

6. He was the regular champion.

7. She is a beautiful soprano.

8. He is a criminal lawyer.

9. He is a rural policeman.

10. His main argument is that he needs more time to work on his project.

習題 353 解答

1. These are the boys (who work hard).

2. The boy (who was lazy) was punished.

3. This is the place (where he lived).

4. Those (whom the gods love) die young.

5. The cat killed the rat (That ate the corn).

6. I know the woman (whose child was hurt).

7. They (who live in glass houses) should not throw stones.

8. The moment (which is lost) is lost for ever.

9. He has lost the watch (you gave him).

10. The books (which keep you most) are those (which makes you think most).

習題 354 解答

1. quite a few Americans that I know

2. the family that lives here

3. the book that she asked about

4. the pen that cost me ten dollars

5. the museum that they are going to visit

6. the doctor that was talking to a patient

7. the doctor that John went to see

8. advice that he gave to some people

9. some people that he gave advice to

10. the country that I come from

11. the laboratory that she is working in

12. the money that he gave to the clerk

13. the clerk that he gave the money to

14. the man that we elected captain

15. the movie actress that she looks like

習題 355 解答

1. Women who / that work in hospitals are to be admired.

2. The doctor who(m) / that she visited is famous.

3. The girl who(m) / that you see at the door is my sister.

4. The people who / that are looking at that house are my parents.

5. All the people who(m) / that I have ever met have disliked him.

6. Who is the girl who / that is sitting at the door?

7. Where is the student who(m) / that you sold your old dictionary to?

8. The man who(m) / that you spoke to in the street is my English teacher.

9. Buy it back from the man who(m) / that you sold it to.

10. What was the name of the girl who / that lost the book which / that you lent her?

習題 356 解答

1. The cigarette (that / which) you are smoking is quite expensive.

2. The fish (that / which) I ate yesterday was not good.

3. The doctor (that / who(m)) she visited is famous.

4. The music (that / which) the orchestra is playing is Strauss waltz.

5. The noise (that / which) you hear is only our dogs fighting.

6. I would like to see the trees (that / which) you picked these apples from.

7. The people (that / who(m)) you were living with in New York are coming to see you.

8. Can you remember the person (that / who(m)) you took it from?

9. That's the knife and fork (that / which) I eat with.

10. What's that music which you are listening to?

11. Here comes the girl (that / who(m)) I am hiding from.

12. Who is the gentleman that is watching the lady (that / who(m)) you spoke to a moment ago?

習題 357 解答

1. food much of which is cold

2. classes some of which met at night

3. coffee all of which has sugar in

4. five answers one of which is completely wrong

5. students most of whom are from China

6. two guests neither of whom had a reservation

7. members each of whom has to pay ten dollars

8. possibilities only a few of which are feasible

習題 358 解答

1. the boy whose brother is a policeman

2. the girl whose progress was remarkable

3. the man whose son is in the navy

4. the friends whose faces I will never fogot

   (these friends, whose faces I will never forget)

5. the man whose English we can't understand

6. the fox whose tail the hunter caught

7. the university whose faculty is mostly Chinese

8. the committee whose advice they aren't asking for

9. the woman whose native language we can't identify

10. the company whose employees are on strike for higher wages

習題 359 解答

1. A child whose parents are dead is called an orphan.

2. This is the girl whose mother is president of the PTA.

3. That's the man whose daughter Betty is going to marry.

4. The client whose stock he was handling died.

5. The man whose name I always forget is coming to tea.

6. The policeman whose helmet you knocked off is at the door.

7. The girl whose mother I was talking to has left the room.

8. A woman whose mind is made up is more obstinate than a man.

9. What's the name of the man whose wife has run away and left him?

10. The boy whose work I showed you is the cleverest boy in the school.

11. He went to a university whose faculty is mostly Catholic.

12. The house in whose windows there is a light is mine.

習題 360 解答

1. the place (that / where) my father works

2. the time (that / when) we had an appointment

3. the way (that) they went home

4. the place (that / where) I bought this dictionary

5. the year (that / when) they met each other

6. the reason (that / why) he left for England

7. the time (that / when) a lot of people travel

8. the day (that / when) we paid a visit to our teacher

9. the place (that / where) the general was defeated

10. the time (that / when) I like to take a walk

11. the place (that / where) she put her necklace

12. the reason (that / why) he could not attend the meeting

13. the manner (that) our teacher explained the problem to me

14. the time (that / when) she arrived home

15. the manner (that) he wrote his report

習題 361 解答

1. I cannot find the place (that / where) I lost it.

2. The hour (that / when) we leave has not been decided.

3. Tell us the reason (that / why) you did not come.

4. I met her the year (that / when) my father died.

5. Is that the house (where / that) Bill was born in?

6. There is no reason (that / why) he should not be admitted.

7. There are times (that / when) such things are necessary.

8. I'll go anywhere (that) you want me to go.

9. We passed the house (where) the fire started.

10. Those were the days (that / when) no one cared to be alive.

11. On the day after we started our car blew up.

12. The year after he enlisted was a momentous one.

13. The woods (where) we camped were filled with mushrooms.

14. Brazil is the place (that / where) most of the coffee comes from.

15. The reason (that / why) he moved is now obvious.

16. Ten o'clock is the time (that / when) they take their coffee break.

習題 362 解答

1. where	2. why	3. when	4. where	5. where
6. where	7. when	8. where	9. why	10. when

習題 363 解答

1. as	2. than	3. than	4. but	5. as
6. as	7. as	8. but	9. as	10. as
11. As	12. than	13. as	14. as	15. but

習題 364 解答

1. There is no child that does not know him.

   Every child knows him.

2. There was no boy that does not fall in love with her.

   Every boy falls in love with her.

3. There is no work that he can not criticize.

   He can criticize every work.

4. There is not a bird that does not do more harm than good.

   Every bird does more harm than good.

5. There is no friend that he cannot find fault with.

   He finds / can find fault with every friend

6. There was not a soldier among them that did not hope to get out alive.

   Every soldier among them hoped to get out alive.

習題 365 解答

1. who(m)	2. who	3. which	4. which	5. who
6. which	7. which	8. which	9. who	10. which
11. who	12. which	13. which	14. which	15. whom

習題 366 解答

1. They have four children, who all of whom go to college.

2. He passed his examination with honors, which made his parents very proud of him.

3. John went fishing last week-end, which is one of the pleasantest ways of spending one's leisure.

4. I gave Mary a box of candies, which pleased her very much.

5. He studied hard in his youth, which contributed to his success in later life.

6. I saw two dwarfs at the circus, neither of whom was over three feet tall.

7. She was dropped when she was a baby, which made her a permanent invalid.

8. We have two spare rooms upstairs, neither of which has been used for years.

9. He came home drunk the other night, which shocked the whole neighborhood.

10. My uncle built several houses, none of which are more than two miles from the station.

習題 367 解答

1. My mother, who lives in Taichung, teaches school.

2. Beth, whose father is rich, spends a lot on her clothes.

3. Geometry, which I know nothing about, seems a very dull subject.

4. The king, whose life has been devoted to his country, deserves his popularity.

5. My sister, who faints at the sight of blood, plans on becoming a nurse.

6. Her clothes, which are made in Paris, are all beautiful.

7. Chess, which is a very old game, is difficult to play.

8. Jane, whose pride was hurt, looked angry.

9. We took a taxi to Kennedy Airport, which was a few miles outside New York.

10. That land, which was once a paddy field, is now very valuable.

11. Switzerland, which is a small country in Europe, is noted for its beautiful scene.

12. The chief of police, whose work is very important, takes care of the public safety.

13. He met my mother, from whom he got the news of my marriage.

14. We, who are all fond of tomatoes, cannot decide whether tomatoes are a fruit or a vegetable.

15. Our refrigerator, whose motor often stops, was made in 1950.

習題 368 解答

1. The best time to talk is at night, when we aren't busy.

2. We went to Rome, where we stopped a week.

3. At sunrise, when it is cold, is too early to go swimming.

4. They traveled together as far as Europe, where they separated.

5. The nicest day in Mary's life was May 5, 1957, when she met Paul.

6. The school library, where nobody will disturb you, is the best place to study.

習題 369 解答

1. A teacher who teaches will be popular.

2. A student who comes to school late will be punished.

3. A pen which / that leaks should be repaired.

4. A person who is an original thinker will make a scientist.

5. Buildings that / which are strong will last many years.

6. A house that / which is painted white is cooler in the summer.

7. Anyone who reads fast can do well in school.

8. People who live in glass houses should not throw stones.

9. An egg that / which is spoiled can't be used for anything.

10. A woman who is in mourning often wears a black dress.

習題 370 解答

1. That is the house (that / which) we have been invited to.

   That is the house to which we have been invited.

2. The gentleman whose foot you trod on is our school master.

3. The building opposite which I live is the Finance Ministry.

   The building (that / which) I live opposite is the Finance Ministry.

4. The spoon (that / which) he was eating the soup with was stolen from a hotel.

5. The fountain around which they are standing was built by the Romans.

   The fountain (that / which) they are standing around was built by the Romans.

6. This is the point beyond which I have never been.

   This is the point (that / which) I have never been beyond.

7. The pen (which / that) I wrote the letter with has a steel nib.

8. I appreciate the kind words (that / which) you have welcomed me with.

9. The dignity with which he repudiated the charge greatly impressed the judge.

10. The tree fell on to a party of fishermen, all of whom were injured.

11. St. John's Glacier, beyond which I've never climbed, is only about 8,000 feet high.

12. He was not such a coward as we took him for.

13. The old man (that / who(m)) you were talking to me about and told me to go and see has died.

14. Miss Taylor, whose father is a millionaire, has several new friends, all of whom are artists.

習題 371 解答

1. a piece of land from which each obtains his food

2. some countries for which it's impossible to predict the outcome

3. the cultivation of land from which they derive all their income

4. the food for which they're always competing among themselves

5. better fertilizer through the use of which productivity will increase

6. medical knowledge advances in which will lengthen the average life span

習題 372 解答

1. The flight on which they arrived originated in San Francisco.

2. Is that the student to whom you put the question?

3. The station over which they broadcast the news was WCBS.

4. The operator is the person from whom they were able to obtain the information.

5. Hsinchuang is the town through which you have to pass to reach Taipei.

6. The person in whom she places her trust is not her father but her brother.

7. He needs a watch by which he can tell the day, the month and the year.

8. The land reform about which the politician spoke is nothing more than a dream.

習題 373 解答

1. that	2. (that)	3. where	4. who / that
5. (that)	6. (that)	7. (that)	8. (that)
9. (that)	10. which	11. (that)	12. where
13. (that)	14. which	15. (that)	16. which
17. whose	18. whose	19. (that)	20. (that)
21. (that)	22. (that)	23. (that)	24. (that)
25. (that)	26. that	27. that	28. that
29. that, (that)	30. (that), whose		

習題 374 解答

1. These are forms that occasionally occur but which should not be taught.

2. The best play (that) Shakespeare wrote but which I haven't read is probably *King Lear*.

3. He's the person (that) I meet at the club every day and who(m) I've invited to dinner tonight.

4. It was the police detective who / that told me to fetch the rifle (that) I had been praticing with.

5. He's the best man (that) I can find who can mend it in an hour.

6. This is the horse that kicked the policeman (that) I saw trying to clear away the crowd who had collected to watch a fight (that) two men had started.

習題 375 解答

1. who / that

2. that / which

3. who / that

4. (That / which)

5. who / that

6. (that / which)

7. (that / who(m))

8. (that / which)

9. (that / which)

10. who / that

11. (that)

12. that / who

13. who / that

14. (that / which)

15. (that / who(m))

16. that / which

17. whose

18. that / who

19. (that / which)

20. (that)

21. (that / where)

22. (that / when)

23. (that / who)

24. (that / who)

25. (that / which)

26. that

27. (that / which)

28. (that)

29. that

30. that

31. (that)

32. as, (that)

33. (that / which),that

34. that, which

35. (that), (that)

36. (that), (that), which

37. who (m), (that), who (m)

38. which, (that), (that)

習題 376 解答

1. They re scholars well known to us.

They're well-known scholars.

2. Birds singing in my garden remind me that spring is here.

Singing birds remind me that spring is here.

3. The income earned abroad amounts to two million dollars.

The earned income amounts to two million dollars.

4. All visitors touring the art museum are asked to sign the guest book.

All touring visitors are asked to sign the guest book.

5. All the guests invited to the party brought their presents.

All the invited guests brought their presents.

6. All vehicles driving along the new highway are required to pay a toll.

All driving vehicles are required to pay atoll.

7. The table loaded with books belongs tothe editor.

The loaded table belongs to the editor.

8. The young mother tenderly kissed the baby sleeping in the cradle.

The young mother tenderly kissed the sleeping baby.

9. The candidates chosen by the committee include Mr. Lee.

The chosen candidates include Mr. Lee.

10. People traveling first-class receive special privileges.

Traveling people receive special privileges.

11. All the afternoon Jack was mourning over the effort wasted by us all.

All the afternoon Jack was mourning over the wasted effort.

12. Children growing up in the city need more exercises.

Growing children need more exercises.

13. Skills acquired through work are very valuable.

Acquired skills are very valuable.

14. I have thrown away the shoes worn out with hiking.

I have thrown away the worn-out shoes.

15. He is one of the workers laid off by the factory.

He is one of the laid-off workers.

習題 377 解答

1. She is a person good to know.

She is a good person to know.

2. He is a man hard to convince.

   He is a hard man to convince.

3. That's a poem nice to remember.

   That's a nice poem to remember.

4. Show me the instrument easiest to play.

   Show me the easiest instrument to play.

5. She always knows a way better to say it.

   She always knows a better way to say it.

6. Bob is the person most convenient to send.

   Bob is the most convenient person to send.

7. We have some decisions hard to make.

   We have some hard decisions to make.

8. Is that a course easy to pass?

   Is that an easy course to pass?

9. That's a course impossible to do well in.

   That's an impossible course to do well in.

10. She's preparing all kinds of things wonderful to eat.

    She's preparing all kinds of wonderful things to eat.

習題 378 解答

1. He'll catch another bus leaving in an hour.

2. You won't see a movie as good as that.

3. They gave me a question too hard to answer.

4. Mr. Lee, our chemistry teacher, speaks excellent German.

5. Who is the girl watering the flower?

6. The boy bitten by a snake has been sent to the hospital.

7. These are advertisements designed to please housewives.

8. It turned out to be a day too hazy for pictures.

9. Students wanting pencils please raise their hands.

10. Whom does the car over there belong to?

11. Bob, a good salesman, charmed them immediately.

12. Have you made a list of machines needing new parts?

13. Those having finished assignments may go home now.

14. You shouldn't have taken on activity as strenous as that.

15. The teacher gave us a subject very easy to talk about.

16. I've never seen a movie as long as *Gone with the Wind*.

17. There's a job for you to do.

18. They need someone to take care of their children while they are away.

習題 379 解答

1. It's a water cooler.

2. It's a pencil sharpener.

3. It's a windshield wiper.

4. It's acan opener.

5. It's a flame thrower.

6. It's weed killer.

7. It's a fire distinguisher.

8. He's a mind reader.

9. He's a trouble maker.

10. He's a home owner.

11. He's a food inspector.

12. He's a movie producer.

13. He's a garbage collector.

14. He's a flute player.

15. He's an elevator operater.

習題 380 解答

1. It's a standard of living.

2. It's water for drinking.

3. They're costs that are rising.

4. It's a fit of coughing.

5. It's a need that presses.

6. It's paper for wrapping.

7. It's a game of guessing.

8. It's a pan for frying.

9. It's a danger that exists.

10. It's a door that revolves.

11. It's gum for chewing.

12. It's a point of turning.

13. It's a mind that inquires.

14. They're privileges of parking.

15. They're facilities for recording.

16. It's a career of acting.

17. It's an agreement that works. 18. It's an analysis that penetrates.

19. It's the experience in teaching. 20. It's a ingredient that soothes.

習題 381 解答

1. It's a tiger that eats man.

2. It's a device for warning early.

3. It's an arena for bullfighting (fighting bulls).

4. They're costs that are ever increasing.

5. It's a living standard that is high.

   It's a high standard of living.

6. It's a working agreement that is perfect.

   It's a perfect agreement that works.

7. It's an effect that lasts very long.

8. It's a tape-recording session thatis long.

   It's a long session of tape-recording.

9. It's a self-winding clock that is reliable.

   It's a reliable clock that winds itself.

10. It's a three-day tour for speech-making (making speeches).

    It's a speech-making tour that lasts three days.

11. It's a eating capacity that is small.

    It's a small capacity of eating.

12. He's a beginning student that is hardworking (works hard).

    He's a hardworking student that (just) begins.

習題 382 解答

1. It's a vóte-gètting campàign.

2. lt's an eŷe-câtching displáy.

3. It's a hîgh withhólding tàx.

4. It's a chéck-càshing sèrvice.

5. He's a fâst-wôrking ingrédient.

6. It's an ôld mining còmpany.

7. It's a sêlf-sêaling énvelope.

8. They're shôrt vísiting hòurs.

9. It's a gôod híding plàce.

10. They're sêlf-gôverning cólonies.

11. It's a nâtional bírd-wàtching sòcìety.

12. It's a lârge néws-gàthering organizàtion.

習題 383 解答

1. whoever finishes first

2. what / whatever happened

3. whichever (one) costs most

4. whenever is convenient

5. who(m)ever he contacted

6. wherever they live now

7. who(m)ever it belongs to

8. what / whatever bothered him

9. whenever he decided to come

10. wherever he used to live

11. whichever (one) he likes a little more

12. whatever way / however she finished her job

習題 384 解答

1. whoever   2. whatever   3. whoever

4. whichever   5. what   6. what

7. Whoever   8. who(m)ever   9. whoever

10. whichever   11. whosever   12. whoever

13. Whatever   14. What   15. whatever

習題 385 解答

1. what   2. what(ever)   3. who(m)ever   4. whoever

5. whatever   6. whatever (whichever)   7. what

8. whatever   9. what   10. what   11. what (ever)

12. what	13. what	14. whichever	15. what
16. what	17. whatever	18. what	19. what
20. what			

習題 386 解答

1. What is really amazing is his intelligence.

   His intelligence is what is really amazing.

2. What she is looking for is something to read on the train.

   Something to read on the train is what she is looking for.

3. What I want to know is her name.

   Her name is what I want to know.

4. What is in the box is the missing diamond.

   The missing diamond is what is in the box.

5. What she does is (to) write to him every day.

6. What she'll look at is the display in the window.

   What she'll do is (to) look at the display in the window.

7. What we're returning by mail is her application.

   What we're doing is returning her application by mail.

8. What I tried to do was remind myself to do it.

9. What a university has to have is responsibility.

   Responsibility is what a university has to have.

10. What they wanted you to do was accept it.

    What they wanted to do was for you to accept it.

11. What they'll urge you to do is think twice.

    What they'll do is (to) urge you think twice.

    What they'll urge is for you to think twice.

12. What isn't important is who he associates with.

    Who he associates with is what isn't important.

13. What impressed me was what he had to say.

    What he had to say was what impressed me.

14. What amazes me is how you can have such a big argument.

    How you can have such a big argument is what amazes me.

15. What they meant to do was ask a couple of questions.

16. What she taught herself to do was speak English.

    What she did was (to) teach herself to speak English.

17. What also came up in the discussion was where he comes from.

    Where he comes from was what also came up in the discussion.

18. What their job is is showing people around.

    Showing people around is what their job is.

19. What she ought to do is go over and over the whole thing.

20. What will determine when we can start is when he gets here.

    When he gets here is what will determine when we can start.

21. What they'll never find is coffee as good as that.

    Coffee as good as that is what they'll never find.

22. What they dressed to do was go out to a movie.

    What they dressed for was to go out to a movie.

23. What she slowed down for before reaching the intersection was a left turn.

    What she slowed down to do before reaching the intersection was (to) make a left turn.

24. What they expect to be able to do is keep up their growing business.

25. What I just can't figure out is why he likes to keep a record of all the people he ever met.

    Why he likes to keep a record of all the people he ever met is what I just can't figure out.

26. What I am certain of is (that) he will succeed.

    That he will succeed is what I am certain of.

27. What he was afraid of was (that) you might object to the plan.

   That you might object to the plan was what he was afraid of.

28. What Mike is is a doctor.

   A doctor is what Mike is.

29. What Jack wanted to be was a hero.

   A hero was what Jack wanted to be.

   What Jack wanted to do was be a hero.

30. Was what you caught by the ear a rabbit?

   Was a rabbit what you caught by the ear?

習題 387 解答

1. It will create a generation incapable of enjoying liberty.

2. We deny evidence of intellectual independence by silencing criticism.

3. It produces demoralization and eventual corruption.

4. The search for subversives discourages independence of thought.

5. In order to get there on time he has to leave before dawn.

6. We want to know where he gets all the time for speech-making.

7. As soon as they all leave we'll have a bite.

8. What he says and does can upset me.

9. What his views are is important.

10. What he does, not what he says, is important.

習題 388 解答

1. Wherever the singer goes, crowds welcome her.

2. Whatever happens, keep calm.

3. I'll discuss it with you whenever you like to come.

4. Whoever you are, you don't belong here.

5. You are certainly right, whatever others may say.

6. The car shouldn't be parked here, whoever carit is.

7. However hard hetries, he'll never succeed.

8. Whomever you'd like to get a letter of recommendation from, you should first ask for his permission.

9. Whichever measure you take, you are bound to offend some people.

10. Whenever she does an exercise she makes mistakes, however hard he tries.

習題 389 解答

1. which
2. whatever
3. whichever
4. whatever (whichever)
5. which
6. what (which)
7. whatever (whichever)
8. which
9. what
10. whatever (whichever)
11. Whatever
12. which
13. what
14. whatever
15. which

習題 390 解答

1. which
2. (that / which)
3. who / that
4. who
5. (that / which)
6. whose
7. as, (that / when)
8. (that / when)
9. whose
10. who (that)
11. which
12. Who(m)ever
13. whichever
14. as
15. than
16. Whosever
17. than
18. which
19. as
20. but
21. which
22. whatever, whenever
23. However, whatever
24. whichever, whoever
25. Whichever, whoever, whenever

習題 391 解答

1. The food here is <u>pretty</u> **good**.

2. An elephant is <u>far</u> **larger** <u>than a horse</u>.

3. He is much **the best** student in class.

4. I'm so **glad** you've come.

5. I'm awfully **sorry** that I hurt your feelings.

6. The patient is little **better** this morning.

7. Bob speaks Chinese remarkably **well**.

8. Jane is not **old** enough to get married.

9. She came too **late** to attend the meeting.

10. He was so **careless** as to forget the appointment.

11. She spoke so **rapidly** that I couldn't understand her.

12. Mary is beautiful, but she is not nearly **tall** enough.

習題 392 解答

1. quite delicious	2. too hot	3. rather heavy

4. a pretty good   5. easy enough

6. a rather silly / rather a silly   7. quite a sudden

8. a very large   9. a very dirty

10. an awful nice   11. rather thoughtless

12. pretty plausible   13. rather cold   14. a very nice

15. not quite a   16. very fortunate

17. somewhat outspoken   18. far too clever

19. far more interesting   20. enough prettier

21. so very sensational   22. rather more sensational

23. quite a good bit better

24. very strong indeed (indeed very strong)

25. quite strong enough   26. far too clever

27. far and away the greatest   28. rather too vague

29. quite strong enough   30. not quite so much better

習題 393 解答

1. much	2. a lot	3. rather	4. too
5. quite	6. by far	7. by far	8. a little
9. quite	10. most	11. a lot	12. a great deal
13. not a little bit		14. quite	15. by far

習題 394 解答

1. very	2. very	3. very (much)
4. very	5. very much	6. (very) much
7. very much	8. very	9. (very) much
10. (very) much	11. very	12. (very) much
13. (very) much	14. very	15. much
16. much	17. very	18. very
19. much	20. much, much	

習題 395 解答

1. terribly funny	2. exceedingly skillful
3. hardly safe	4. awfully nice
5. (an) extremely dirty	6. highly qualified
7. fairly well	8. remarkably clever
9. exceptionally beautiful	10. simply overjoyed
11. literally packed	12. sadly deficient
13. noticeably increased	14. considerably greater
15. markedly improved	16. incomparably the best
17. decidedly heavier	18. appreciably lighter
19. surprisingly fast	20. immensely fond
21. only slightly wounded	22. indisputably evident
23. (a) highly amusing	24. deeply appreciative

25. relatively prosperous	26. remarkably well
27. moderately large	28. dreadfully cross
29. (an) uncommonly miserable	30. —miserably poor
31. —hopelessly ill	32. —piercingly cold
33. highly pleased	34. greatly better
35. considerably more	36. diametrically opposed
37. increasingly difficult	38. strikingly different
39. entirely ignorant	40. barely enough

習題 396 解答

1. shightly	2. extremely	3. barely	4. fairly
5. moderately	6. simply	7. barely	8. perfectly
9. wholly	10. absolutely		

習題 397 解答

1. fairly	2. rather	3. rather	4. fairly
5. fairly	6. rather	7. rather	8. fairly
9. rather	10. rather		

習題 398 解答

1. straight ahead	2. far beyond
3. right under	4. far beyond
5. straight up	6. right behind
7. far ahead	8. right in
9. three miles away	10. ever since
11. simply fun	12. right from
13. three blocks	14. a long way away
15. a little wayoff	16. three doors
17. far beyond	18. straight to

19. far beyond

20. straight out

21. three days after

22. immediately after

23. straight into

24. Immediately on

25. as soon after the election as possible

習題 399 解答

1. sure

2. easier

3. better

4. more intelligent

5. ready

6. worse

7. profound

8. saltier

9. careful

10. further (farther)

11. more expensive

12. more difficult

13. better

14. tall

15. severe

16. popular

17. latest

18. shorter

19. farther

20. later

21. last

22. latest

23. farther (further), farther (further)

24. last

25. latest, last

習題 400 解答

1. John is the same height as Bob.

2. Jane is not the same weight as Alice.

3. The camera is the same price as the typewriter.

4. Your coat is not the same size as mine.

5. The station is the same distance as the post office.

6. This book is the same thickness as that one.

7. This piece of wood is the same hardness as that one.

8. Mr. Higgins is the same age as Mrs. Higgins.

習題 401 解答

1. The church is twice as old as the school.

   The church is twice older than the school.

2. The steak is half as big as the plate.

3. Bob worked three times as hard as his brother.

   Bob worked three times harder than his brother

4. Jane is ten times as charming as Anne.

   Jane is ten times more charming than Anne.

5. The movie is not half as good as the one we saw last week.

習題 402 解答

1. Come as soon as possible.

2. Paul will try as hard as possible.

3. I tried to explain the problem as patiently as I could.

4. He said he would come here as quickly as possible.

5. Mary promised to stay there as long as she could.

6. The boy shouted as loudly as possible.

7. Mr. Lee treated his servant as kindly as he could.

8. Get as much firewood as you can.

習題 403 解答

1. Your hotel is the same as mine.

   Our hotels are the same.

2. They come from the same country.

   He comes from the same country as she does.

3. His nationality is different from hers.

   Their nationalities are different.

   They are of different nationalities.

4. He is like you.

   You and he are alike.

5. I had my training at the same school as he did (had).

   We had our training at the same school.

6. He's like her.

   They're alike.

7. Your analysis was different from mine.

   We (and you) have different analyses.

   Our analyses were different.

8. His job is the same as hers.

   Their jobs are the same.

9. You are like him.

   You and he are alike.

10. His (great) ambition is different from hers.

    They have different (great) ambitions.

    Their (great) ambitions are different.

習題 404 解答

1. busy	2. happy	3. helpless	4. free
5. hard	6. clear	7. quiet	8. dull
9. poor	10. light	11. old	12. nervo
13. strong	14. deaf	15. blind	

習題 405 解答

1. like	2. as	3. like	4. like
5. as	6. as; as	7. like	8. like
9. like	10. as	11. as; as	12. like

習題 406 解答

1. It was a stone like a diamond.

   It was a diamondlike stone.

2. His hands were as cold as ice.

   His hands were ice-cold.

3. It was a substance like chalk.

   It was a chalklike substance.

4. Her skin was as white as snow.

   Her skin was snow-white.

5. The night was as black as pitch.

   The night was pitch-black.

6. He lived a life which was like a dream.

   He lived a dreamlike life.

7. We enjoyed the atmosphere which was like that of home.

   We enjoyed the homelike atmosphere.

8. His intention was as clear as crystal.

   His intention was crystal-clear.

習題 407 解答

1. It was five feet too long.

2. He had one glass too many.

3. His watch was 15 minutes (too) slow.

4. He's two years too young (to get a license).

5. His temperature is two degress too high.

6. They gave her a hat two sizes too large.

7. The letter weighs one ounce too heavy (for 31-centpostage).

8. He got here 30 minutes too late.

9. The police caught him 15 miles per hour (too) fast.

10. She has two eggs too few.

習題 408 解答

1. He calls home as often as three times a week.

2. The fisherman is as old as 96.

3. She was born as early as in 1890.

4. We waited for them as long as half an hour / a half hour.

5. The concert lasted as long as two hours.

6. The airline weighed in our luggage at as heavy as 50 pounds.

7. They were able to drive as far as from here to the next town.

8. The top of the mountain is as high as four miles above sea level.

9. The thermometer on the porch reads as low as 19 degrees.

10. We usually order as many as three or four dozen at a time.

習題 409 解答

1. Chemistry is as difticult as Mathematics (is).

2. The salesman is as pleased as the customers (are).

3. Your mother is not as/so tall as your father (is).

4. You didn't look as happy as your brother (did).

5. He has as many books as she (does / has).

6. Does he have as much money as he has power?

7. Miss King is as competent as our former secretary (was).

8. Do you study as hard now as (you did) then?

9. The editor must be as well-informed as the writer.

10. Did the second string play as well as the first one (did) ?

11. He drives as dangerously today as (he did) yesterday.

12. Mr. King made money as rapidly as Mr. Jones (did).

13. Mrs. Jones spent money as rapidly as Mr. Jones made money.

14. Jim plays basketball as brilliantly as Bob does football.

15. Mr. Fogg is as severe as his son is naughty.

16. Did you take as many courses last semester as (you do) now?

習題 410 解答

1. Iron is more useful than gold (is).

2. Wordsworth is a better poet than Cowper (is).

3. The streets of Taipei are wider than those of Hsinchu (are).

4. Bob looks better than John (does).

5. Betty behaved worse than Alice (did).

6. Mrs. Jacobson is more eccentric than Mr. Jacobson (is).

7. I bought a more comfortable car than John did.

8. I drive more dangerously today than (I did) yesterday.

9. I bought a less comfortable car than my neighbor did.

10. He writes better prose than his teacher (does).

11. John has a bigger car than Bill (does / has).

12. I know a duller man than George (is).

13. This house is more solidly built than that (one) (is).

14. The car is bigger than the one my neighbor has 〔my neighbor's〕.

15. John bought a bigger car than (the one) he sold.

16. I bought a bigger car in New York than (the one I did) in Chicago.

17. She made more progress than he (did).

18. It is easier to go by bus than (it is) by train.

19. He has more customers than he can handle.

20. Mary is less sad than (she is) angry 〔more angry than (she is) sad〕.

21. They have less ability than (they have) enthusiasm.

22. It's less easy for him to answer questions than (it is) to ask them.

23. It's less easy for her than for him to ask questions 〔easier for him than for her to ask questions〕.

24. It's less easy for her to ask questions than (it is) for him to answer them 〔easier for him to answer questions than for (it is) for her to ask them〕.

25. I bought a bigger car than my neighbor expected me to (buy).

習題 411 解答

1. Bob has more enthusiasm than he has intelligence.

2. Bob has more enthusiasm than Jack does.

3. TV is more interesting than the radio is.

4. TV is more interesting than it is educational.

5. Cats are more of a pleasure than they are of a nuisance.

6. Cats are more of a pleasure than dogs are.

7. New York City has more Puerto Ricans than San Juan does.

8. New York City has more Puerto Ricans than it has Greeks.

9. Driving across the country is more interesting than it is convenient.

10. Driving across the country is more interesting than flying across is.

習題 412 解答

1. The book is no thicker than that.

2. Ten friends are as many as I have.

3. The room was no bigger than that.

4. One hundred dollars is as much as he can pay.

5. I could go no more quickly than that.

6. 20 hours is as long as they played chess.

7. We could compromise no more than that.

8. 60 miles an hour is as fast as the car runs.

9. I can go along with you no further (farther) than that.

10. 100 words a minutes is as quickly as he can read.

習題 413 解答

1. better	2. taller	3. best	4. proudest
5. best	6. lighter	7. largest	8. hotter
9. more ferocious		10. most intelligent	
11. most useful	12. most interesting		13. highest
14. highest	15. rarest		16. most generous
17. sweetest	18. largest		19. gentlest
20. vaguest	21. last		22. best

習題 414 解答

1. The harder you work, the more money you make.

2. The sooner you get here, the sooner we will be able to start out.

3. The higher you go, the better the scenery will be.

4　The more he read, the less he understood.

5. The more I heard about it, the more anxious I became.

6. The longer we stayed there, the less we liked the place.

7. The more money he makes, the more he wants

8. The more learned a man is, the more modest he usually is.

9. The sooner we get there, the more likely we are to get seats.

10. The more places you travel to, the more you will find out about the world.

習題 415 解答

1. Lead is the heaviest of all metals.

   No other metal is so / as heavy as lead.

2. You don't know him any better than I (do).

   You krow him no better than I (do).

3. David was stronger than any other man / all other men.

   David was the strongest of all (men).

4. *Sakuntala* is better than any other drama in Sanskrit.

   No other drama in Sanskrit is so / as good as *Sakuntala*.

5. Shakespeare is the greatest of all English poets.

   No other English poet is so / as great as Shakespeare.

6. The tiger is more ferocious than any other animal (all other animals).

   No other animal is so / as ferocious as the tiger.

7. Iron is the most useful of all metals.

   No other metal is so / as useful as iron.

8. The sword is not so / as mighty as the pen.

9. Charles is one of the most diligent boys.

Charles is more diligent than any other boy(s).

10. John came earliest of all the students.

No other student came so / as early as John.

習題 416 解答

1. Tell me a story bette than this.

Tell me a better story than this.

2. I don't know a boy braver than Tom.

I don't know a braver boy than Tom.

3. We've seen a school library much bigger than this.

We've seen a much bigger school library than this.

4. I never read a book more exciting than the Treasure Island.

I never read a more exciting book than the Treasure Island.

5. Did you ever meet a person more careless than our brother?

Did you ever meet a more careless person than our brother?

6. You won't find a camera less expensive than this one.

You won't find a less expensive camera than this one.

7. Could you give me a book easier to understand?

Could you give me an easier book to understand?

8. He always knows a way better to say it.

He always knows a better way to say it.

9. Charles is the person most convenient to sent our mail to.

Charles is the most convenient person to sent our mail to.

10. She's preparing all kinds of things wonderful to eat.

She's preparing all kinds of wonderful things to eat.

習題 417 解答

1. English is an easier language to learn than Russian.

   English is an easier language than Russian to learn.

2. This is a harder word to pronounce than that.

   This is a harder word than that to pronounce.

3. This is a more interesting lesson to study than the other.

   This is a more interesting lesson than the other to study.

4. John is a more convenient person to send than the others.

   John is a more convenient person than the others to send.

5. These are more difficult problems to deal with than the previous ones.

   These are more difficult problems than the previous ones to deal with.

6. Mr. Hill is a better person to ask for help than Mr. Tower.

   Mr. Hill is a better person than Mr. Tower to ask for help.

7. Fords are more economical cars to keep than Buicks.

   Fords are more economical cars than Buicks to keep.

8. Buicks are more comfortable cars to drive in than Fords.

   Buicks are more comfortable cars than Fords to drive in.

習題 418 解答

1. soon / early, possible

2. many, books, can

3. as, often, as, to

4. good, any

5. nice, to, me, ever

6. happy, can, be

7. good, dead

8. much, ask

9. without, much, saying

10. much, responsibility, mine

11. much, to

12. as, much, write

13. so, much, as

14. much, again

15. as, expensive, as, same, price, as, as, much, as

16. as (/ so), thick, as, same, thickness, as, thinner, than, thicker, than

習題 419 解答

1. more, than, read
2. more, than, ever
3. more, than, enough
4. not, any, more
5. more, than
6. more, than
7. more, frightened, hurt, rather, than
8. more, than, ten, ago
9. No, more, than
10. not, more, than, most
11. no, more, than
12. no, more, a, than
13. no, more, than, as, as, are
14. not, more, not, as, than
15. no, more, able, than, I, am
16. no, more, than, fly, not, any, more, fly, not, just, as
17. no, less, than, as, as
18. not, less, than, least
19. no, less, than, as, as
20. no, less, than
21. worth, little, than
22. nothing (little), less, than
23. little (no), better, than
24. It, nothing (little), less, than, to, such
25. more, less
26. bigger, and, bigger
27. more, and, more, interesting
28. less, and, less, interested
29. more, than, rather, than
30. more, than, rather, than, not, so, much, as
31. The, more, the, better
32. The, more, time, the, less, results
33. all, the, better (more), because (as)
34. all, the, more, for
35. not, any, the, less, because
36. not, any, the, less, for
37. none (not), the, less
38. much (still / even), less, to
39. the, less, because (as)
40. neither, more, less, than

習題 420 解答

1. very
2. possible, possible
3. imaginable, imaginable
4. the, second, largest
5. the, third, tallest, in
6. most
7. make, of, make, best, of
8. had, best (better), better, keep

9. not, least

10. in, least (slightest)

11. The, least

12. least, best

13. less, as (so), eloquently, as, more, eloquently, than

14. the, biggest, city, bigger, than, other, city (cities), no city, as, big, as

15. ① most, frequently (after), ② more, frequently (after), than, any, ③ other, member, as, frequently (after), as, ④ other, members, less, frequently (after), than, ⑤ more, time, than, any, ⑥ other, other, member, as, much, time, as, ⑦ other, members, less, time, than

習題 421 解答

1. John is tall enough to reach the ceiling.

2. The story is easy enough (for you) to understand.

3. Jack is too short to play in the team.

4. Dick was so excited as to start shouting.

5. He ran too quickly for me to catch.

6. The battery is strong enough to last forty-eight hours.

7. She is not so weak as to give up her plan.

8. She is still too young to marry you.

9. She is still too young (for you) to marry.

10. Dick is clever enough to solve any problem.

11. This problem is simple enough for Dick to solve.

12. She is too good a wife (for Tom) to leave.

13. It is too dangerous a job for him to have anything to do with.

14. It is too late for us to go to the movies.

15. The weather is warm enough for you to be outside.

16. He has enough time to give an interview.

17. She has too little time to play bridge this evening.

18. I am not confident enough to give a speech in public.

19. Do you know him well enough to borrow money from him?

20. We were so fortunate as to be in London for the Coronation.

習題 422 解答

1. that bad a situation
2. so good a movie
3. the best possible solution
4. a five-mile-wide canyon
5. a taller person than Mr. Taylor
6. a rather nice person to talk about

   (rather a nice person to talk about)
7. so unbelievable a story
8. a very easy subject to talk about
9. a good enough man for us to send to U.S.
10. as long a movie as *Gone with the Wind*
11. the worst imaginable situation
12. a more cooperative employee than Miss Ford
13. too horrible a possibility to think about
14. that important a development
15. as good a movie as that
16. too hazy a day for pictures
17. a ten-year-old boy
18. too important a day for us to forget
19. as good a book as any that I ever read
20. an important enough document to require immediate attention

習題 423 解答

1. John is so nice that every body likes him
2. The lecture was so long that the audience grew impatient

3. I was so shocked that I didn't know what to say

4. She was so clever that she solved all the problems at once.

5. His story was so funny that I couldn't help laughing.

6. She was so foolish that she believed everything he told her.

7. He was such a good runner that I couldn't catch him.

8. He ran so quickly that I couldn't catch him.

9. He was so crazy that he tried to jump down from the top of the house.

10. He worries so much about his financial position that he can't sleep at night.

習題 424 解答

1. She is so nice that everybody likes her.

2. She is such a nice girl that everybody likes her.

3. The room is so big that we can have a party here.

4. It is such a big room that all your family can live in it.

5. The news is so good that I can hardly believe it.

6. The dress is so old that I can't wear it any longer.

7. Yesterday was such a hot day that we stayed home.

8. Alice has such a good voice that she should study singing.

9. The weather is so hot that I don't feel like going out.

10. I had such a severe headache that I couldn't sleep all night.

習題 425 解答

1. so, that, enough, to

2. so, that, enough, to

3. enough, for, me

4. too, for, him, to

5. too, young, to

6. clear, enough, for, you, to

7. too, slippery, for, us, to

8. so, lucky, as, to

9. so, as, enough

10. too, dim, to, be, used

11. well, enough, to

12. so, fat, that, can't

13. so, strong, that, will   14. so, weak, that, will

15. so, quick, can't, him = so, quickly, can't, him = such, runner, can't

習題 426 解答

1. firmly	2. firm	3. directly	4. hard
5. hardly	6. directly	7. direct	8. hard
9. Hardly	10. easy	11. easily	12. hardly
13. hard	14. directly	15. directly	16. mighty
17. hardly	18. hard（hardly 意思不同）		19. direct
20. highly	21. hardly	22. closely	23. close
24. closely	25. clearly	26. clearly	27. clear
28. sharp	29. sharply	30. loudly	31. right
32. wide	33. widely	34. wide	35. tightly
36. lately	37. largely	38. soundly	39. sure
40. flatly			

習題 427 解答

1. in English（介詞片語）

2. suddenly（副詞）during the conference（介詞片語）

3. yet（副詞）when you came（副詞子句）

4. carefully（副詞）by several experts（介詞片語）

5. often（副詞）with his secretary（介詞片語）in the morning（介詞片語）

6. as soon as you finish the work（副詞子句）

7. successfully（副詞）unless he follows the directions（副詞子句）

8. quietly（副詞）into the room（介詞片語）because the boy was sleeping（副詞子句）

9. always（頻度副詞）here（場所副詞）since we moved to this city（副詞子句）

10. here（時間副詞）early（狀態副詞）with your friend（介詞片語）tomorrow morning（時間副詞）if you want to see the manager（副詞子句）

習題 428 解答

1. Where did they take a walk in the morning?

2. When do they like to sit under the tree?

3. How did they learn the poem?

4. Why are you (we) fighting? / What are you (we) fighting for?

5. How do most city dwellers go to work?

6. Where did she hang the picture?

7. Where is the ship sailing?

8. How fast is the car running?

9. Why was she trembling?

10. How did he get the job?

習題 429 解答

1. on	2. in	3. at	4. ✕	5. on
6. in	7. in	8. in	9. in	10. on
11. ✕	12. at	13. in	14. at	15. at
16. at	17. at	18. in	19. at	20. on
21. at	22. on	23. in	24. in	25. at
26. at	27. in	28. at	29. at	30. in
31. at	32. at	33. on	34. in	35. on
36. at	37. at	38. in	39. ✕	40. at

習題 430 解答

1. in, on	2. in, in
3. in, on	4. at, at
5. in, at	6. at, on
7. by, by	8. in, on

習題 431 解答

1. for	2. for
3. during	4. for
5. since	6. During
7. since	8. during
9. since	10. since

習題 432 解答

1. at	2. since
3. from	4. since
5. from	6. on
7. in	8. from
9. since	10. from

習題 433 解答

1. in	2. through
3. during	4. during
5. during	6. in
7. during	8. during
9. in	10. throughout

習題 434 解答

1. at	2. toward(s)	3. till (until)
4. by	5. before	6. by, before
7. Toward(s)	8. till (until)	9. By
10. till (until)		

習題 435 解答

1. by	2. around	3. on
4. till	5. since	6. till, before
7. till (until)	8. after	9. through
10. for	11. in	12. in (during), at
13. at (by), on	14. by	15. In
16. after	17. after	18. of
19. at, at	20. on	21. on
22. on	23. On	24. within
25. by	26. from	27. With
28. From	29. since	30. for
31. during (for)	32. during	33. in
34. at (till, until)	35. at	36. On (upon)
37. After	38. behind	39. at (on)
40. in (within)		

習題 436 解答

1. from now on	2. for the time being
3. in a (little) while	4. once in a while
5. at the moment	6. All of a sudden
7. from time to time	8. on the spur of the moment
9. in no time	10. after a while
11. All at once	12. at once
13. once and for all	14. at length
15. after all	

習題 437 解答

1. since last night	2. through	3. around
4. behind	5. since	6. at

7. in   8. since   9. since

10. before long   11. on   12. at

13. behind   14. Day after day

15. in no time   16. for the time being

17. once and for all   18. from time to time

19. At the moment   20. once in a while

習題 438 解答

1. in   2. in   3. at, in   4. at

5. in   6. On   7. on   8. at, in

9. at, in   10. at   11. in   12. at, in, in

13. on   14. on   15. in, on, at   16. at, in

17. at, in   18. in, on   19. on, in   20. on (in), on

習題 439 解答

1. on, over   2. on, on (over)

3. below   4. on, over

5. under   6. on

7. over   8. beneath (under (neath))

9. under   10. above

11. over   12. on

13. over   14. over

15. under   16. on

17. beneath (under (neath))   18. above

19. beneath (under (neath)) (= directly under) cf. below the bridge (=lower down the stream)

20. on   21. on

22. above   23. below

24. under (beneath, under (neath))   25. above

習題 440 解答

1. between   2. among (amid (st))   3. inside

4. outside   5. amid (in)   6. between

7. among   8. Among   9. amid (in)

10. between   11. among   12. between

13. among   14. outside   15. outside

習題 441 解答

1. The tiger was inside the cage.

2. The car was running behind ours.

3. Our apartment is directly under yours.

4. The bicycle is in back of the car.

5. He was standing in front of me in the cafeteria line.

6. Tell the servant to leave the suitcase at the bottom of the stairs.

7. What is there in the cabinet over the sink?

8. The temperature is now above freezing point.

9. The weight of the car is below two tons.

10. You will find the word at the top of the page.

習題 442 解答

1. behind   2. in front of   3. in front of

4. in front of   5. behind (in back of)   6. ahead of (behind)

7. after   8. behind

9. after   10. behind

習題 443 解答

1. into   2. out of   3. into

4. into   5. out of, into   6. out of

7. into, in(to)   8. into

9. outside   10. inside

習題 444 解答

1. across   2. through   3. along

4. beyond   5. through   6. across

7. along   8. beyond   9. across

10. across (over)   11. along   12. beyond

習題 445 解答

1. around   2. around (about)   3. around

4. against   5. aroundg   6. against

7. around (about)   8. about

9. against   10. around

習題 446 解答

1. to   2. for   3. toward(s)

4. for   5. for   6. toward(s)

7. toward(s)   8. to

9. to   10. to (in)

習題 447 解答

1. in, in   2. on   3. in

4. of   5. on   6. to

7. in   8. in

9. on   10. to

習題 448 解答

1. by (beside, near)
2. beside (by, near)
3. beside (cf. standby = support) / near
4. by
5. past
6. beside (near)
7. by (beside, near)
8. to
9. past
10. near

習題 449 解答

1. The car drove *out of* town in the middle of the night.

2. He walked slowly *away from* the door.

3. They walked *up* the street singing merrily.

4. Suddenly the cat jumped *on* (*onto*) the table.

5. They sailed *down* the river in a boat.

6. He came *from* Taipei *to* Tainan.

7. They have always wanted to move *into* the city.

8. Bob was afraid of going *up* the ladder.

9. This is a letter *to* Jack *from* his girl friend Betty.

10. He was startled when the car moved rapidly *toward* (*s*) him.

習題 450 解答

1. at	2. on	3. up	4. on top of	5. off
6. down	7. onto	8. on	9. through	10. above
11. ahead of	12. up	13. onto	14. at	15. to
16. off	17. at	18. about	19. in	20. over
21. into	22. among	23. into	24. to	25. on

習題 451 解答

1. to
2. under
3. by
4. before

5. over

6. on

7. on (to)

8. to, to

9. at

10. on

11. below

12. on (through, across)

13. in (to)

14. on (in)

15. through (across)

16. to

17. from

18. to

19. at, on

20. around (about)

21. across

22. up, down

23. at (by)

24. at

25. at

26. within

27. beyond

28. between

29. at, in (during), at, in

30. in, at

31. into, up (down, along)

32. on, into

33. on

34. out of (outside)

35. in (at)

36. in, above

37. against

38. about

39. (a)round

40. through (in)

41. over

42. amid(st)

43. among

44. across, in

45. through

46. on

47. among

48. in

49. behind

50. up, down

51. at

52. by (at)

53. in

54. in

55. on

56. under (neath) (beneath)

57. under (neath) (beneath)

58. on

59. to

60. in

習題 452 解答

1. for	2. in	3. from	4. at	5. for
6. at	7. off	8. from	9. for	10. off

習題 453 解答

1. by, in	2. by, on	3. by, on
4. by, on	5. by, on	6. by, on
7. by	8. on〔over〕	9. by
10. over (on)	11. over (on)	12. by

習題 454 解答

1. by	2. with	3. with	4. by
5. by	6. on	7. in	8. in
9. in	10. by	11. with	12. in
13. on	14. with	15. with	16. by
17. in	18. in, in	19. with, in	20. by, by

習題 455 解答

1. by	2. with	3. like	4. in (with)	5. with
6. like	7. with, with	8. by	9. like	10. with, with
11. with	12. like	13. with	14. like	15. by, in
16. by	17. with	18. with	19. in	20. with

習題 456 解答

1. with fluency	2. with rapidity	3. with triumph
4. with tenderness	5. with calmness	

習題 457 解答

1. They were running with their ears erect.

2. The dog ran away with his tails between his legs.

3. She followed her guide with her head down.

4. He was sitting on the steps with his back against the wall.

5. He was seated on the bench with his arms resting on his knees.

6. She sat there with her eyes fixed on the ground.

7. I lay down to sleep with a heavy weight removed from my mind.

8. The servant found Sir Isaac Newton standing before the fire with the egg in his hand and his watch boiling in the saucepan.

習題 458 解答

1. He learned English by listening to the radio.

2. She cannot manage without (having) servants.

3. I reached his family by telephoning / phoning.

4. She left for the States without telephoning / phoning

5. He cannot eat with (using) chopsticks.

6. I can tell his feelings by looking at his face.

7. They got to work by riding the subway.

8. I can't teach without (using) a blackboard.

9. He ended his story with laughing.

10. They attacked without giving any warning.

11. She returned her application by sending it through the mail.

12. He left the office without promising anything.

習題 459 解答

1. with pride
2. with ease
3. with honor
4. with honesty
5. with regularity
6. with beauty

7. with diligence 8. with fury 9. with sympathy

10. with enthusiasm 11. without hope 12. with great charm

習題 460 解答

1. from 2. for 3. through

4. for 5. through 6. for

7. from 8. for (from) 9. for

10. through 11. for 12. through

13. for 14. through 15. for

16. for 17. from 18. for

19. through 20. through

習題 461 解答

1. out of (through) 2. from 3. from (out of)

4. from 5. out of 6. through

7. for 8. for 9. out of

10. from 11. for, for 12. for, out of

習題 462 解答

1. For, of 2. for, of 3. to

4. for, of 5. with, to 6. in

7. For, of 8. on, of 9. of

10. by, of 11. to 12. by, of

13. with, of 14. in, of 15. on

16. with, of 17. in, of 18. in, to

19. with, of 20. in, of 21. In, of

22. by, of 23. on (in), of 24. with, of

25. in, for 26. For, of 27. by, of

28. for, of 29. by, of 30. for, of

習題解答

31. in, of	32. by, of	33. in, of
34. in, of	35. in, of	36. in, to
37. in, of	38. in, to	39. in, of
40. to	41. in, for	42. to, by

習題 463 解答

1. He was upset because of / on account of the late hour.

2. She was unhappy because of / on account of a poor grade.

3. They didn't buy the house because of / on account of its small rooms.

4. He couldn't sleep because of / on account of your talking loudly outside.

5. He felt depressed because of / on account of his personal problems.

6. I was worried because of / on account of your not arriving in time.

7. I have trouble walking because of / on account of my bad fall.

8. He got into trouble because of / on account of our not warning him in advance.

9. She had trouble getting to see the play because of / on account of the great demand for tickets.

10. I couldn't hear what you said because of / on account of the noise in the room.

習題 464 解答

1. Except	2. Besides	3. without
4. with	5. except	6. Besides
7. besides	8. except	9. instead of
10. without	11. in spite of	12. with
13. Instead of	14. in spite of	15. without
16. with (without)	17. Besides	18. besides
19. without	20. in spite of	

習題 465 解答

1. to	2. with	3. with
4. In, to	5. With, of	6. as, as
7. in, with	8. in, of	9. For
10. For (With)	11. For (After)	12. in, of; with (in), to
13. with (in), to	14. of	15. with (in), to
16. in, with	17. in, with	18. As
19. in, with	20. with (in), to	

習題 466 解答

1. except	2. in spite of	3. in respect to
4. concerning	5. Except	6. with
7. with	8. about	9. After all
10. In respect to	11. except	12. according to
13. with	14. regardless of	15. as well as
16. as for	17. as for	18. Instead of
19. despite	20. despite	

習題 467 解答

1. Without	2. in spite of	3. instead of
4. Besides	5. On	6. with
7. without	8. without	9. without
10. than		

習題 468 解答

1. d   2. h   3. f   4. g   5. i   6. b   7. a   8. c   9. j   10. e

習題 469 解答

1. In spite of / Despite her bad cold, …

2. In spite of / Despite the high price. …

3. In spite of / Despite my coming late, …

4. In spite of / Despite his being rude (his rudeness), …

5. In spite of / Despite the warm uniforms, …

6. In spite of / Despite his parent's disapproval, …

7. In spite of / Despite seldom studying, …

8. In spite of / Despite my mentioning it several times, …

9. In site of / Despite some skill, …

10. In spite of / Despite not having the necessary skills, …

11. In spite of / Despite having just read the book, …

12. In spite of / Despite the late hour, …

13. In spite of / Despite his expressed love for her, …

14. In spite of / Despite the unbearably hot weather, …

15. In spite of / Despite never having been to Japan, …

習題 470 解答

1. In case of rain, …

2. … in case of illness.

3. … in case of the cold weather.

4. In case of a fire, …

5. … in case of a motor trouble.

6. … in case of a bad weather.

7. … in case of a bad cold.

8. … in case of a sudden emergency.

9. In case of his arriving before I get back, …

10. … in case of my absence (my being away).

習題 471 解答

1. *while* he was eating breakfast

2. *because* it was raining

3. *Even though* it was snowing very hard

4. *so* I expected you

5. *Since John's* answers weve incomplete

6. *as soon as* I found out the guests had arrived

7. *ever since* I entered the high school

8. *if* I'm not late

9. *when* he speaks English with friends

10. *Whenever* he wants to talk to his friends

習題 472 解答

1. I always went to the ball games with my brother before he went in the army.

2. He happily accepted our offer without hesitation when we suggested it.

3. I seldom make mistakes in spelling if I'm careful.

4. He will soon speak English fluently if he studies his lessons carefully.

5. The mother quietly walked into the room because the baby was sleeping.

6. Get up early tomorrow morning if you don't want to miss the train.

7. The temperature quickly dropped to 30 degrees as soon as the wind changed.

8. I'll gladly help you with your homework whenever I have time.

9. Have you ever been absent from class because you were sick?

10. He willingly entertains us with his violin whenever we ask him to do so.

習題 473 解答

1. when	2. while	3. when
4. while	5. when	6. as
7. while	8. while (as)	9. as (when)
10. when	11. as	12. When

習題 474 解答

1. before   2. After   3. whenever   4. whenever   5. before

6. whenever   7. After   8. before   9. before   10. before

習題 475 解答

1. until (till)   2. since

3. Now (Now that)   4. Now (Now that)

5. since   6. Now (Now that)

7. since   8. since

9. until (till)   10. since

習題 476 解答

1. as soon as   2. Once

3. as long as   4. no sooner, than

5. Once   6. Directly

7. scarcely (hardly), before (when)   8. once (now)

9. Now   10. no sooner, than

11. Now   12. as long as

13. Now   14. Once

15. As (so) long as   16. The moment

17. No sooner, than   18. as (so) long as

19. as long as   20. Scarcely (Hardly), before (when)

習題 477 解答

1. the, moment   2. the, time   3. The, moment

4. The, year (day)   5. the, day〔year〕   6. the, time

7. the, time   8. the, day

習題 478 解答

1. When

2. before

3. until (till, before)

4. until (till)

5. once (now)

6. as

7. as soon as

8. Now

9. as (so) long as

10. As soon as

11. until (till)

12. After

13. once

14. Once

15. till (until)

16. but

17. since

18. scarcely (hardly), before (when)

19. Scarcely (Hardly), before (when)

20. but that

習題 479 解答

1. While John was running for the train, he got out of breath.

   → While running for the train, John got out of breath.

2. After I did all I could, I calmly awaited the results.

   → After doing all I could, I calmly awaited the results.

3. Before I give my answer, I will ask you some questions.

   → Before giving my answer, I will ask you some questions.

4. While I'm studying, I like to play the radio.

   → While studying, I like to play the radio.

5. After he made a great effort, he at last finished his task.

   → After making a great effort, he at last finished his task.

6. Before I read that book, I must finish this one.

   → Before reading that book, I must finish this one.

7. While Alice was getting dressed, she kept looking at the clock.

   → While getting dressed, Alice kept looking at the clock.

8. After Bob finished his homework, he went out to play.

   → After finishing his homework, Bob went out to play.

9. After I left school, I began studying German.

　　→ After leaving school, I began studying German.

10. While Betty was lying in bed, she thought about her vacation.

　　→ While lying in bed, Betty thought about her vacation.

習題 480 解答

1. When, before

2. soon, possible

3. While, in, the, hospital

4. After, visiting

5. When, asked

6. called, for

7. while, on, his, way, home

8. than, had I, before (when)

9. Whenever, Every, but

10. no, than, as, as, The moment

11. hat, did, greet, Whenever, somebody, without greeting

12. Every, that

13. while, a, child

14. when dearly bought

習題 481 解答

1. where

2. wherever (everywhere)

3. Wherever

4. where

5. where (wherever)

6. Wherever

7. Where (wherever)

8. Where

9. where

10. wherever (anywhere)

習題 482 解答

1. as

2. as if (though)

3. as

4. as

5. as if (though)

6. as

7. as

8. as if (though)

9. as

10. as, as if (though)

習題 483 解答

1. as though tired   2. as if crazed

3. to be   4. like

5. as though thoroughly frightened   6. as if to ask

習題 484 解答

1. because   2. Since

3. because (as)   4. As (Since)

5. As (Since)   6. that

7. because   8. Since (As)

9. that   10. because

習題 485 解答

1. Being a careless fellow, he forgot all about it.

2. It being stormy, she stayed home.

3. Having nothing to do, I went swimming.

4. Being a shy little thing, she said nothing.

5. Not receiving any letter, I wrote to him again.

6. Being a good girl, she is liked by all.

7. It being Sunday, we did not go to school.

8. Having read the book, I could answer the question.

9. There being no taxi, we had to walk.

10. Not knowing what to do, the boy started crying.

11. Having finished his exercise, he put away his books.

12. The fog being very dense, the plane was forced to alight.

13. Night coming on, we went home.

14. The tiger is renowned through all the countryside, being so cunning and ferocious.

15. There being no expense connected with the plan, it was quickly adopted.

習題 486 解答

1. Being friendless
2. Feeling
3. Having learned
4. knowing
5. The case having been decided
6. with, so much away
7. because, his presence
8. (being) written
9. Having been
10. for, to

習題 487 解答

1. lest
2. so that
3. lest
4. in order that
5. lest
6. for fear
7. that
8. so that
9. so that
10. lest
11. in order that
12. lest
13. for fear
14. so that
15. Lest

習題 488 解答

1. ··· that she may study social work.

2. ··· that it may take you to the station.

3. ··· that he might improve the condition of the people.

4. ··· that I may be free tomorrow.

5. ··· that they may learn things.

6. ··· that they might see better.

7. ··· that they might study English.

8. ··· that he may keep his family in comfort.

9. ··· that her daughter might go abroad.

10. ··· that every student might understand.

習題 489 解答

1. for, to
2. me, sign
3. for everyone to see
4. for us to live

5. for everyone to be satisfied   6. so as to (in order to)

7. in order for, to   8. so as not to (in order not to)

9. for you to eat   10. so as not to

習題 490 解答

1. so, that	2. such, that	3. so, that
4. so	5. so, that	6. so, that
7. such, that	8. such, that	9. so, that
10. such, that	11. so, that	12. such, that
13. so, that	14. so, that	15. such, that

習題 491 解答

1. He became so nervous that …

2. He speaks such good English that …

3. He had so much intelligence that …

4. He spoke so many languages that …

5. I was so hungry that …

6. He walked so slowly that …

7. It is such a long address that …

8. The story is so short that …

9. Bob has such a good memory that …

10. The teacher gave so many assignments that …

習題 492 解答

1. I was too distressed to speak.

2. The days were too hot for us to go outdoors.

3. He was too proud to learn.

4. He ran too quickly for me to catch him.

5. The book is easy enough for us to understand.

6. The weather is warm enough for us to go out to play.

7. I was so stupid as to believe his story.

8. The problem was too difficult for us to solve.

9. The car is cheap enough for everybody to buy.

10. We were so fortunate as to arrive there just in time.

11. It is never too late to mend.

12. He is not too proud to work for bread.

   (He is not so proud as not to work for bread.)

13. He is too clever for me to keep pace with.

14. His success was so unexpected as to arouse suspicion.

15. The artificial flowers are too skillfully made to be distinguished from the natural flowers.

16. He spoke in too low a voice to be heard from the other end of the room.

習題 493 解答

1. He speaks so fast that he can't be understood.

2. The tree is so high that I can't climb it.

3. I hope he will not be so weak that he yields.

4. The news is so good that it can't be true.

5. You are so tall that you can hang the picture.

6. The book is so easy that we can understand it.

7. The bed is so big that we can both sleep in it.

8. He is so fond of spending money that he can't become rich.

9. Do you know him so well that you're able to borrow money from him?

10. You're not so foolish that you believe all you read in the newspapers, I hope.

11. Yesterday was so cold that we couldn't go swimming.

12. The story was so bad that it couldn't be liked by children.

13. He is not so foolish that he would do that.

14. He was so brave that he astonished the world.

15. When a straight line meets another so that it makes the adjacent angles equal to each other, it's called a perpendicular.

習題 494 解答

1. If we have nine players, we can start a baseball team. / Unless we have nine players, we can't start a baseball team.

2. If you tell me what your trouble is, I can help you. / Unless you tell me what your trouble is, I can't help you.

3. If Bob studies hard, he will get a scholarship. / Unless Bob studies hard, he won't get a scholarship.

4. If there is a sudden frost, the flowers won't bloom. / Unless there is a sudden frost, the flowers will bloom.

5. If you have an appointment, you can see the doctor. / Unless you have an appointment, you can't see the doctor.

6. If you don't ask him, he won't tell you the answer. / Unless you ask him, he won't tell you the answer.

7. If the tires are properly inflated, the car will drive well. / Unless the tires are properly inflated, the car won't drive well.

8. If the nation is not free, it can't be strong. / Unless the nation is free, it can't be strong.

9. If you don't keep your promises, you'll lose your friends. / Unless you keep your promises, you'll lose your friends.

10. If we advertise in the newspaper, we will sell a lot of merchandise. / Unless we advertise in the newspaper, we won't sell a lot of merchandise.

習題 495 解答

1. if	2. unless	3. If	4. If	5. Unless
6. If	7. unless	8. If	9. unless	10. unless

習題 496 解答

1. If Jack had not gotten up on time, he would not have caught the bus. / Had Jack not gotten up on time, he would not have caught the bus.

2. If today were a holiday, you could go to the beach. / Were today a holiday, you could go to the beach.

3. If Alice had had a cold, she wouldn't have gone to school. / Had Alice had a cold, she wouldn't have gone to school.

4. If I were accepted, I would go to university. / Were I accepted, I would go to university.

5. If I had known you were hungry, I would have offered you dinner. / Had I known you were hungry, I would have offered you dinner.

6. If there were enough money for a car, I wouldn't buy a scooter. / Were there enough money for a car, I wouldn't buy a scooter.

7. If he had had enough money, he would have bought a car. / Had he had enough money, he would have bought a car.

8. If the dog had not been tied up, it would have bitten you. / Had the dog not been tied up, it would have bitten you.

9. If I had not had something to do, I would have come yesterday. / Had I not had something to do, I would have come yesterday.

10. If he had not stopped the train in time, there would have been casualties. / Had he not stopped the train in time, there would have been casualties.

習題 497 解答

1. Suppose	2. unless	3. If
4. in case	5. if	6. unless
7. so long as	8. in case	9. provided
10. unless	11. supposing	12. provided
13. so long as	14. provided that	15. unless

16. Provided   17. Unless   18. so long as

19. Unless   20. on condition that

習題 498 解答

1. Should, happen   2. Were, mine

3. Had, known   4. If, weren't (Were, not)

5. unless   6. If, were not

7. If you, then   8. if you are

9. Winning   10. if any

11. if not sooner   12. if ever

13. unless caught young   14. To master

15. if caught young   16. Turning to the right

17. considering, being considered   18. so to speak

習題 499 解答

1. No matter what is bothering you, don't think about it anymore. / Whatever is bothering you, don't think about it anymore.

2. No matter where George goes, he gets along well with people. / Wherever George goes, he gets along well with people.

3. No matter how strong the enemy are, we will drive them out of the country. / However strong the enemy are, we will drive them out of the country.

4. No matter what you find within this room, it is for sale. / Whatever you find within this room, it is for sale.

5. No matter whose book this is, you must return it to him at once. / Whoever's book this is, you must return it to him at once.

6. No matter what orders he gives, they must be obeyed. / Whatever orders he gives, they must be obeyed.

7. No matter who cooked it, I would like to eat some. / Whoever cooked it, I would like to eat some.

8. No matter when I call on him, he is always busy. / Whenever I call on him, he is always busy.

9. No matter what I did, no-one paid any attention. / Whatever I did, no one paid any attention.

10. No matter how much she practices, she will never be a pianist. / However much she practices, she will never be a pianist.

11. No matter which boy broke the glasses, he must pay for them. / Whichever boy broke the glasses, he must pay for them.

12. No matter which one you took, you should give it back to George. / Whichever one you took, you should give it back to George.

習題 500 解答

1. whichever, whoever
2. whenever, who(m)ever
3. Whatever, whoever
4. Whenever, however
5. Whatever, who(m)ever
6. who(m)ever
7. Whichever, whoever, whenever
8. who(m)ever, whatever
9. Whoever, whatever
10. whoever, wherever, however, whenever

習題 501 解答

1. Though (although)
2. while (whereas)
3. Whether
4. Though (Although)
5. while (whereas)
6. even though (even if)
7. Whether
8. while (whereas)
9. Whether
10. Notwithstanding
11. though
12. though
13. as (though)
14. as (though)
15. while (whereas)

習題 502 解答

1. No matter
2. but
3. Say what
4. Though, again
5. Hard as (However hard)
6. Though (Although), perhaps
7. However, may
8. Whatever
9. though (although)
10. for all, wealth
11. For all, learning
12. Calm or worried
13. Whether he is a
14. You may, yet
15. Woman as
16. as he is
17. though
18. rain or shine
19. notwithstanding (nevertheless, still)
20. Say what

習題 503 解答

1. except that
2. but that
3. except that
4. But that
5. except that
6. Except that
7. But that
8. But that

習題 504 解答

1. according as
2. so (as) far as
3. The, the
4. So (As) far as
5. in proportion as
6. according as
7. So (As) far as
8. according as
9. as, as
10. as (so), as
11. as, so
12. according as
13. the, the
14. as, as
15. So (As) far as
16. As, so
17. The, the
18. as, as
19. As
20. than
21. than
22. In proportion as

習題 505 解答

1. As, so will
2. Ten, six, as (what), five, three
3. according to, work
4. thiat, am
5. except for
6. But, you helped
7. as, or, to, your
8. according to our income
9. as he succeeds
10. isn't, so (as) far as
11. You made, If, had not
12. Except for, of
13. so (as), as, than, other, the biggest
14. Though a whig, becausea whig
15. In, of being
16. as compared with

習題 506 解答

1. Unfortunately
2. feeling unwell
3. who was laughing
4. According to the paper
5. waving a bigstick
6. The vans having arrived
7. Rain or shine
8. encouraged by the result
9. anxious about Mother
10. Whoever is elected

習題 507 解答

1. Unfortunately, things went from bad to worse. / Things unfortunately went from bad to worse. / Things went from bad to worse, unfortunately.

2. Unluckily, John did not arrive on time. / John unluckily did not arrive on time. / John did not arrive on time, unluckily.

3. Apparently, Mr. Dale did not love his wife. / Mr. Dale apparently did not love his wife. / Mr. Dale did not love his wife, apparently.

4. Obviously, Sam did not know what he was saying. / Sam obviously did not know what he was saying. / Sam did not know what he was saying, obviously.

5. Possibly, he has misunderstood what I said. / He possibly has misunderstood what I said. / He has misunderstood what I said, possibly.

6. Naturally, Bob did not agree to your plan. / Bob naturally did not agree to your plan. / Bob did not agree to your plan, naturally.

7. Interestingly, no one found out about their marriage until a month later. / No one interestingly found out about their marriage until a month later. / No one found out about their marriage until a month later, interestingly.

8. Reportedly, he has made a fortune in real estate business. / He reportedly has made a fortune in real estate business. / He has made a fortune in real estate business, reportedly.

9. Supposedly, he did not like the idea very much. / He supposedly did not like the idea very much. / He did not like the idea very much, supposedly.

10. Admittedly, he was the best player in school. / He admittedly was the best player in school. / He was the best player in school, admittedly.

11. Curiously, he is willing to relinquish his control. / He curiously is willing to relinquish his control. / He is willing to relinquish his control, curiously.

12. Not surprisingly, the whole economy has collapsed. / The whole economy not surprisingly has collapsed. / The whole economy has collapsed, not surprisingly.

習題 508 解答

1. b	2. h	3. m	4. n	5. d
6. n	7. k	8. g	9. f	10. o (a)
11. e	12. l	13. c	14. i	15. d
16. g	17. a (o)	18. g	19. j	20. e
21. k	22. p	23. b	24. l	25. k
26. g	27. c	28. t	29. a	30. p
31. r	32. q	33. t	34. t	35. r

習題 509 解答

1. Needing a haircut, John went to the barber shop. / John, needing a haircut, went to the barber shop. / John went to the barber shop, needing a haircut.

2. Being alarmed, Alice turned off the gas. / Alice, being alarmed, turned off the gas. / Alice turned off the gas, being alarmed.

3. Hearing the noise, the man ran into the street. / The man, hearing the noise, ran into the street. / The man ran into the street, hearing the noise.

4. Being pleased by the compliment, Betty sang another song. / Betty, being pleased by the compliment, sang another song. / Betty sang another song, being pleased by the compliment.

5. Knowing nothing about it, Susan didn't say anything. / Susan, knowing nothing about it, didn't say anything. / Susan didn't say anything, knowing nothing about it

6. Having nothing better to do, we might play cards. / We, having nothing better to do, might play cards. / We might play cards, having nothing better to do.

7. Watching the play, the principal smiled his approval. / The principal, watching the play, smiled his approval. / The principal smiled his approval, watching the play.

8. Walking and crawling, he made his way back to the plane. / He, walking and crawling, made his way back to the plane. / He made his way back to the plane, walking and crawling.

習題 510 解答

1. Eager to help, the child climbed onto the roof.

2. An excellent cook, Mrs. Lee cooks every meal herself.

3. Very tired, Susan went to bed early.

4. Only a small boy at the time, I didn't understand the difficulty.

5. Anxious to know the result, Jack picked up the telephone.

6. A forgotten man, Mr. Pane lives alone in the hut.

7. A shy little thing, Julie just smiled and nodded.

8. Full of may strange ideas, the boy set out to look for a fairy.

習題 511 解答

1. The day being a fine one, we had a fine view of the city.

2. (With) his hand trembling violently, he gave the watch to the boy. / He gave the watch to the boy, (with) his hand trembling violently.

3. (With) his arms rested on his knee, he was seated on the bench. / He was seated on the bench, (with) his arms rested on his knee.

4. Them being reassured, no obstacle remained.

5. (With) tears streaming down her face, she looked in my face. / She looked in my face, (with) tears streaming down her face.

6. Her eyes shining with joy, she handed the letter to me.

7. The dinner being ready, the butler sounded the gong.

8. His voice shaking with emotion, he told me he would never forget me.

9. With his head slightly to one side, he stood silent. / He stood silent, with his head slightly to one side.

10. With her heart full of love and tenderness, she said her prayers at home. / She said her prayers at home, with her heart full of love and tenderness.

習題 512 解答

1. Eager to please her parents, Mary prepared her lessons very carefully.

2. The rain having stopped, we resumed our walk.

3. A shy little thing, Alice said nothing.

4. My girlfriend having stood me up, I went to the show alone.

5. Other things being equal, the simplest explanation is the best.

6. Not having received the notice, I did not attend the meeting.

7. Smiling prettily, she gave me her hand.

8. Not knowing what to do, she stood their smiling.

9. Everything being in order, we saw no objection to go ahead.

10. The troops having been given their orders, there was nothing to do but wait.

11. Wanting power, he couldn't be tempted by money.

12. Henry being already overburdened with work, Mr. Douglas assigned the job to Paul.

13. There being no survivors, the exact causes which led to the accident will never be known.

14. Sitting sewing in the garden, Susan's thoughts were easier than her fingers.

15. The walls being covered with books that stretched to the ceiling, they sat in a loft library.

習題 513 解答

1. We stopped to have a rest.

2. He got up to answer the bell.

3. They ran to help her.

4. John went to the station to see his friend off.

5. Bob studied hard to gain a prize.

6. I am waiting to hear your explanation.

7. Dick has called to see you.

8. The fox jumped up to get the grapes.

9. She cooked the dinner for you to eat.

10. They are waiting for him to make the final decision.

習題 514 解答

1. They came to attend the concert.

2. They went to hear the radio program.

3. Bob went to the restaurant to eat lunch.

4. Betty bought the meat to make sandwiches.

5. Mary went to the kitchen to get some matches.

6. Susan went to the store to buy the coat.

7. George came here to find a chair.

8. Charles went to the barbershop to have a haircut.

9. Everybody works hard to earn a living.

10. I'm going to see Mr. Lee to get some advice.

習題 515 解答

1. Bob went to the bank to cash checks.

2. Mary went to the shoe store to buy a pair of shoes.

3. He got up early so as to catch the first train.

4. They came here to study English.

5. We practice constantly so as to learn to speak English.

6. Bob took a taxi so as not to miss the concert.

7. We hurried so as not be late.

8. Jack hurried through his work to catch the train.

9. He shouted at the top of his voice to be heard.

10. She saved the money for her daughter to go abroad.

11. The teacher explained that passage again and again for every student to understand it.

12. For everybody to understand it, write it in simple language.

習題 516 解答

1. Why does she have to step outside? / What does she have to step out for?

2. Why will I drop over tomorrow? / What will I drop over tomorrow for?

3. Why does he need to study? / What does he need to study for?

4. Why do I ask a lot of questions? / What do I ask a lot of questions for?

5. Why are they applying for a bank loan? / What are they applying for a bank loan for?

6. Why are they applying to the local bank? / What are they applying to the local bank for?

習題 517 解答

1. She trembled to see the stranger come in.

2. I could not help laughing to see his funny face.

3. He shuddered to think of what might have happened to him.

4. They rejoiced to hear the news of victory.

5. We all grieved to hear the death of such a great and good man.

6. He wept to hear the sad news.

7. She smiled to see her husband so happy.

8. I trembled to think of the danger ahead of me.

9. The girl blushed to hear her name called.

10. He did not bat an eyelid to see her come toward him.

習題 518 解答

1. He trembled to think of being sent to prison.

2. He wondered to hear the steam-whistle.

3. She rejoiced to see her son.

4. He shuddered to see her friend's corpse.

5. She blushed to think of becoming Mrs. Hill.

習題 519 解答

1. She awoke to find the house on fire.

2. The poor man sank, never to rise again.

3. I offered to assist him, only to be turned down.

4. Few people live to a hundred years old.

5. He did his best only to fail again.

6. They grew up to become handsome lads.

7. The good old days have gone to never return.

8. One day you will wake up to find your daughter a woman.

9. They escaped the sword only to be perished by famine.

10. He opened his eyes to find that he had rolled from the rock to the grass.

習題 520 解答

1. (In order) for our children to go to college, we need more money.

2. (In order) to gain a prize, Bob must study hard.

3. (In order) for everybody to have one, we must buy more books.

4. (In order) to use our time more wisely, we must realize that our time is limited.

5. (In order) for foreigners to understand your Chinese, you shouldn't speak too fast.

6. (In order) for my aunt to read it, I must write the letter neatly.

7. (In order) to emphasize his point, he struck his fist on the table.

8. (In order) to understand thoroughly, she read the passage again and again.

9. (In order) for everybody to understand it, the story must be short and simple.

10. (In order) to learn to speak English, we should practice constantly.

11. (In order) to explain the situation more clearly, he went to see the manager again.

12. (In order) for me to enjoy it, a poem must be either realistic or humorous.

習題 521 解答

1. Peter was happy, until he got married with his wife.

2. Peter, insulted, left the room angrily.

3. It was, as it were, a case of excess irritation.

4. Mr. Benjamin, unfortunately, couldn't afford to buy a new car.

5. One should probably, when in doubt, say nothing.

6. To emphasize his point, he jabbed me vigorously in the chest.

7. I knew, when I heard the news, that there was no more hope.

8. Jim Bob, having gone ahead, directed the operation.

9. The men, by working double shifts, got the job done in two weeks.

10. He knew, nevertheless, that there would be a trouble.

11. She guessed, although there was little evidence, that there was something fishy.

12. The last bus having gone, they had to walk all the way home.

13. Johnson, knowing what he had to do, didn't hesitate.

14. Mr. Jackson decided, after he saw what had happened, to reorganize the company.

15. To the great surprise of everyone who was present, Charles turned out to have a beautiful tenor voice.

習題 522 解答

1. Steven, not feeling very satisfied, asked one more question. / Not feeling very satisfied, Steven asked one more question.

2. Mr. Wilson, feeling bad about it, apologized. / Feeling bad about it, Mr. Wilson apologized.

3. St. Isadore Cathedral, built in 1612, caved in. / Built in 1612, St. Isadore Cathedral caved in.

4. The boy, not knowing anything about it, said nothing. / Not knowing anything about it, the boy said nothing.

5. The man, getting out of the car, twisted his ankle. / Getting out of the car, the man twisted his ankle.

6. The girl, forgotten by her friends, wandered off by herself. / Forgotten by her friends, the girl wandered off by herself.

7. The lady, fainting from heat, collapsed on the sofa. / Fainting from heat, the lady collapsed on the sofa.

8. Chicago, being determined to have the convention, made new concessions. / Being determined to have the convention, Chicago made new concessions.

9. President Johnson, knowing what he had to do, did not hesitate. / Knowing what he had to do, President Johnson did not hesitate.

10. Miss Davis, not wanting to anger her, pretended to agree. / Not wanting to anger her, Miss Davis pretended to agree.

11. The suspect, confronted with the evidence, made a full confession. / Confronted with the evidence, the suspect made a full confession.

12. The knave, smiling an ugly little smile, drew a knife from his pocket. / Smiling an ugly little smile, the knave drew a knife from his pocket.

13. The captain, having never been to the island before, addressed the natives in English. / Having never been to the island before, the captain addressed the natives in English.

14. The lawyer, being aware that his client did not have a very good case, decided to bribe the judge. / Being aware that his client did not have a very good case, the lawyer decided to bribe the judge.

15. George, being a man willing to risk all to get what he wanted, did not hesitate for a moment. / Being a man willing to risk all to get what he wanted, George did not hesitate for a moment.

習題 523 解答

1. Men <u>and</u> women are welcome.

2. The doctor warned him not to smoke <u>or</u> drink.

3. The violinist played brilliantly <u>but</u> dispassionately.

4. I'll pick you up at eight <u>and</u> get you back home by midnight.

5. After eating dinner <u>and</u> taking a long nap, he felt much better.

6. I don't know when he left town <u>or</u> why he wanted to do so.

7. He said that he was very tired <u>and</u> that he was going home to rest.

8. Mr. Black's speech, <u>though</u> he read it fervently, made no impression.

9. I want you to play <u>because</u> when you do, I feel relaxed.

10. If you like me, you will go away, <u>and</u> if you love me, you will stay away.

習題 524 解答

1. The old woman slipped and fell on the pavement.

2. The thief moved quickly and quietly.

3. He walked into the house and up the stairs.

4. After dinner and a long nap, he went out for a ride.

5. His love and respect for his father is most touching.

6. He professed his love for and allegiance to his king.

7. I'll inform you if and when he comes.

8. We can and will succeed.

9. Mistakes have been made and will continue to be made in that office.

10. He has and will always contribute to that cause.

習題 525 解答

1. The girl and her mother enjoyed the movie.

2. You can keep it or throw it away.

3. We decided to leave at dawn, for we had many miles to ride.

4. His mother was a peasant woman, but his father was a famous artist.

5. Paul or Bob must have known it.

6. He was tired but happy.

7. He walked slowly yet steadily.

8. You will have to report this immediately or you will be in serious trouble with the police.

9. He has experience as well as knowledge.

10. You must tell the truth or say nothing.

11. They usually played chess or watched television in the evening.

12. They couldn't find any firewood, so they simply chopped up some of the furniture.

13. He looked everywhere for his keys and wallet.

14. He gave me money as well as advice.

15. She was very pretty but rather hard to get along with.

16. None of the teachers knew what had happened nor could the students offer any explanation.

17. He had excellent manners yet everybody distrusted him.

18. My friends as well as I were betrayed.

19. Mr. Lee is always busy, nor does Mrs. Lee have much free time.

20. Children were tired and cross, nor were their parents in a much better humor.

21. Does he sing as well as dance?

22. I don't know when he left town or why he wanted to do so.

23. Anyone who does not like the new policy of this company and would like to resign is free to do so.

24. He married a woman who was very intelligent and charming but couldn't cook at all.

25. She left the white hat, white dress, and black shoes.

26. He was contented, happy, and wealthy.

27. He told me to shut up, mind my own business, and leave him alone.

28. He gave her a ring and diamond bracelet, and kissed her.

29. He owned a nice home, rented a cabin at the beach, and was on the point of buying a new car.

30. He just wanted to loaf a little, do a little fishing, and try to regain his strength.

習題 526 解答

1. He should try, and he will.

2. I shouldn't be unhappy, but I am.

3. I didn't expect to enjoy myself, but I did.

4. They don't seem to be very happy, and they aren't.

5. He meant to write it down, but he forgot to.

6. We reminded them to pick us up, and they did.

7. You didn't give them an answer before, and you'll have to now.

8. He won't need to use his own money, and he shouldn't have to.

9. She wants to take out a loan, and they are allowing her to.

10. I'm not trying to find out now, but I will try to later.

習題 527 解答

1. He can speak or understand Russian,

2. It's cold but sunny outside.

3. Did you give him a ring or write him a note?

4. It's on the floor or near the window.

5. Do we meet again at seven or eight?

6. I know Dick, but not Bob.

7. This restaurant serves cocktails, but the one on the corner serves beer only.

8. Manuscripts are available at the library, but not at the bookstore.

9. Are manuscripts available at the library or the bookstore?

10. Did she say yes or not?

習題 528 解答

1. and	2. but	3. but	4. or	5. or
6. and	7. or	8. but	9. and	10. but
11. or	12. or	13. and	14. but	15. but
16. and, but	17. and	18. or	19. and	20. and
21. or / but	22. and	23. and	24. and	25. and

習題 529 解答

1. The boys, the girls, and the dogs chased the cat.

2. He should, must, and will win the contest.

3. Mary is tall, blond, blue-eyed.

4. He is a tall, dark, handsome, young man.

5. The boy who was here, who left the note, and who disappeared was Bob Tower.

6. He walked out to the porch, looked carefully around the garden, and jumped.

7. Some books are to be tasted, others to be swallowed, and some few to be chewed and digested.

8. I had an egg, a piece of toast, a glass of orange juice, and a cup of coffee.

9. Because he didn't care for the country, because the beach had no appeal to him, and because the mountain always scared him, he decided to travel during his vacation.

10. A huge celebration dinner was given for all the officers in the party, for all those who had contributed sizable amounts of money to their campaign, and for all the party workers who had helped bring about their victory at the polls.

習題 530 解答

1. Bob laughed, and Dick cried. / Bob and Dick laughed and cried, respectively

2. John loves Mary, and Harry loves Alice. / John and Harry love Mary and Alice, respectively.

3. Tom is six years old, and Jack is eight years old. / Tom and Jack are six and eight years old, respectively.

4. He lives in Boston, and she lives in Philadelphia. / He and she live in Boston and Philadelphia, respectively.

5. A training college for men is to be built in Taipei, and a training college for women is to be built in Hsinchu. / Training colleges for men and for women are to be built in Taipei and Hsinchu, respectively.

6. John took a position in a bank, Bob took a position in a school, and Dick took a position in a shipping firm. / John, Bob, and Dick took positions in a bank, school, and shipping firm, respectively.

習題 531 解答

1. I laughed and laughed.

2. He waited and waited.

3. She read it over and over.

4. We climbed down and down.

5. They argued for hours and hours.

6. They went around and around to the top of the lighthouse.

7. Prices went up and up until nobody could afford to buy them.

8. I tried again and again to reach you.

9. Why do we have to go over and over the same material?

10. I hit and hit him until he died.

習題 532 解答

1. John hit the boy, and Bill, the girl.

2. My brother likes music, and I, painting.

3. I have studied German, and my sister, French.

4. Nancy told the story badly, but Jane, marvelously.

5. Mr. White plans to go to North America, but Mrs. White, South America.

6. Mr. Jones has decided to start for Japan on Monday, and Mr. Johnson, on Tuesday.

習題 533 解答

1. Jane resembles Grace.

2. Charles is married to Susan.

3. The president conferred with the dean on the matter.

4. This rope is equal to that rope in length.

5. This pencil is different from that one in color.

6. The sand is mixed with the loam.

7. John agrees with Bill that Harry is an idiot.

8. The earth is identical to the moon in their chemical composition.

9. The secretary deferred from the treasurer in their opinions.

10. John's resemblance to Bill is very striking.

習題 534 解答

1. Work hard, and you will pass the examination.

2. Hurry up, or you will be late for the train.

3. Go straight on, and you will see a church.

4. Put on your overcoat, or you will catch a cold.

5. Work well, and you will be rewarded.

6. Make one step, and you will be a dead man.

習題 535 解答

1. Bob doesn't eat meat. Nor does he eat fish.

2. She didn't use sugar in her coffee. Nor did she use cream.

3. He didn't have cigarettes. Nor did he have matches.

4. There is no paper in the desk. Nor are there pencils.

5. The hats are not in the closet. Nor are the coats.

6. Cash wasn't available. Nor were checks.

7. Jack hasn't admitted it. Nor has he denied it.

8. Tom didn't see us. Nor did he hear us call.

9. I don't know. Nor do I care.

10. I have not gone there. Nor will I ever go.

11. I didn't see it. Nor did anybody else.

12. He can't do it. Nor can I do it. Nor can you do it. Nor can anybody do it.

習題 536 解答

1. but	2. yet	3. but / for	4. and	5. yet	6. for
7. or	8. or	9. and	10. and / but	11. for	12. so
13. for	14. yet	15. or	16. or	17. for	18. but

習題 537 解答

1. He's poor, but happy.

2. You haven't got much time, neither have I.

3. Don't sit at this table, nor any other table.

4. They didn't find her a seat, but I did.

5. He handed her the money and went out.

6. The phone is out of order, so is the other one.

7. Spain is in Europe, so is Portugal.

8. The post office doesn't sell cigarettes, nor does the bank.

9. Arabic is a Semitic language, but Turkish isn't.

10. She thought for a moment, but didn't say anything at all.

11. You shouldn't leave him a big tip, nor should they.

12. Is this table alright, or do you prefer another one?

13. We supposed it was morning, for the roosters were making a lot of fuss.

14. He kept failing the examinations, so he decided to withdraw from his physics class.

習題 538 解答

1. B́ill saw the accident, and J́im did, t́oo.

2. Mr. J́ones quit smoking, and Í did, t́oo.

3. T́hey couldn't get tickets, and wé couldn't, éither.

4. Mr. Ẃhite isn't a doctor, and Mr. B́lack isn't, éither.

5. B́ill can swim, but Jim ćan't.

6. Ẃe weren't alarmed, but they ẃere.

7. J́im doesn't like school, but his sister d́oes.

8. T́his suitcase is lighter than t́hat one.

9. T́his picture is as expensive as t́hat one.

10. Our house is b́igger than theirs, but theirs is préttier.

11. This chair is ṕrettier than that one, but it isn't as ćomfortable.

12. Bobby is ýounger than Jim is, but he's a better player.

13. We work hárder than they do, but we don't get as much d́one.

14. This book cost f́ive dollars and this one t́hree dollars.

15. This book cost five d́ollars and this one three ṕounds.

16. It's his ẃife that I don't ĺike.

17. The one that I don't ĺike is his ẃife.

18. It's his ẃife that's always ńasty.

19. The one that's always ńasty is his ẃife.

20. It's a little śympathy that he ẃants.

21. What he ẃants is a little śympathy.

22. This isn't an éasy book, but it's a góod one.

23. Mary isn't a béautiful child, but she's very prétty.

24. He works for the cíty government, not the státe government.

25. That isn't my fávorite picture, but I líke it very much.

26. I have thrée children, not fóur.

27. I've met Mr. White, but I've never met Mrs. White.

28. Is the letter ín the desk, or ón the desk?

29. Does John sit in frónt of Bill, or in báck of him?

30. Is he getting ín the taxi, or óut of it?

31. Can you tell whether he's going úp the hill, or coming dówn?

32. Is he fór the proposal, or agáinst it?

33. Is he walking tóward the office, or áway from it?

34. She is úpstairs, not dównstairs.

35. He is ínside, not óutside.

36. I told you to take your coat óff, not put in ón.

37. I asked you to turn the volume dówn, not turn it úp.

38. I asked you to háng your coat up, not thrów it on the floor.

39. (Does John always beat you at tennis?) He úsually wins, but he doesn't álways win.

40. (Is Mr. Jones thoughtful at home?) He's not álways thoughtful, but he's úsually thoughtful.

41. (Isn't Mrs. Jones a teacher at your school?) Yes, she is á teacher. But she isn't mý teacher.

42. (Is that the best way to do it?) Well, it's á way to do it. But I'm not sure it's thé best way.

43. (Didn't you find a lot of money?) I found sóme money, but not véry much.

44. (Isn't that Mr. Johnson?) Well, it's á Mr. Johnson. But it isn't thé Mr. Johnson. I mean his name ís Johnson, but he isn't thé famous Mr. Johnson.

45. (Isn't this the book you were looking for?) Well, it's á book, but it isn't thé book.

46. (Do you know Mrs. Jones?) Well, I know á Mrs. Jones. But I don't know whether it's the śame one.

47. (What do you think of George's point of view?) Well, it's á point of view. But it's not mine.

48. Is he éighteen or níneteen?

49. Did you say "śixty-seven" or "séventy-seven"?

50. Did you say "eńcouraged" or "díscouraged"?

51. Do "díslike" and "únlike" have the same meaning?

52. Did you óverestimate or únderestimate?

53. I said malígnancy, not malígnity.

54. They were at once śimilar and díssimilar.

55. I said she was a Frénch teacher, not a frésh teacher.

56. That happened both in frevolutionary and póstrevolutionary France.

習題 539 解答

1. You must either tell the truth or say nothing.

   Either you tell the truth, or you say nothing.

2. He was not only thoughtless but also insolent.

   Not only was he thoughtless, but he was also insolent.

3. She either forgot about the party or didn't want to come.

   Either she forgot about the party, or she didn't want to come.

4. Peter is both lazy and careless.

5. Both Paul and Bob work hard.

6. Jane likes neither pork nor beef.

   Neither does Jane like pork, nor does she like beef.

7. Not the girls but the boys were at fault.

8. Bob was either mad or a very shrewd young man.

   Either Bob was mad, or he was a very shrewd young man.

9. Bob was neither mad nor ignorant.

   Neither was Bob mad, nor was he ignorant.

10. Either Shakespeare wrote carelessly, or we have corrupt texts of some of his plays.

11. Neither the old man nor his sons can be trusted.

12. There was not six but one member.

13. He came to the office not only late but also quite disheveled.

    Not only did he come to the office late, but he also came to the office quite disheveled.

14. It turned out to be not an oil well but a very dry whole.

15. Either Mom will fix dinner, or Dad will take us out.

16. Both the girls and their mother want new job.

17. Both Joe and Mary are coming to the party.

18. She was both a pretty girl and a good cook.

19. Paul helped in both the kitchen and the yard.

20. Either the parents who disciplined the child or the grandparents who spoiled her are to blame.

習題 540 解答

1. Neither his father nor his mother is alive.

2. The great poet and novelist is dead.

3. Extravagances as well as parsimony are to be avoided.

4. A good and useful man has passed away.

5. Kindness as well as justice is to be our guide.

6. Every leaf and every flower is stripped off the tree.

7. To take pay and then not to work is dishonest.

8. The long and the short of the matter is this.

9. The cow as well as the horse eats grass.

10. One or the other of these fellows has stolen the watch.

11. Man's happiness or misery is in a great measure in his own hands.

12. Curry and chicken is my favorite dish.

13. Bread and butter is fattening.

14. Mr. Johnson or his employers are mistaken.

15. Iron as well as gold is found in China.

16. Jack, and not you, has won the prize.

17. Neither Bob nor I am willing to do that.

18. Not only you but also your brother is lazy.

19. Two and two is four.

20. Sugar and water makes syrup.

習題 541 解答

1. I'm too tired to go; besides, it is too late.

   I'm too tired to go; it is, besides, too late.

   I'm too tired to go; it is too late, besides.

2. The window was open; that is, the whole place was open.

   The window was open; the whole place was open, that is.

3. Do what you are told; otherwise, you will be punished.

   Do what you are told; you will, otherwise, be punished.

   Do what you are told; you will be punished, otherwise.

4. I see your point of view; still, I don't agree with you.

   I see your point of view; I don't, still, agree with you.

   I see your point of view; I don't agree with you, still.

5. I have noted his better behavior; nonetheless, I cannot change my decision.

   I have noted his better behavior; I cannot, nonetheless, change my decision.

   I have noted his better behavior; I cannot change my decision, nonetheless.

6. We have not yet reached a decision; however, our opinion of your plan is favorable.

   We have not yet reached a decision; our opinion of your plan is, however, favorable.

   We have not yet reached a decision; our opinion of your plan is favorable, however.

7. He was the only candidate; therefore, he was elected.

   He was the only candidate; he was, therefore, elected.

He was the only candidate; he was elected, therefore.

8. She was very tired; nevertheless, she kept on working.

She was very tired; she, nevertheless, kept on working.

She was very tired; she kept on, nevertheless, working.

She was very tired; she kept on working, nevertheless.

9. I did not like the house; moreover, it was too high-priced.

I did not like the house; it was, moreover, too high-priced.

I did not like the house; it was too high-priced, moreover.

10. He is the popular candidate; consequently, he will be elected.

He is the popular candidate; he will, consequently, be elected.

He is the popular candidate; he will be elected, consequently.

11. She didn't like him very much; nevertheless, she decided to invite him.

She didn't like him very much; she, nevertheless, decided to invite him.

She didn't like him very much; she decided, nevertheless, to invite him.

She didn't like him very much; she decided to invite him, nevertheless.

12. He knew what he wanted; however, he didn't know how to get it.

He knew what he wanted; he didn't, however, know how to get it.

He knew what he wanted; he didn't know how to get it, however.

13. I don't like skating; furthermore, the ice is too thin.

I don't like skating; the ice is, furthermore, too thin.

I don't like skating; the ice is too thin, furthermore.

14. Her father had been active in politics; indeed, he had once run for governor.

Her father had been active in politics; he had once, indeed, run for governor.

Her father had been active in politics; he had once run for governor, indeed.

15. He had never been out of Japan; in fact, he had never been twenty miles from Tokyo.

He had never been out of Japan; he had never been, in fact, twenty miles from Tokyo.

He had never been out of Japan; he had never been twenty miles from Tokyo, in fact.

16. The coach was not on speaking terms with any of the players; hence, team morale was rather low.

The coach was not on speaking terms with any of the players; team morale was, hence, rather low.

The coach was not on speaking terms with any of the players; team morale was rather low, hence.

17. There seemed no chance of coming to an agreement; therefore, it was decided to break off negotiations.

There seemed no chance of coming to an agreement; it was, therefore, decided to break off negotiations.

There seemed no chance of coming to an agreement; it was decided to break off negotiations, therefore.

18. The floods had damaged many of the railroad bridges; accordingly, all trains were running late.

The floods had damaged many of the railroad bridges; all trains were, accordingly, running late.

The floods had damaged many of the railroad bridges; all trains were running late, accordingly.

19. Each attack left him weaker than the one before; thus, he crept softly into the arms of death.

Each attack left him weaker than the one before; he, thus, crept softly into the arms of death.

Each attack left him weaker than the one before; he crept softly into the arms of death, thus.

20. France was fearful of Germany; besides, she was bound by a treaty to come to the aid of Russia.

France was fearful of Germany; she was, besides, bound by a treaty to come to the aid of Russia.

France was fearful of Germany; she was bound by a treaty to come to the aid of Russia, besides.

習題 542 解答

1. because　　2. Because　　3. for　　4. for　　5. because; for　　6. because; for

7. for　　　　8. because　　9. for　　10. for　　11. because　　　12. Because

習題 543 解答

1. She was very pretty, but she was rather hard to deal with.

2. They were very tired; nevertheless, they still had miles to drive.

3. There seemed no chance of coming to an agreement; therefore, it was decided to break off negotiations.

4. The outside temperature was around eighty; also, it was rather muggy.

5. The river was filled with crocodiles; moreover, they seemed to be of a particularly vicious sort.

6. The plan had certain weakness, yet we decided to adopt it.

7. I heard my name on the loud speaker, so I hurried to the information desk.

8. France was fearful of Germany; besides, she was bound by a treaty to come to the aid of Russia.

9. Because Charles would not help, Bob was angry.

10. Although he had used no word that was not in the dictionary, he got an F on the paper.

11. The Prime Minister's adherents were already gathering in the streets; consequently, the army had to move fast.

12. Franklin hit on the notion of a circulating library, for it was hard to get books in America at that time.

13. John was anxious to make a good impression because he needed the job badly.

14. Though he wasn't much interested in the project, Bob was determined to do his best.

15. There was little evidence; nevertheless, he guessed that there was something fishy.

參 考 書 目

　　本書的編成得力於下列參考書之處甚多，特列於後，不在書內另做詳註。

Allen, W. Stannard. *Living English Structure*

Bach, Emmon Werner. *An Introduction to Transformational Grammar*

Chomsky, Noam Avram. *Syntactic Structures*

Chomsky, Noam Avram. *A Transformational Approach to Syntax*

Crowell, Thomas Lee Jr. *A Glossary of Phrases with Prepositions*

Curme, George O. *Principles and Practice of English Grammar*

Dixson, Robert J. *Complete Course in English*

Dixson, Robert J. *Graded Exercises in English*

Francis, W. Nelson. *The Structure of American English*

Gleason, H. Allan Jr. *An Introduction to Descriptive Linguistics*

Gleason, H. Allan Jr. *Linguistics and English Grammar*

English Language Services. *The Key to English Series*

English Language Services. *English Grammar Exercises*

Fraser, Bruce. *The Verb-Particle Combination in English*

Hill, A. Archibald. *Introduction to Linguistic Structures*

Hill, A. Archibald. *The New Linguistic Method*

Hayden, Rebecca E., *et al Mastering American English*

Hornby, Albert S. *A Guide to Patterns and Usage in English*

Hornby, Albert S., *et al. The Advanced Learner's Dictionary of Current English*

Jespersen, Otto. *Essentials of English Grammar*

Lado, Robert & Fries. Charles C. *English Sentence Patterns*

Langendoen, D. Terence. *The Study of Syntax*

Langendoen, D. Terence. *Essentials of English Grammar*

Lees, Robert B. *The Grammar of English Nominalizations*

Nichols, Ann E. *English Syntax*

Myers, Louis McCorry. *American English*

Rand, Earl. *Oral Approach Drills*

Roberts, Paul. *Uuderstanding Grammar*

Roberts, Paul. *Understanding English*

Roberts, Paul. *Patterns of English*

Roberts, Paul. *English Sentences*

Roberts, Paul. *English Syntax*

Roberts, Paul. *The Roberts English Series*

Rosenbaum &Jacobits. *English Transformational Grammar*

Ross, Janet & Doty, Gladys. *Writing English*

Rutherford, William E. *Modern English*

Stageberg, Norman C. *An Introductory English Grammar*

Stockwell, Robert P., *et al. Integration of Transformational Theories on English Syntax*

Whitford, Harold C. & Dixon, Robert J. *Handbook of American Idioms and Idiomatic Usage*

Corder S. Pit. *An Intermediate English Practice Book*

Virginia & Robert Allen. *Review Exercises for English as a Foreign Language*

The National Council of Teachers of English. *English for Today*

國家圖書館出版品預行編目（CIP）資料

觀察・類推・條理化：分析性的英語語法 / 湯廷池編
著. -- 初版. -- 臺北市 : 元華文創股份有限公司,
2023.11

　　冊 ；　公分

　ISBN 978-957-711-346-7 (下冊:平裝)

　1.CST: 英語教學　2.CST: 語法　3.CST: 中等教育

524.38　　　　　　　　　　　　　　　112018442

觀察・類推・條理化：分析性的英語語法（下冊）

湯廷池 編著　許淑慎 監修

發 行 人：賴洋助
出 版 者：元華文創股份有限公司
聯絡地址：100 臺北市中正區重慶南路二段 51 號 5 樓
公司地址：新竹縣竹北市台元一街 8 號 5 樓之 7
電　　話：(02) 2351-1607　　傳　　真：(02) 2351-1549
網　　址：www.eculture.com.tw
E-mail：service@eculture.com.tw
主　　編：李欣芳
責任編輯：立欣
行銷業務：林宜葶
出版年月：2023 年 11 月 初版
定　　價：新臺幣 630 元

ISBN：978-957-711-346-7 (平裝)

總經銷：聯合發行股份有限公司
地　址：231 新北市新店區寶橋路 235 巷 6 弄 6 號 4F
電 話：(02)2917-8022　　　　傳　真：(02)2915-6275